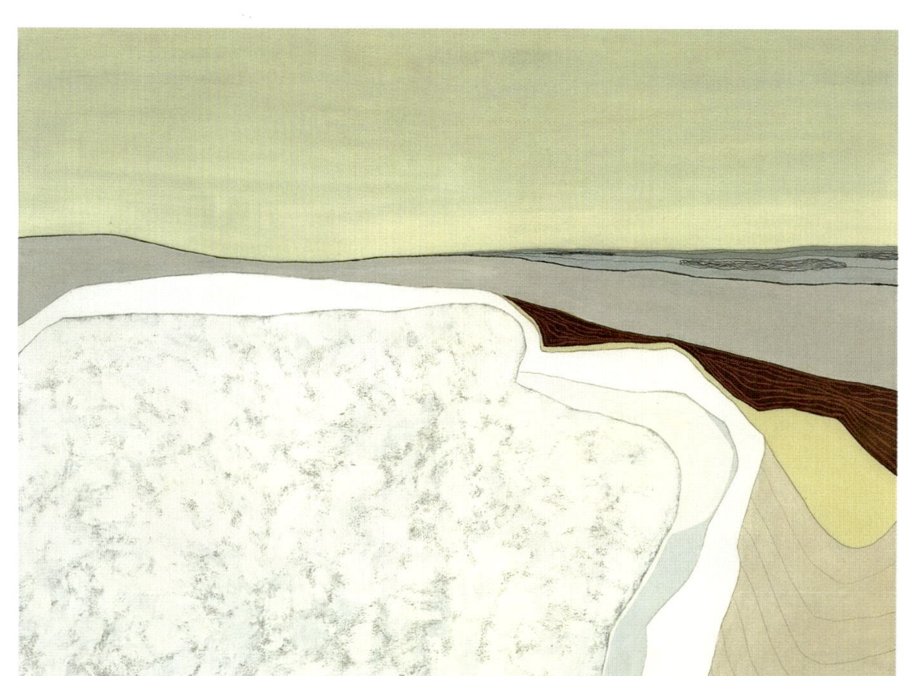

philip hughes tracks

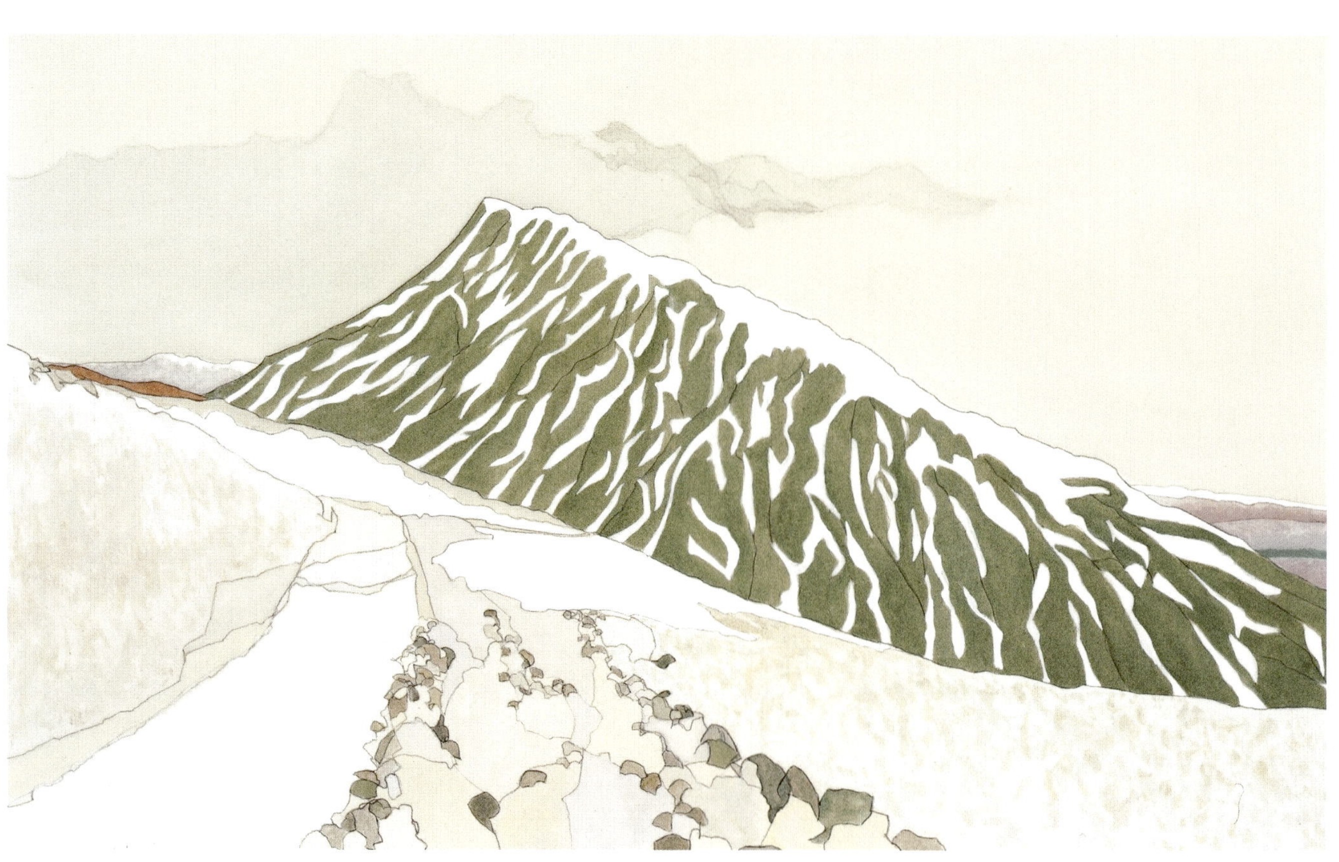

philip hughes tracks

walking the ancient landscapes of britain

with an introduction by kay syrad

with 148 illustrations

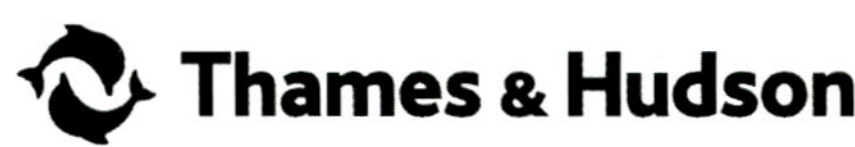
Thames & Hudson

FOR PSICHE, WITH LOVE

PHILIP HUGHES's work is based mainly on landscape with a special interest in remote areas, archaeology, topography and maps. He has had over forty one-man exhibitions, including many with public galleries in the UK, France, Mexico and Australia. His work is held internationally in numerous public and private collections.

KAY SYRAD is a novelist and poet. Her publications on artists include the Thames & Hudson monograph *Chris Drury: Silent Spaces*.

First published in the United Kingdom in 2012 by Thames & Hudson Ltd, 181A High Holborn, London WC1V 7QX

First paperback edition 2019

Tracks: Walking the Ancient Landscapes of Britain
© 2012 and 2019 Thames & Hudson Ltd, London

Introduction © 2012 and 2019 Kay Syrad
Other texts © 2012 and 2019 Philip Hughes
Artworks by Philip Hughes © 2012 and 2019
Philip Hughes

Maps pp. 55 and 97 courtesy Collins Bartholomew Ltd; p. 87 courtesy English Heritage; pp. 105, 121, 135, 151 and 169 reproduced by permission of Ordnance Survey on behalf of HMSO © Crown Copyright 2012. All rights reserved. Ordnance Survey Licence number 100051433.

British Library Cataloguing-in-Publication Data
A catalogue record for this book is available from the British Library

ISBN 978-0-500-29536-6

Printed and bound in Slovenia by DZS-Grafik d.o.o.

To find out about all our publications, please visit **www.thamesandhudson.com**. There you can subscribe to our e-newsletter, browse or download our current catalogue, and buy any titles that are in print.

ACKNOWLEDGMENTS
Many have helped with so many aspects of this book. To them my great thanks. I should like to single out Julie Melrose, who has worked with me on this project for years, and who has played such an important role.

I should also like to thank the staff of Thames & Hudson who have helped create this book – the structure, the design, the editing and the production. It has been a pleasure to work with such a creative and friendly team.

NOTES TO THE READER
Spellings of place names are variable, particularly in transcriptions from Scottish Gaelic. Differences may therefore be observed between spellings in the text and on the maps shown.

Measurements for artworks are given in centimetres.

Page 1
UFFINGTON CASTLE, BERKSHIRE | 1964
gouache on paper
82 × 100

Page 2
SCHIEHALLION | 2005
tempera, aquacryl & acrylic on paper
30 × 50

CONTENTS

Always, everywhere, people have walked, veining the earth with paths,
visible and invisible, symmetrical and meandering.
THOMAS A. CLARK[1]

Topography displays no favorites; North's as near as West.
More delicate than the historians' are the map-makers' colors.
ELIZABETH BISHOP[2]

What is most startling and unique about Philip Hughes's work is how his drawings and paintings enhance our sensitivity to the history and form of our landscape. He achieves this by quietly asserting his cartographic and geological knowledge within an artistic practice that is characterized by the tension between representation and abstraction, between precision and the surreal. By this method, he brings to our attention what often remains invisible to others: the quartz veins in rock on the Islay coast, for example, or the exact placing of a tumulus or stone circle in relation to both its surrounding landforms and other Neolithic monuments. Inspired and informed by maps, aerial photographs and the latest electronic survey techniques, Hughes's clean, spacious compositions, with their arresting blocks of colour, make contemporary some of the most ancient and formidable landmarks of the British Isles.

Hughes has painted and exhibited all over the world. He was one of the first to take up an Artist's Fellowship in Antarctica with the British Antarctic Survey, and he has made substantial bodies of work in Australia and France. *Tracks* is the first comprehensive overview of the drawings and paintings he has made in Great Britain – mostly during the last twenty years, although some works date much further back, including one of the Ridgeway in Wiltshire from 1964. During this time Hughes has walked the ancient paths from Orkney in Scotland down to Logan Rock in Cornwall – drawing and painting Neolithic settlements such as Maes Howe; standing stones at Stenness, Avebury and Stonehenge; mountains of special geomorphic and geological interest such as Schiehallion in Scotland and the Three Peaks in Yorkshire; and visiting and re-visiting sites of mysterious and outstanding beauty such as Silbury in Wiltshire.

It is not only the mountains and monuments themselves that Hughes is concerned with, but the paths leading to the sites – the crossing of Rannoch Moor, for example, or the shorter path towards Stonehenge. Each section of this book thus represents a track, shown in part on a map

SILBURY IN MIST | 2008
aquacryl, pastel & gouache on paper
71 × 100

that acts here not as a guide but as an image, a visual preface. Each map is of a different type, from the Bartholomew half-inch series, to geological and archaeological maps (of Orkney or Hadrian's Wall, for example), to contemporary digital Ordnance Survey plat maps (Stonehenge, for example). It is with this cartographic assistance that the artist chooses his site. Attracted by its archaeological or topographical significance, or by a resonance that cannot easily be explained, he completes each pencil drawing in one sitting, working outside. Only later does he select his palette of colours – pastels, gouache, acrylic, aquacryl – not so much to represent the tones and hues observed at the time of drawing, but, driven to make visible what is poetic or spiritual in his chosen location, to express something intangible, emotional. This method is exemplified in his series of drawings and paintings of Silbury Hill.

Silbury Hill is the oldest, tallest artificial earth mound in Europe. Set on the Kennet plain in Wiltshire, it stands forty-six metres high and covers an area of five acres, constructed between the late Neolithic and early Bronze Ages. Stonehenge and the great stone circle of Avebury are nearby. Hughes's first sketchbook drawings of the Hill in 2007 are respectful, simplifying what he apprehends into accurate, sympathetic lines, completing the drawings in situ and later giving naturalistic colour to the outlines of the vast, solid mound, represented from many different perspectives and different times of day (see below left and p. 138). The drawings are sometimes accompanied by text noting the artist's viewpoint, the weather, and perhaps asking questions about the siting of the mound in the landscape and in particular in relation to the great stone circle at Avebury. These are inquiry drawings, seeking knowledge about Silbury's origins and meaning by concentrating on topography, placing and scale.

Then on several occasions between 2008 and 2010 Hughes returned to Silbury. The results of these visits are a series of four large paintings in which Silbury is no longer a green mound, but instead rises up ghostly grey, almost imperceptible in mist; or appears as a light- and dark-yellow disc that could spin or take flight;

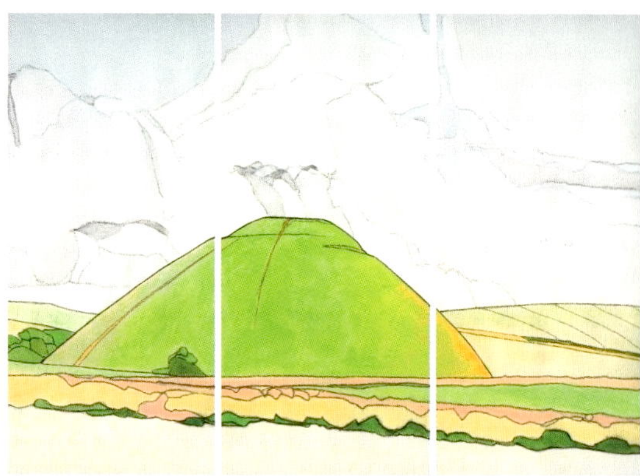

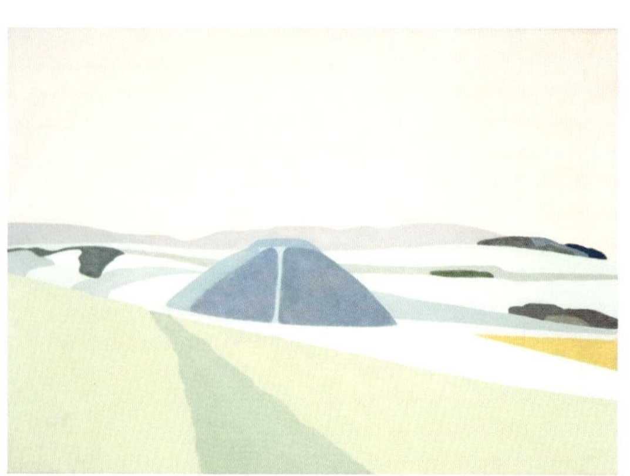

or distant, authoritative, in a muted blue-grey. This time a different level of inquiry is taking place. These paintings still retain topographical integrity in terms of scale and positioning, but they are more dramatically an exploration and expression of Hughes's spiritual response. I say 'exploration' first because there is a lightness of touch in the compositions here, reflecting a humility towards even attempting to represent this most extraordinary and still largely unexplained phenomenon in the landscape, while it is in the artist's choice of colours that resides the uncontainable, spiritual – yet more confident – 'expression'. In this series, the use of colour gives poetic elevation to the Hill: we are presented with the *idea* of Silbury, of the Hill, as symbol.

In the blue version, for example (opposite right and pp. 140–41), Silbury is no longer rooted in the grass plain but instead floats against a sea of hills. It is the blue-grey that gives the Hill independence and levity. It is off-centre, with a track leading the eye towards and beyond it. There is a geometric imperative here, the painted Hill consisting of two blue triangles separated by a white path, while a triangle of yellow points towards the Hill from the right. The blue hill is pure form among other pure forms, with exact, subtle arcs and curves. Hughes says this is the version that most closely represents what he *feels* about Silbury Hill. The colours suggest that his feeling is one of surrender: one imagines the breath falling away in a sigh at the encounter with the Hill's immensity and shape and mystery. In this painting, the top of Silbury almost reaches the sky, stopped only by a narrow stretch of pale grey-pink. It appears separated from the ground by its colour, and, in this way, the Hill lifts off: impervious, impenetrable and eternal.

The more haunting version, however, is *Silbury in Mist* (p. 7), which is the artist's favourite, perhaps because the painting gives a particular sense of the Hill's loneliness in time and space, its near-indivisibility from the sky, and our difficulty in seeing its original purpose. Silbury was long thought to be a burial mound, but excavations have found no remains. In contrast, the nineteenth-century geologist Moses Cotsworth proposed that Silbury's height relates to its function as a great shadow hill to mark the progress of the sun.[3] Other theories

SILBURY: 10 AM 20 JUNE 2007 | 2007/08
aquacryl, pastel, gouache & print on paper
48 × 67

SILBURY | 2008
acrylic on canvas
70 × 98

ABOVE SILBURY | 2008
aquacryl, pastel & gouache on paper
71 × 100

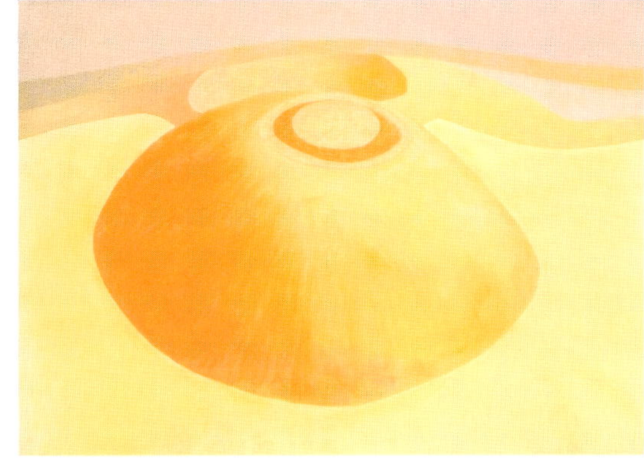

include Tom Brooks's mathematical explanation, which is that 'pre-historic monuments form a series of isosceles triangles spiralling out from Silbury Hill',[4] with the triangle pointing to the next monument and thereby creating a system of directions across hundreds of miles. It is interesting to consider Hughes's blue, geometric Silbury alongside this theory.

Thirdly, the aerial view of Silbury (p. 9), painted from a photograph, gives the Hill a more archetypal form, now painted in deep cadmium yellow, spinning as if over a sandy desert, ancient, giving a sense of time passing. The deep blush-shadow to the left, the nipple-like circles on top, the cut-away circle and lines behind an echo or shadow rising towards the horizon – all suggest an inner landscape that poignantly symbolizes our human relationship to the cosmos, which might be described as an uneasy juxtaposition of vulnerability and power.

Finally, the Hill appears in elemental orange, encircled by water (below and p. 143). Its painted relationship to the River Kennet is not accidental, there being early evidence of tracks from the river to the mound, but also, more significantly, the Hill is very near Swallowhead Springs, the head of the Kennet. In the painting, the representation of water literally adds another layer to our understanding: Silbury, like many earth mounds, has a moat – a ring of water whose function is thought to be a 'sighting object, as it reflected light from the sky (and perhaps at times a beacon on the ley) when seen from a distance'[5] – but here in the painting the blue 'ring of water' is in fact the river, imagined both as a moat and a sighting object for the viewer of the Hill.

In this last Silbury painting, Hughes is re-drawing the map in relation to his own metaphysical orientation – an example perhaps of what Edward Casey names 're-implacement', in which 'places are altered and transmuted even as they are reinstated in paintings and maps'.[6] Indeed, there is a dramatic relationship between Hughes's paintings and the maps he studies. The maps, and sometimes official mapping photographs, provide him with ordered information that no doubt appeals to his sensibilities as a trained engineer (maps being at the meeting point between art and science), but he proceeds in full recognition of the aesthetic choices that must be made by the mapmakers, of the potential and

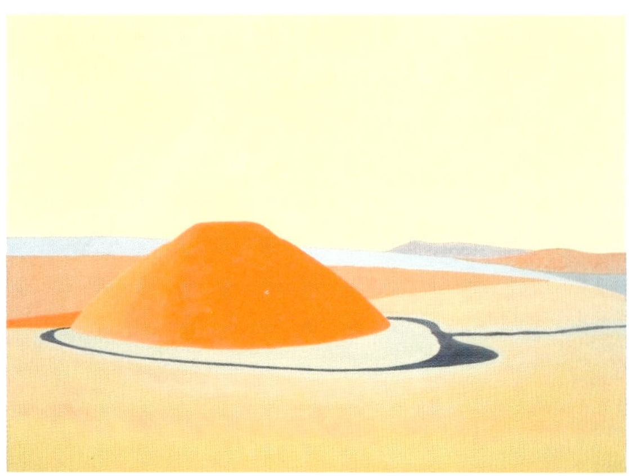

left
SILBURY AND THE KENNET | 2009
acrylic on canvas
70 × 98

opposite
INGLEBOROUGH | 1998
acrylic on board with print
79 × 130

actual misrepresentation of proximity and distance for political ends, and, as the variety of maps presented in this book illuminates, acutely aware of the historically and culturally specific nature of how we perceive, organize and represent the land we occupy. Compare, for example, the beautiful pale blue against brown and grey in the old geological Orkney map (p. 19) with the very sculptural quality of the map of Rannoch with its steep contour lines (p. 55), or the map of the stones at Stonehenge (p. 121). Sometimes Hughes also incorporates the map itself into a work (see the Three Peaks series, below and pp. 98–103) or uses grid lines (as in *Walls: West Penwith*, p. 115, or *Sarsen Stones, Below Overton Down*, p. 153), although even where the final work is in dialogue with or actually includes

a section of a map, ultimately all the works originate in drawing.

Hughes says he does not choose colours with conscious intent, although he does often try to reproduce the colours found in maps. The weather and the time of day or year the drawing was made may have an influence on his colour palette, or may not signify at all. Colour is used to convey the quality of the artist's experience of the place at a particular moment. In paintings made in Australia, for example (not shown in this book), Hughes uses hugely vibrant reds and oranges to express the drama of scale as well as to echo actual earth colours. The choice of colours renders the images either naturalistic or surreal: colours have intrinsic properties, material effects, which have been

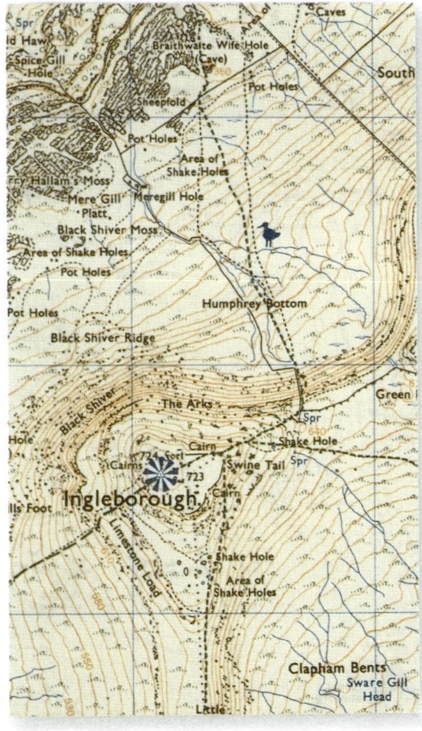

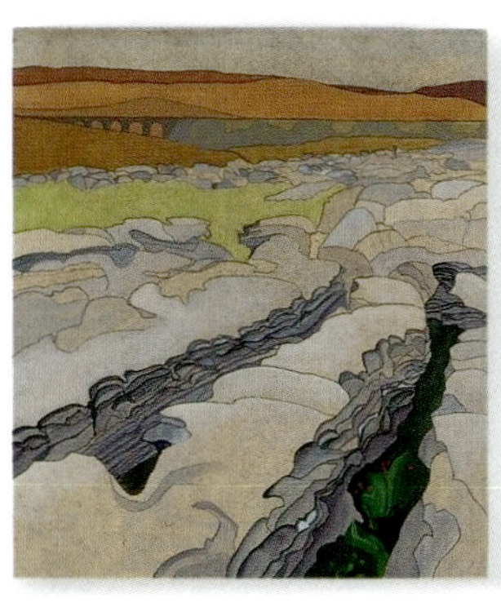

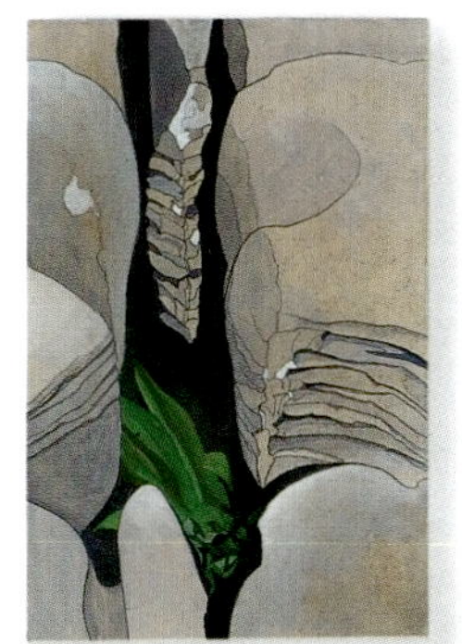

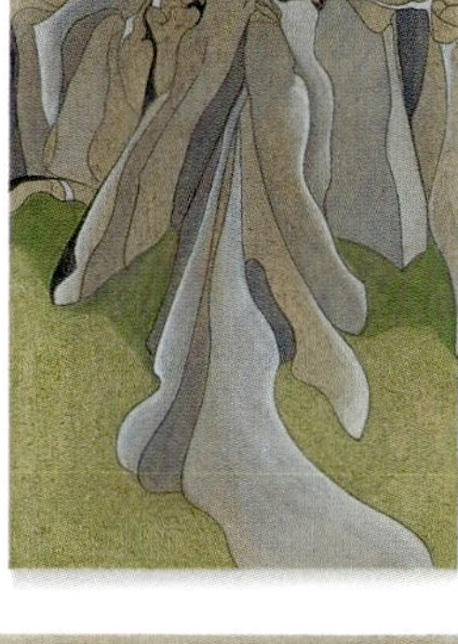

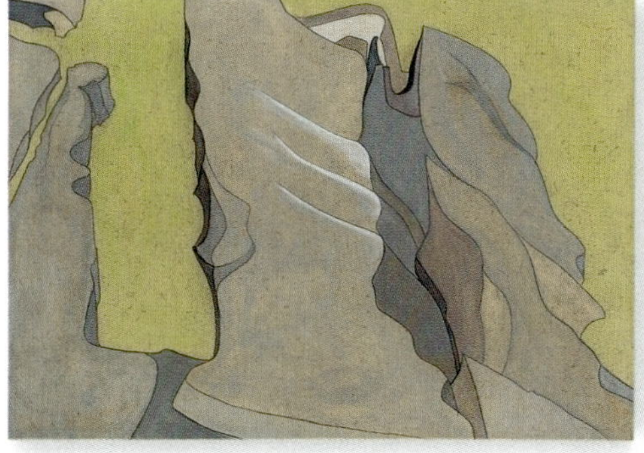

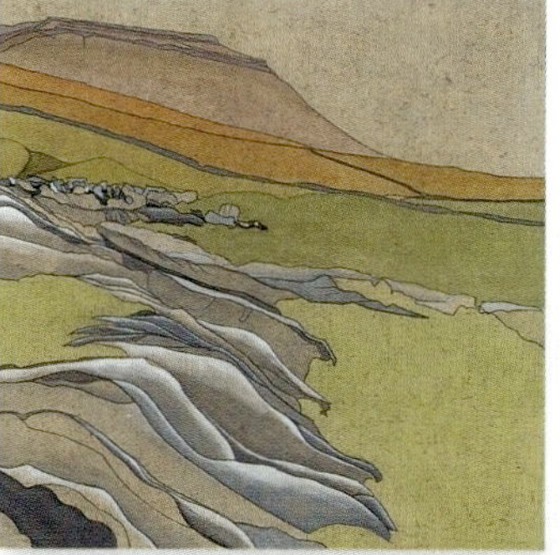

described anthropomorphically – by Kandinsky, for example – as profound (blue),[7] or as having equanimity (green), or the power to create a sense of motion or tranquillity. Indeed, going back to the Silbury paintings, it is as if Kandinsky was describing the effect of the colours on our optical experience of Hughes's Silbury mound when he wrote in 1912:

If two circles are [...] painted respectively yellow and blue, a brief contemplation will reveal in the yellow a spreading movement out from the centre, and a noticeable approach to the spectator. The blue, on the other hand, moves into itself, like a snail retreating into its shell, and draws away from the spectator. The eye feels stung by the first circle while it is absorbed into the second.[8]

It is interesting how this optical experience echoes the experience of the walker: Hughes is after all approaching Silbury Hill on foot from a variety of directions, the Hill looming and receding in different lights, at different seasons, its apparent transmogrification altering the consciousness of the artist. This is a crucial aspect of Hughes's work. He is informed not only by prior historical or geographical knowledge, by his memory and experience of other, similar landforms, and by his disciplined looking, but also, and particularly, by the kinaesthetic knowledge that is gained by walking to, from, around and between the sites. In making walking fundamental to his epistemology, to his conceptualization of landscape, it has been argued that Hughes has a connection to the school of land artists who emerged in the late 1960s. As William Packer puts it in the catalogue to Hughes's retrospective show in Scotland in 1990:

Where the contemporary artist has made his contribution to the tradition of the artist-traveller is in taking the journey itself as an entity, to be considered in its own formal terms and dimensions of time as well as space. Philip Hughes is just such a modern peripatetic, standing both for the tradition in its long established sense of the experience of the landscape expressed as an accumulation of single images, and also with such as Richard Long and Hamish Fulton for their more consciously temporal abstracted and conceptual record and celebration.[9]

Long and Fulton were questioning the relationship between nature and culture; contesting 'the dichotomies that hold the self apart from [...] place'; interested in the way in which place may be regarded as 'constitutive of one's sense of self'.[10] Another land artist, Chris Drury, a trained classical sculptor, began 'making walks' in wild places with Fulton in the early 1980s, refusing to draw or paint what he encountered, as that would be, as he saw it, to separate himself from nature in order to observe it. Instead he made interventions – cairns or rough shelters – out of materials to hand, 'as a means of opening a space for nature to dwell within the imagination',[11] photographing then destroying them before moving on. Long and Fulton were the first to make walks as artworks, a kind of performance art that sought to demonstrate how it is impossible to represent the earth *as such*. As Amanda Boetzkes argues, 'In contrast to landscape painting, which attempts to mask human presence or naturalize human dominance, earth art explores the point of contact between the body and the earth.'[12] This is true of Long's *Ten Mile Walk, England* (1968), a walk in a straight line across the high moorland of Exmoor, in southwest England, represented as an artwork only by his drawing a straight line across a map of the area. It is 'sculptural in its articulation of a passage through space'.[13]

In contrast to Hughes, however, Long and Fulton are interested in stone circles only in passing; they carry the same weight as say 'a barking dog' or 'a passing eagle', or even 'a fragment of conversation' or 'a song in the head'. But in marking the ground with lines and circles, Long shows both our abiding inclination towards geometry and the desire for human intervention; a wish to mark and differentiate from nature. Hughes's work explores the past using line and colour, while Long and Fulton are trying to break new ground by linking to our very distant past, before any attempt in the West to represent landscape *as* landscape. However, Hughes reflects the significance of his walking in the paintings themselves, sometimes in views of the track – Ridgeway, for example (pp. 156–59); or in his observation of objects along the way (see Islay, p. 79, or the Three Peaks, pp. 102–03); in his incorporation of maps; in the setting of ancient sites as seen one from the other, in the examples of Orkney (see p. 22) or Silbury and Avebury (p. 147); or in the juxtaposition of close-up views with long views. Sometimes the walk is represented by written comments on the work itself.

On the temporal question, it is true that many of Hughes's *Tracks* paintings give a strong sense of both arrival and departure – his own moving through the landscape – and the weather is often recorded with his sketches; moreover, he is concerned with prehistory and the effects of time on stone (exposure, geological strata) and on landforms. He is interested in cartographic changes and anomalies, and the use of electronic survey techniques that trace the normally unseen history of prehistoric sites – in Maes Howe, for example (below left and pp. 20–21).

On the other hand many of the paintings have a static quality: no movement of light or water, no clouds, no trees bending in wind. In this way, the paintings are always abstract, the external world reduced or contained within inert blocks of colour

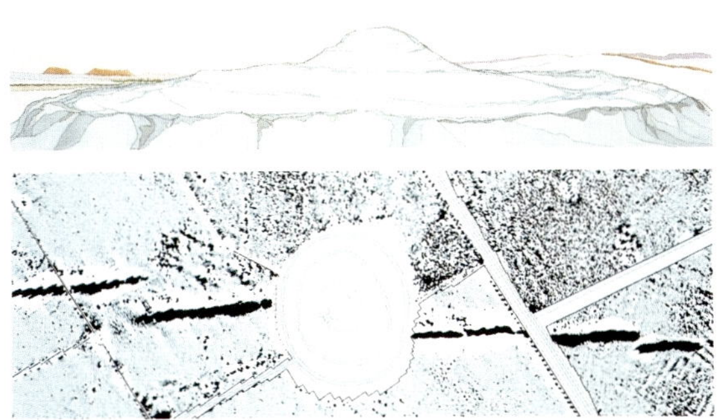

MAES HOWE | 2009
aquacryl & gouache on paper & print
72 × 105

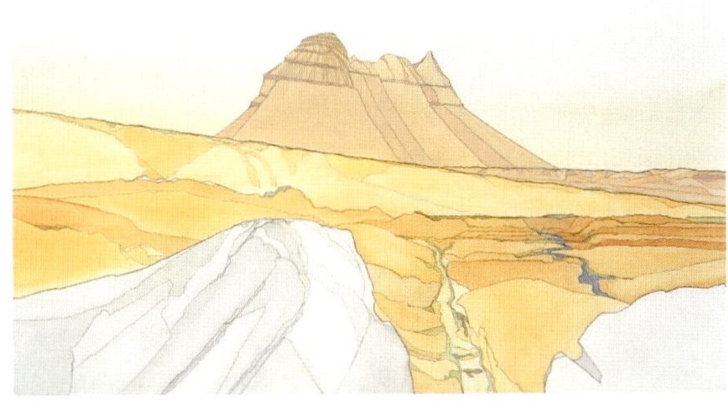

INVERKIRKAIG TO SUILVEN, SCOTLAND | 2004
acrylic & gouache on paper
67 × 101

… and yet, as scars and seams, edges and curves (see, for example, *Inverkirkaig to Suilven, Scotland*, p. 13, or *Bostal Bottom*, pp. 180 and 181), the forms present the movement of time – history, both human and non-human.

Hughes's work can also be described as conceptual in its classical detachment, in its scientific basis in geology and geomorphology, and in its method of repeated, serial attempts to describe and analyze, as in the Buachaille Etive Mòr series (see opposite left, p. 59 and pp. 61–64). Moreover, its *process* is apparent – sketches showing through as part of the paintings, and sketches and paintings presented together as a work; or the use of text as part of the work describing place, time, weather, or asking questions of the site; use of aerial images and maps – all in an acknowledgement that the subject is not containable within a single painting. It has been argued that, philosophically, Hughes's work is concerned with our human relationship to vastness, to wilderness (for example, Rannoch Moor), evoking Burke's theory of the sublime, yet it remains resolutely modern or even post-modern in that the paintings embody a tension between the singularity of the topographical representation and the plurality of possible optical experiences. It is an analysis, rather than the presentation, of a romantic 'grand truth' about landscape.

What is significant is the dialectical movement between abstraction and representation in this work. It is as if there are two artists here: almost a Cartesian split between mind and body, the rational and the intuitive. The rational man draws his object using his prior knowledge of geology and landforms, trained in perspective and concerned with accuracy. He disciplines himself to complete the drawings in situ in an act of faithfulness and integrity. This work is representational. Back in the studio, within a long tradition of landscape painting, he applies colour in a way that brings into relief the *forms* he has encountered. This aspect, rather than a particular mountain or ridge, is his main aesthetic concern, and in this way he is an abstract painter. The colours signify the feelings experienced – the spiritual, emotional and aesthetic effect upon the artist of these dramatic forms, which are surreal, utopian, visionary, transformatory; subjective and romantic, yet rendered universal, classical, eternal by restraint and discipline (only *these* colours, *these* washes), sometimes intimate, sometimes remote. The work thus balances on a pinpoint between classical and romantic – vast and complex landscapes simplified to colour blocks separated by curves and lines, cast from an exquisite palette of muted washes sometimes bringing to mind Georgia O'Keeffe. But a quick comparison of Hughes's *Buachaille Etive Mòr* (opposite left) with, say, O'Keeffe's *Pedernal* reminds us of what is particular to Hughes's work: his emphasis, here in these *Tracks* paintings, is less on *what* – not the mountain itself – than on *where* the mountain is. In this way, like the early earth or land artists, Hughes makes works that 'reenact or thematize the phenomenological experience of space, opening a reconsideration of the earth itself not merely as a spatial envelope for the art object but as an active component of it'.[14]

Tracks is therefore an appropriate title for this book, on the one hand denoting a journey, 'taking the journey itself as an entity', and on the other hand connoting the idea of tracing or following a light, making light or fire – Alfred Watkins uses the word 'ley' to denote an ancient sighted track, that is, one that is aligned with the sun or a star, arguing that early meanings of 'leye' include 'light', 'flame', 'blaze', 'fire'. The artist's journey thus *illuminates* both the land itself and our human relationship to it: it is *over there*, you can walk towards it and beyond it, but there is a sense in which you cannot arrive.[15]

Hughes has a further link to the land art movement in the spectre of Joseph Beuys, who had a profound influence on artists such as Long, Fulton and Drury. Beuys's drawings have been seen as mental doodles, a kind of visible stream of consciousness, but some remarks he made about drawing illuminate an element of Hughes's work:

Drawing is the first visible form in my works … the first visible thing of the form of the thought, the changing point from the invisible powers to the visible thing[…] You have also incorporated the senses … the sense of balance, the sense of vision, the sense of audition, the sense of touch.

And everything now becomes modified by other creative strata within the anthropological entity, the human being…[16]

Unlike the Impressionists – whose 'revolutionary gesture' was to go outside and paint the light, putting paint straight on the canvas – Hughes always makes preliminary drawings. As with Beuys, Hughes's first visible mark is a line. The line may appear to be representational and made in a bid for objectivity, but it is already and inevitably subjective in that a frame has been made by the artist's site lines; he has chosen which stone, mountain, track on which to focus; he has a sense of social responsibility in accurately recording – for history – signs from prehistory. Yet he is, precisely, interested in the abstractness of lines, created by geology or by humans – the abstract land drawing of the White Horse at Uffington in Wiltshire, for example (below) – as well as in the tracks or the alignments created by mounds and stones, which Hughes also in fact regards as Neolithic art installations. He has

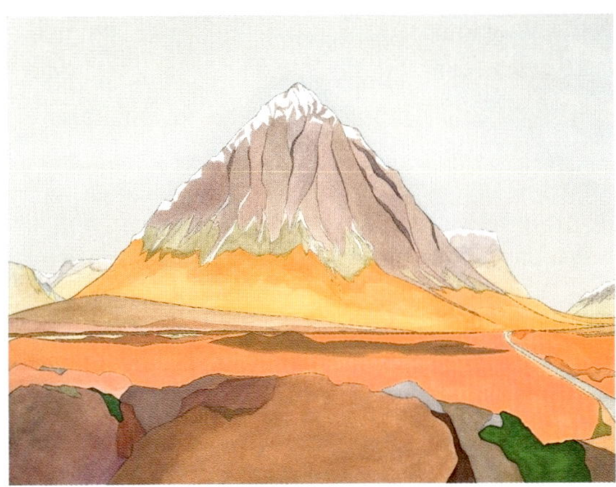

BUACHAILLE ETIVE MÒR 15 NOV 2006 | 2006
acrylic, aquacryl & gouache on paper
57 × 75

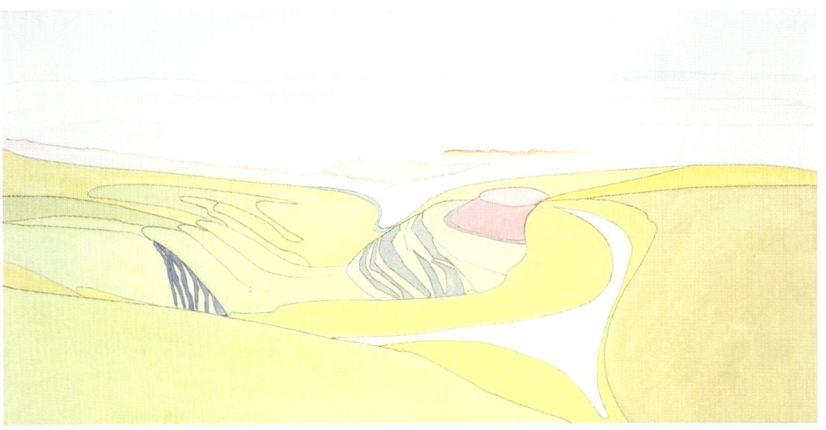

FOG BENEATH THE WHITE HORSE, UFFINGTON | 2003/04
gouache on paper
31 × 62

read the geologist Richard Fortey's comprehensive account in *The Hidden Landscape* of the impact of different types of rock on the character of social and cultural life; he has studied local maps; he has walked the landscape surrounding his object. He is *aware* of a hidden landscape. He has even, many times, drawn Mont Ventoux, which he can see from his studio window in France, and which Petrarch climbed and was 'probably the first man to express the emotion on which the existence of landscape painting so largely depends'.[17]

So the artist begins with all this knowledge and experience, but it is within the raw physical process of drawing that he will learn about the rhythms and patterns in the placing of his object, the nuances of its weathering over time. It is bleak: he is aware of biting wind on his face and scalp as he sits, utterly still, before his object, which has already and always been his subject. He attempts to draw what he sees; yet, to invoke Leonardo da Vinci, 'Line does not exist in nature; the marks of a drawing have a symbolic relationship to experience.'[18] Or, as Chris Drury puts it, 'Culture is the veil through which we experience nature.'[19]

But there is another link to Beuys, in that in later life he re-categorized his work as anthropological: by 'appropriating mythical and anthropological accounts of early cultures … the artist shifted the role of draftsmanship from private disclosure to public instruction – and a more concrete idea of drawings as objects'.[20] There is a sense of the anthropological in Hughes's work, too – in his method of 'participant-observation', in which he not only observes but also experiences the rhythms and routines, not of communities but of places. Nevertheless there are human ghosts in the earthworks and landforms encountered and drawn by Hughes, with evidence in the tracks, the mounds, the stones of *homo faber*, Stone Age man in particular, navigating, constructing, making tools. This is also the temporal aspect of Hughes's work, giving time *form* in his depictions of exposed rock, the remaining stones from a once great stone temple, fragments of Hadrian's Wall, the rapidly crumbling Seven Sisters cliffs in Sussex, and ancient trackways such as the South Downs Way and the Ridgeway. And in this way, Hughes's work, like Beuys's and Long's, is – after all – romantic. As Bernice Rose says:

The romance of the fragment is part of the romance of ruins; they are places where the past and present become eternally one – aesthetic and static. In drawing, there is a parallel romance, as the very marks of the ravages of time – the losses as well as the accretions – contribute to the feeling that the whole past of the drawing has come together in one instantaneous, present, aesthetic moment. Indeed, 'incompleteness' as part of the romantic tradition of drawing profoundly influenced the aesthetic of the nineteenth century.[21]

Thus, by this formulation, Philip Hughes's quest to understand the placing of these ancient artefacts and mounds is satisfied not by studying archaeology or geology, but by solving the mystery of the missing elements spatially, kinaesthetically, in form and colour.

NOTES

1   From 'In Praise of Walking', in *Distance and Proximity*, Edinburgh: Pocketbooks (2000), p. 15.

2   From 'The Map', in *Elizabeth Bishop: Complete Poems*, London: Chatto & Windus (1983), p. 3.

3   See also R. Hippisley-Cox, *The Green Roads of England* (1914), London: Garnstone Press (1973), pp. 12–13. Hippisley-Cox gives credence to Cotsworth's theory, which was that by placing a 95-foot pole on top of Silbury Hill a shadow was created, falling onto a stone placed to the north on the level meadows of the Kennet, the daily gauge being about 4 feet, almost exactly that of the Great Pyramid. In the Sussex town of Lewes, near which Hughes has a home, there is a mound from which one can see both the sunrise and the sunset on the shortest day of the year. The name 'Lewes' comes from 'hlaw', meaning 'place of the burial mounds'.

4   In J. Leary and D. Field, *The Story of Silbury Hill*, Swindon: English Heritage (2010), p. 177.

5   Alfred Watkins, *The Old Straight Track* (1925), London: Abacus (1976), p. 45.

6   Edward S. Casey, *Representing Place: Landscape Paintings and Maps*, Minneapolis: University of Minnesota (2002), p. xv.

7   In *Dictionnaire des couleurs de notre temps*, Paris: Bonneton (1999), cited by Philippe Rekacewicz in 'Confessions of a Map-maker', www.forum onpublicdomain.ca (2006), Michel Pastoureau suggests blue is, for maps, 'the favourite colour of all western countries because it is neither aggressive nor transgressive'.

8   Wassily Kandinsky, *Concerning the Spiritual in Art* (1912), trans. Michael T. H. Sadler, New York: Wittenborn (1955), p. 57.

9   William Packer (1990), cited in *Philip Hughes: Scotland*, London: Frances Kyle Gallery (2007).

10 E. S. Casey (2001), 'Between geography and philosophy: what does it mean to be in the place-world?', *Annals of the Association of American Geographers*, 91, p. 684, cited in Jon Anderson, 'Talking whilst walking: a geographical archaeology of knowledge', in *Area* (2004), 36.3, Royal Geographical Society with the Institute of Geographers, p. 255.

11 Amanda Boetzkes, *The Ethics of Earth Art*, Minneapolis and London: University of Minnesota Press (2010), p. 124.

12 Ibid, p. 17.

13 Ben Tufnell, *Land Art*, London: Tate Publishing (2006), p. 11.

14 Amanda Boetzkes, op. cit., p. 26.

15 Alfred Watkins, op. cit., pp. 158–60.

16 Cited by Bernice Rose, 'Joseph Beuys and the Language of Drawing', in Ann Temkin and Bernice Rose (eds), *Thinking is Form: The Drawings of Joseph Beuys*, Philadelphia and New York: The Philadelphia Museum of Art and MoMA (1993), p. 73.

17 Kenneth Clark, *Landscape into Art*, London: John Murray (1953), p. 7. Extraordinarily, Hughes's Italian wife, Psiche, is a direct descendant of Petrarch.

18 Ann Temkin and Bernice Rose, op. cit., p. 74.

19 Chris Drury (1995), cited in Chris Drury and Kay Syrad, *Silent Spaces*, London: Thames & Hudson (1998), p. 6.

20 Ann Temkin and Bernice Rose, op. cit., p. 75.

21 Ibid, p. 76.

ORKNEY

Maes Howe to Skara Brae

The island of Mainland in Orkney has one of the largest concentrations of ancient sites in Britain, matched only by the area around Avebury and Silbury in Wiltshire. I first visited Orkney some twenty-five years ago and did paintings of the main sites (Stenness, p. 28; Brodgar, p. 29; and Skara Brae, p. 37). But it was in preparation for an exhibition of drawings of Britain's stone circles at the Pier Arts Centre in Stromness that I really got to know the island, returning many times. Orkney has a magic that draws visitors back time and time again. Indeed, I have met many who have chosen to move there.

The landscape is relatively flat, except for the island of Hoy. Most striking is the mixture of inland lochs and sea lochs. They are so intertwined that it is sometimes hard to tell them apart. This intermingling of land and loch gives an extraordinary light reflected from all the water. There is a great feeling of space. And in the centre of this lie the ancient monuments.

The track links the tomb of Maes Howe with the Neolithic village of Skara Brae on the western coast. Central to this is the joining of the stone circles of Stenness and Brodgar by a narrow isthmus between the Lochs Harray and Stenness, shown on the section of geological map. I have tried to give the feel of this connection, as well as the drama of these two very different circles.

Recently I have worked with a group of archaeologists in Orkney, led by Dr Jane Downes at Orkney College. New techniques of electronic scanning have been developed that show buried objects and disturbances of the land without archaeologists having to excavate. The plots that come out of these scans are visually striking in their own right. Thanks to Dr Downes and her team, I have been able to link these scans with paintings of the ancient sites, creating composite works (pp. 30–33).

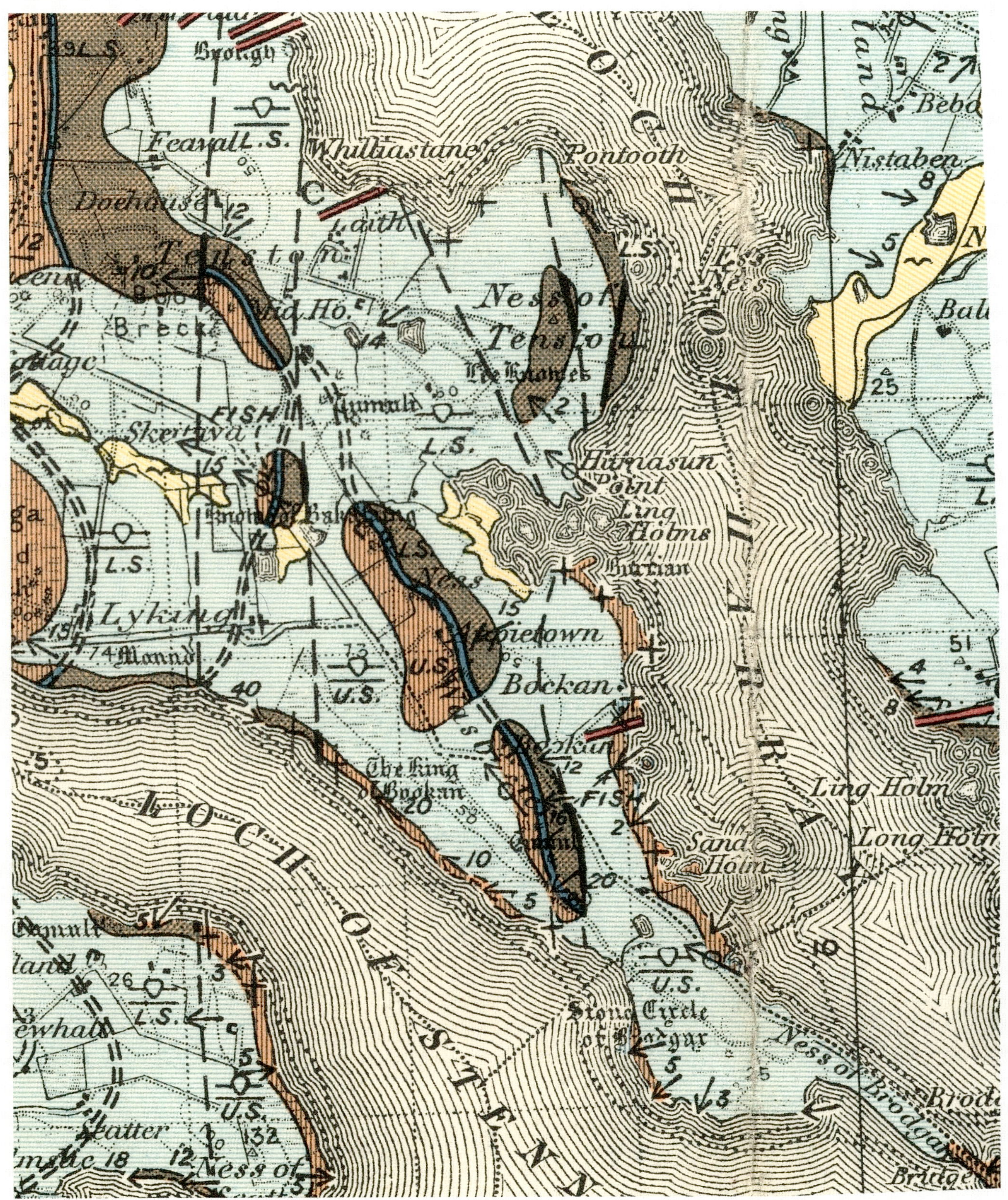

Brough
Feaval L.S.
Whulliastane
Pontooth
Nistaben
Doehouse
Teiston
Ness of
Tenston
Laith
Breck
Old Ho.
Hymald
The Knowes
Humasun
Point
Ling
Holms
Skerrawa
FISH
L.S.
Knowe of Baking
L.S.
L.S.
Lyking
Appietown
Bockan
Bockan
L.S.
Mound
U.S.
U.S.
The King
of Bockan
FISH
Ling Holm
Long Holm
Sand
Holm
LOCH OF STENNA
Stone Circle
of Brodgar
Ness of Brodgar
Brodgar
Bridge
Voy
Newhall
L.S.
U.S.
U.S.
U.S.
Vatter
Ness of

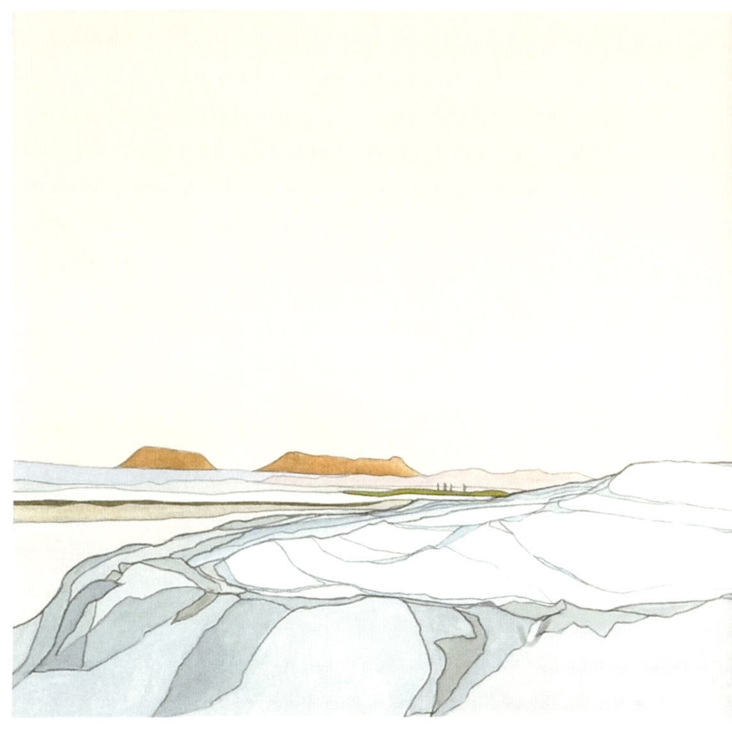

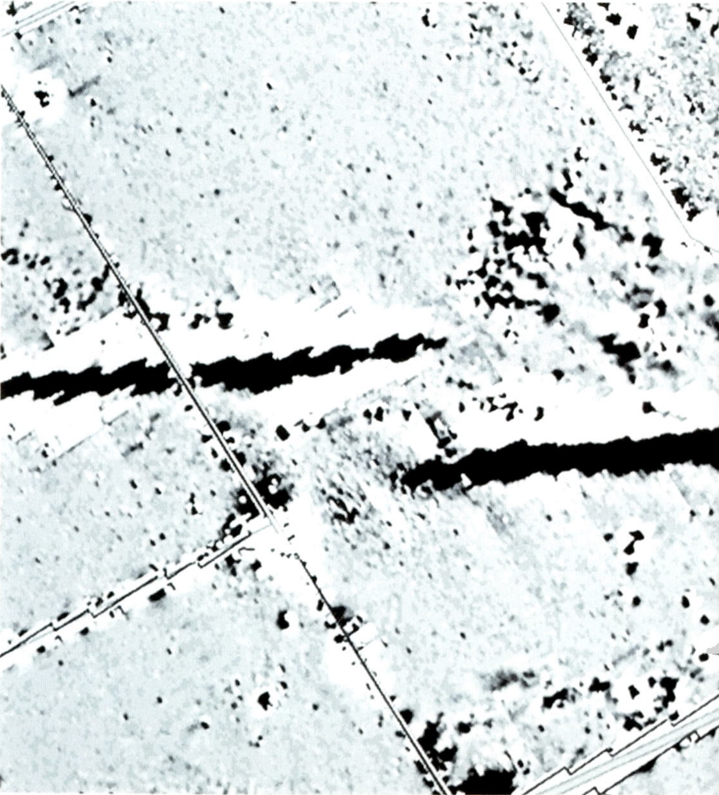

MAES HOWE | 2009
aquacryl & gouache on paper & print
72 × 105

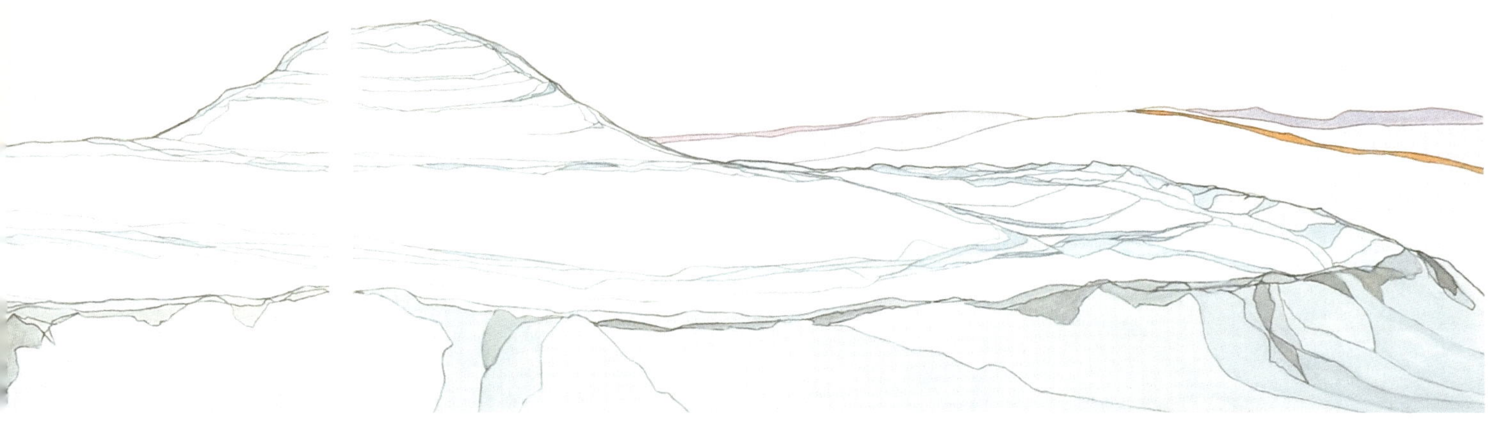

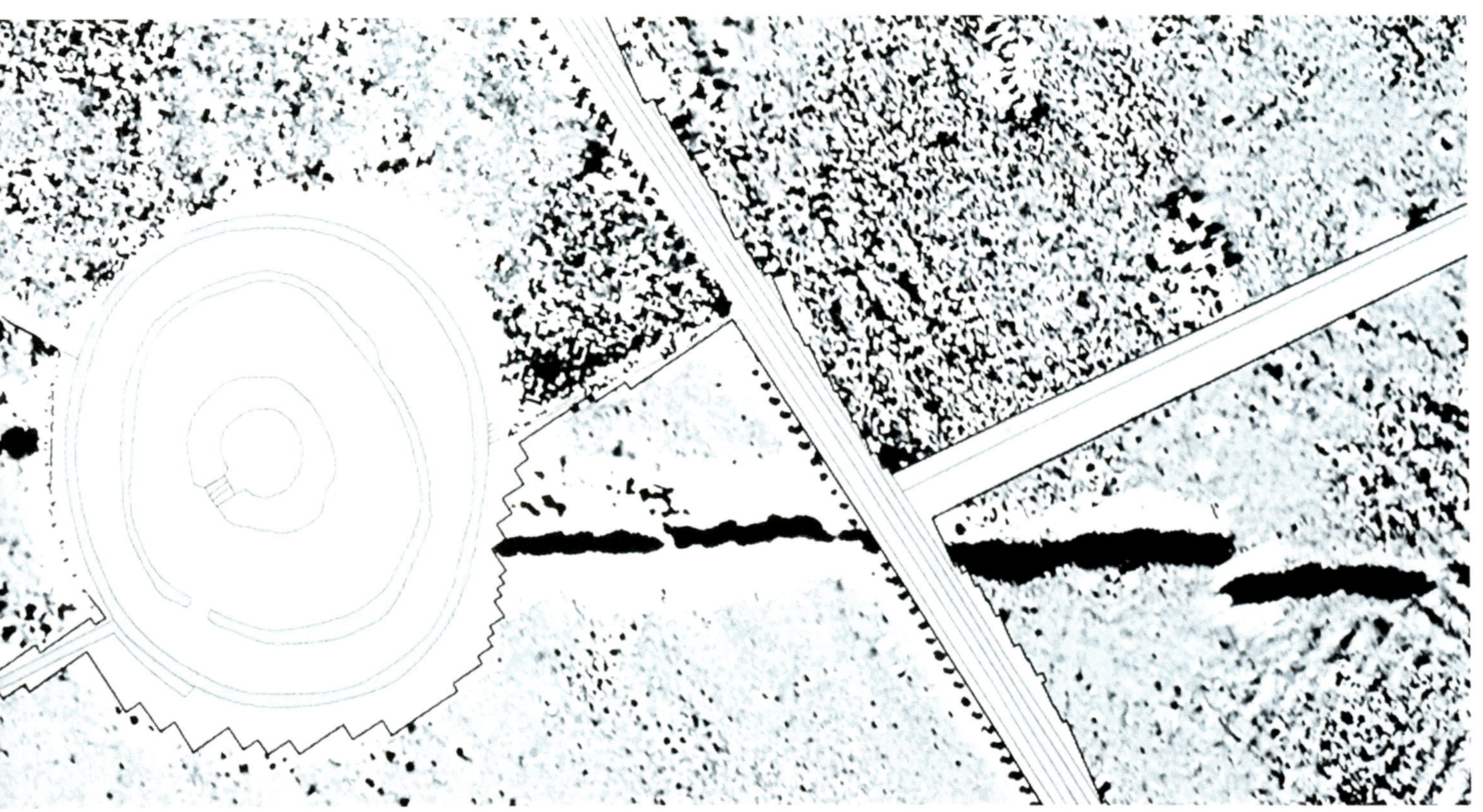

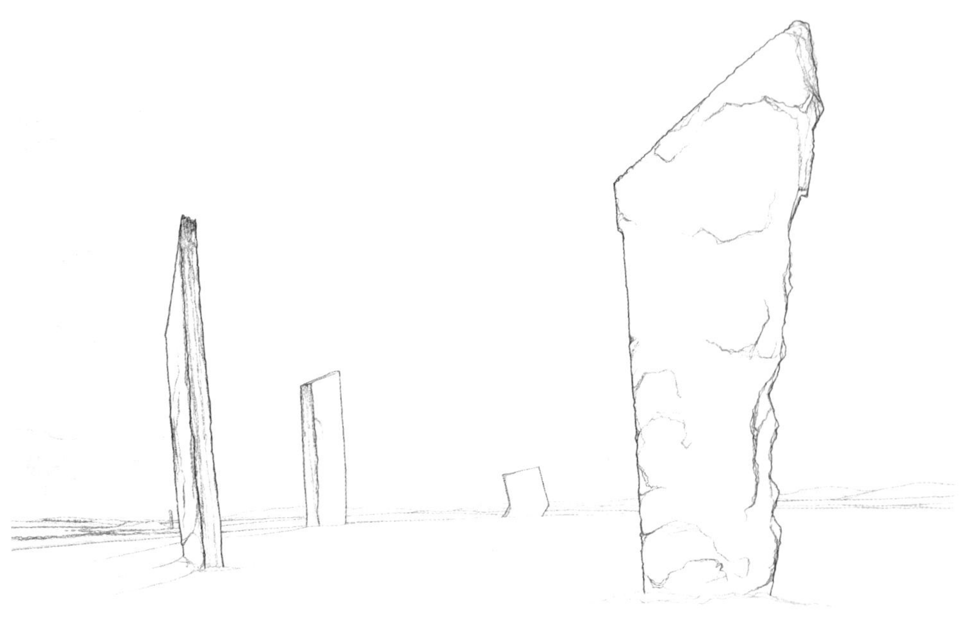

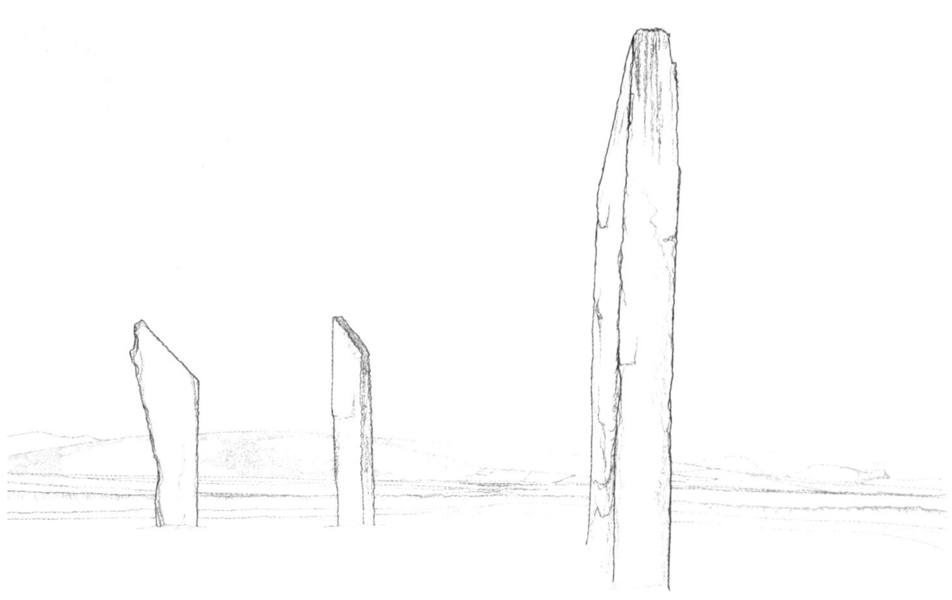

STENNESS: BRODGAR BEYOND 17 JUNE 2008 | 2008
pencil on paper
86×118

STENNESS: HOY BEYOND 18 JUNE 2008 | 2008
pencil on paper
86×118

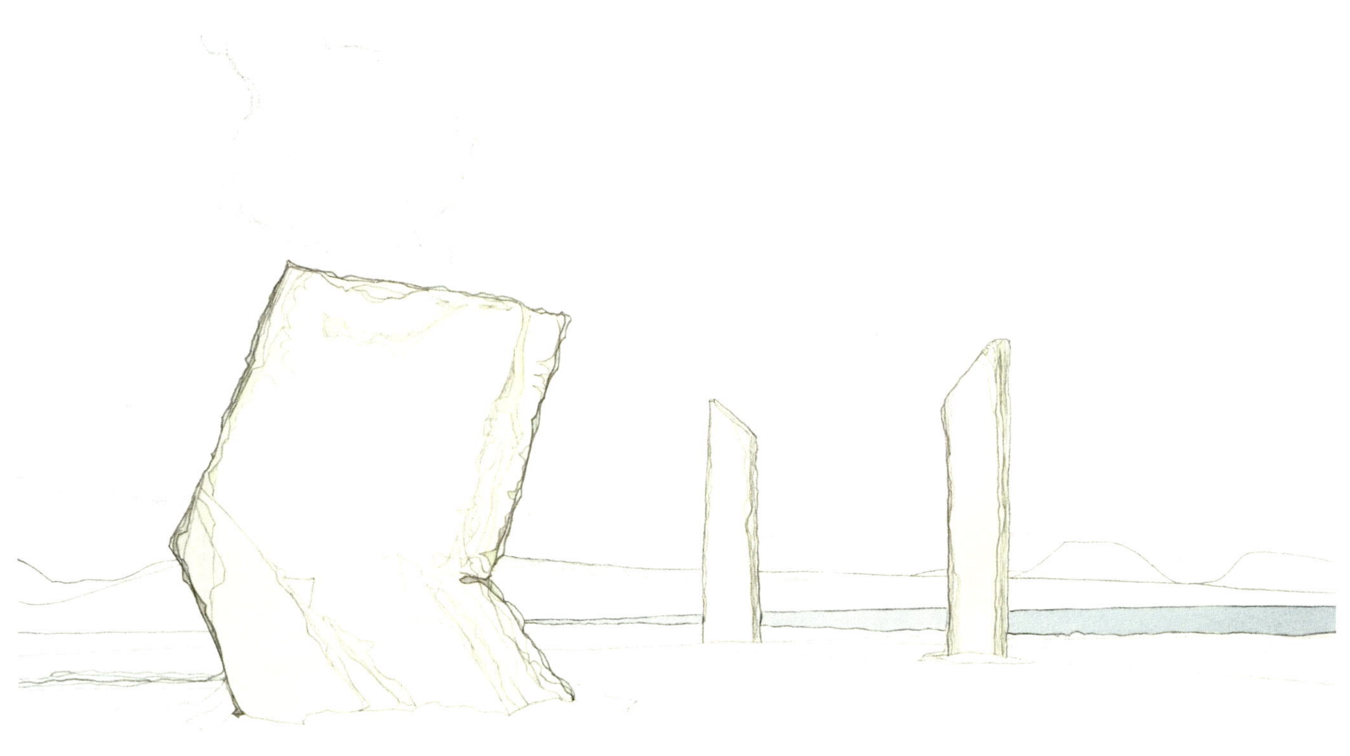

STENNESS 16 FEB 2006 | 2006
acrylic & pencil on paper
32 × 52

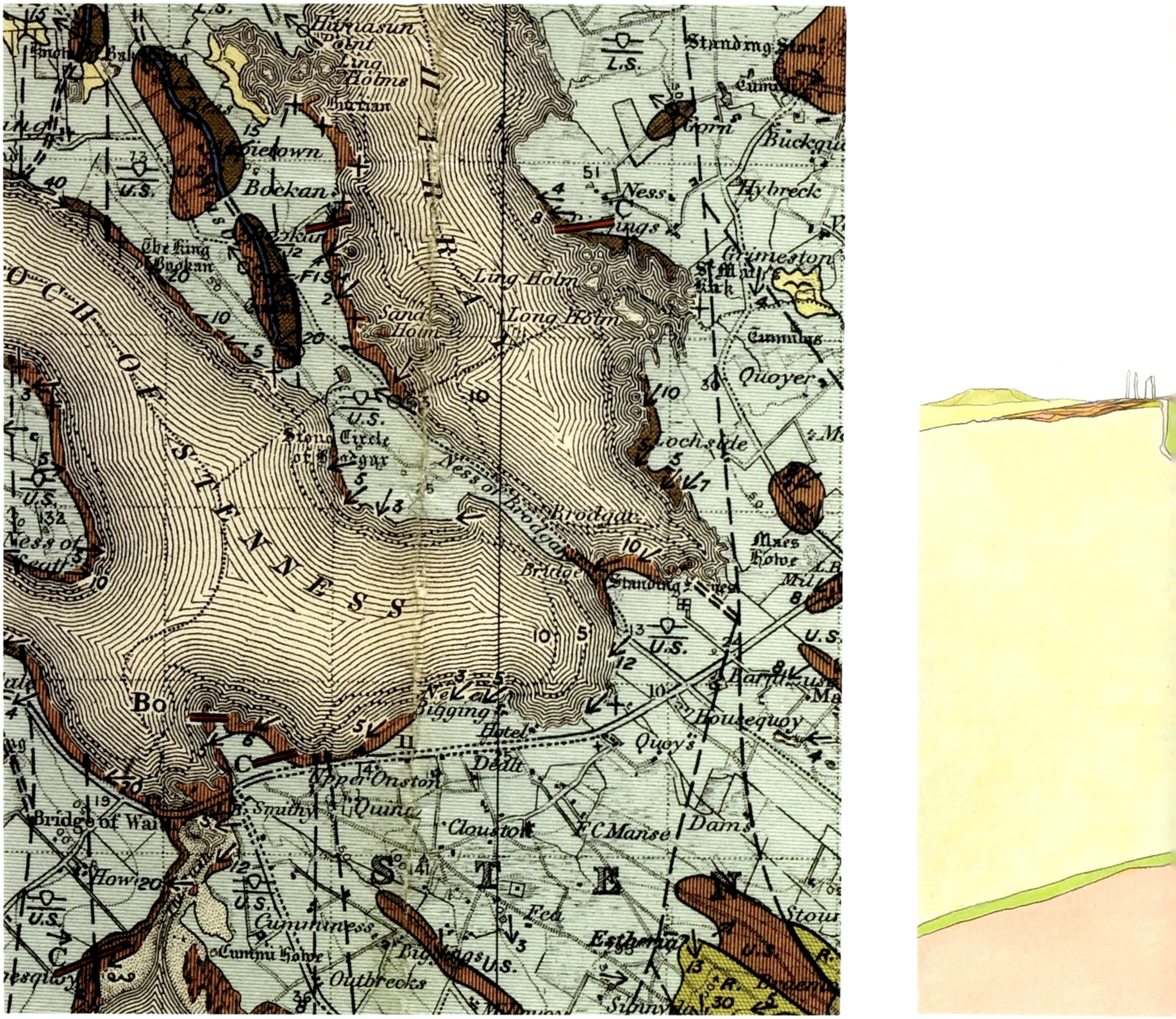

BRODGAR AND THE TWO LOCHS | 2009
aquacryl & gouache on paper & print
40 × 96

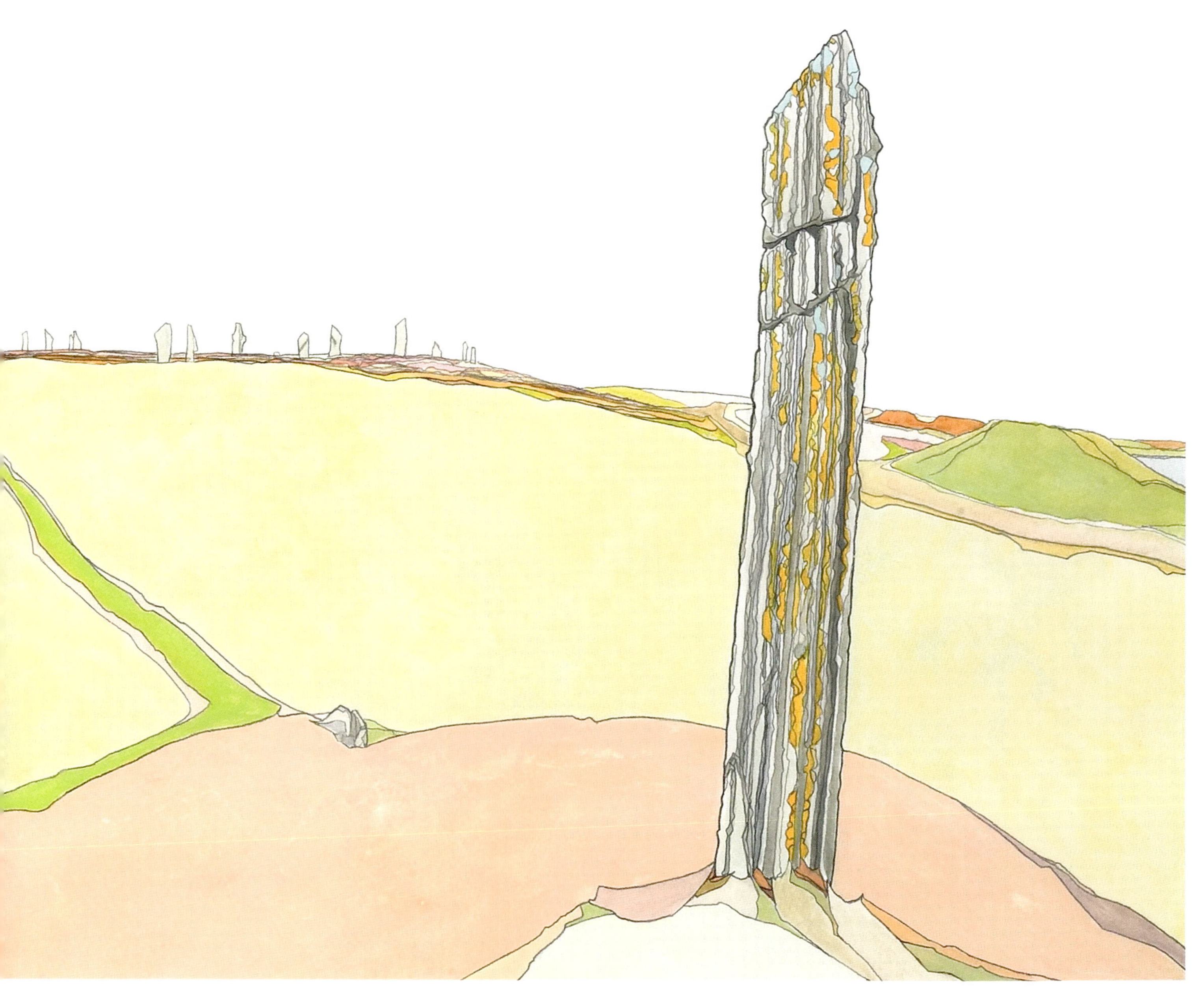

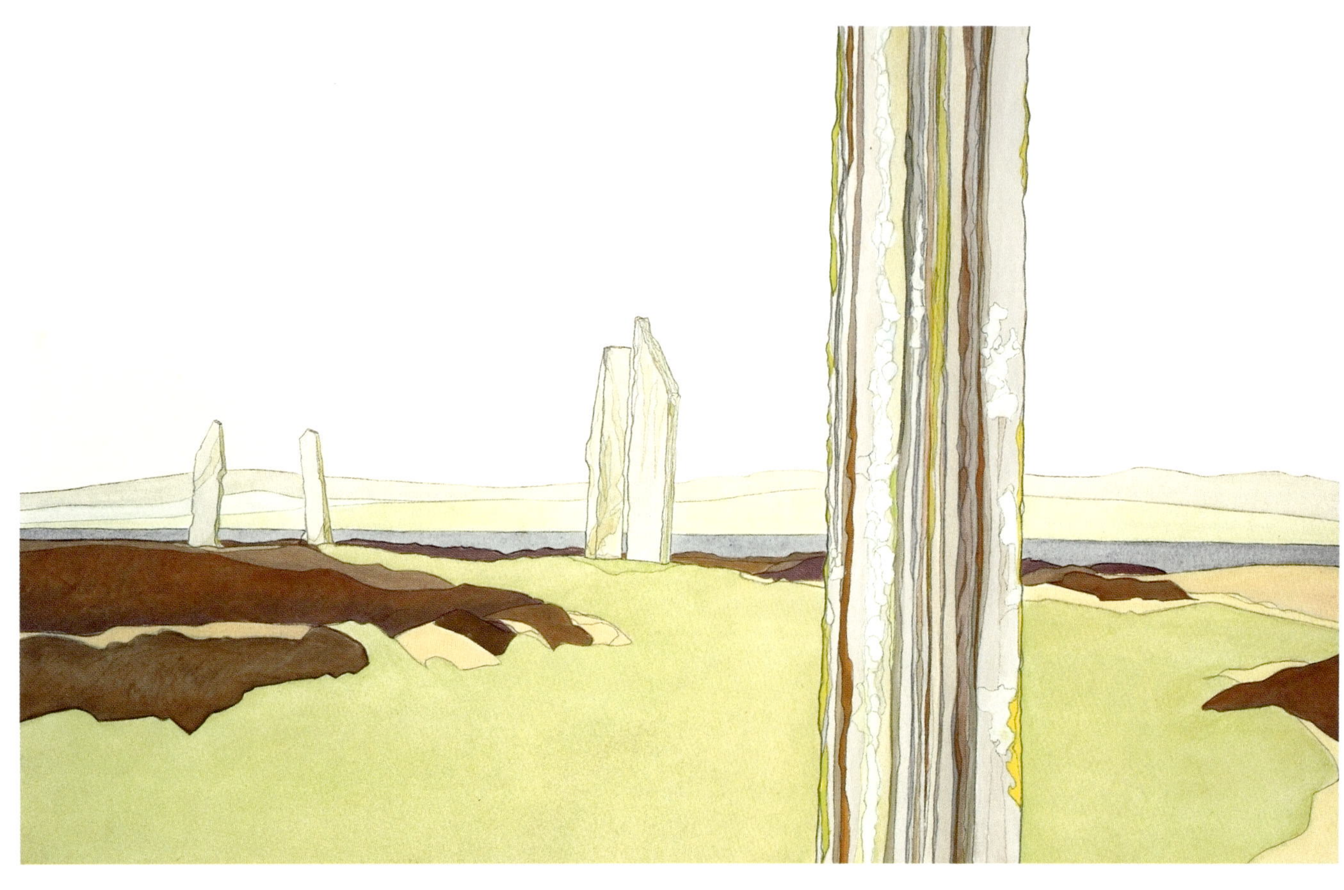

BRODGAR 21 FEB 2006 | 2006
aquacryl & gouache on paper
32 × 52

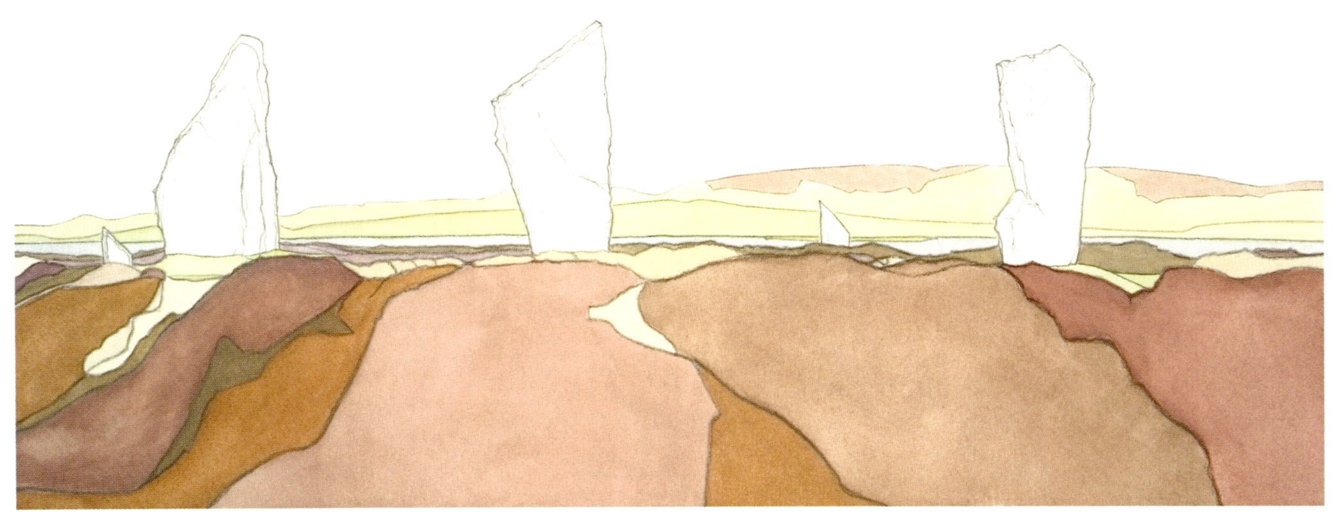

BRODGAR 21 FEB 2006 | 2006
aquacryl & gouache on paper
32 × 52

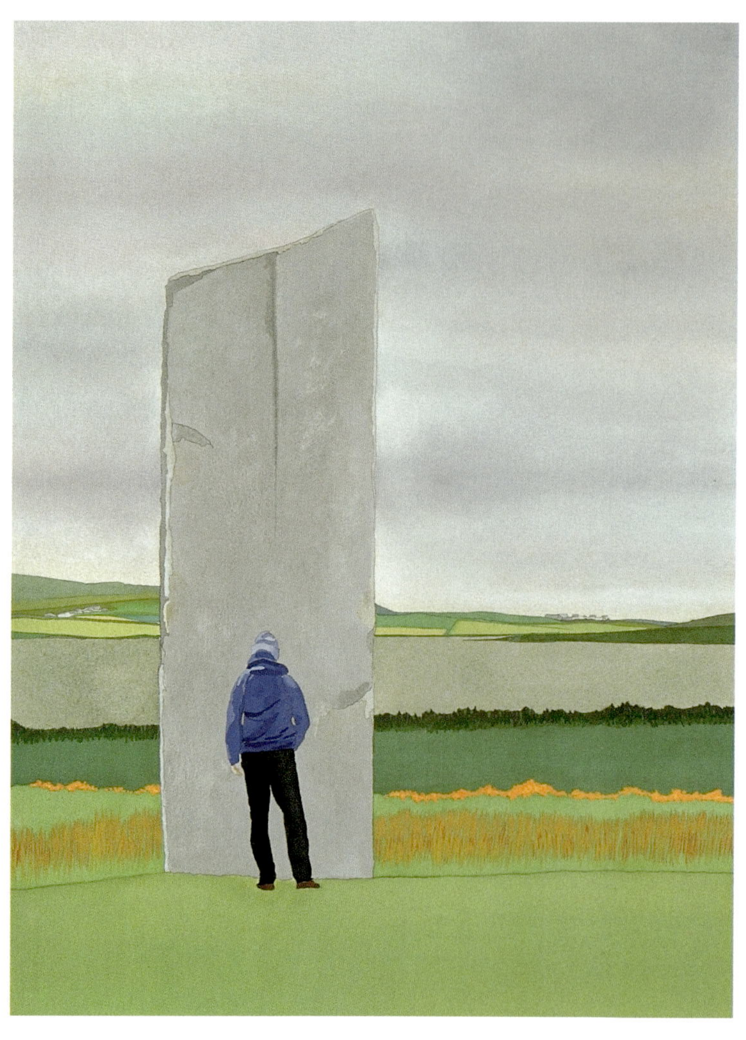

FIGURE AND STONE, STENNESS | 1987

gouache on paper

75 × 57

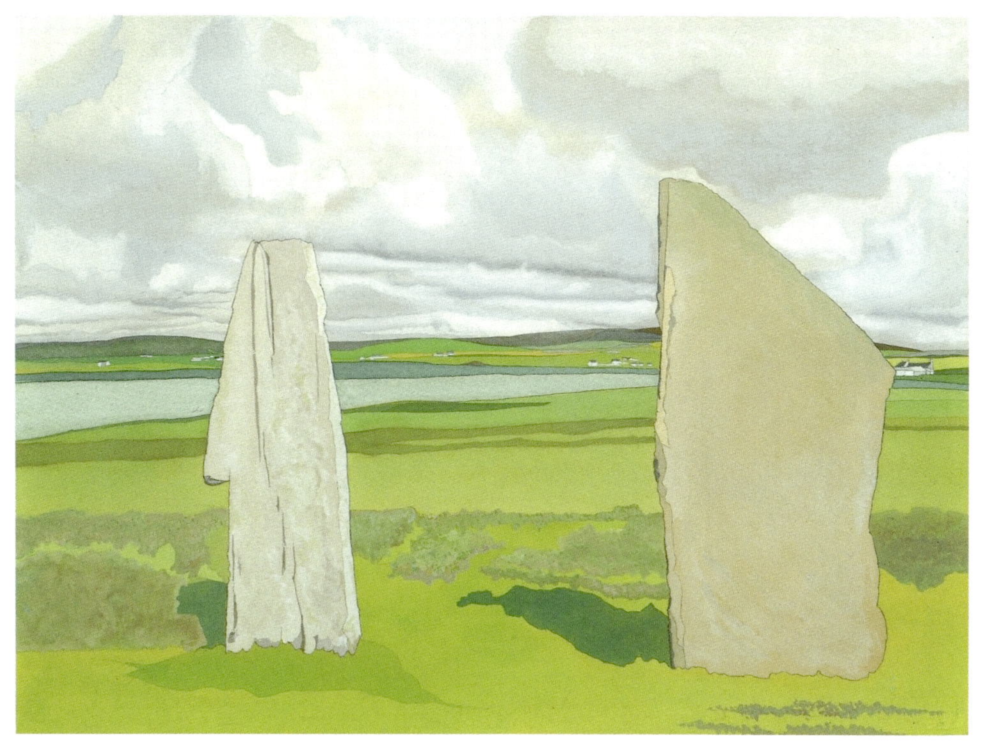

BRODGAR AND LOCH HARRAY | 1987
acrylic on paper
57 × 76

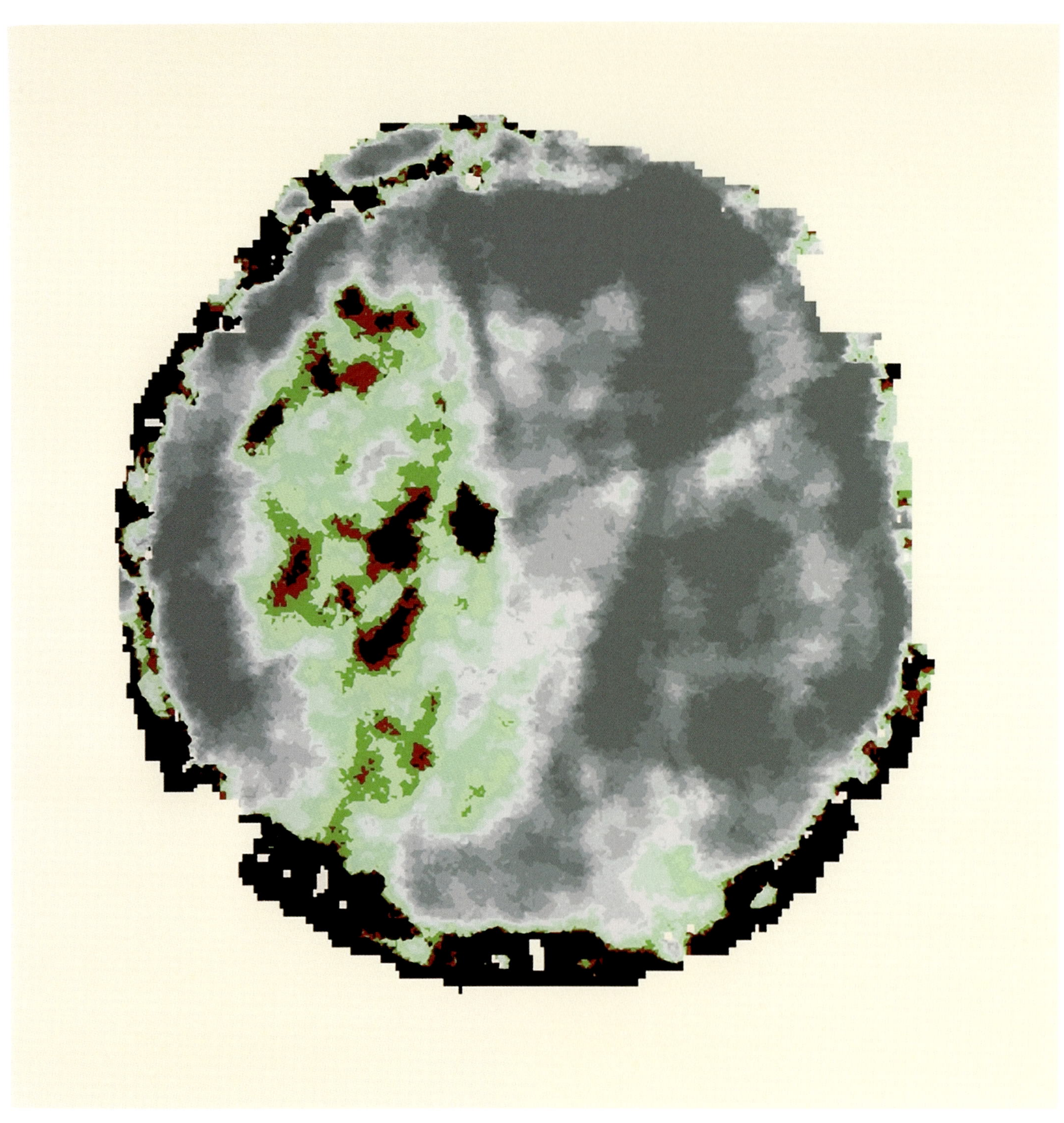

BRODGAR CIRCLE: GREEN | 2009
aquacryl & gouache on paper & print
50×110

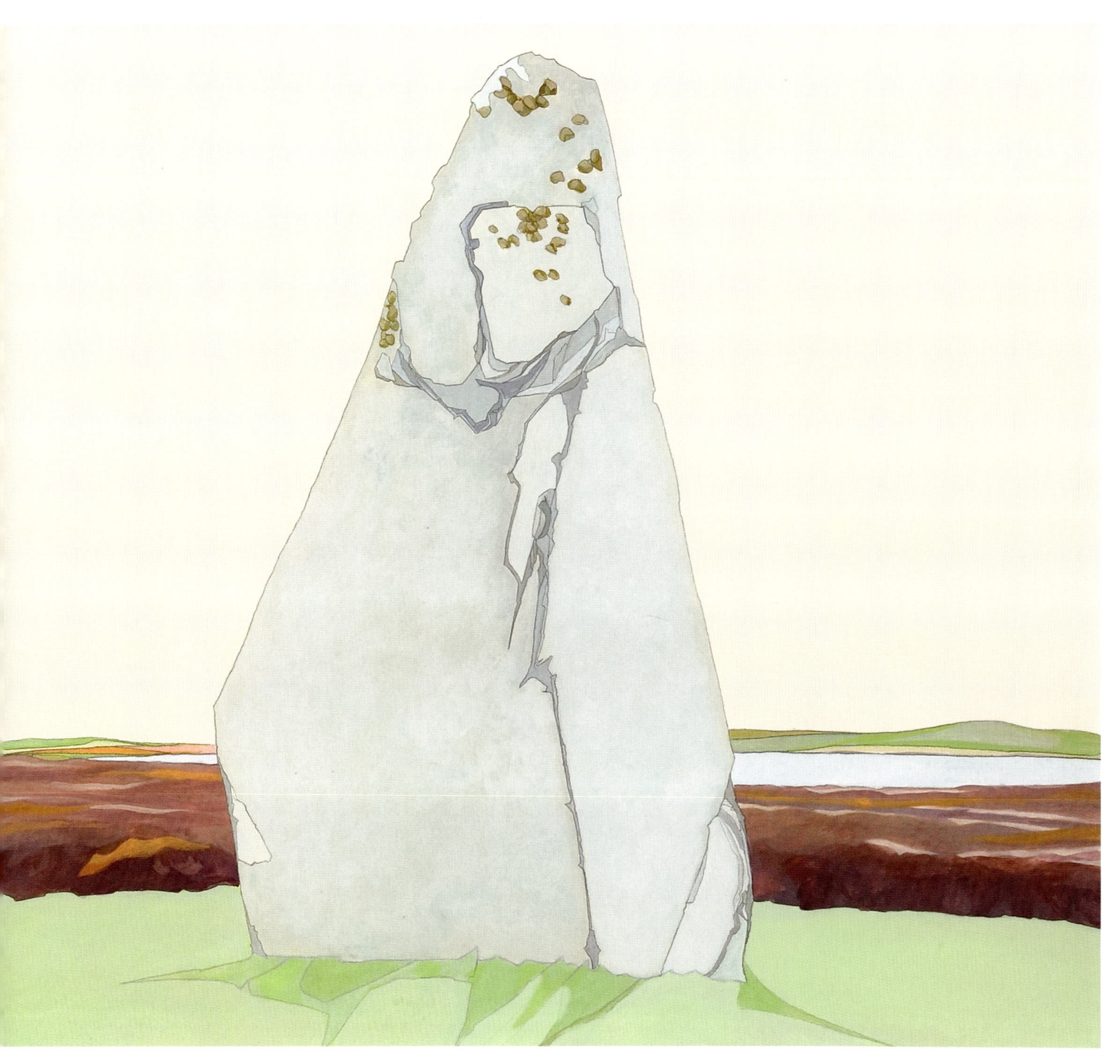

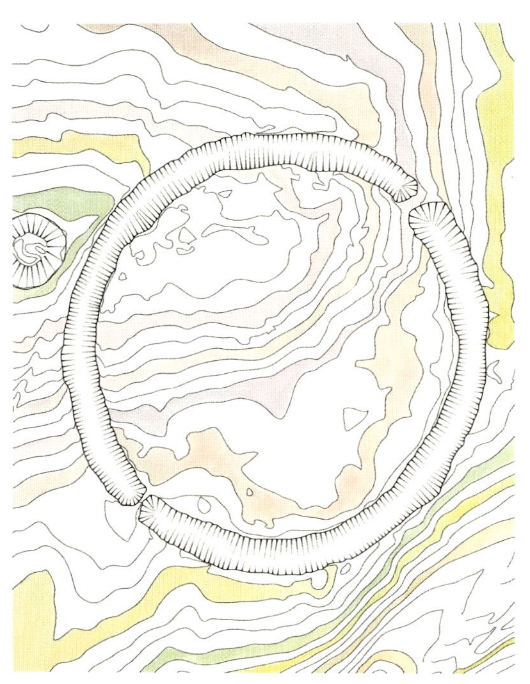 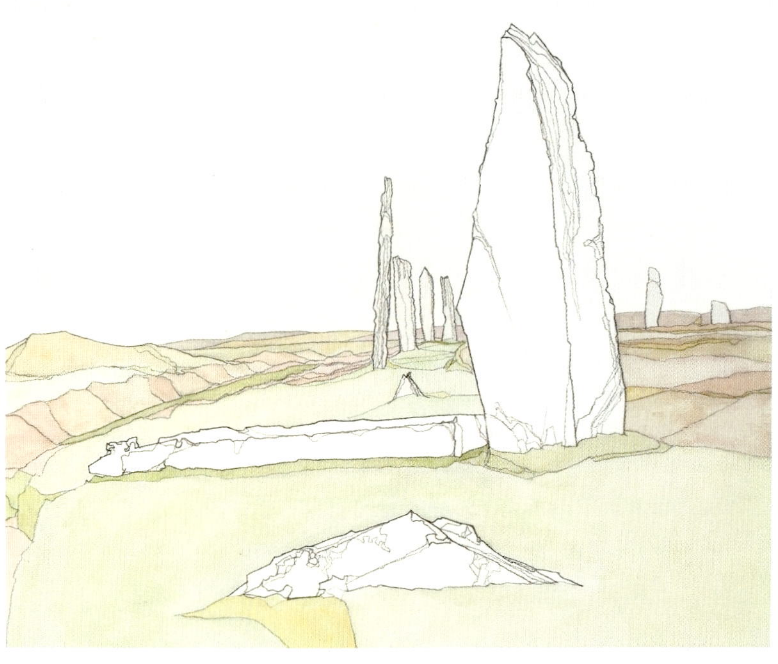

BRODGAR RING | 2009
aquacryl & gouache on paper & print
50×102

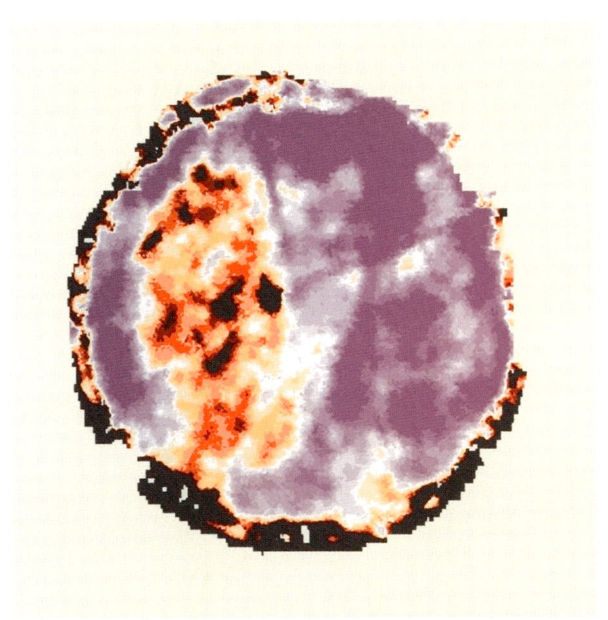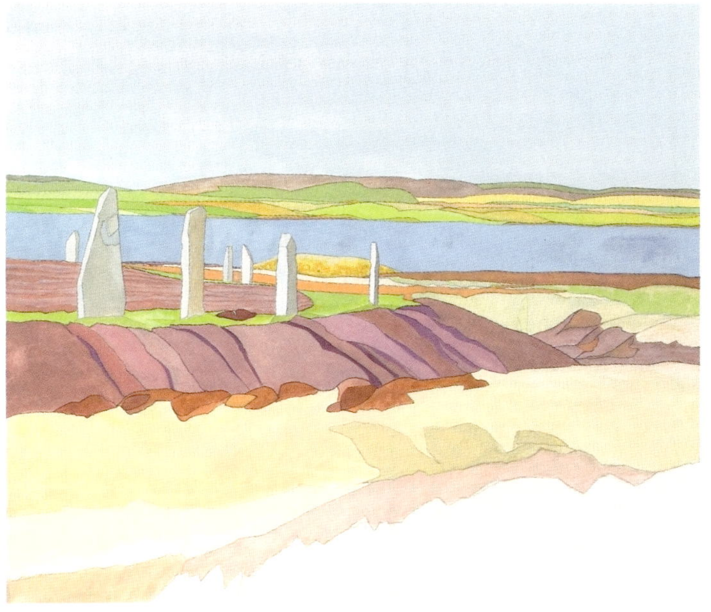

BRODGAR CIRCLE: HEATHER | 2009
aquacryl & gouache on paper & print
50 × 110

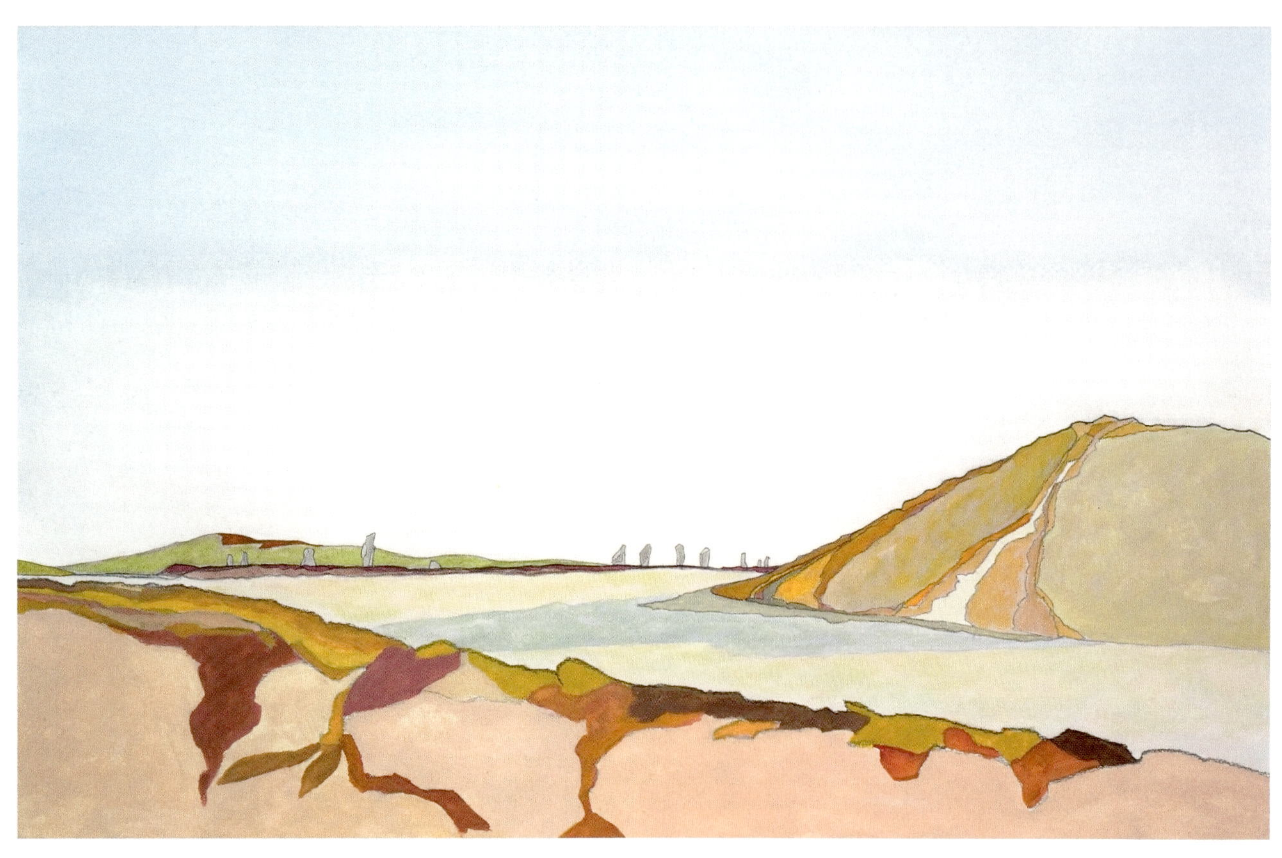

SALT KNOWE AND BRODGAR RING | 2010

aquacryl & gouache on paper

31 × 50

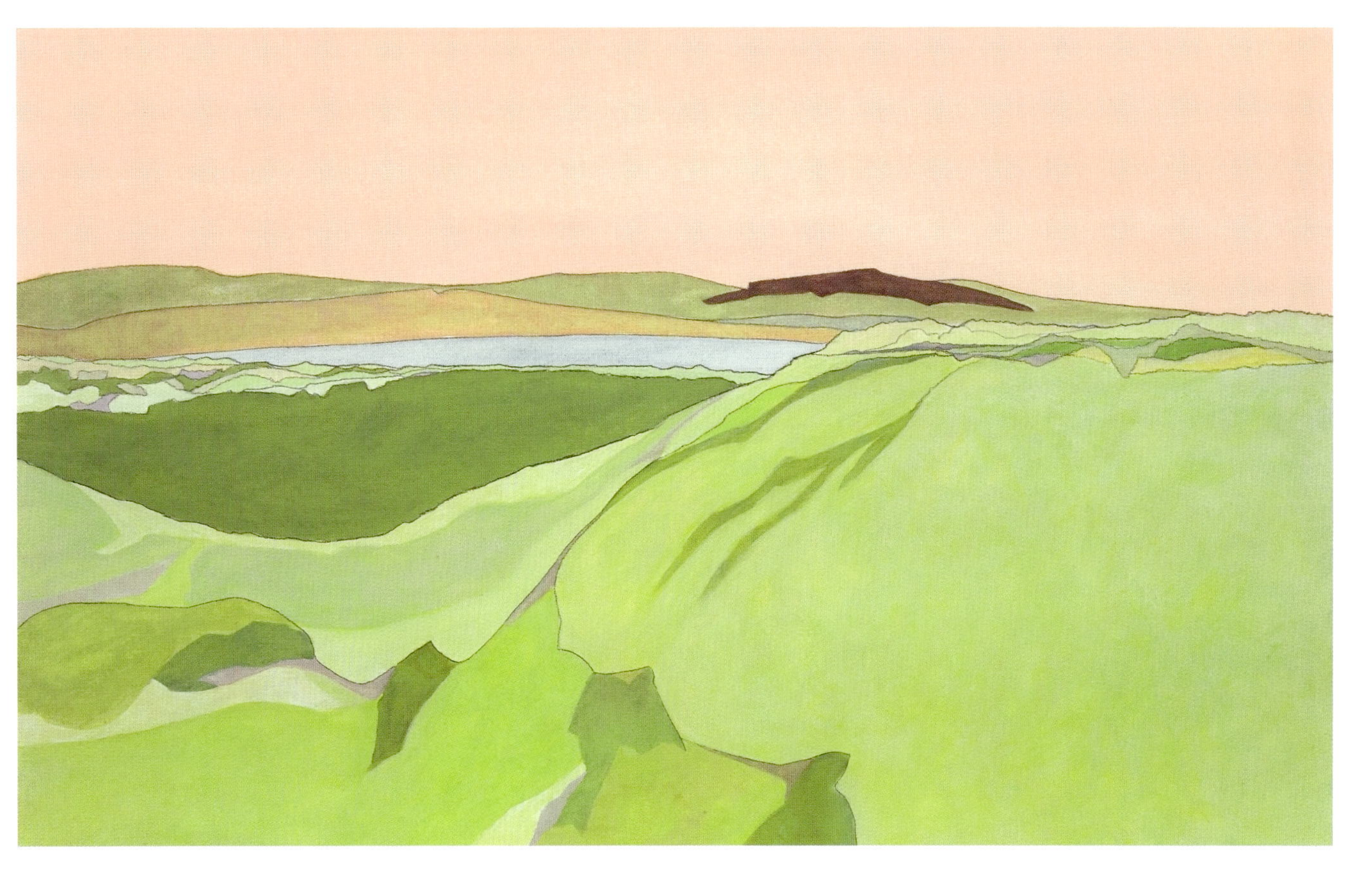

BOOKAN: THE HENGE | 2010
aquacryl & gouache on paper
31 × 50

I first came to Skara Brae some twenty-five years ago. We camped in the sand dunes just beside the houses of the Neolithic village. All was open; we just clambered around.

What a contrast today. There is a large visitors' centre, and fences and railings and made-up paths throughout. True access is forbidden.

Such is progress in this once so beautiful place.

17 JAN 2010

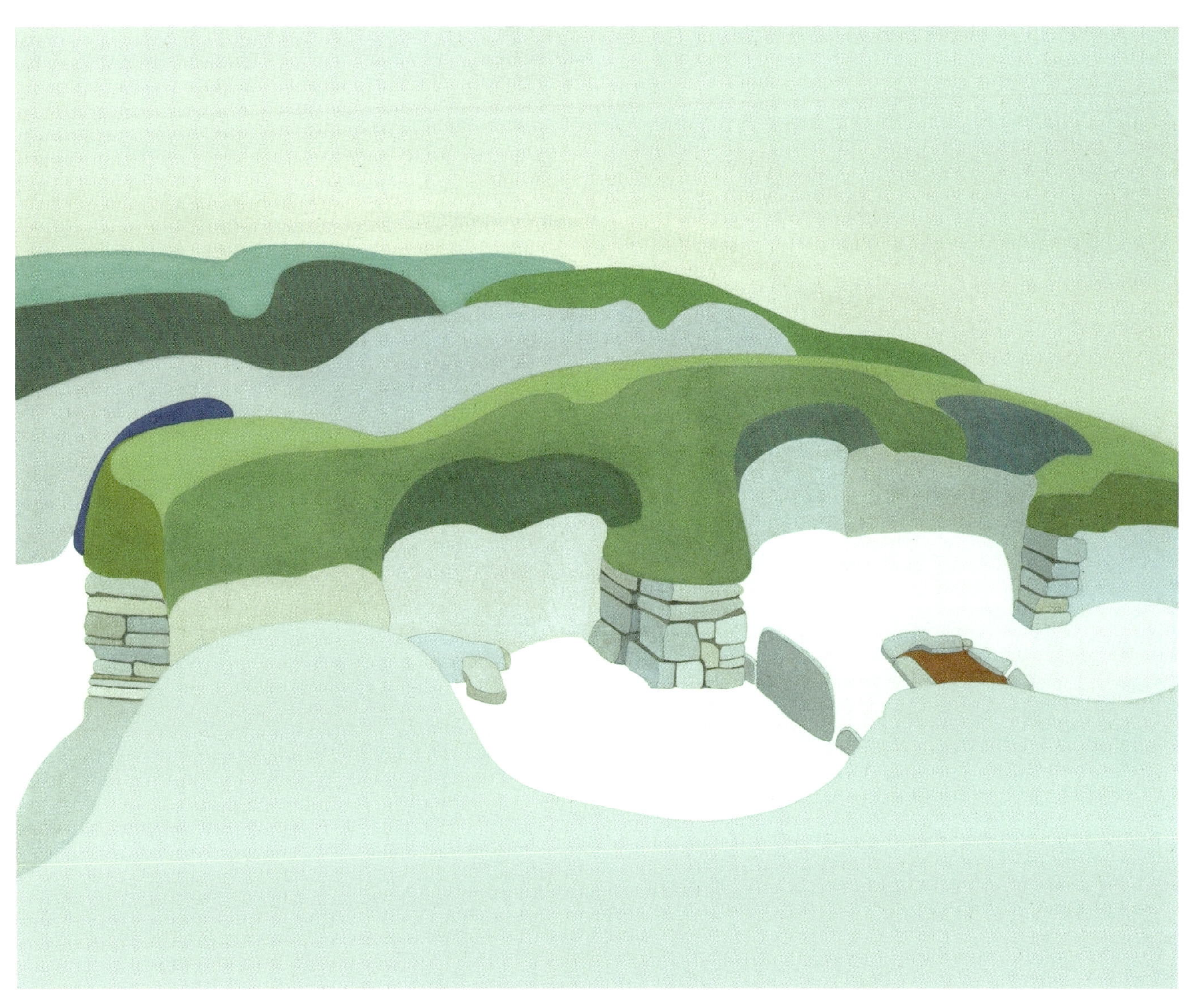

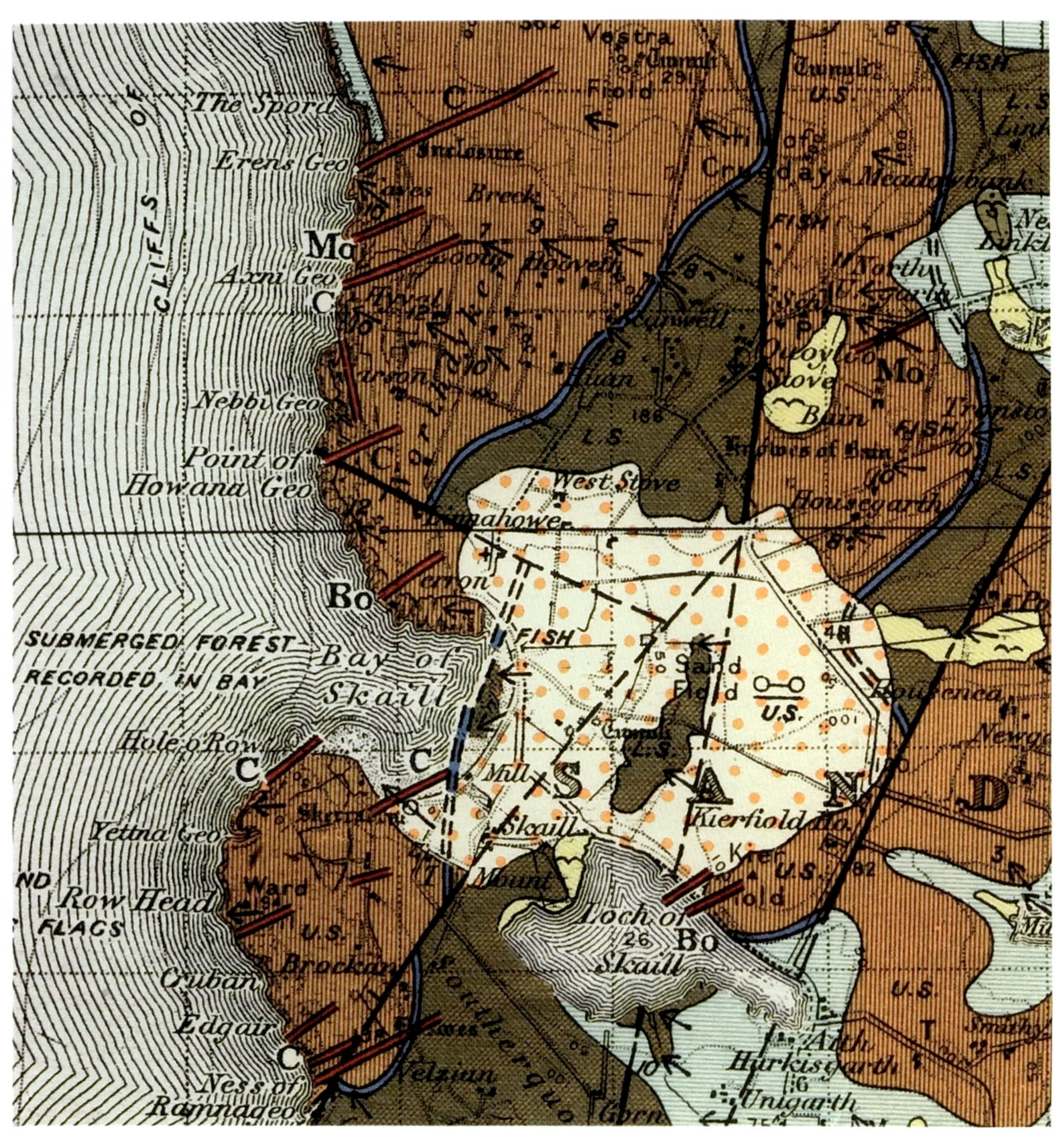

SKARA BRAE AND THE BAY OF SKAILL | 2009

aquacryl & gouache on paper & print

40 × 100

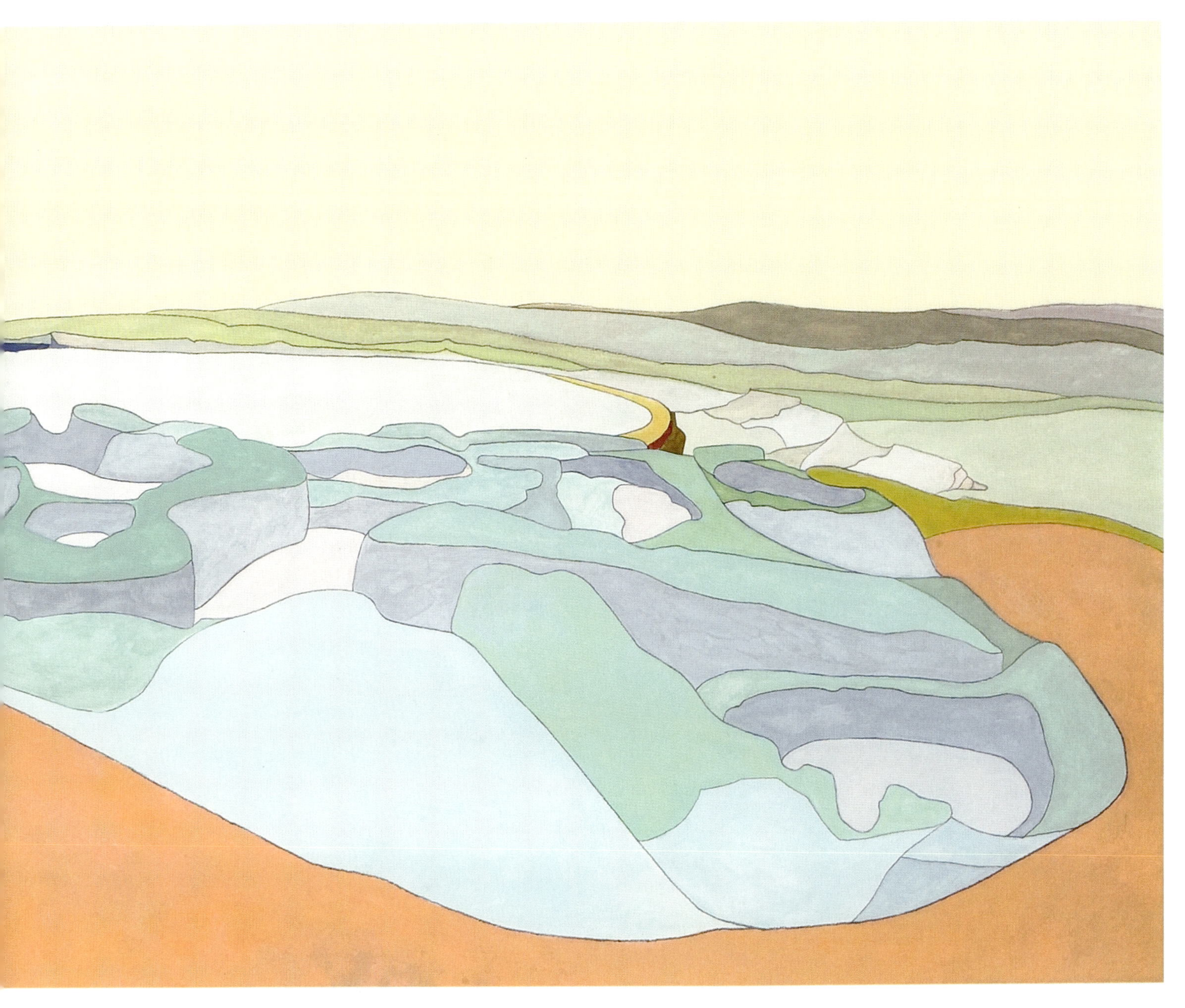

ASSYNT

Three tracks to Suilven – from Inverkirkaig, from Lochinver and from Elphin

Assynt, in the far northwest of Scotland, has the most dramatic landscape in Britain. Geology rules. The base is Lewisian gneiss. Very old, and hard, it takes the form of a myriad of small rounded hills interspersed by lochs and lochans. This same type of landscape can be seen in parts of the Outer Hebrides. The difference in Assynt is that 900 million years ago this gneiss was overlaid with a red sandstone named after the area of Torridon to the south, where it also appears.

This layer of sandstone has been completely eroded except for a few remaining parts that now appear as mountains. So these mountains have not been pushed up from below, as are most, but are just the remains of this sheet of sandstone. Perhaps I concentrate too much on the geology, but it is so apparent to all, even the uninitiated like myself. It is my favourite part of all the country. Each return reinforces the immense impact it has on me.

The mountains include Quinag, Canisp, Stac Pollaidh, Suilven, Cul Mor and Cul Beag. Most striking of these is Suilven in the centre of the group. The view from the summit is spectacular.

You see all the other separate peaks like giant castles set in this mass of water – the small lochans. While not very high (731 metres), it is quite a climb. It is steep, and the difficulty is increased by the need to walk a minimum of eight miles to reach the base.

There are three tracks into Suilven. One starts from the west at Lochinver and arrives at the northern flank (p. 42). The other, also from the west, starts at Inverkirkaig and leads to the south flank (p. 47). The third starts from the east at Elphin (p. 45). Each track gives a very different aspect of the mountain. I attempt to show that, and also the way these mountains group together as a family.

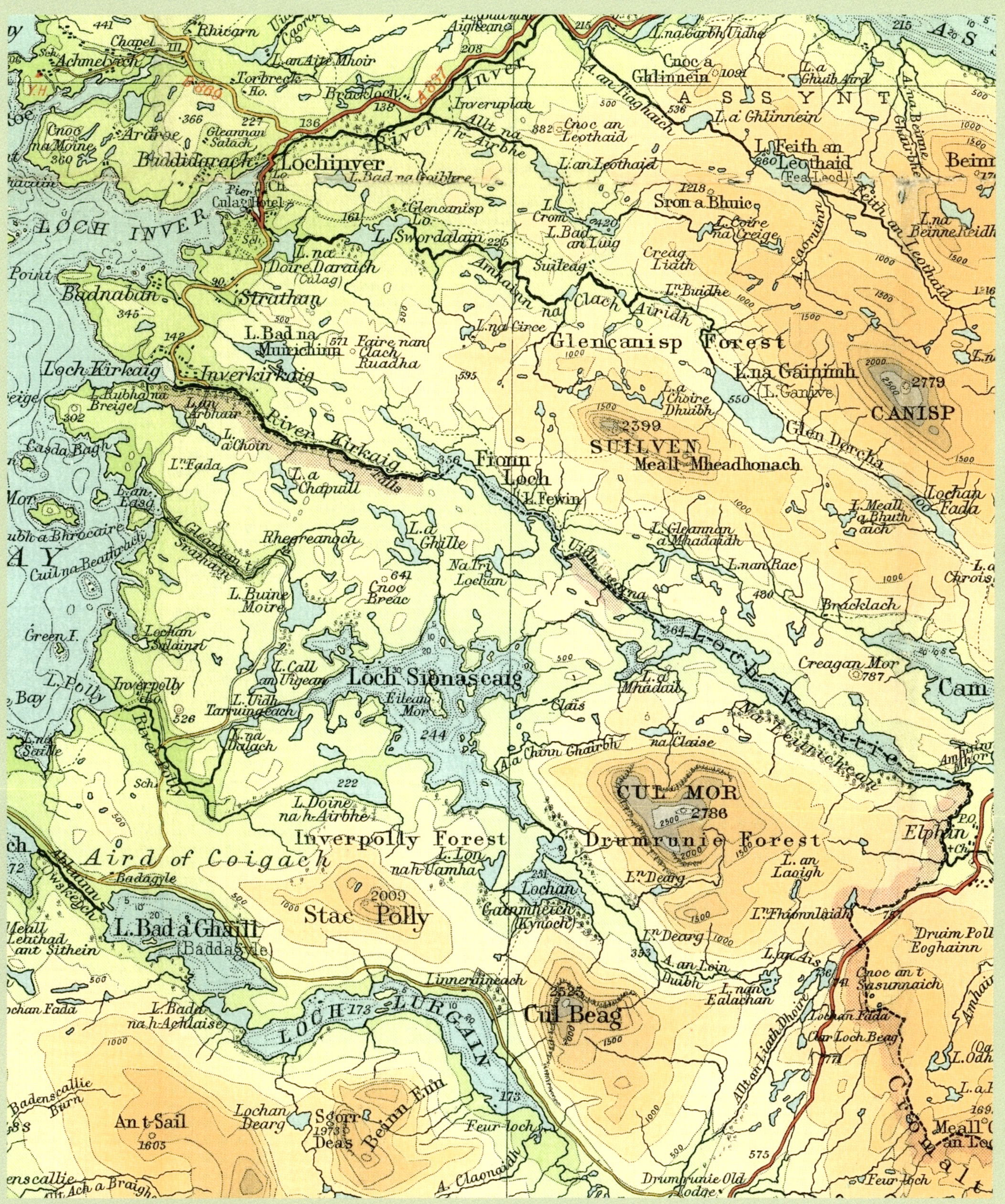

Rhicarn
Chapel
Achmelvich
Torbreck Ho.
L. an Aite Mhoir
Aigheau
L. na Garbh Uidhe
As
Cnoc a Ghlinnein
A na Ghuib Aird
A na Beinne
Brackloch
River Inver
Inverupian
Allt na h-Airbhe
A ' an Tsaghaich
ASSYNT
A na Beinne
Cnoc na Moine
Ardroe
Buddidurach
Gleannan Salach
Cnoc an Leothaid
L. a Ghlinnein
L. Feith an Leothaid
(Fea Leod)
Beinn
Lochinver
Culag Ho.
Ch
Glencanisp Lo.
L. an Leothaid
Sron a Bhuic
Keith an Leothaid
L. na Beinne Reidh
Pier
Culag Hotel
L. Bad na Cailbre
L. Crom
L. Bad an Luig
Creag Liath
L. Coire na Creige
L. na
L. na Doire Daraich (Culag)
Strathan
Am Amhainn na Clach
Suileag
L. Buidhe
Auridh
Glencanisp Forest
L. Bad na Muirichinn
Faire nan Clach Ruadha
L. na Circe
L. na Gainimh (L. Ganive)
CANISP
Loch Kirkaig
Inverkirkaig
L. Rubha na Breige
Lan Arbhair
L. Choire Dhuibh
2399
Glen Dorcha
Casda Bagh
L. a'Choin
L. Fada
River Kirkaig
Fionn Loch
SUILVEN
Meall Mheadhonach
L. Meall a Bhuth aich
Lochan Fada
L. an Easg
L. a Chapuill
L. Fewin
Uidh Fhearna
L. Gleannan a Mhadaidh
L. nan Rac
L. a Chrois
Cul na Bheathrach
Rhegreanach
Na Iri Lochan
Bracklach
Cnoc Breac
L. Buine Moire
L. Call an Uijean
Loch Sionascaig
Eilean Mor
Creagan Mor
Loch Veyatie
Cam
Green I.
L. Polly
Inverpolly
L. Uidh Tarruingeach
Clais
L. a Mhadaid
na Claise
Cul na Saille
Sch
L. Doine na h-Airbhe
A Chinn Ghairbh
CUL MOR
2786
Am Mhor
Inverpolly Forest
Aird of Coigach
L. Lon na h-Uamha
Drumrunie Forest
Elphin
Badagyle
Lochan Gaineimeleich (Kynoch)
L. an Laoigh
L. Bad a Ghaill (Baddagyle)
Stac Polly
2009
L. Dearg
L. Fhionnlaidh
Druim Poll Eoghainn
Metall Leathad an t Sithein
L. Dearg
Cnoc an t Sasunnaich
Linnerineach
A an Toin Duibh
Lochan Fada
Car Loch Beag
L. Bad na h-Achlaise
LOCH LURGAN
Cul Beag
2525
L. nan Ealachan
Lochan Fada
L. Odh
Lochan Fada
An t-Sail
1605
Lochan Dearg
Sgorr Deas
Beinn Enn
Feur loch
Drumrunie Old Lodge
Allt an Liath Dhoire
Meall an Teo
Badenscallie Burn
Ach a Braigh
A. Claonaidh
Feur loch

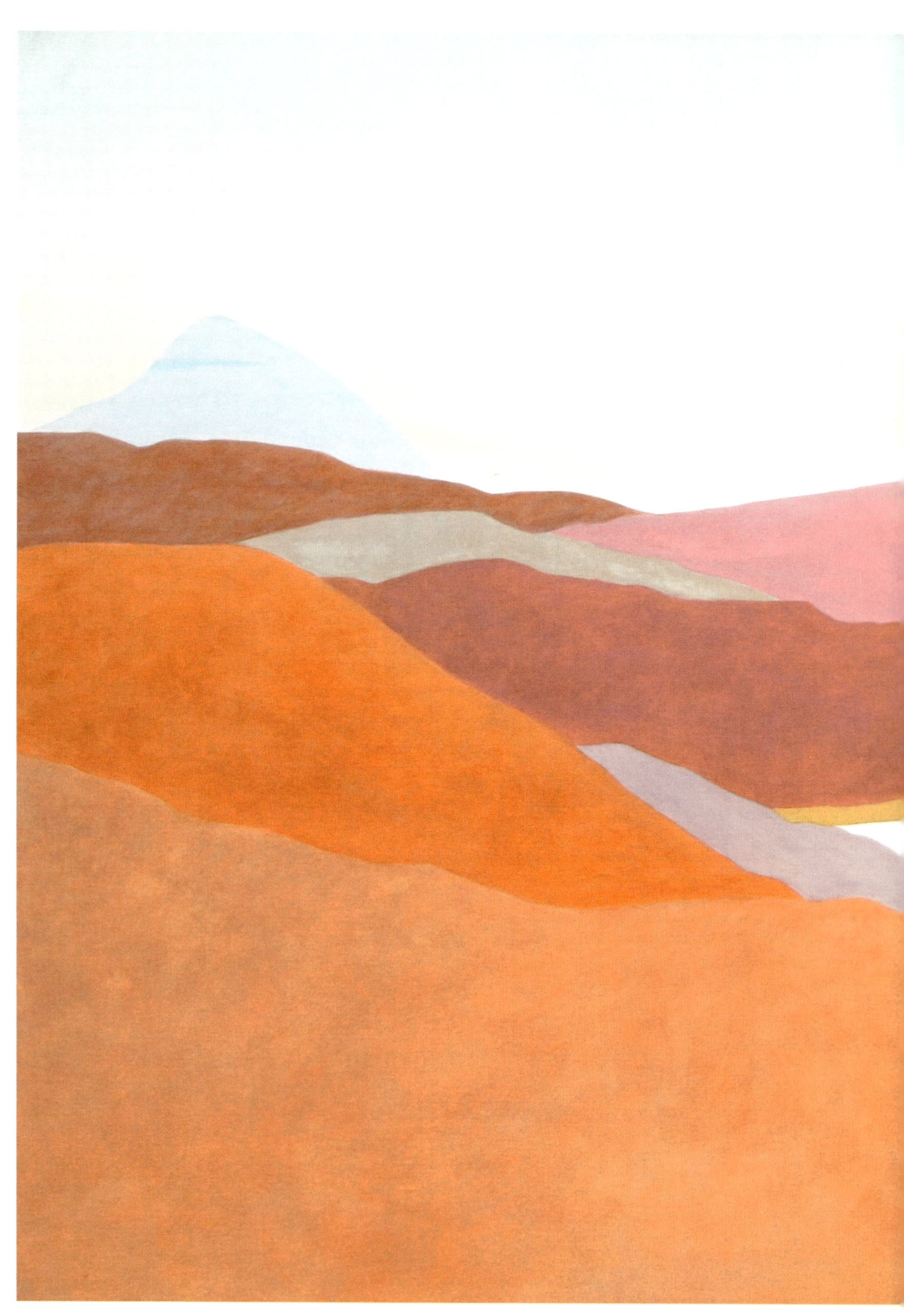

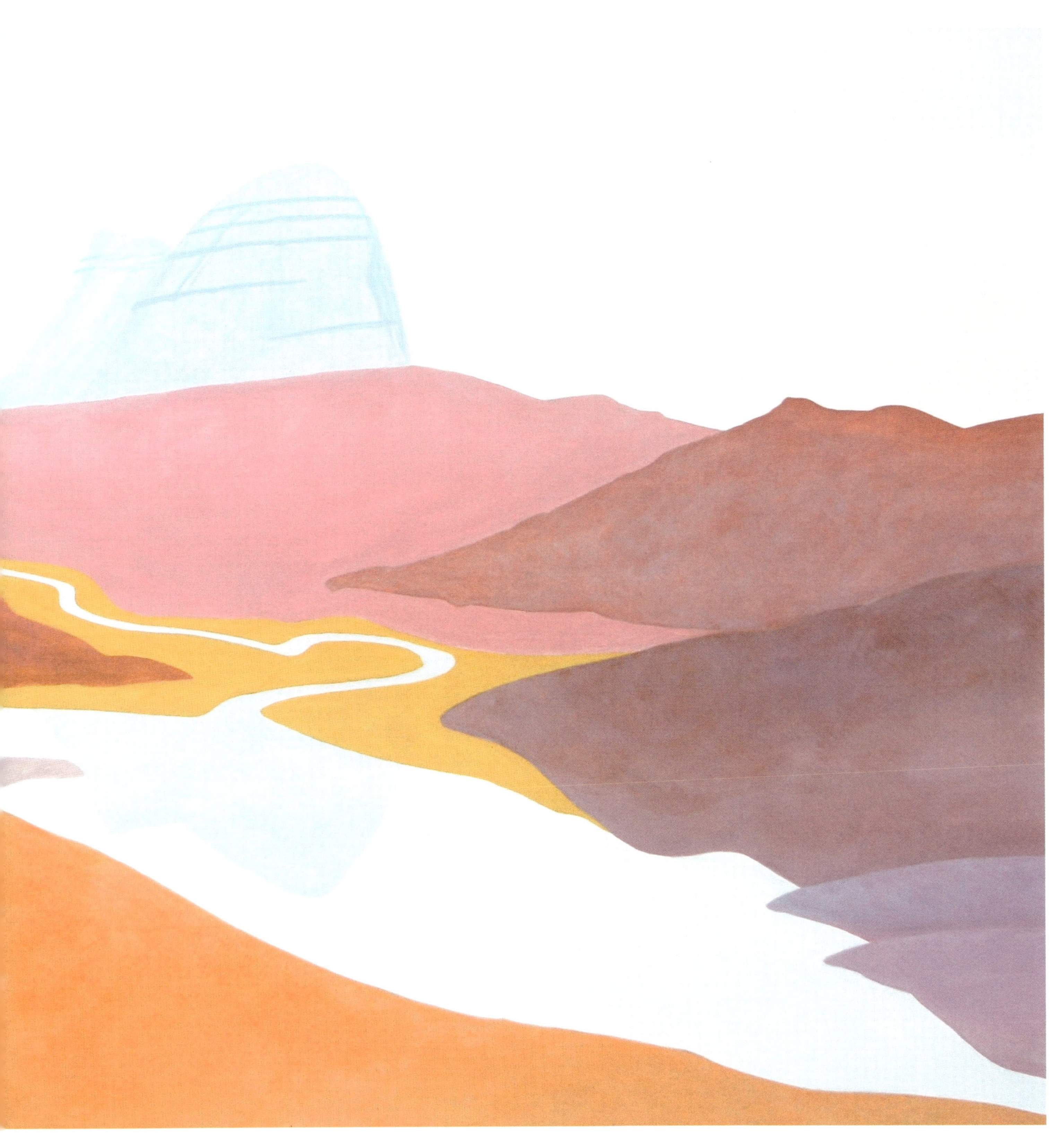

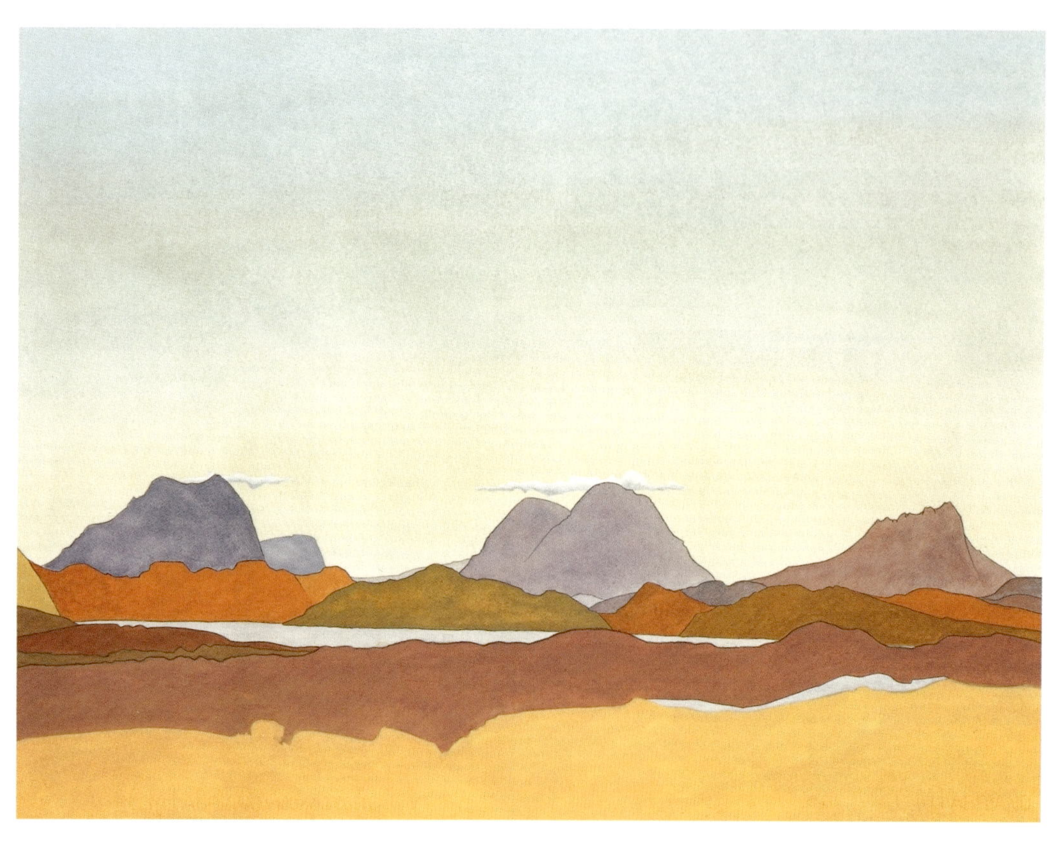

SUILVEN, CANISP, CUL MOR, STAC POLLAIDH | 2004/05
acrylic & gouache on paper
57 × 75

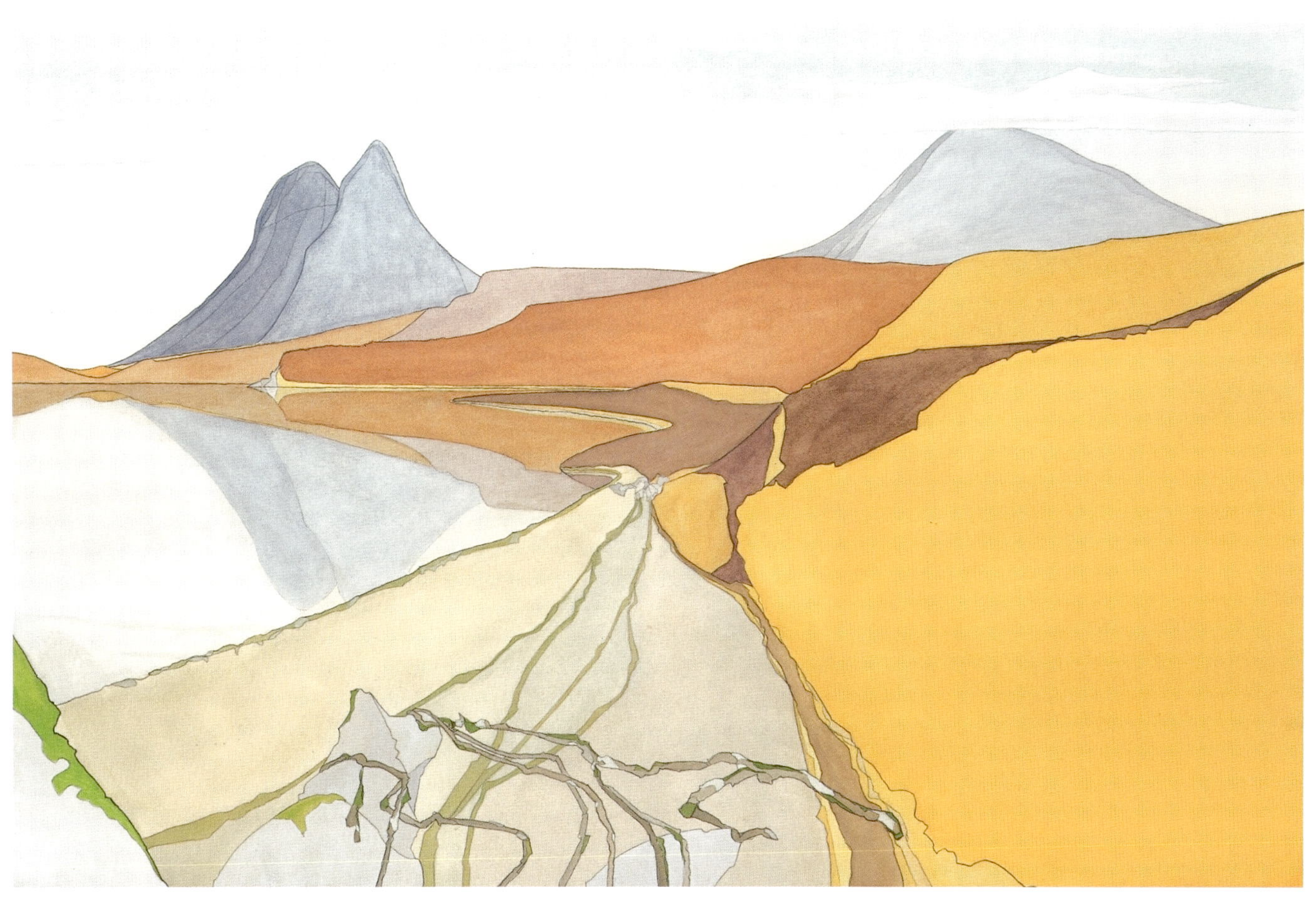

ELPHIN TO SUILVEN | 2004
acrylic & gouache on paper
67 × 101

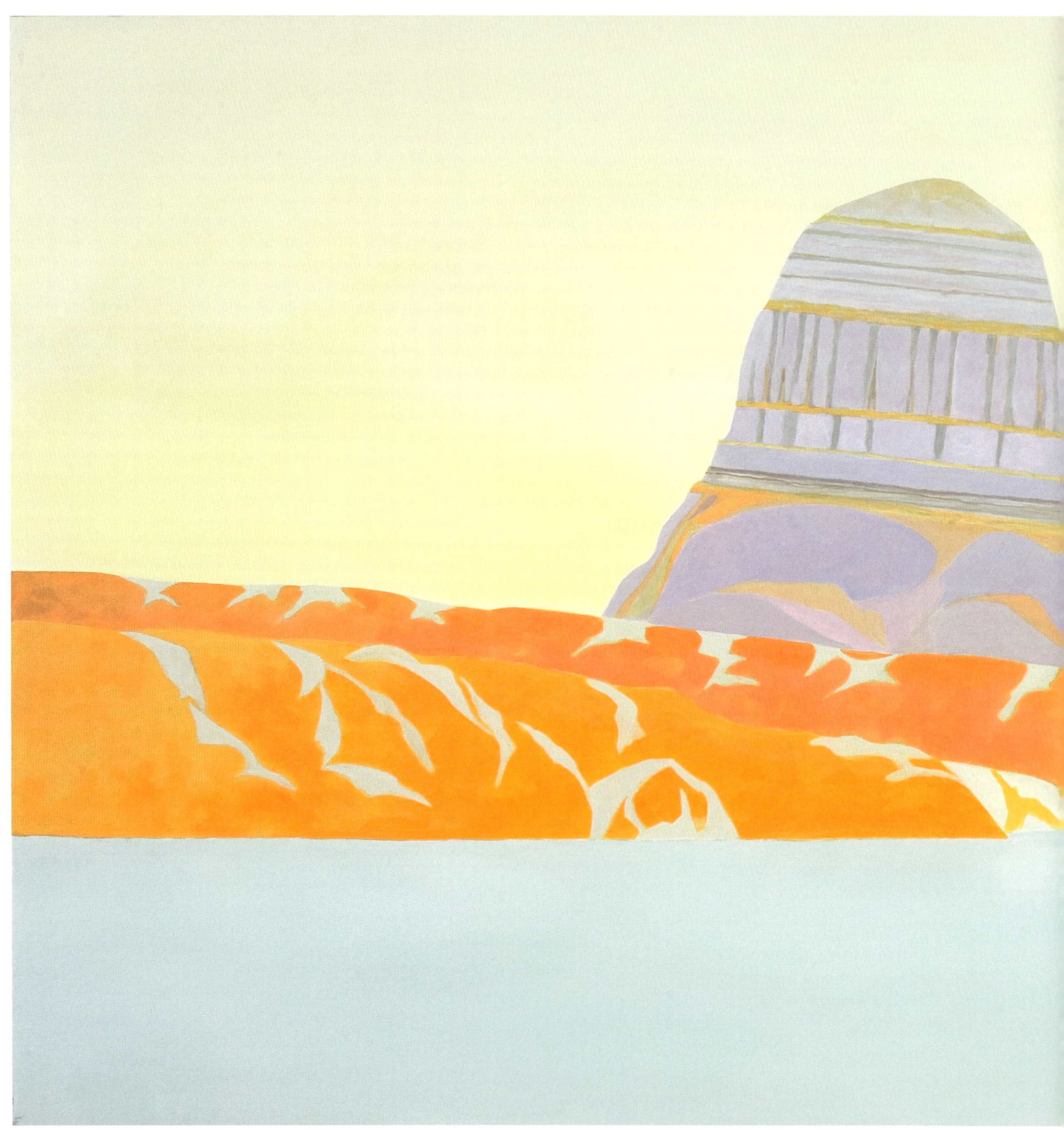

 ASSYNT

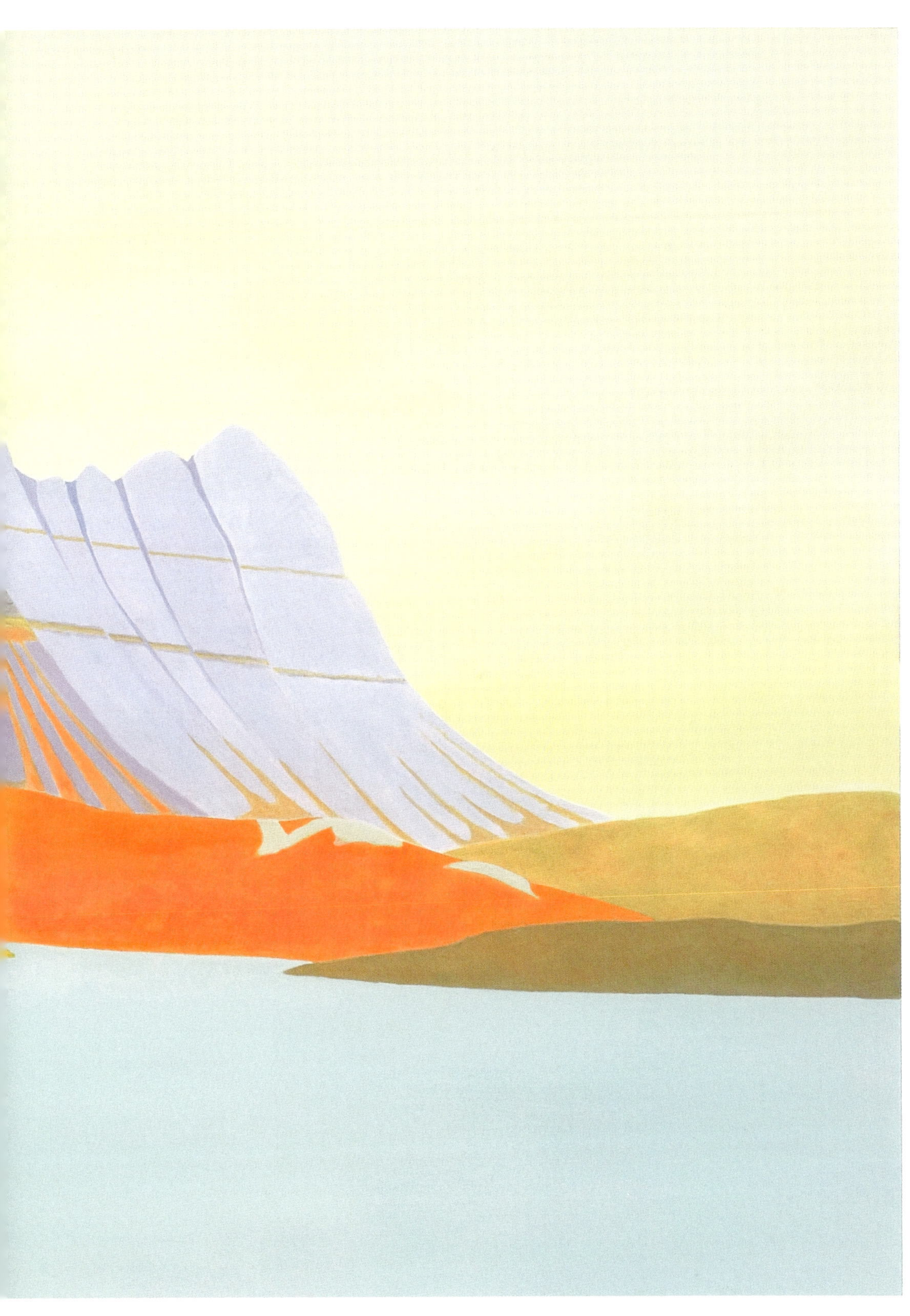

INVERKIRKAIG TO SUILVEN | 2007
acrylic on canvas
80 × 140

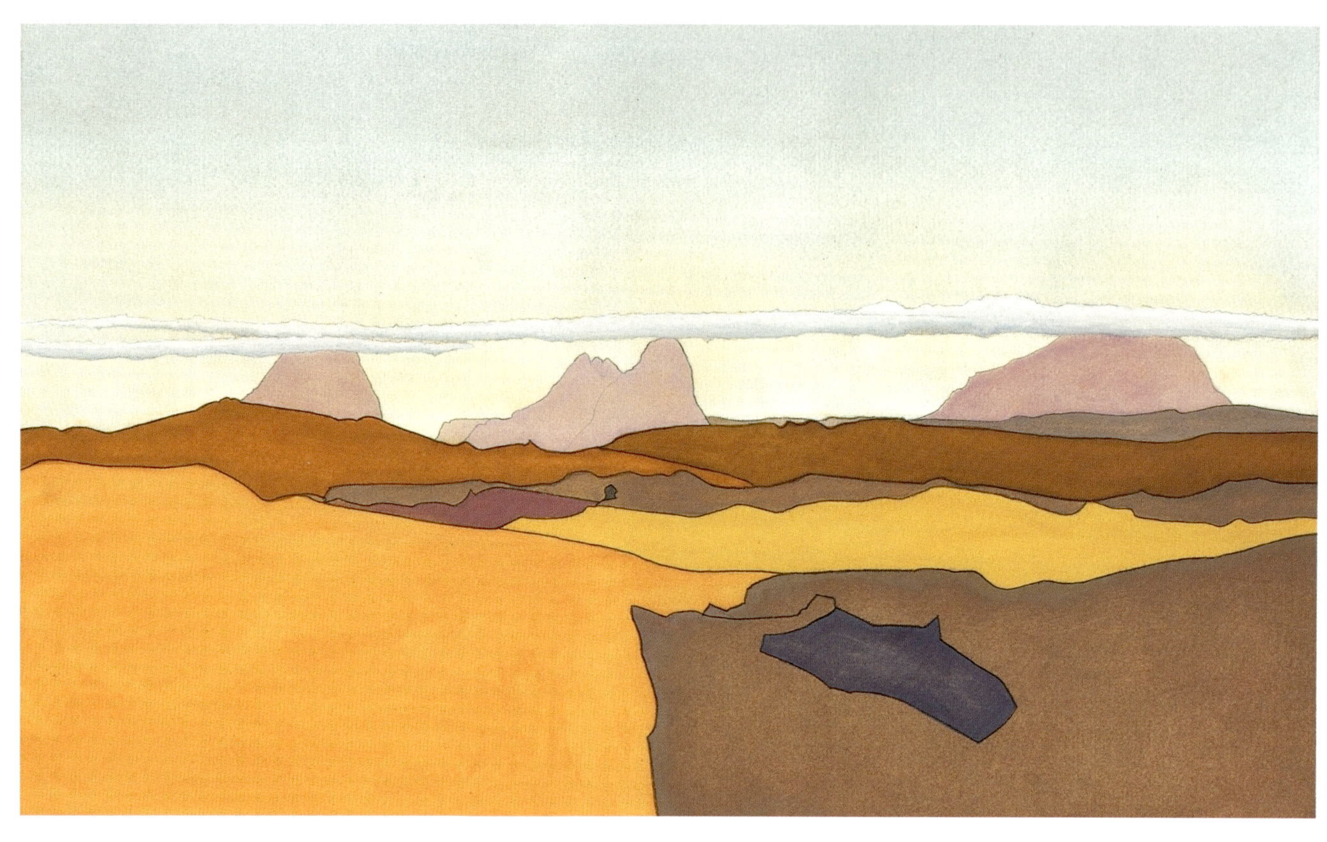

CANISP – SUILVEN – CUL MOR | 2004
aquacryl & gouache on paper
30 × 50

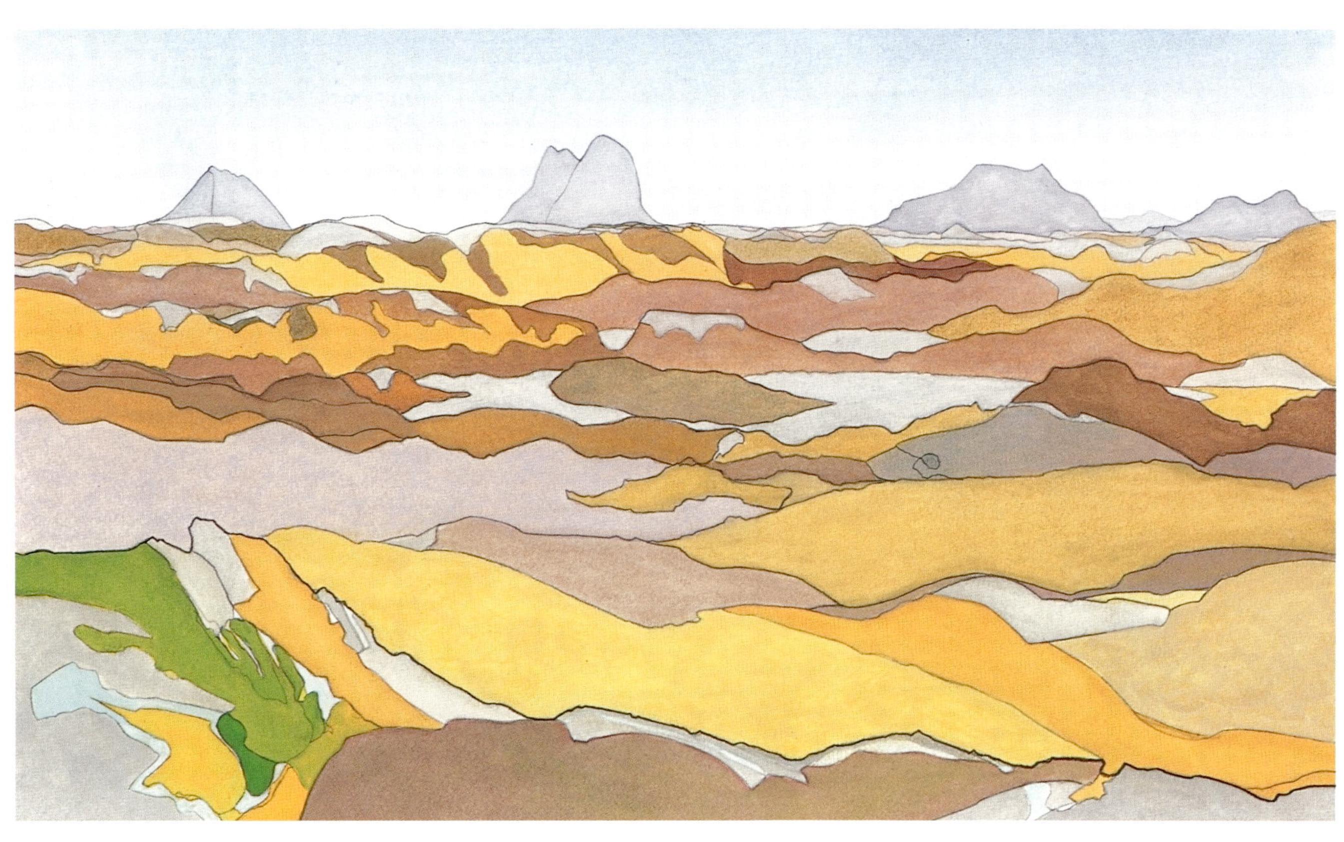

CANISP, SUILVEN, CUL MOR AND CUL BEAG | 2004
aquacryl & gouache on paper
30 × 50

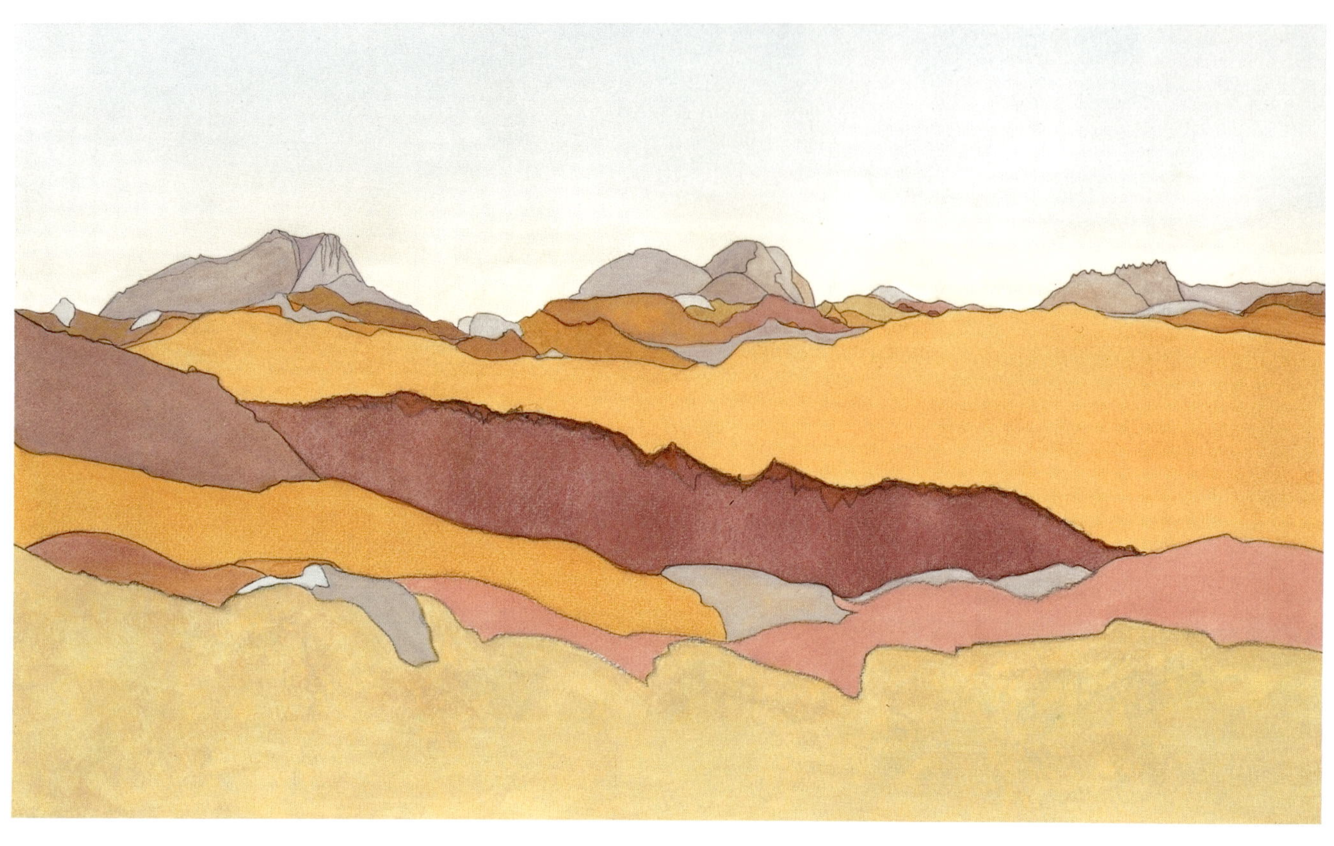

CUL MOR, CUL BEAG AND STAC POLLAIDH | 2004
aquacryl & gouache on paper
30 × 50

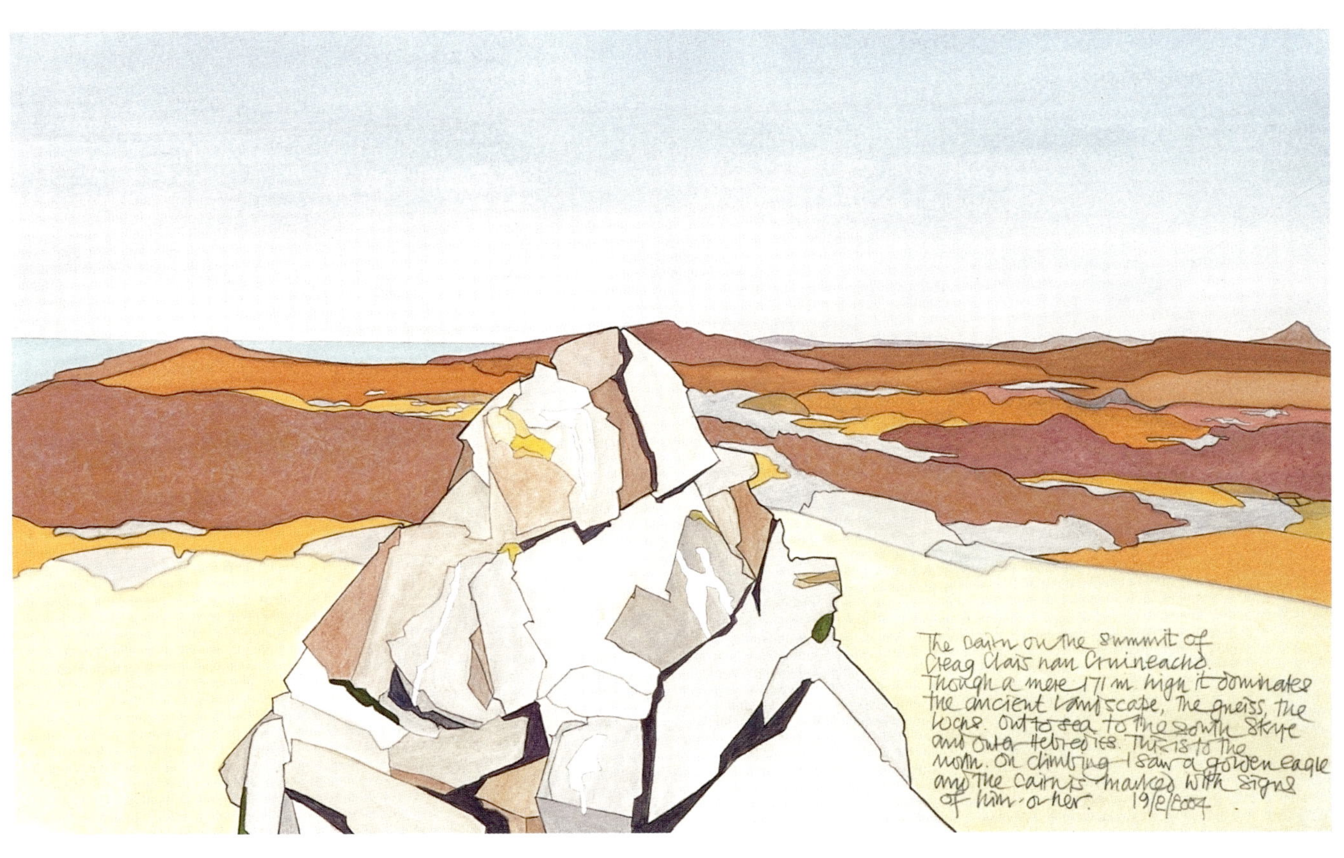

LOOKING NORTH FROM CREAG CLAISNAM NAN CRUINEACHD | 2004

aquacryl & gouache on paper

30 × 50

Though a mere 175m high, the cairn on the summit of Creag Claisnam nan Cruineachd dominates the ancient landscape. The gneiss, the lochs out to sea to the south, Skye and the Outer Hebrides. On climbing I saw a golden eagle, and the cairn is marked with signs of him or her.

19 FEB 2004

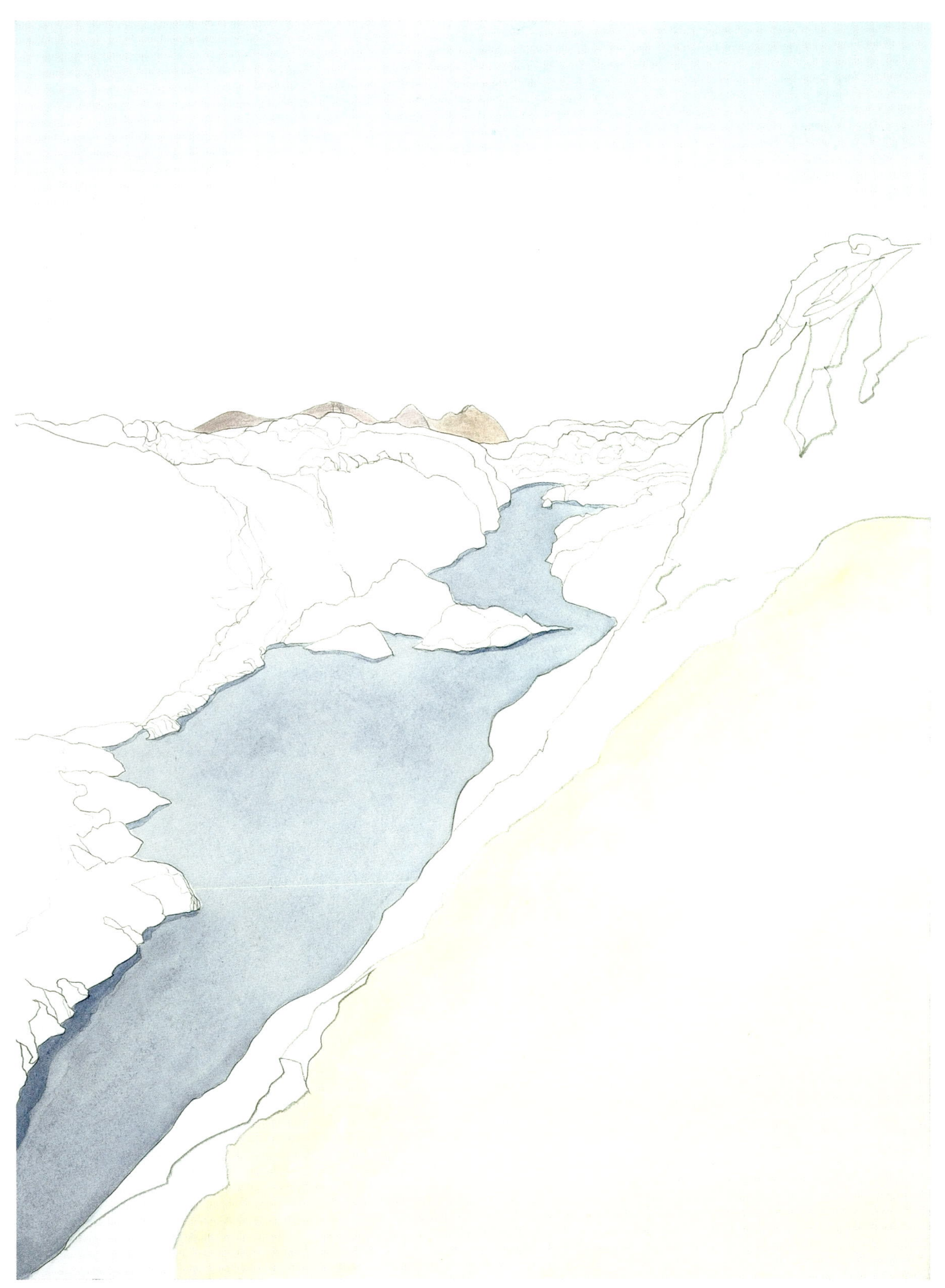

RANNOCH MOOR

Crossing the whole of Rannoch Moor, from Schiehallion to Loch Etive on the west coast

Rannoch Moor is among the bleakest lands in Britain. It lies in the Central Highlands between Loch Rannoch in the east and Buachaille Etive Mòr and the entrance to Glen Coe in the west. This track I have extended to the east, starting at the iconic mountain of Schiehallion, and to the west to Glen Etive, descending to the sea at Loch Etive.

The heart of this walk remains Rannoch Moor itself. Even in good weather it has a feeling of desolation like an ancient world before we criss-crossed the land with habitations and roads. In bad weather – rain, snow, fog – it is almost terrifying.

To cross the centre of the moor is a two-day walk; at least it is so for me. You start at Rannoch railway station. This can be reached directly from London on the overnight sleeper. Then you walk westwards, always towards the pyramid profile of Buachaille Etive Mòr at the head of both Glen Coe and Glen Etive. I had to camp overnight in the centre of the moor. There is nowhere else to stay. Although flat, the track in parts is very difficult, almost lost in the peaty bog.

So why am I drawn to this place? I suppose because it is the closest one comes to 'wilderness' in Britain. When in the centre, you look eastwards towards the sharp Schiehallion (p. 57). This peak is so pointed that it was used in the eighteenth century for experiments into the force of gravity: the then Astronomer Royal suspended plumblines to see how far they would be pulled from the vertical and towards the mountain – what was at the time called 'the attraction of mountains'. A plaque at the site also commemorates Schiehallion as the place where contour lines were first used, as a way for the Royal Observatory Greenwich to survey the great mountain.

Striking as Schiehallion and Rannoch Moor are, it is Buachaille Etive Mòr that holds my attention. I have done a whole series of paintings of the mountain (pp. 61–64). Glen Coe lies to the north. Although magnificent, the experience of the glen is spoiled by the main road that has been blasted through. The old small road followed the movement of the land. All this is lost with the new road. But Glen Etive to the south remains wonderful – indeed, one of the finest in Scotland. The road and walk finish in a dead end at Loch Etive (pp. 68–69). All there is at the end of the road is a red phone box. It worked. I wonder if it still does?

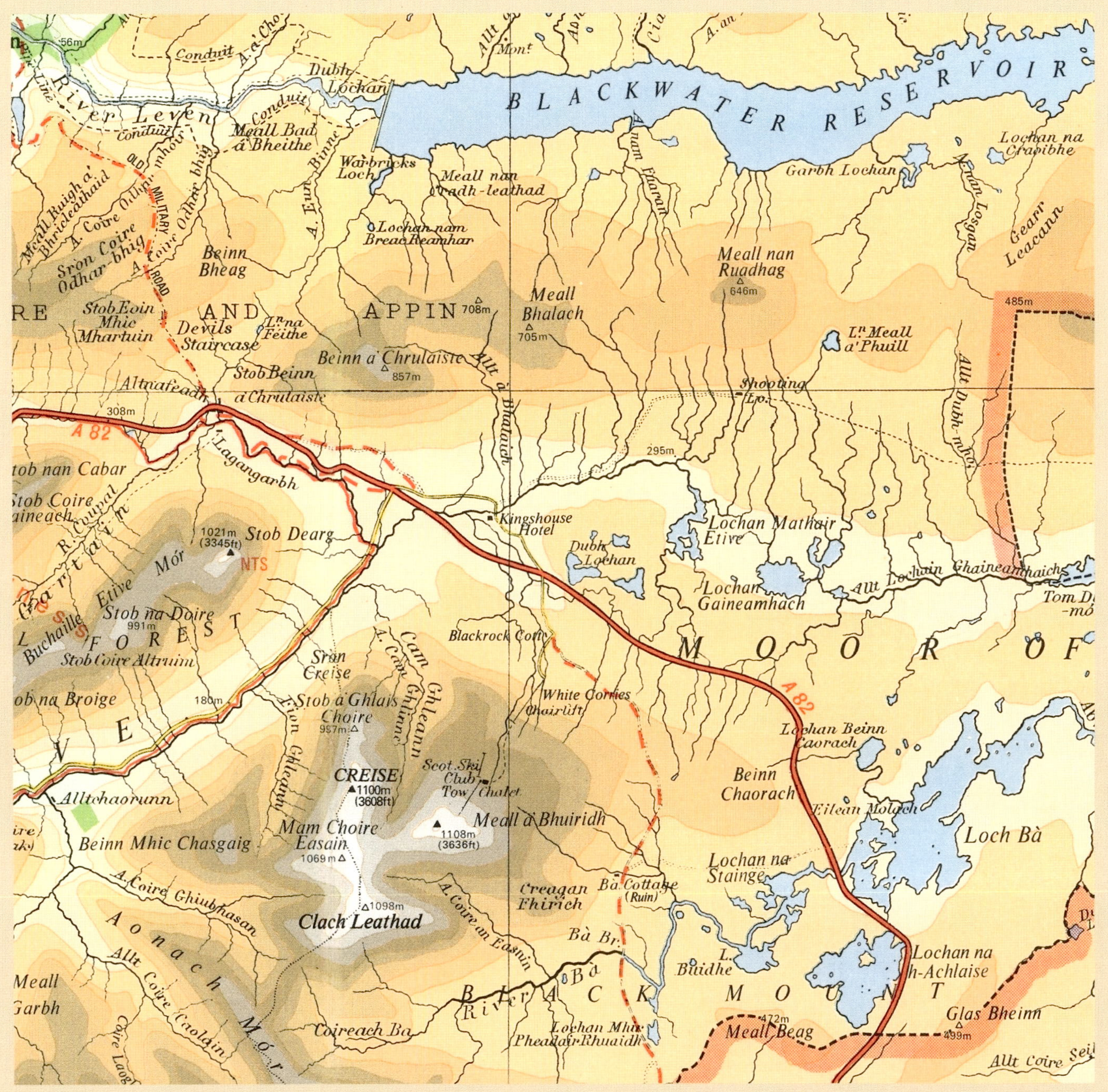

BLACKWATER RESERVOIR
River Leven
Conduit
Dubh Lochan
Meall Bad a' Bheithe
Warbricks Loch
Meall nan Uradh-leathad
Garbh Lochan
Lochan na Crapibhe
Meall Ruigh a' Bhaicleathaid
A. Coire Odhar bhig
Sron Coire Odhar-bhig
Beinn Bheag
Lochan nam Breac Reamhar
Meall nan Ruadhag
646m
Gearr Leacann
Allt Losgan
OLD MILITARY ROAD
Stob Eoin Mhic Mhartuin
Devils Staircase
L. na Feithe
APPIN
708m
Meall Bhalach
705m
L. Meall a' Phuill
485m
Altnafeadh
Stob Beinn a' Chrulaiste
Beinn a' Chrulaiste
857m
Shooting Lo.
A 82
308m
Lagangarbh
295m
Stob nan Cabar
Stob Coire Gaineach
Rannoch
Kingshouse Hotel
Lochan Mathair Etive
Allt Lochain Ghaineamhaich
Tom Da -mó
1021m (3345ft)
Stob Dearg
NTS
Etive Mór
Dubh Lochan
Lochan Gaineamhach
MOOR OF
Buachaille
Stob na Doire
991m
FOREST
Blackrock Cottie
Stob Coire Altruim
Sron Creise
Cam Ghleann A. Coire Ghlinne
White Corries Chairlift
A 82
Lochan Beinn Caorach
Stob na Broige
180m
Stob a' Ghlais Choire
957m
Scot Ski Club Tow / Chalet
Beinn Chaorach
Eilean Molach
Alltchaorunn
CREISE
1100m (3608ft)
Meall a' Bhuiridh
Loch Bà
Beinn Mhic Chasgaig
Mam Choire Easain
1069 m
1108m (3636ft)
Lochan na Stainge
A. Coire Ghiubhasan
1098m
Creagan Fhirich
Bà Cottage (Ruin)
Lochan na h-Achlaise
Clach Leathad
A. Coire an Easain
Bà Br
L. Buidhe
Glas Bheinn
499m
Meall Garbh
Allt Coire Caoldin
River Bà
BLACKMOUNT
472m
Meall Beag
Coire Laog
Coireach Bà
Lochan Mhic Pheadair Rhuaidh
Allt Coire Sei

Yesterday I needed crampons for the
climb of Meall nan Tarmachan. This path
to nearby Schiehallion is much easier. Seen
from here to the south you get no idea of
the sharp wedge form of the mountain,
which led to the famous experiments on
gravity.

22 FEB 2005

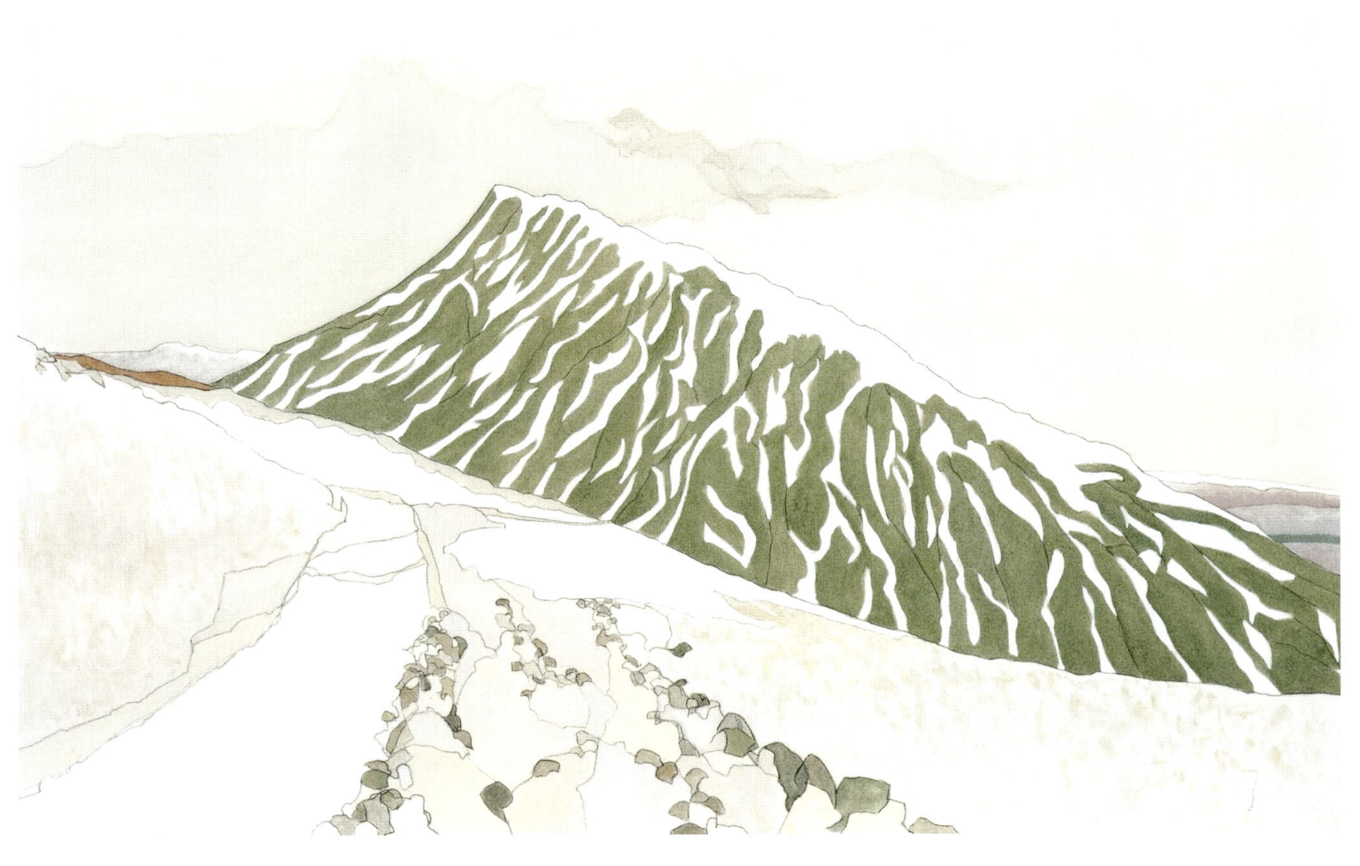

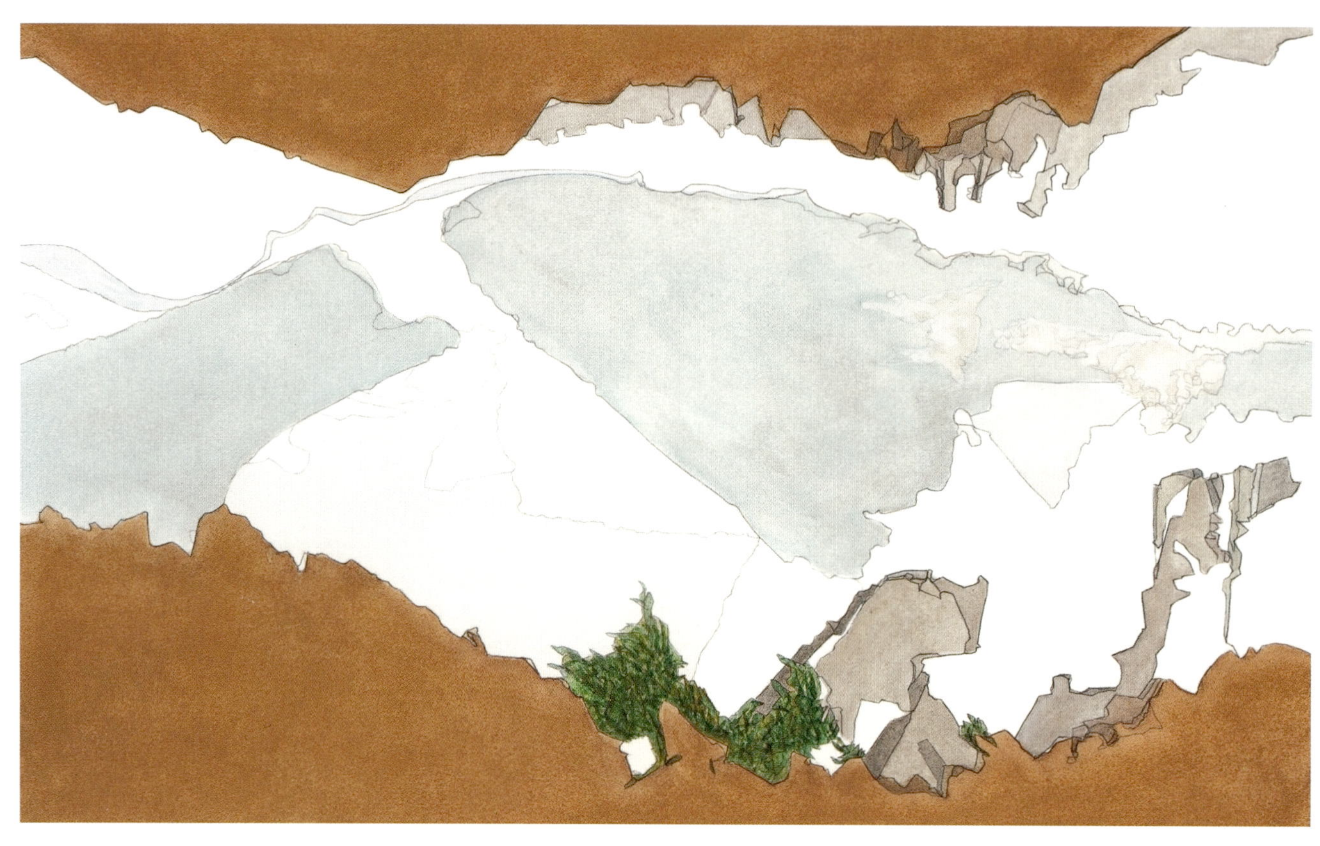

ALLT COIRE PHEIGINN | 2005
tempera, aquacryl & acrylic on paper
30 × 50

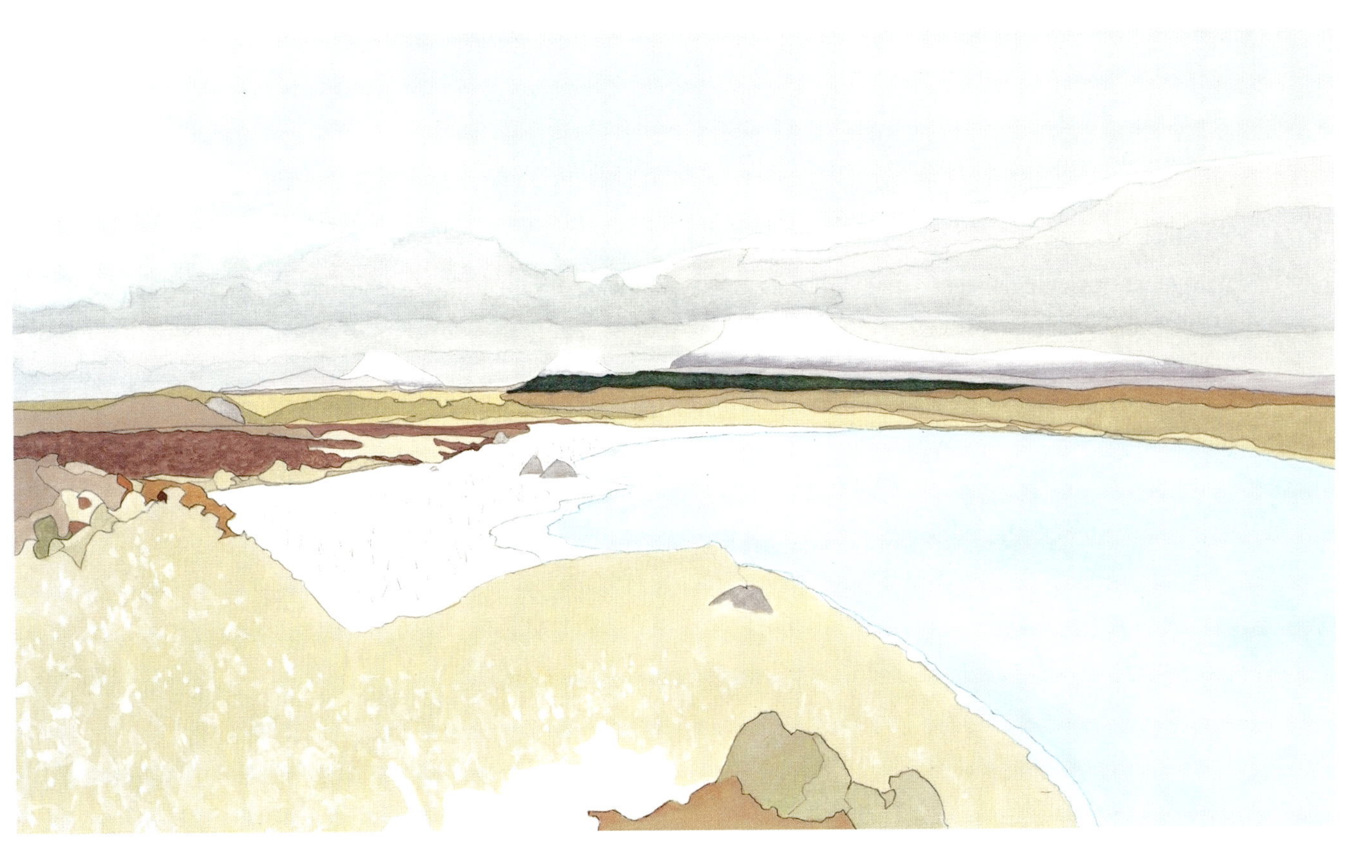

BUACHAILLE ETIVE MÒR ACROSS LOCH LAIDON | 2005
tempera, aquacryl & acrylic on paper
30 × 50

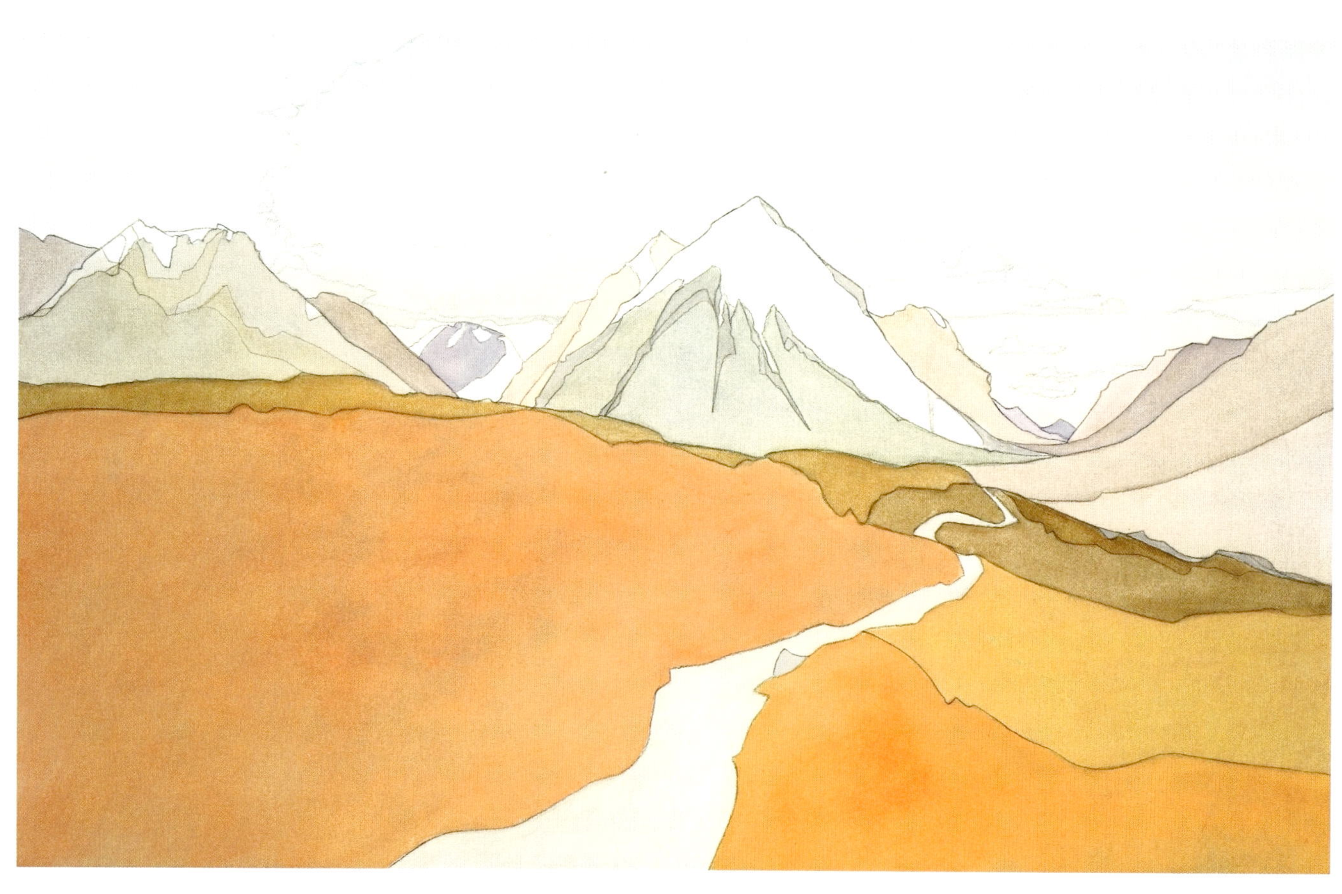

GLEN COE ACROSS RANNOCH MOOR | 2006
tempera, aquacryl & acrylic on paper
30 × 50

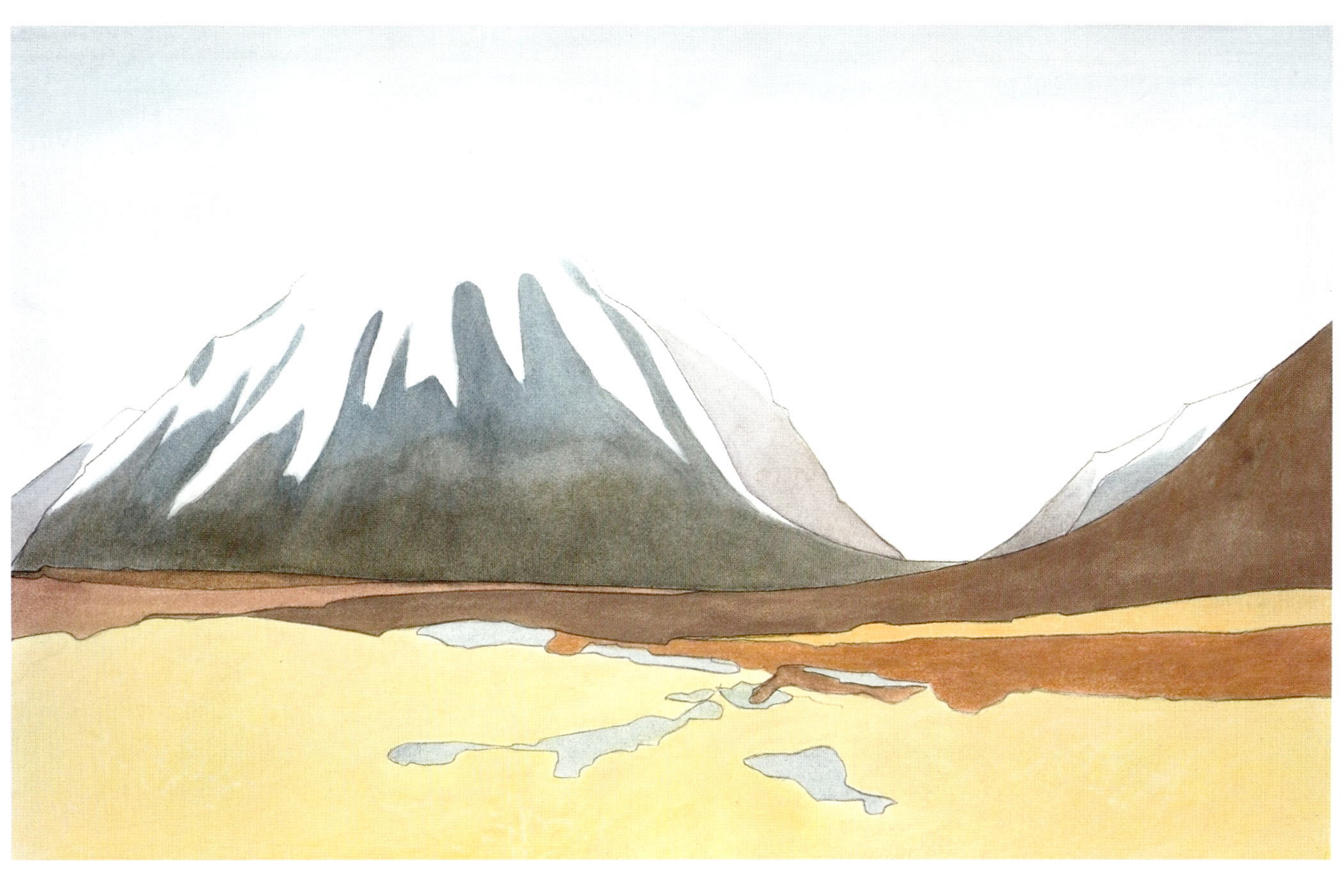

BUACHAILLE ETIVE MÒR 15 FEB 2006 | 2006
aquacryl & gouache on paper
32 × 51

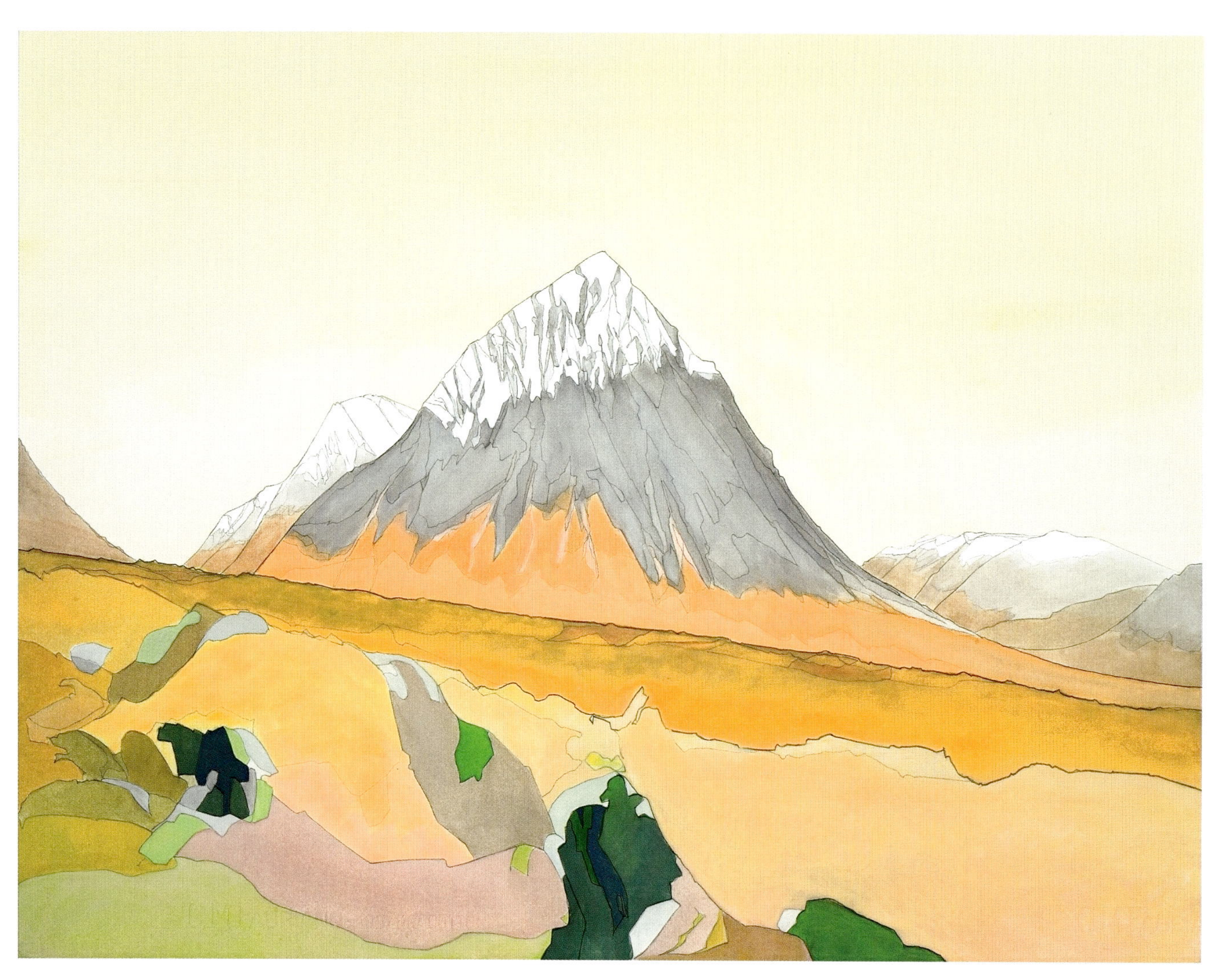

BUACHAILLE ETIVE MÒR 16 NOV 2006 | 2006
acrylic & aquacryl on paper
57 × 75

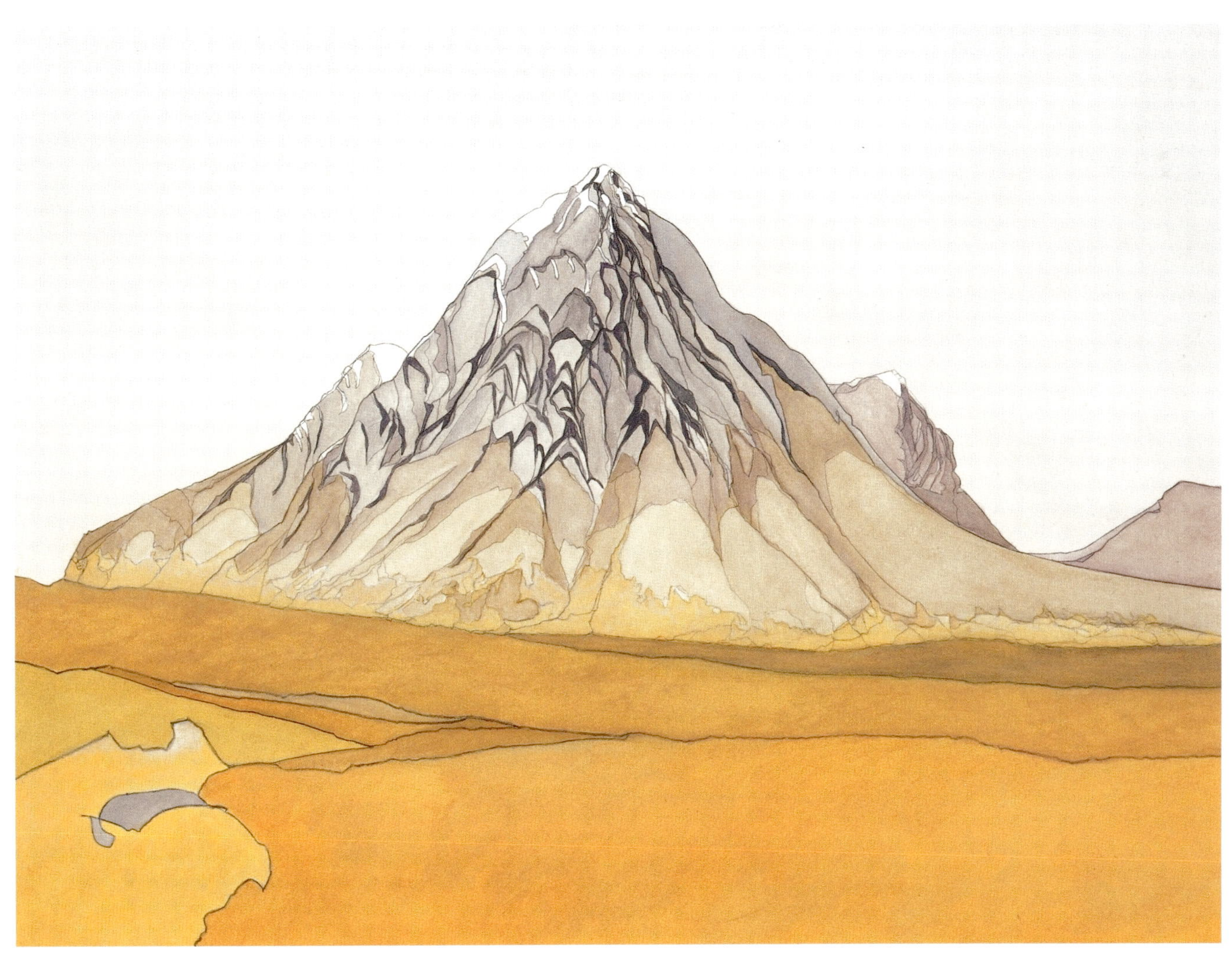

BUACHAILLE ETIVE MÒR I | 2004
aquacryl & gouache on paper
57 × 75

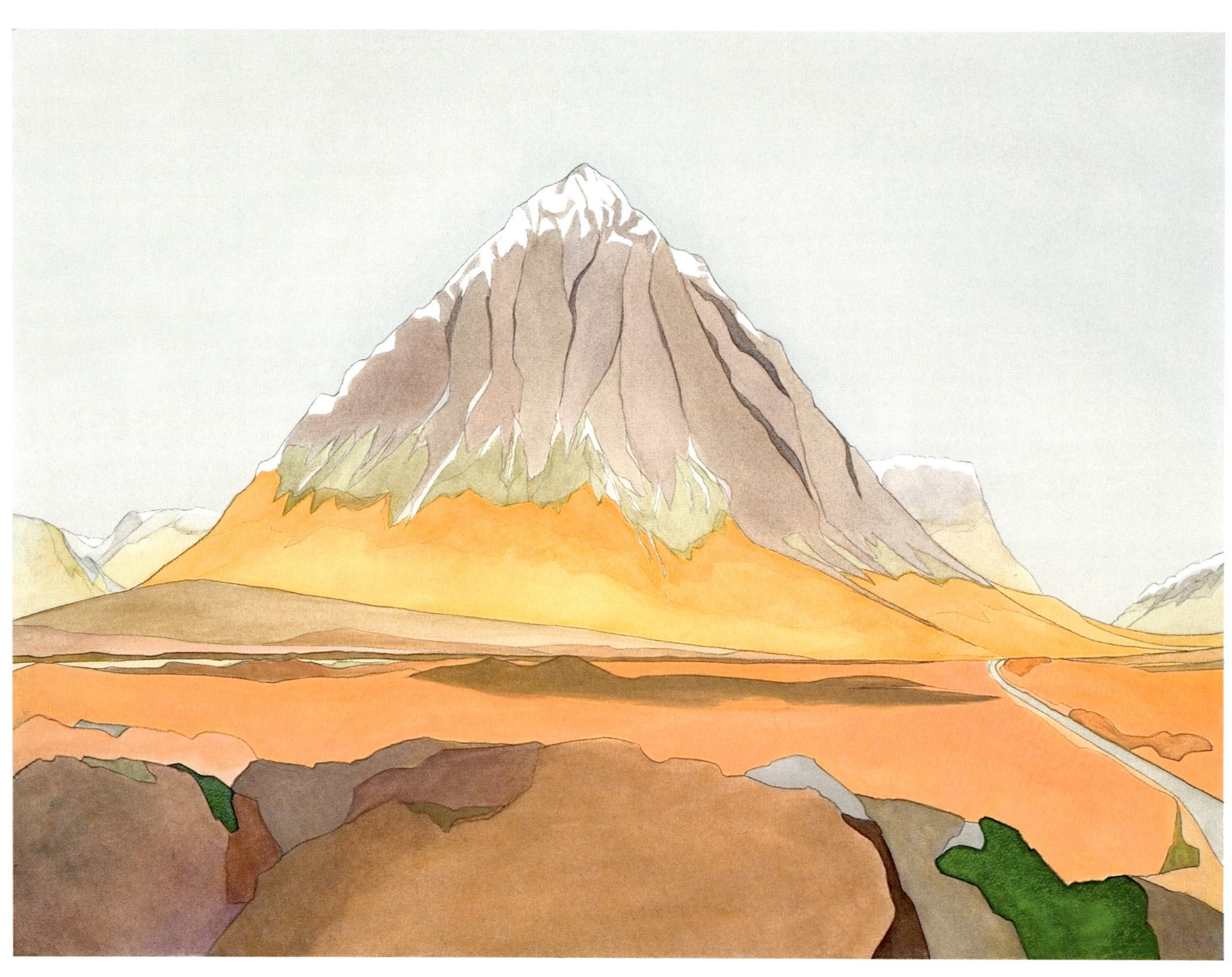

BUACHAILLE ETIVE MÒR 15 NOV 2006 | 2006
acrylic & aquacryl on paper
57 × 75

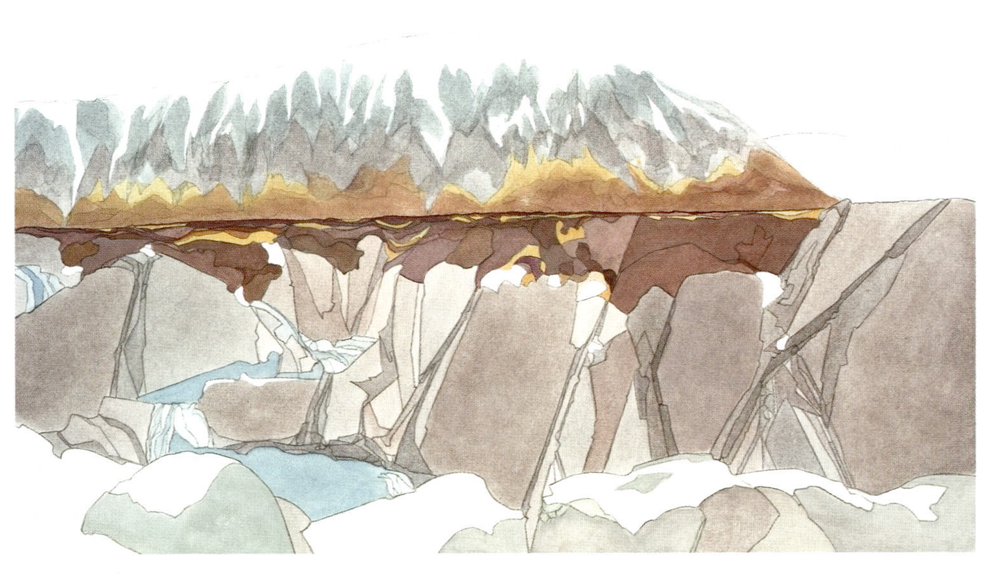

BEINN A'CHRULAISTE | 2006
tempera, aquacryl & acrylic on paper
30 × 50

The track runs from the main road across the Moor to the old road, which is now the West Highland Way. It must have been quite used once upon a time for there are bridges, laid stones. Now at times it is hardly visible.

The rain, rain, rain leaves a series of puddles and it is a difficult choice between jumping these or walking in the bog.

17 NOV 2006

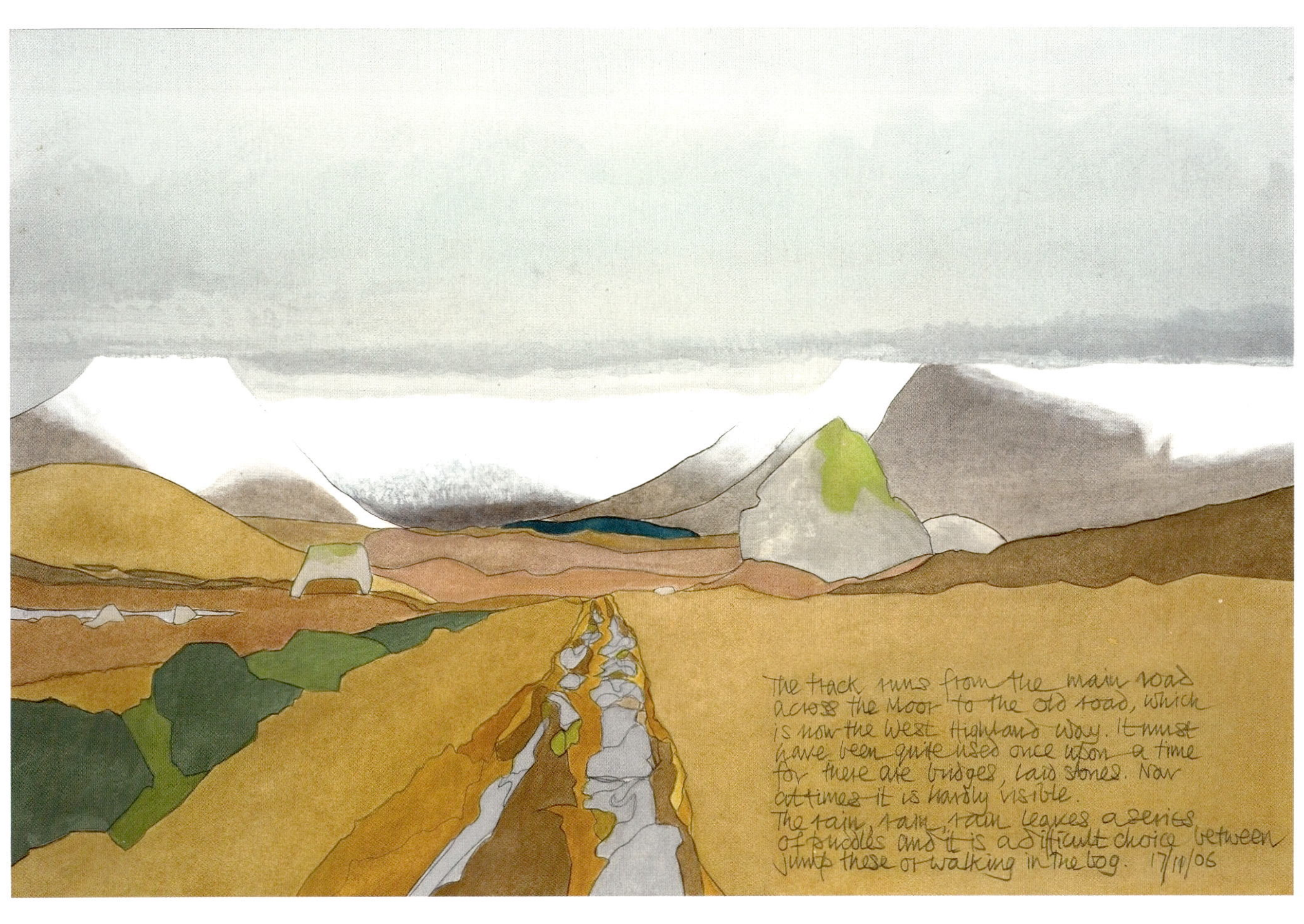

The track runs from the main road
across the Moor to the old road, which
is now the West Highland Way. It must
have been quite used once upon a time
for there are bridges, laid stones. Now
at times it is hardly visible.
The rain, rain, rain leaves a series
of puddles and it is a difficult choice between
jump these or walking in the bog. 17/11/06

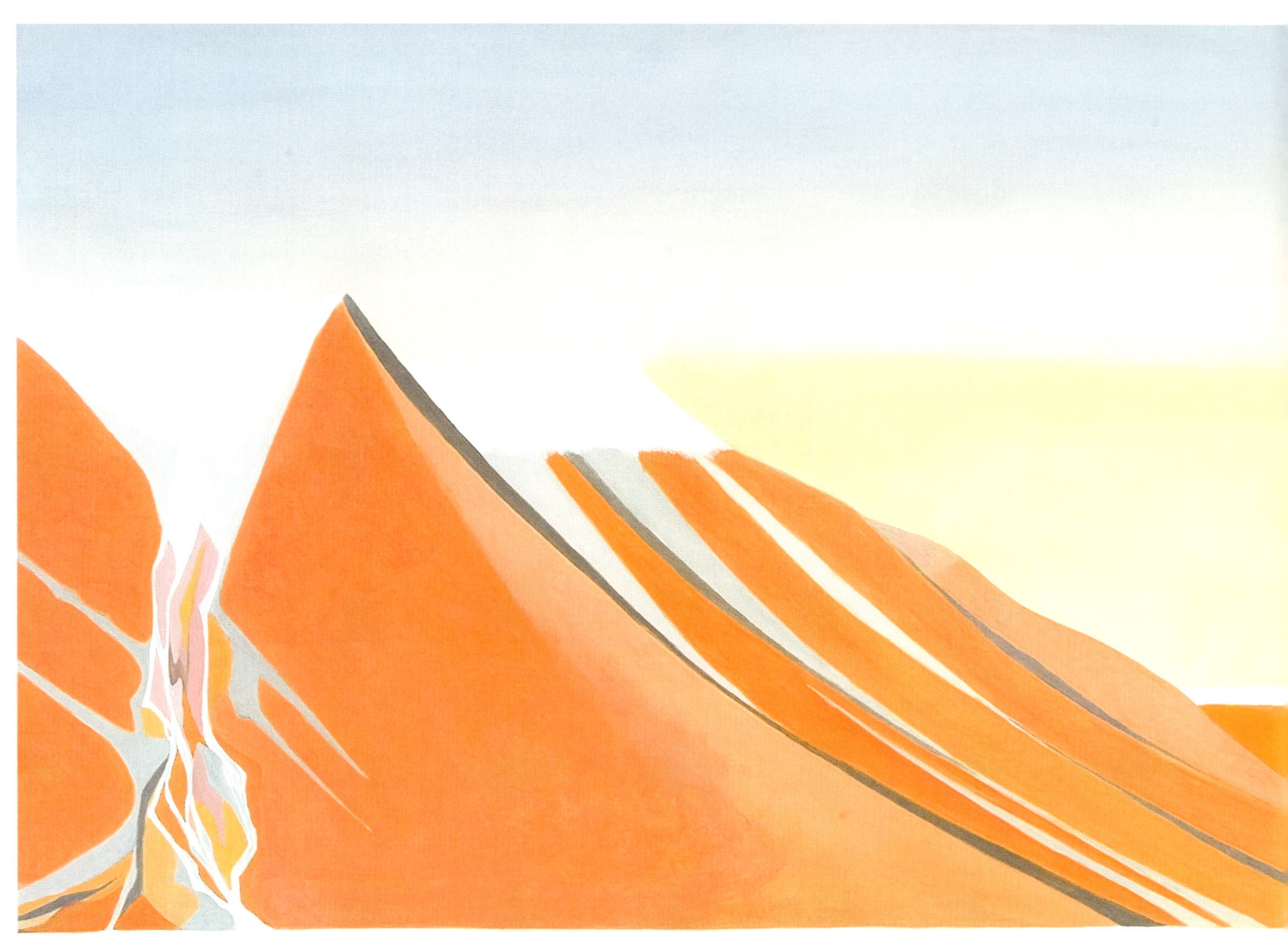

LOCH ETIVE II | 2007
acrylic on canvas
65 × 150

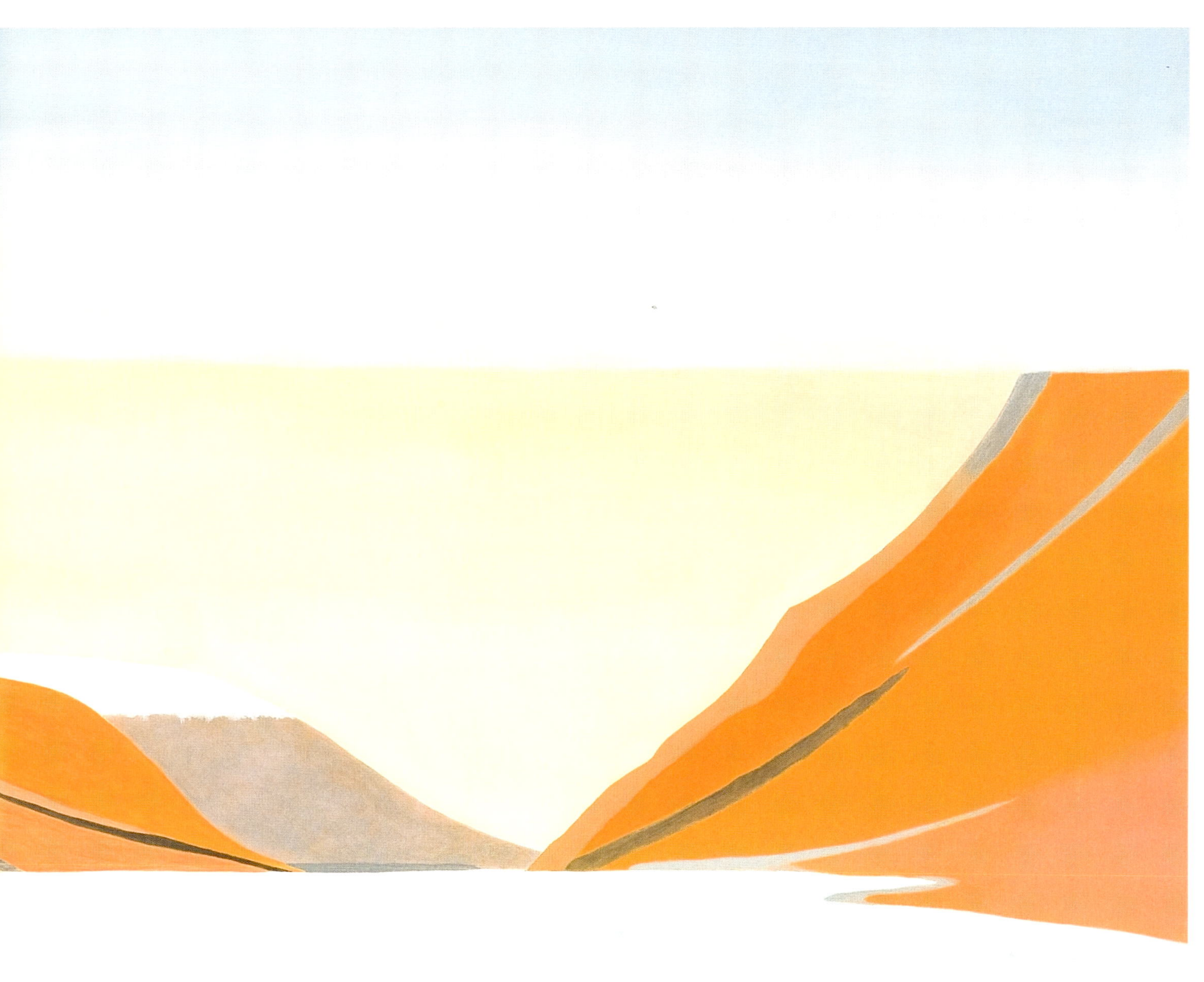

ISLAY • THE WEST COAST

A three-day walk along the whole west coast of Islay, finishing with the view across to Jura to the north

Islay is the island of whisky. What a magical string of names: Laphroaig, Lagavulin, Bruichladdich, Bunnahabhain and more. The island seems scented by the peaty aroma of the distilleries. Then there are the geese. In season the whole island is densely covered with the birds. The farmers are paid by the number of geese grazing on their land, as compensation for letting them eat all their grass.

To me the attraction of going to Islay was to walk the length of the western coast. I took three days. Clearly it could be done quicker, but I was forever stopping to draw en route. The west of Islay is not very exciting, except for the coast which is a wonder of rock forms and small valleys cutting down to the sea. I have tried to represent this walk with a series of composite works showing fragments of the land side by side with maps, both geological and standard (pp. 72–75). This was the start of my including maps directly into my work. Subsequent examples can be seen in the sections on the Three Peaks and in Orkney. The contrast of the detailed rocks and walls can best be seen in the nine-part work (p. 79).

On the third day of the walk I came across the huge carcass of a whale that I suppose had been washed ashore in a storm. I found this fascinating and did a whole series of drawings leading to subsequent paintings (pp. 83 and 84). These are in complete contrast to the rock forms. In a way they are out of place, but such was the impact of this scene that it became *the* image of the track.

The last view is across the straits to Jura, with its mountains, The Paps. Such a contrast to the flatness of Islay. Jura is superb, wild; but that is a different story.

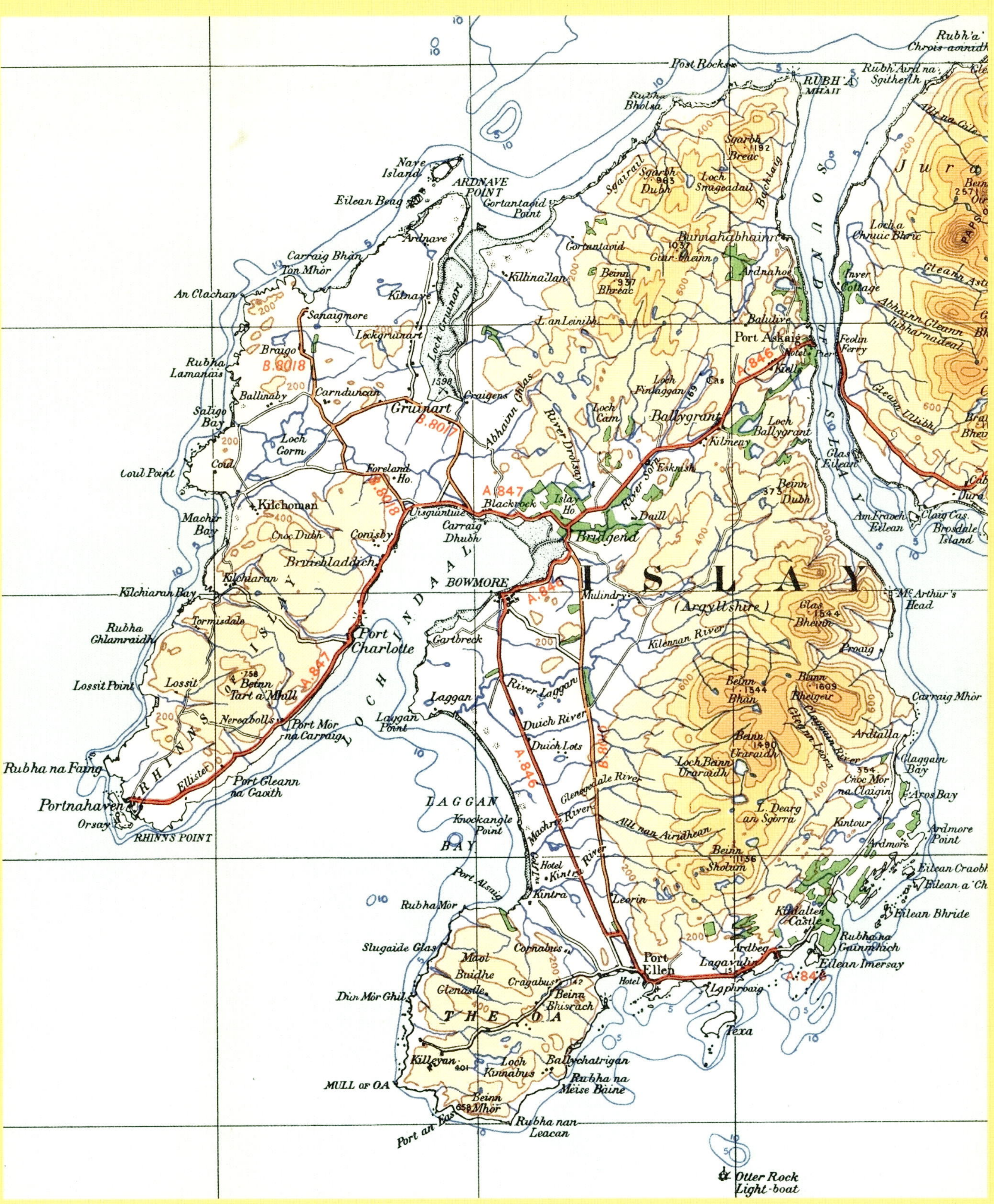
Rubh'a'
Chrois-aonridh
Rubh'a
Post Rocks
RUBH'A
MHAIL
Rubh' Aird na
Sgutherth
Rubha
Bholsa
Tir na Gil
Nave
Island
Sgarbh
Breac
1192
Bachlag
Eilean Beag
ARDNAVE
POINT
Sgarbh
963
Loch
Smageadail
J U R A
Beinn
257
Och
Ardnave
Cortantavid
Point
Bunnahabhain
Ardnahoe
Loch a
Chnuic Bhric
Carraig Bhan
Ton Mhòr
Killinallan
Beinn
337
Bhreac
1037
Giar-bheinn
Inver
Cottage
Gleann Ast
An Clachan
Cortantavid
Abhainn Gleann libharnadeal
Beinn
Bh
Sanaigmore
L. an Leinibh
Balulive
Loch
Grúinart
Rubha
Lamanais
Braigo
B.8018
Lochgruinart
Port Askaig
Feolin
Ferry
Hotel
Pier
A.846
600
Ballinaby
Carnduncan
200
Loch
Finlaggan
Kiells
Gleann Uillibh
Saligo
Bay
Gruinart
1598
Craigens
B.8017
Loch
Cam
Ballygrant
Loch
Ballygrant
Glas
Eilean
Bra
Bhev
Cab
Coul Point
Loch
Gorm
Abhainn Chàs
Foreland
Ho.
River Sorn
Kilmeny
Esknish
Coul
A.847
Blackrock
Islay
Ho.
Beinn
373
Dubh
Kilchoman
400
B.8018
Visguintuie
Carraig
Dhubh
Daill
Am Fraoch
Eilean
Clag Cas
Jura
Macher
Bay
Cnoc Dubh
Conisby
Bridgend
Brosdale
Island
Bruichladdich
BOWMORE
I S L A Y
McArthur's
Head
Kilchiaran Bay
Kilchiaran
Mulindry
(Argyllshire)
Glas
1544
Bheinn
Rubha
Ghlamraidh
Tormisdale
A.846
Kilennan River
Proaig
Lossit Point
Lossit
Beinn
758
Tart a' Mhull
Port
Charlotte
Gartbreck
200
Beinn
1544
Bhan
Blonn
1609
Rheigeir
Carraig Mhòr
River Laggan
A.847
Laggan
Laggan
Point
Nereabolls
Port Mór
na Carraige
Duich River
Beinn
1490
Uraraidh
Gleann Lyora
354
Ardtalla
Rubha na Faing
Ellister
Port Gleann
na Caoth
Duich Lots
Glenegedale River
Loch Beinn
Uraraidh
Cnoc Mór
na Claigin
Claggain
Bay
Portnahaven
L. Dearg
an Sgorra
Kintour
Aros Bay
Orsay
LAGGAN
Knockangle
Point
Machrie River
Allt nan Airidhean
Beinn
1156
Sholum
Ardmore
Point
RHINNS POINT
BAY
Kintra
River
Leorin
Eilean Craobh
Eilean a' Ch
Rubha Mór
Hotel
Kintra
Kildalton
Castle
Eilean Bhride
Slugaide Glas
Port Alsaig
Copnahus
200
Ardbeg
Lagavulin
Rubha na
Gainimhich
Eilean Imersay
Maol
Buidhe
Cragabus
Beinn
Bhisrach
Port
Ellen
Hotel
Laphroaig
A.846
Dún Mór Ghil
Glenastle
142
THE OA
Killeyan
Loch
Kinnabus
401
Ballychatrigan
Texa
Beinn
658
Mhòr
Rubha na
Meise Bàine
MULL OF OA
Port an Fheadain
Rubha nan
Leacan
Otter Rock
Light-boat

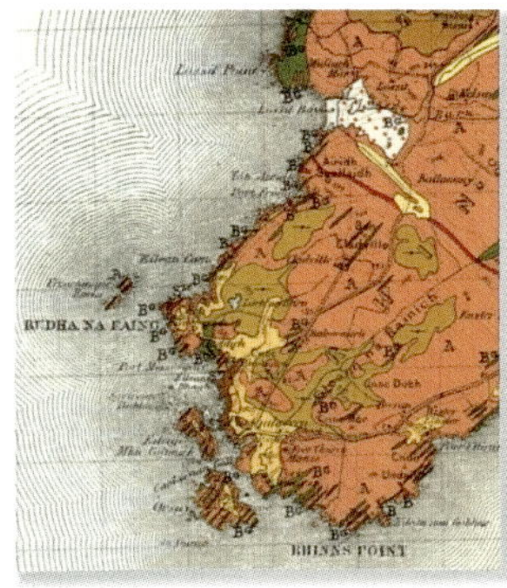
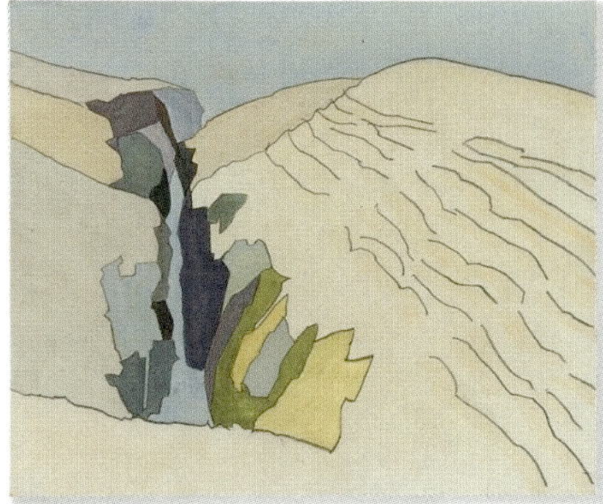
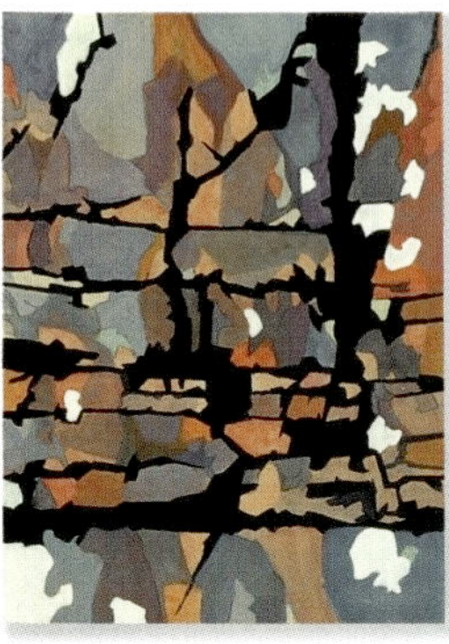
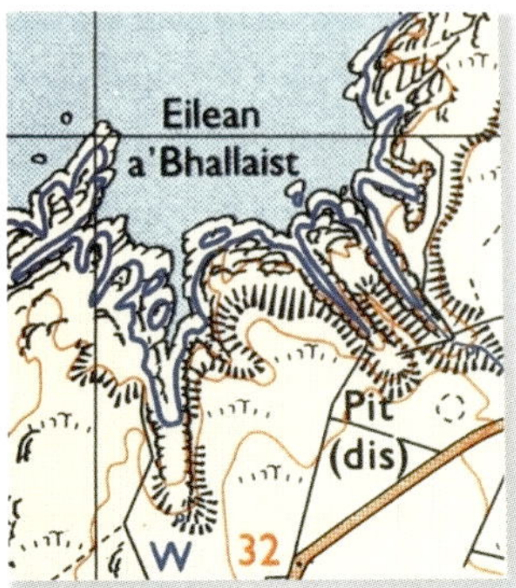
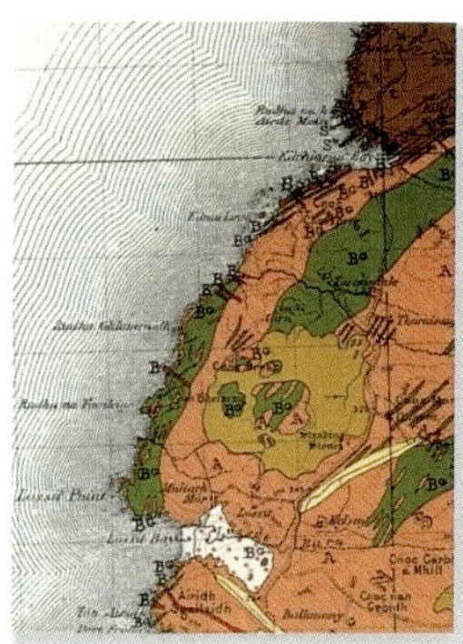
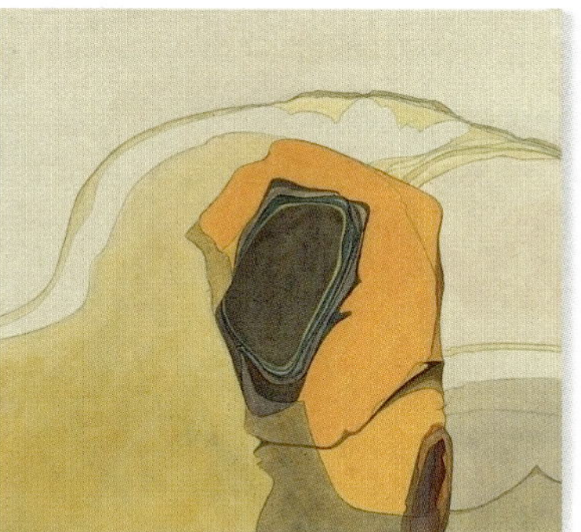
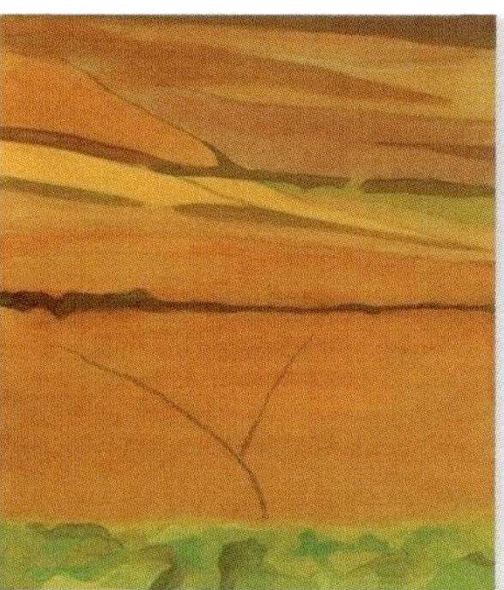
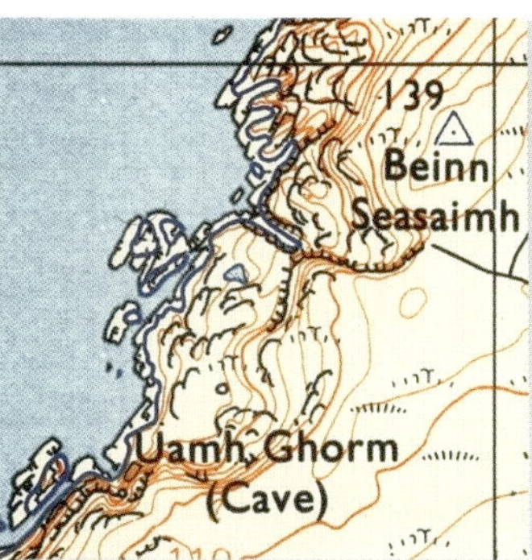

RUDHA NA FAING TO LOSSIT BAY, ISLAY | 1996/97
print & acrylic on board
50×130

LOSSIT BAY TO KILCHIARAN BAY, ISLAY | 1996/97
print & acrylic on board
50×130

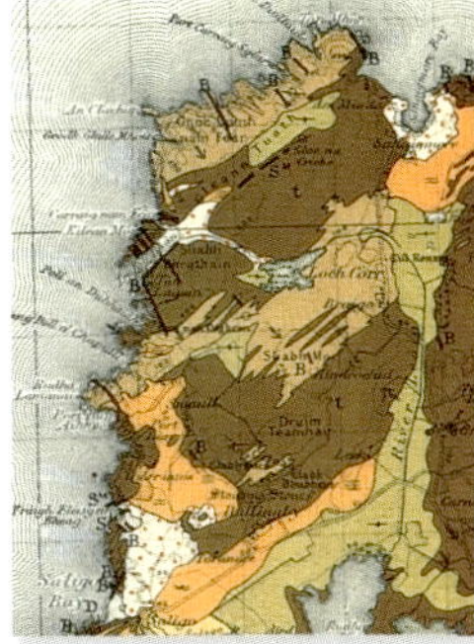
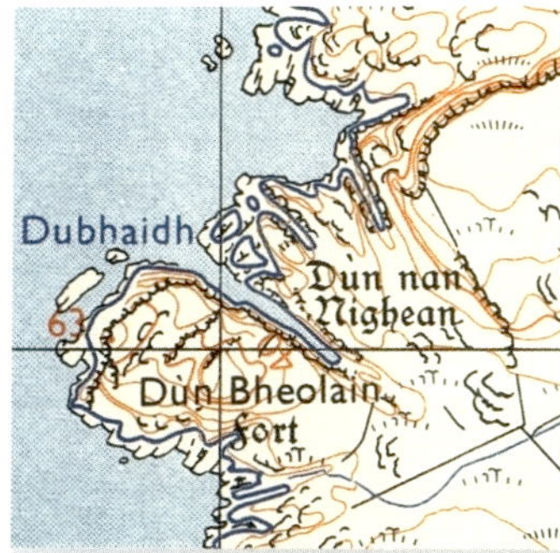

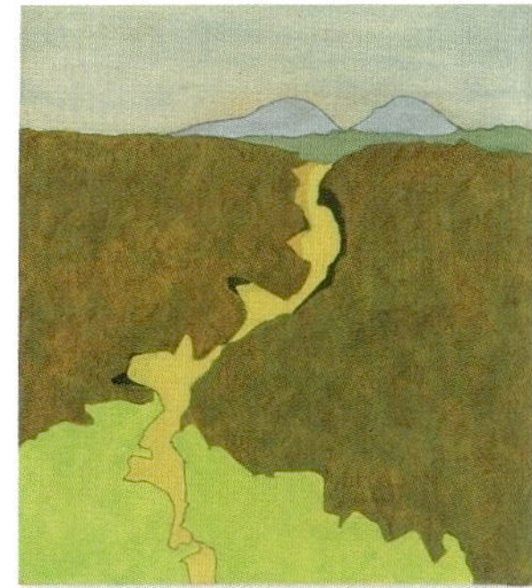
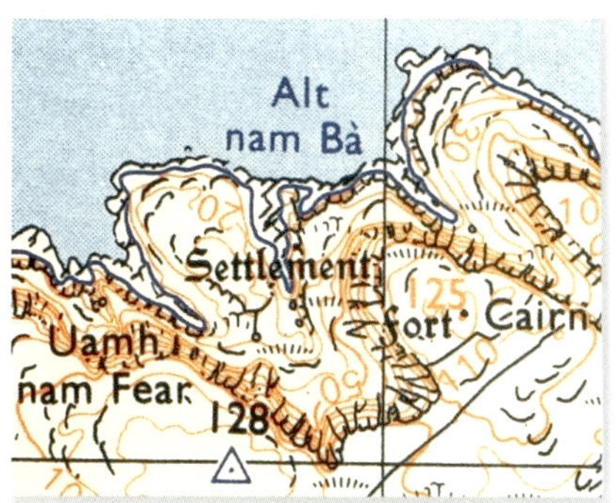

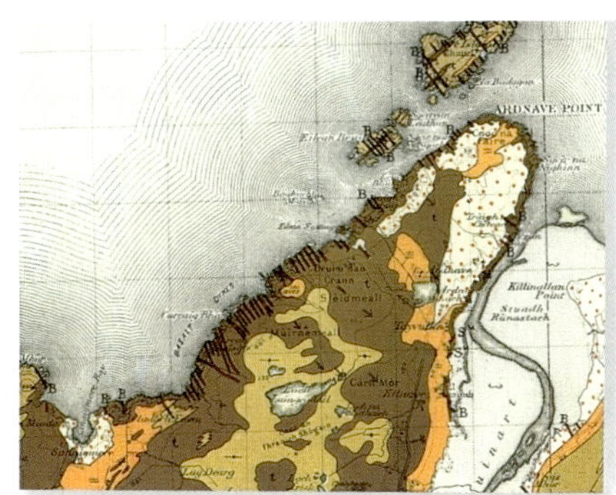

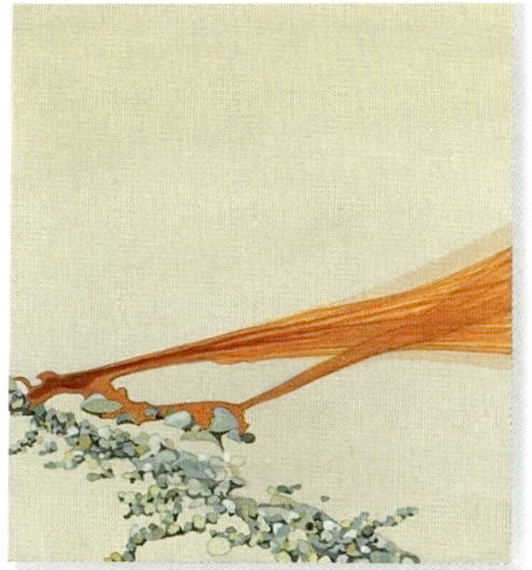
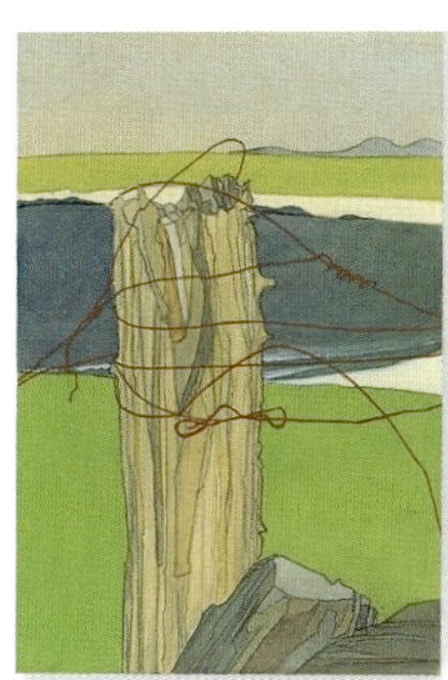
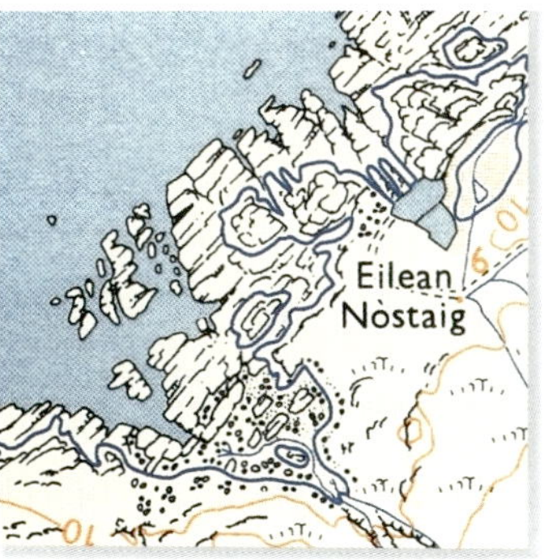

SALIGO BAY TO SANAIGMORE BAY, ISLAY | 1996/97
print & acrylic on board
50 × 130

SANAIGMORE BAY TO ARDNAVE POINT, ISLAY | 1996/97
print & acrylic on board
50 × 130

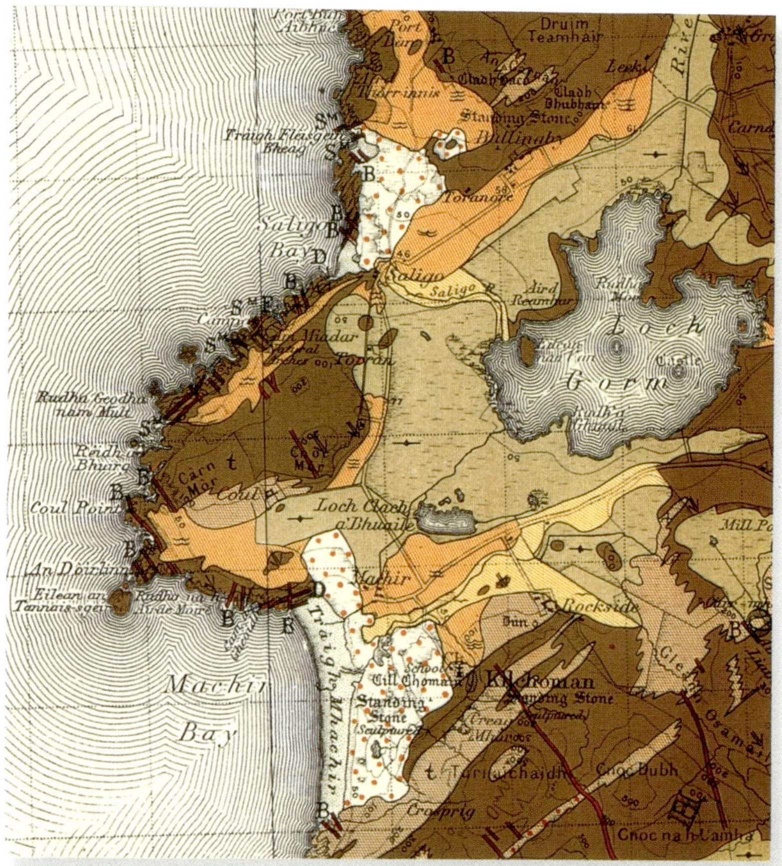

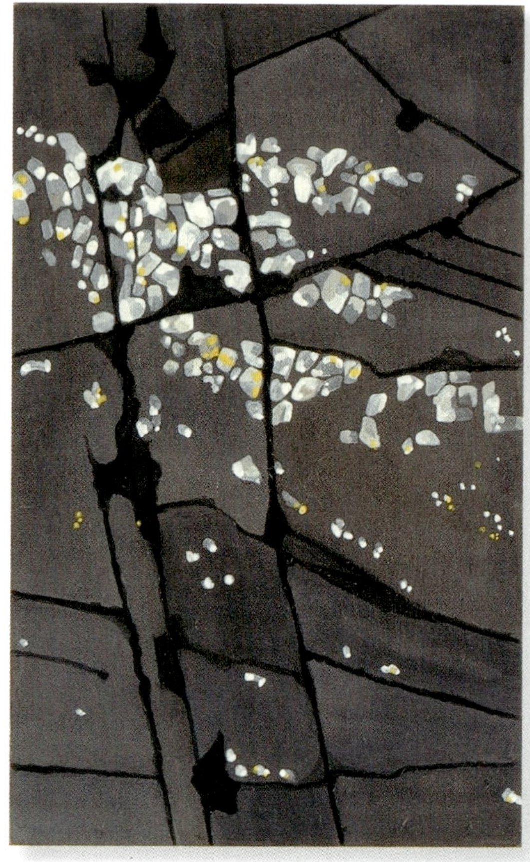

MACHIR BAY TO SALIGO BAY, ISLAY | 1996/97
print & acrylic on board
50 × 130

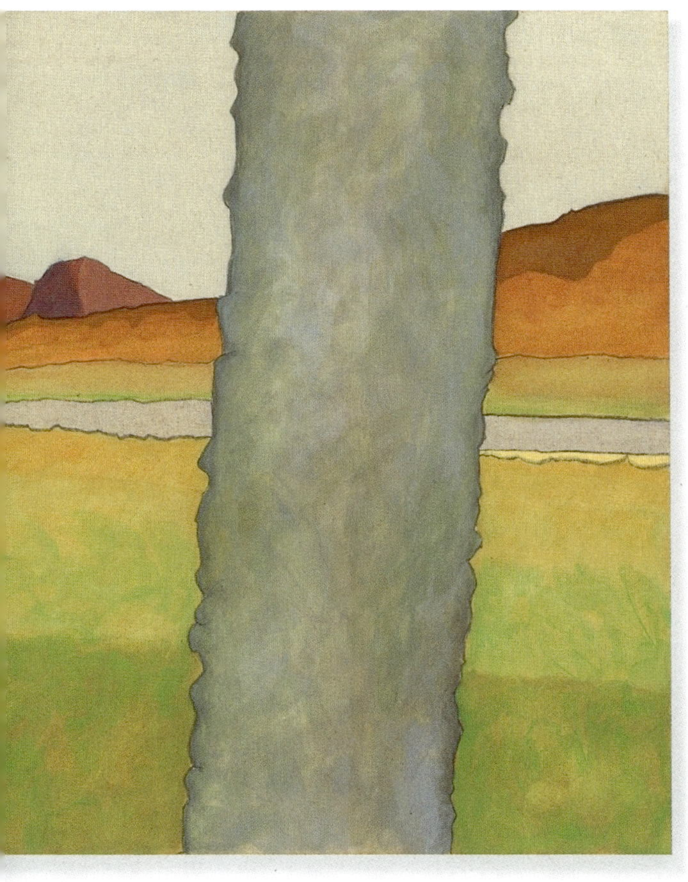

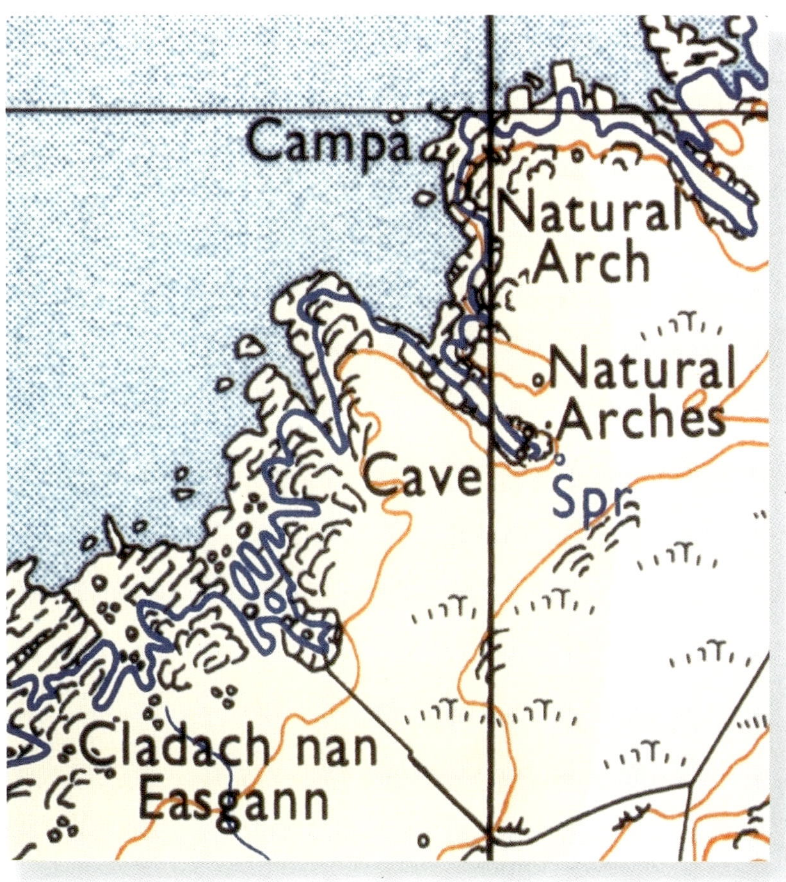

Campä
Natural
Arch
Natural
Arches
Cave
Spr
Cladach nan
Easgann

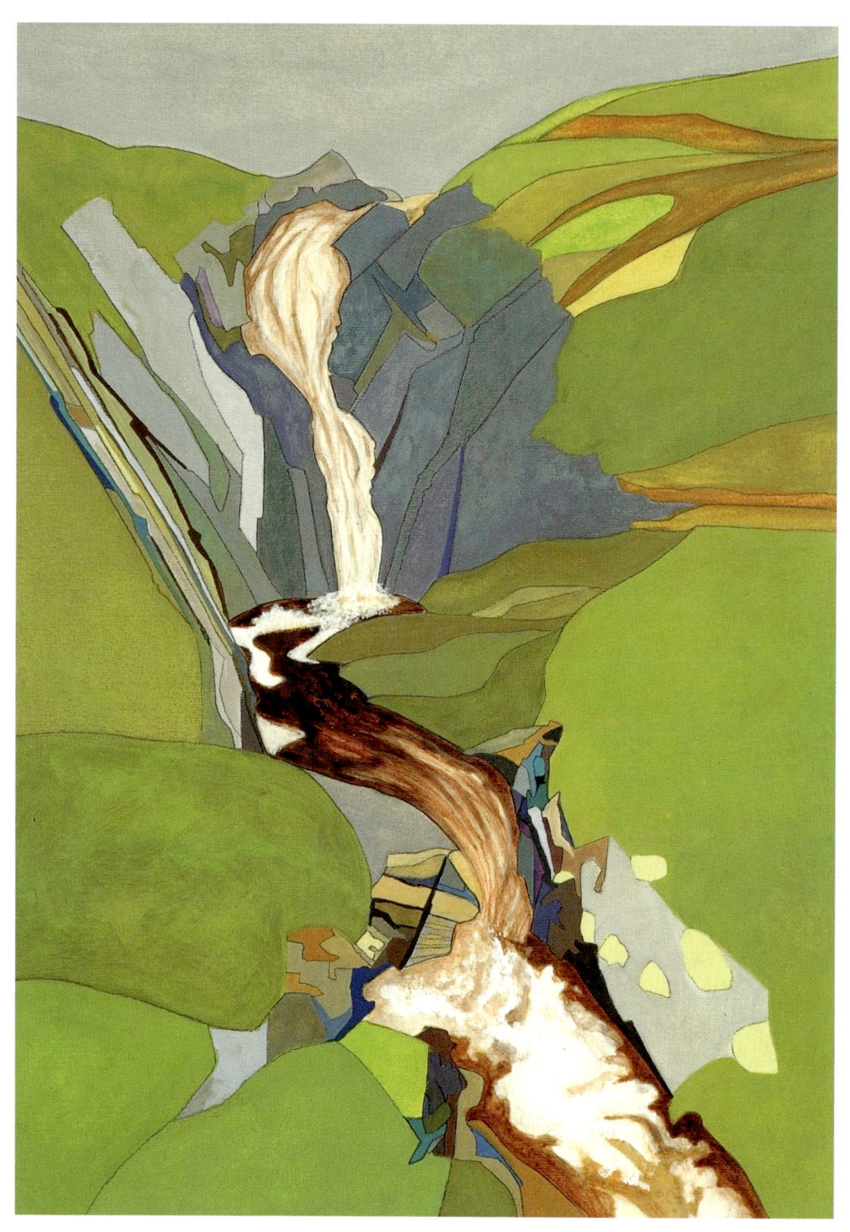

WATERFALL ON ALT A'GHLINNE | 1996/97
acrylic & gouache on paper
35 × 25

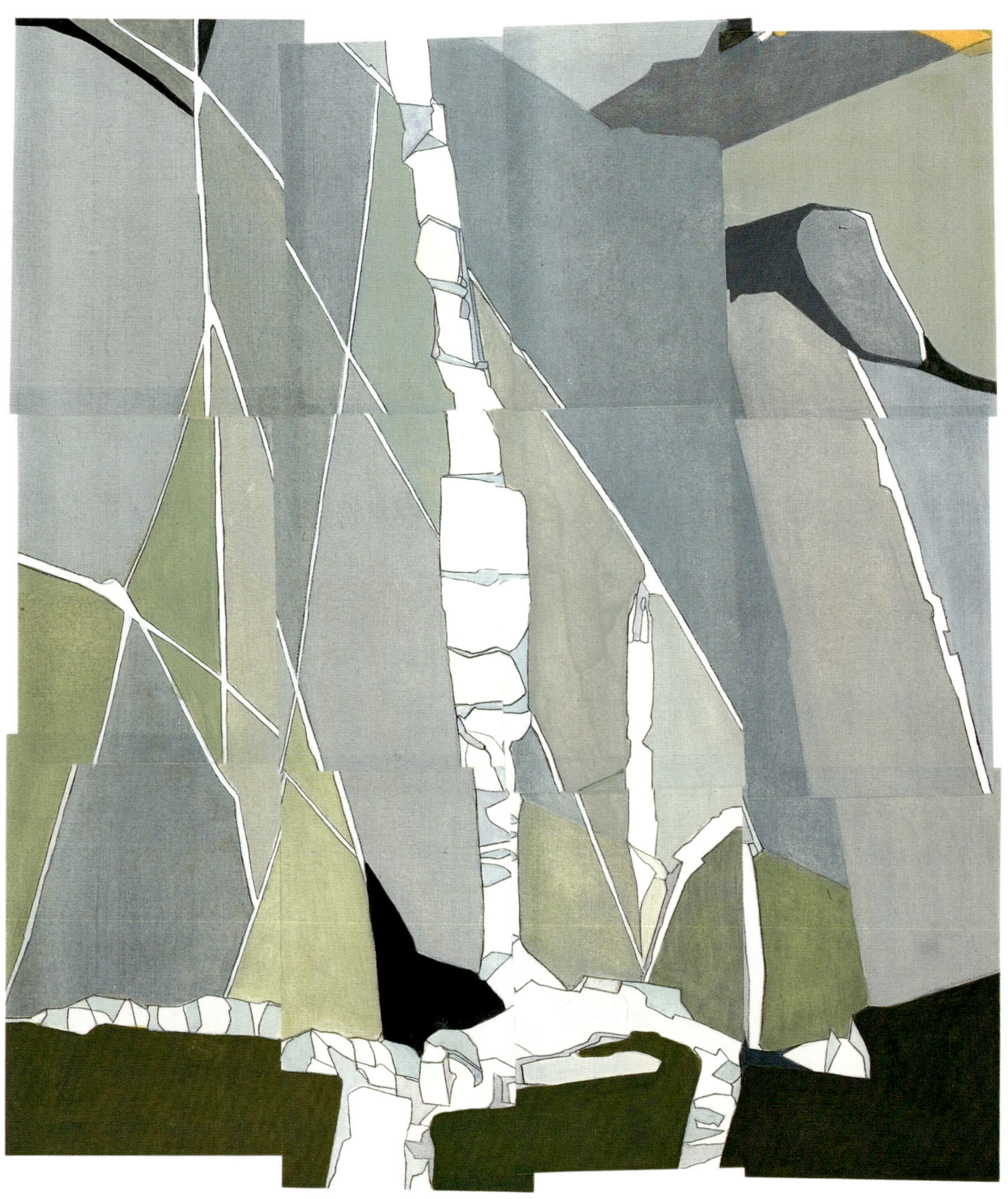

QUARTZ VEINS II | 1996
print & acrylic on board
80×65

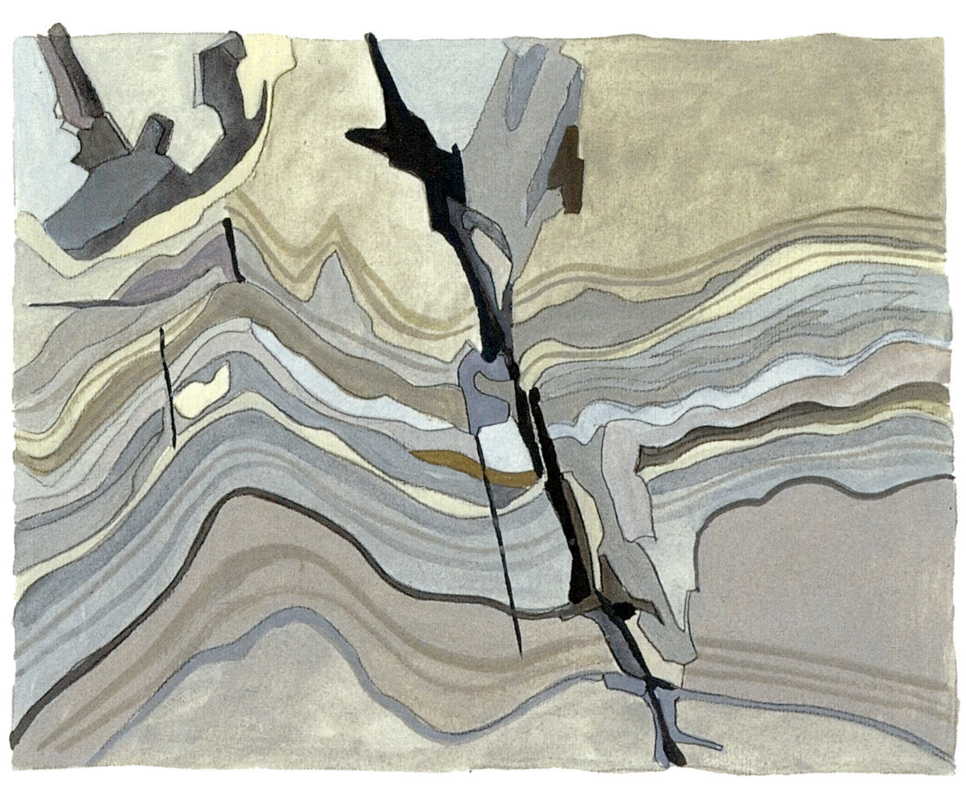

FROM KILCHIARAN TO MACHIR BAY 14 MAY 1996 (AND DETAIL) | 1996
acrylic & gouache on paper
100×70 (detail 16×21)

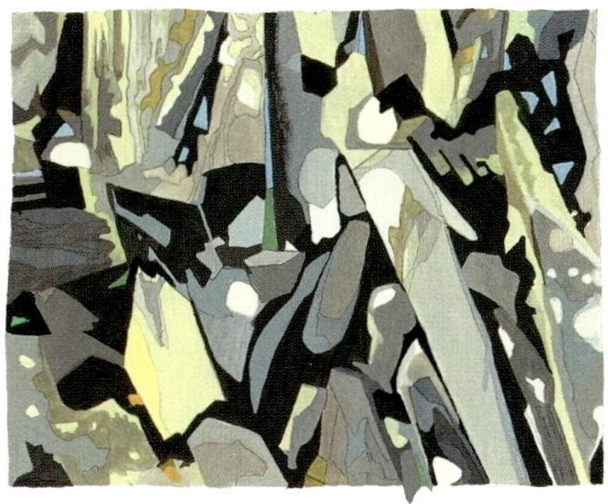
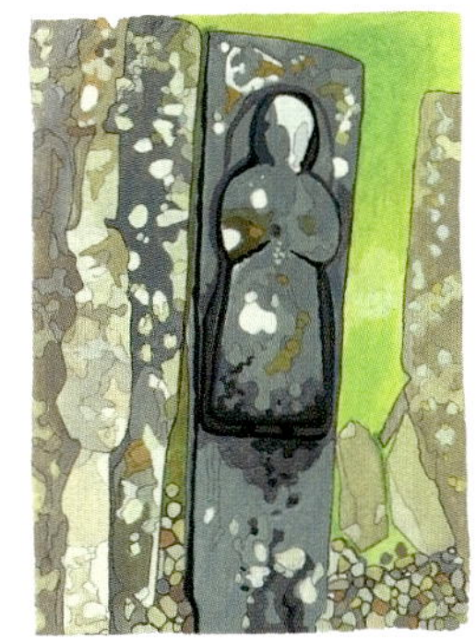
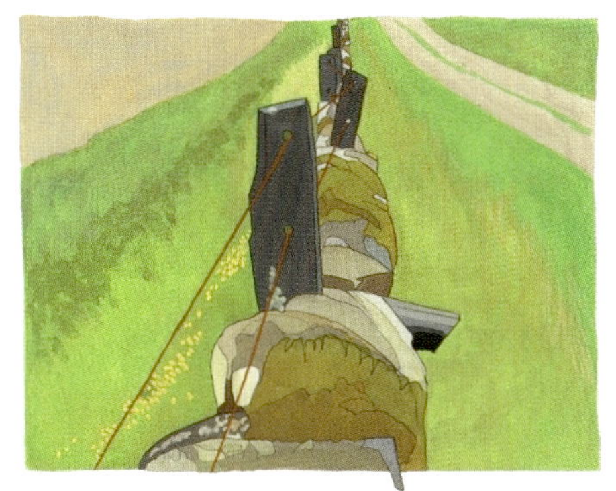
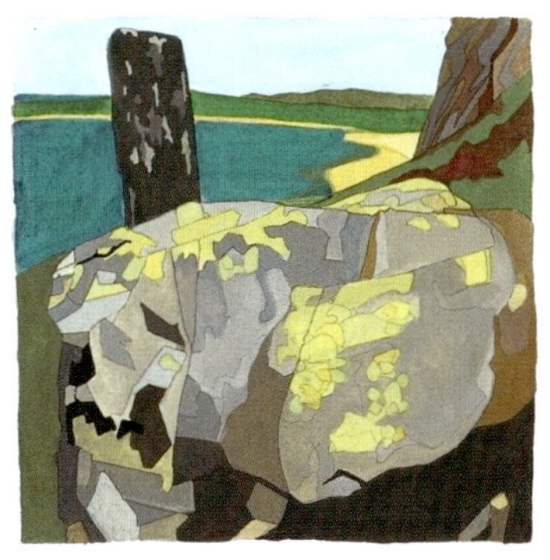
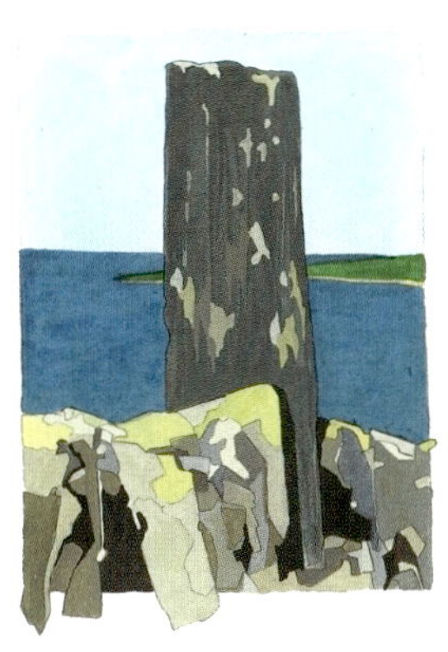
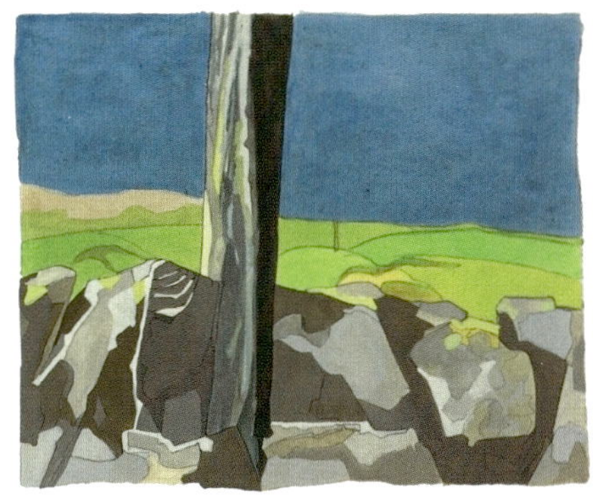
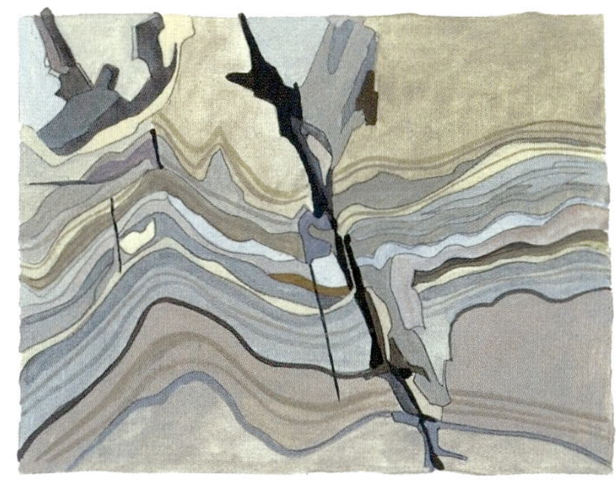
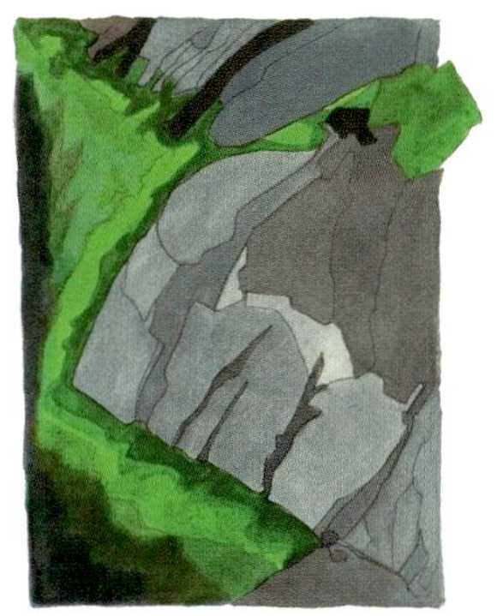
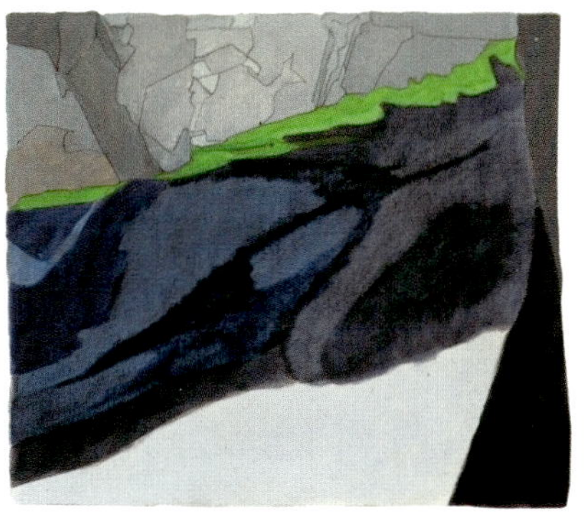

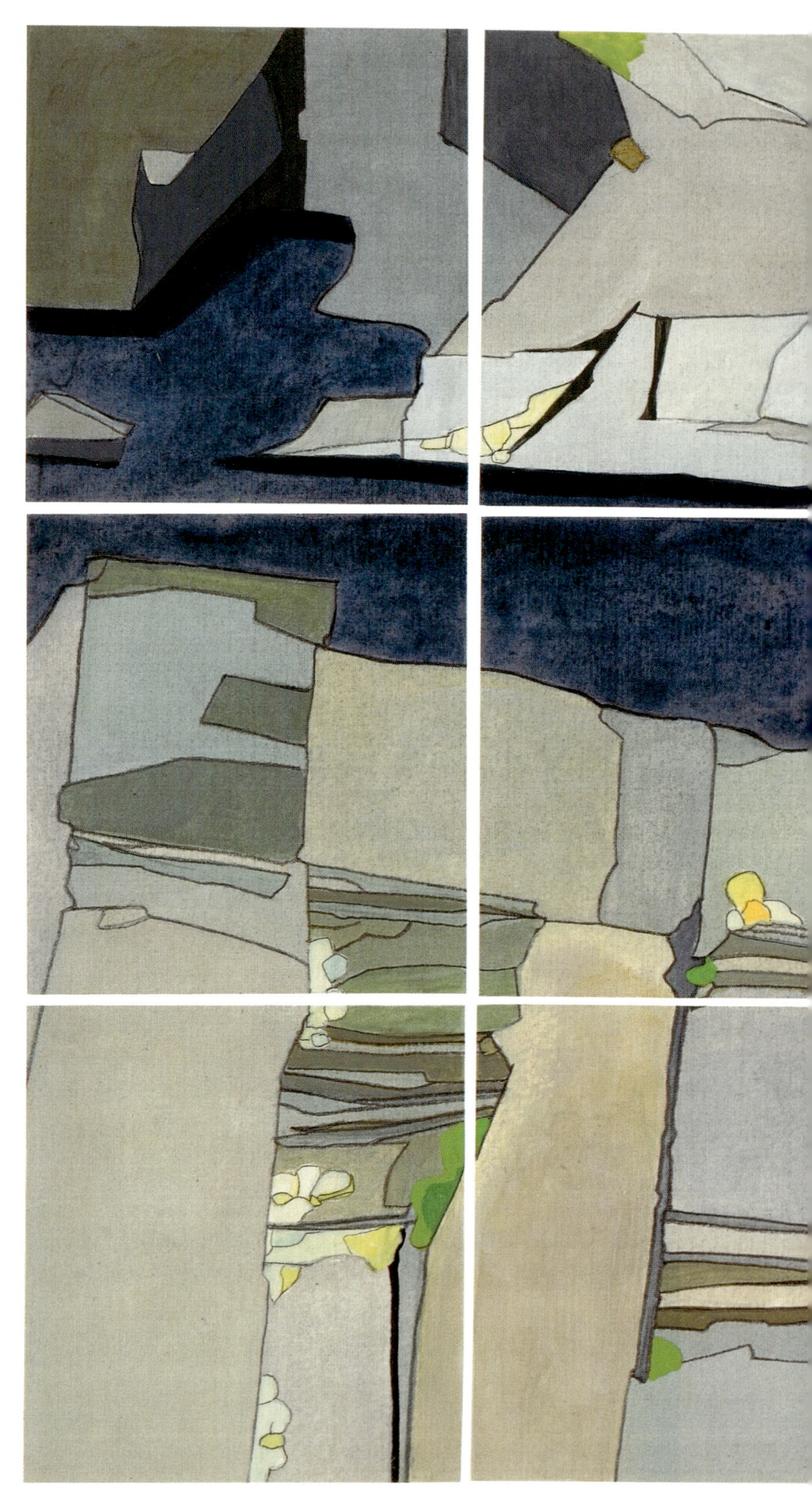

ROCK POOL II | **1996/97**
print & acrylic on board
62 × 100

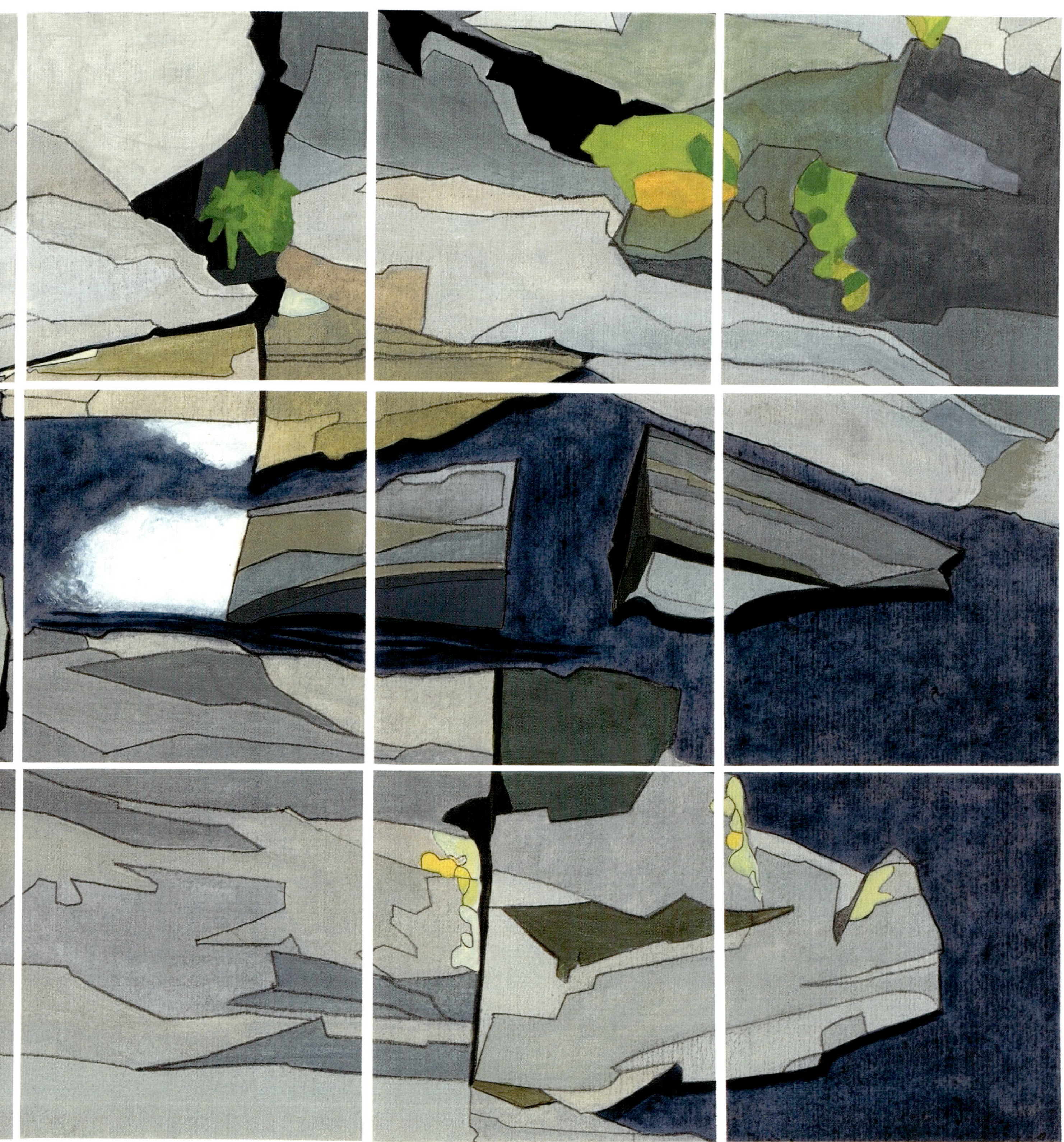

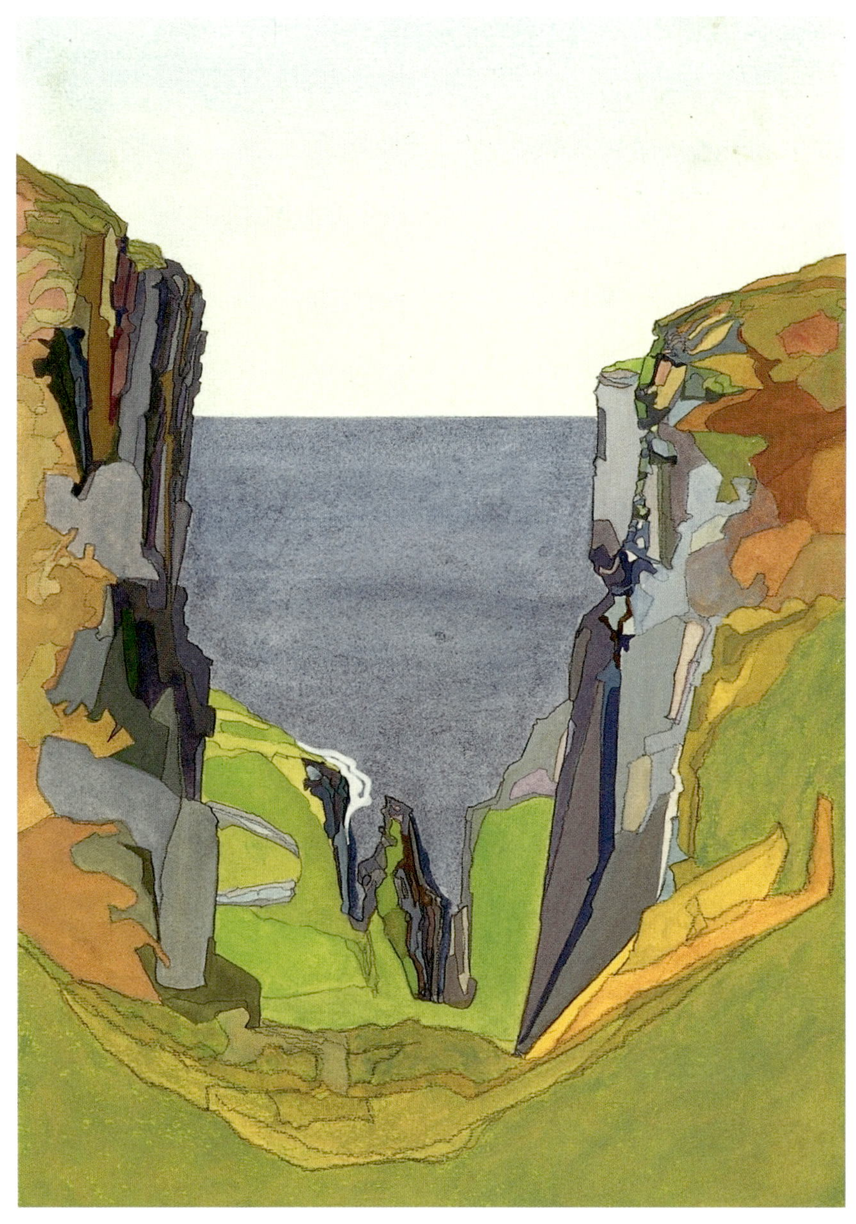

THE SETTLEMENT AT ALT NAM BÀ, ISLAY | 1996
acrylic & gouache on paper
35 × 25

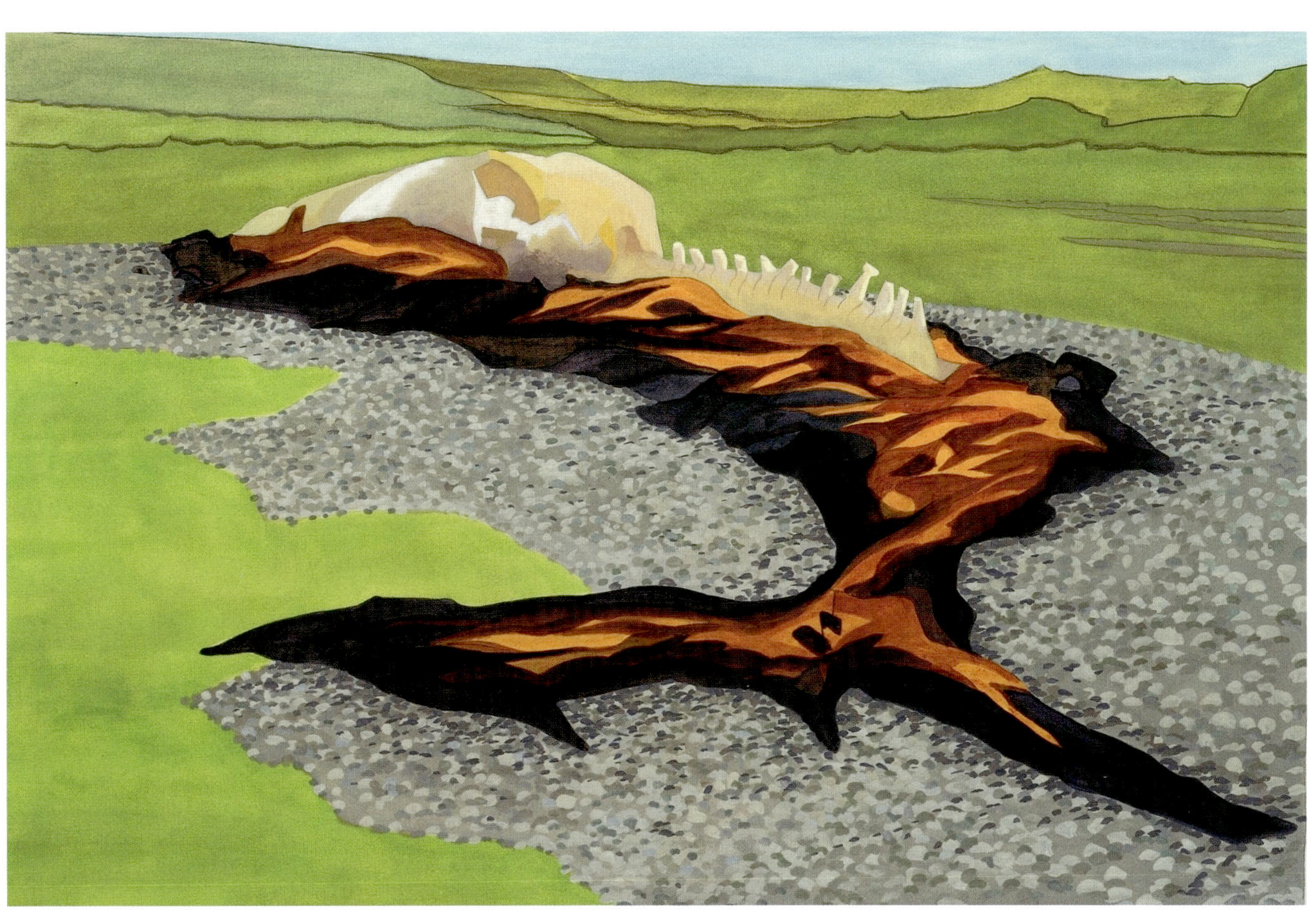

BEACHED WHALE AT CAMPA MAY I | 1996
acrylic & gouache on paper
70 × 100

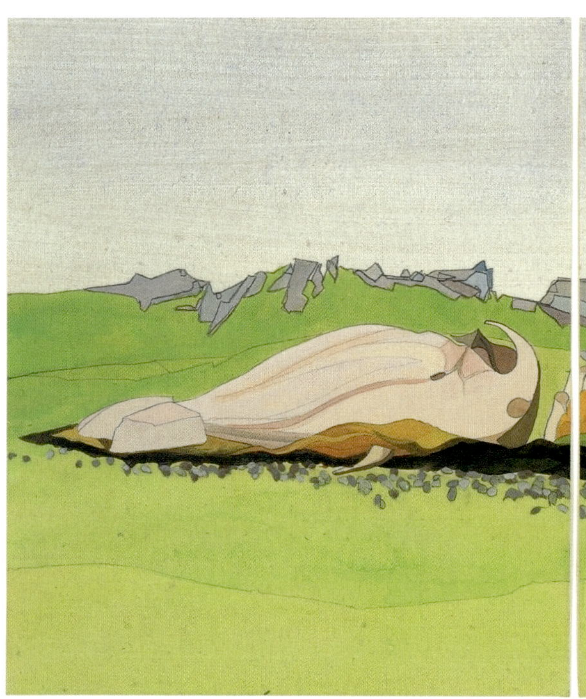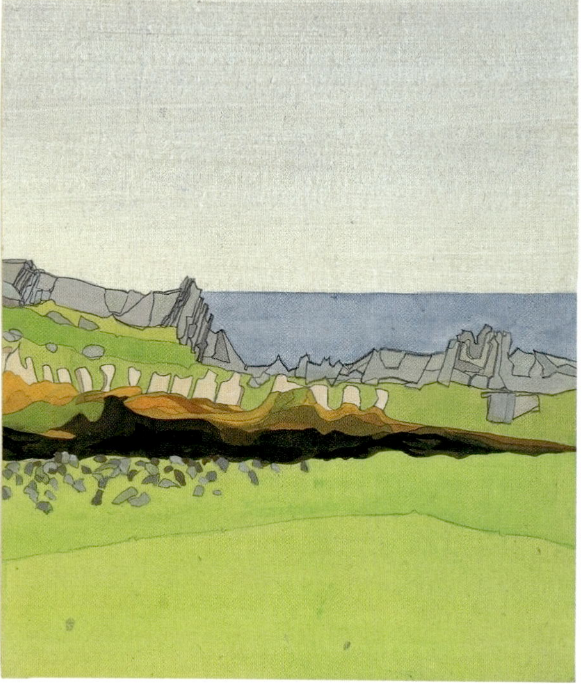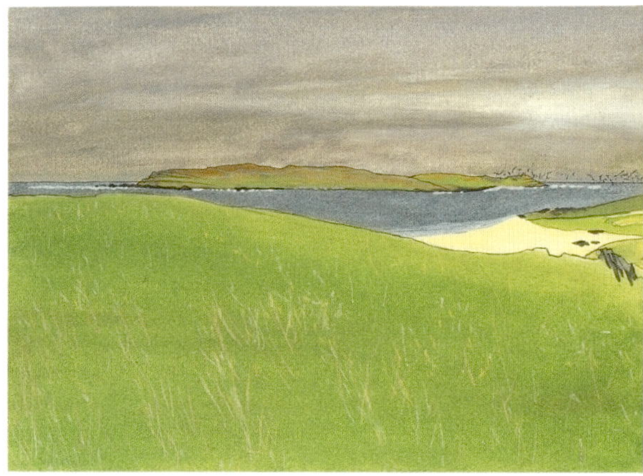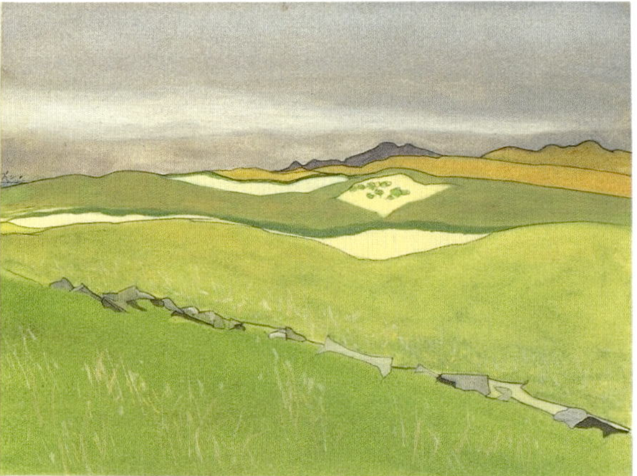

BEACHED WHALE AT CAMPA MAY II | 1996
acrylic & gouache on paper
29 × 50

ARDNAVE POINT, ISLAY | 1996
acrylic & gouache on paper
25 × 68

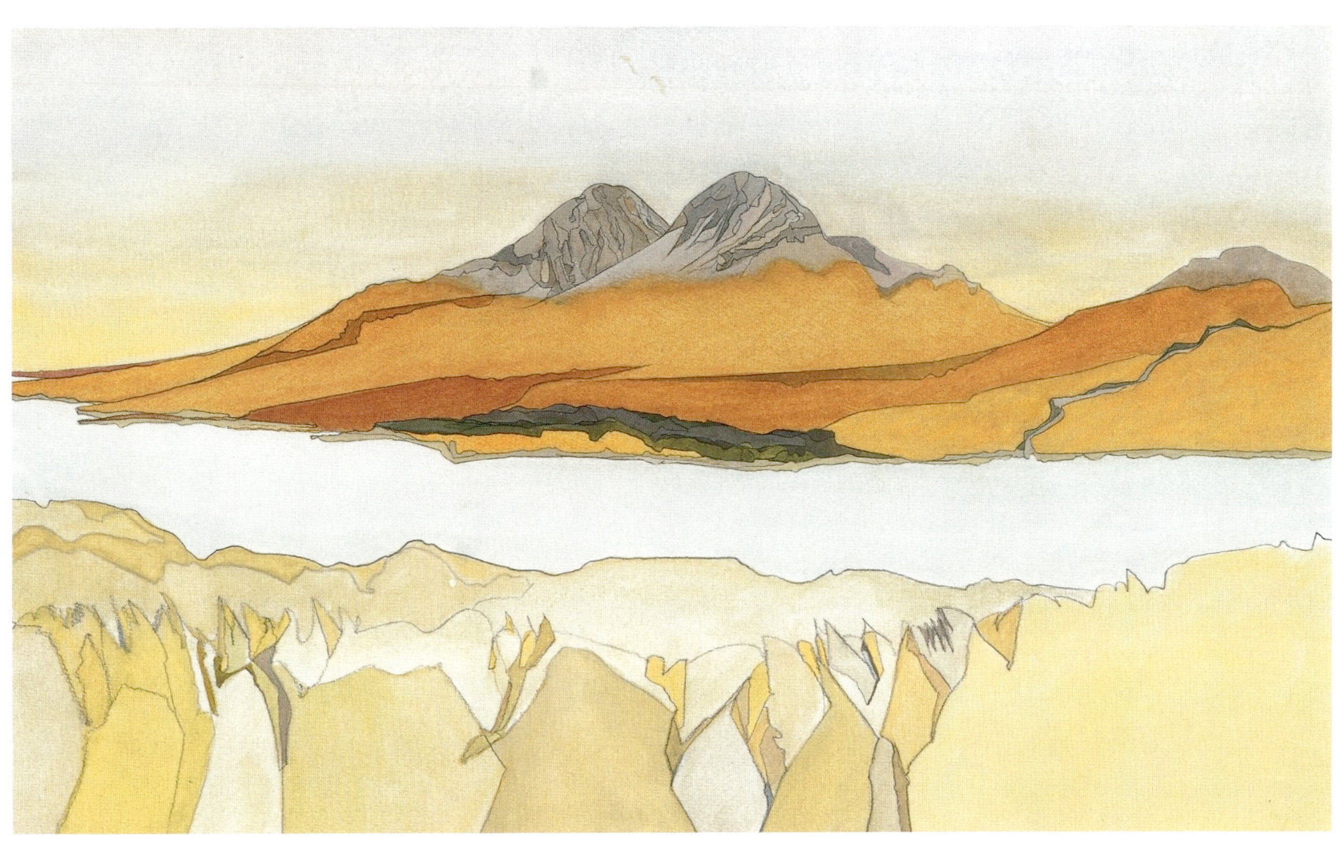

THE PAPS FROM ISLAY I | 2004
aquacryl & gouache on paper
30 × 50

HADRIAN'S WALL

Housesteads to Milecastle

The line of Hadrian's Wall runs right across the country, over one hundred miles from Newcastle to Bowness-on-Solway. The finest stretch is either side of the Roman fort of Housesteads. This is shown on the map of Roman sites. It was this stretch that I walked over a three-day period.

My arrival in February was dramatic. It was quite early in the day, deep in snow. It was so deep that it had discouraged the guardians who would have taken my entry fee. The car park was completely empty, so I had the whole fort to myself. The snow was piled up in large drifts against the walls. I thought of the Roman soldiers stationed so far from home in such bleak conditions.

The wall itself surprised me. I didn't expect to see it in such good condition. Restored or not, it looked like a carefully made wall with fine stonework. My other impression, though, was that it was smaller than I had imagined. Perhaps I was influenced by all those views of the Great Wall of China. This is a very different affair. Notwithstanding, I was impressed, especially by the way the wall snaked across the land. It does seem like a real frontier. To the south the land is flat – well, flatter. To the north the hilly landscape stretches away.

Perhaps because of the snow I saw few other people during the three days I was walking. It was sunny and clear. I have a photograph as the screensaver on my computer. Each day I am reminded of the wall in the snow.

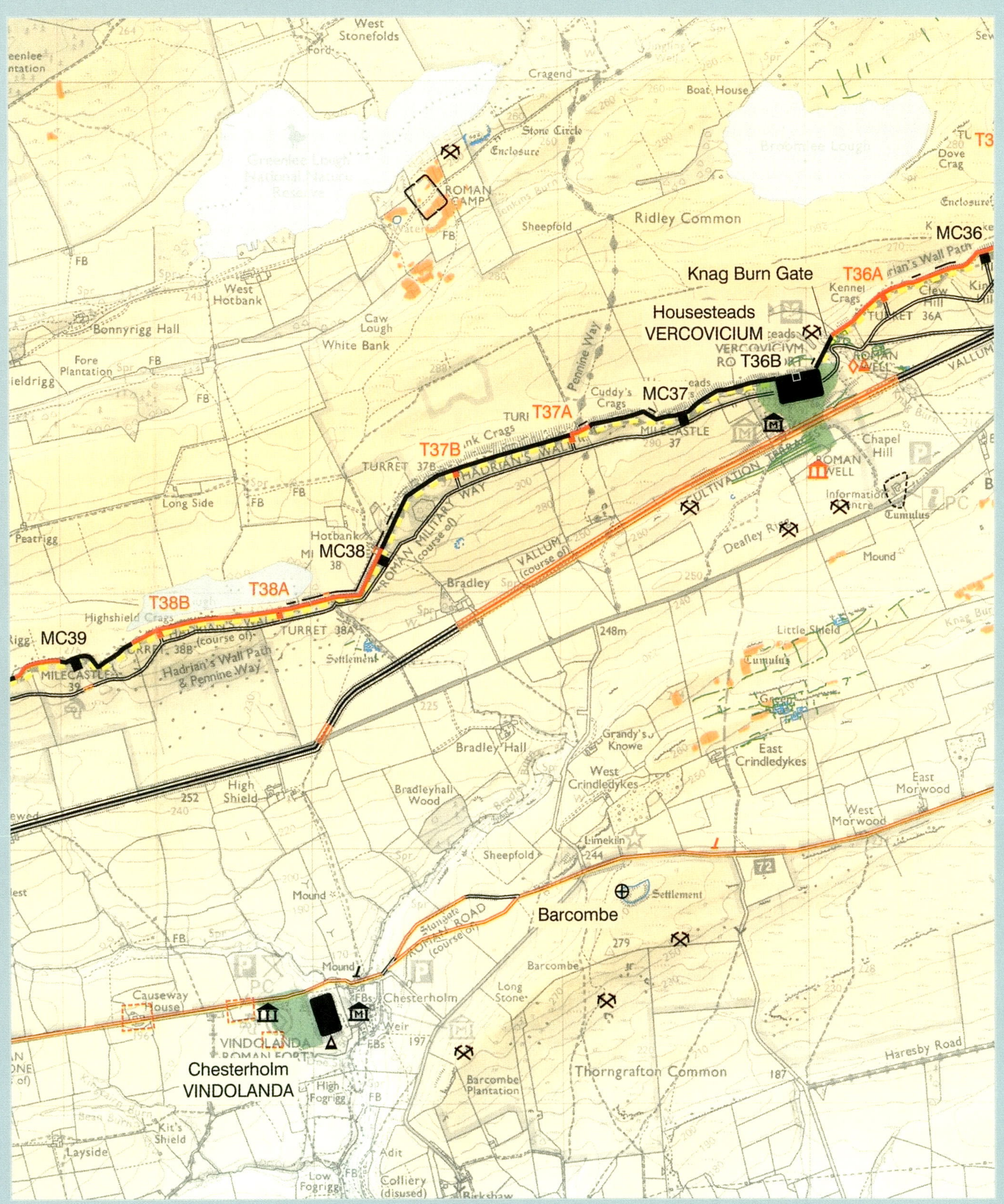

West Stonefolds
Cragend
Boat House
Greenlee Lough
National Nature Reserve
Stone Circle
Enclosure
ROMAN CAMP
Broomlee Lough
T3
Dove Crag
Enclosure
MC36
Ridley Common
Sheepfold
Knag Burn Gate
T36A
Kennel Crags
Clew Hill
TURRET 36A
West Hotbank
Bonnyrigg Hall
Caw Lough
White Bank
Pennine Way
Housesteads
VERCOVICIUM
VERCOVICIUM
ROMAN
T36B
VALLUM
Fore Plantation
Fieldrigg
Cuddy's Crags
MC37
Chapel Hill
ROMAN WELL
TURRET
T37A
MILECASTLE 37
ROMAN WELL
T37B
HADRIAN'S WALL
CULTIVATION
Information Centre
Tumulus
Long Side
ROMAN MILITARY WAY (course of)
VALLUM (course of)
Deafley Rigg
Mound
Peatrigg
Hotbank
MC38
Bradley
Little Shield
T38B
T38A
248m
Tumulus
Highshield Crags
HADRIAN'S WALL
TURRET 38A
MC39
MILECASTLE 39
Hadrian's Wall Path & Pennine Way
Settlement
225
East Crindledykes
East Morwood
High Shield
252
Bradley Hall
Grandy's Knowe
West Crindledykes
West Morwood
Bradleyhall Wood
Limekiln
Sheepfold
Settlement
Barcombe
Stanegate ROMAN ROAD (course of)
Barcombe
Long Stone
Thorngrafton Common
Haresby Road
Causeway House
Chesterholm
VINDOLANDA ROMAN FORT
VINDOLANDA
Weir
High Fogrigg
Barcombe Plantation
Layside
Kit's Shield
Low Fogrigg
Adit
Colliery (disused)
Birkshaw

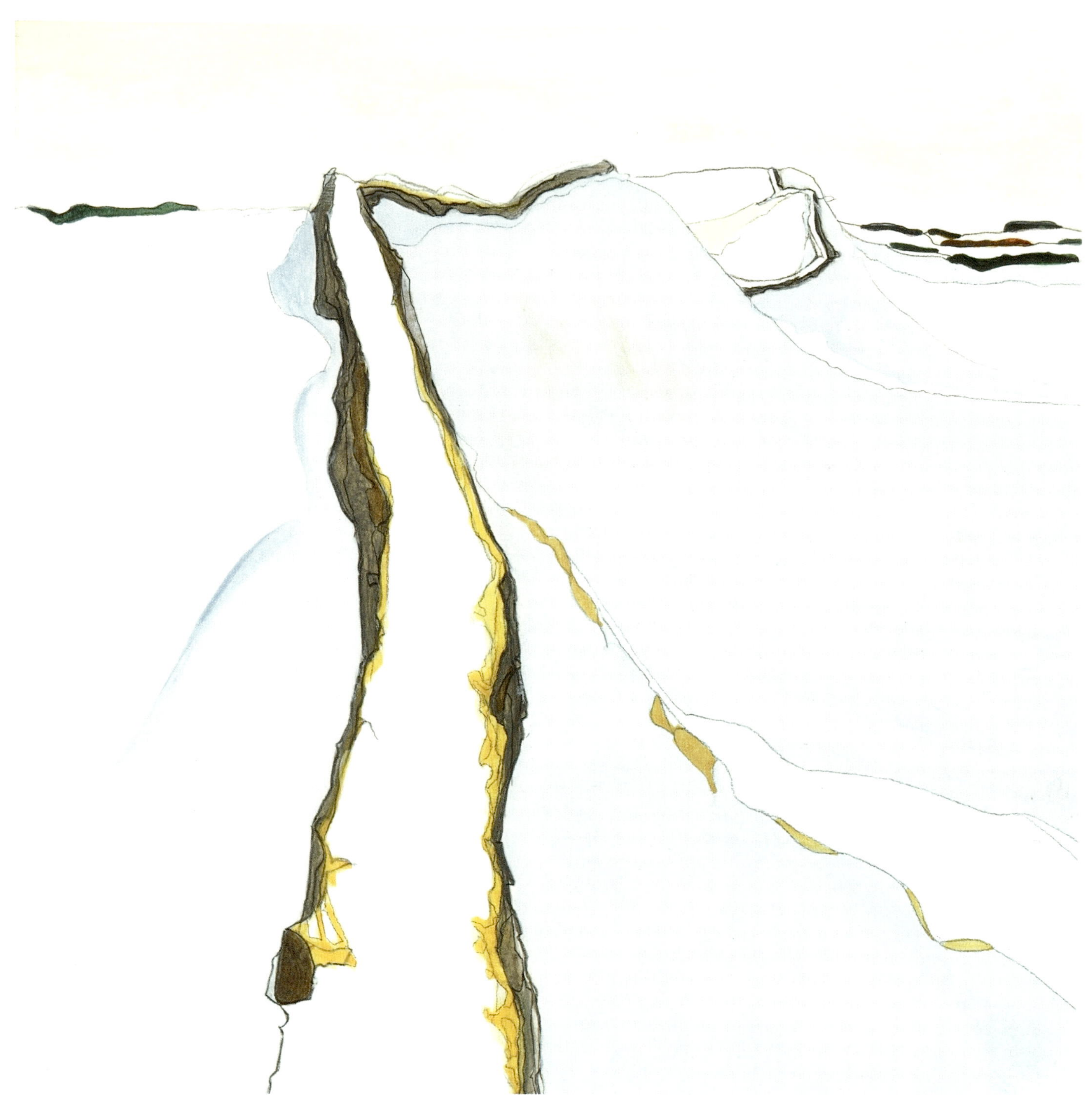

HADRIAN'S WALL: WEST FROM HOUSESTEAD CRAGS | 2003
mixed media on paper
25 × 59

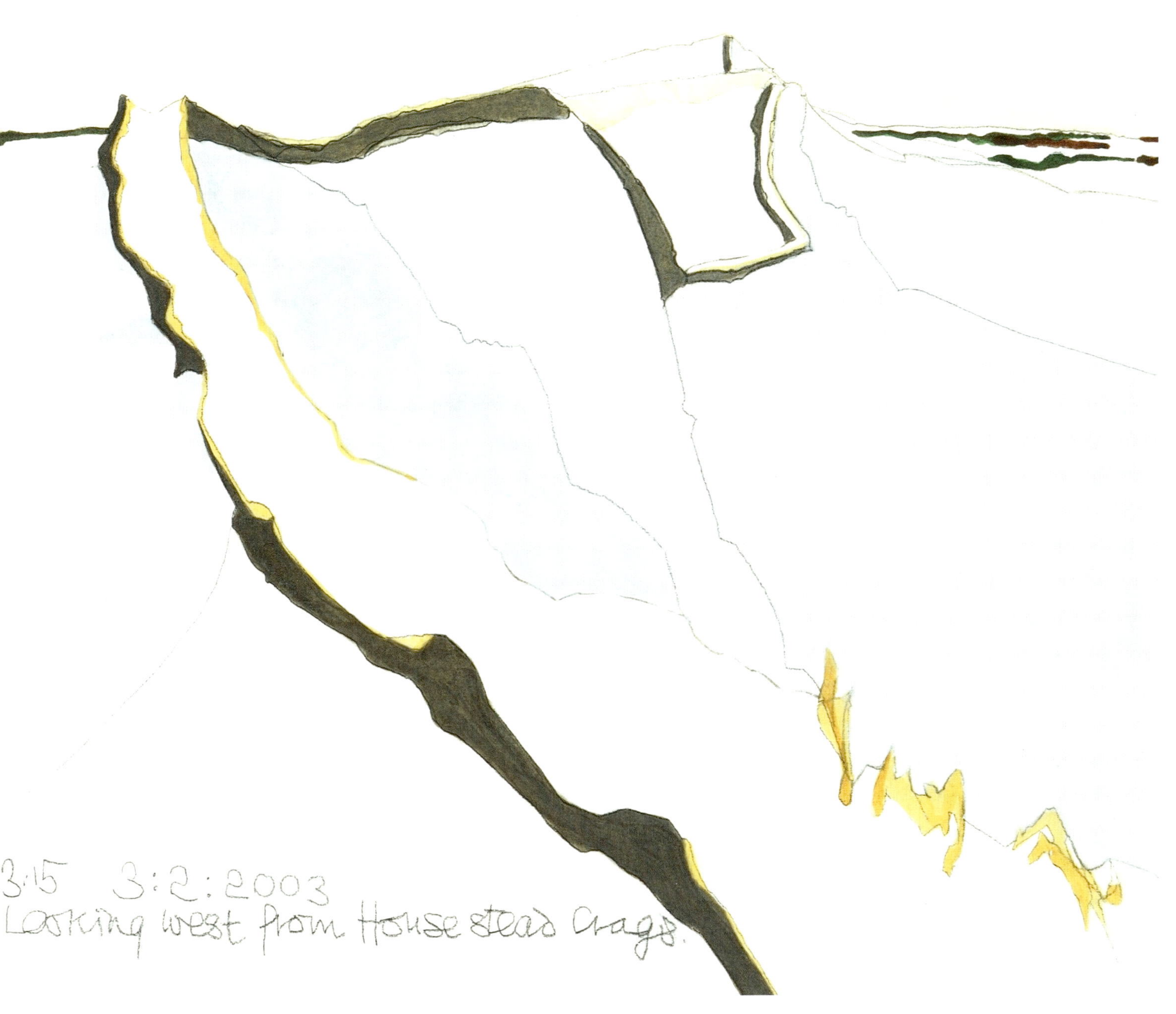

3:15   3:2:2003
Looking west from Housestead Crags.

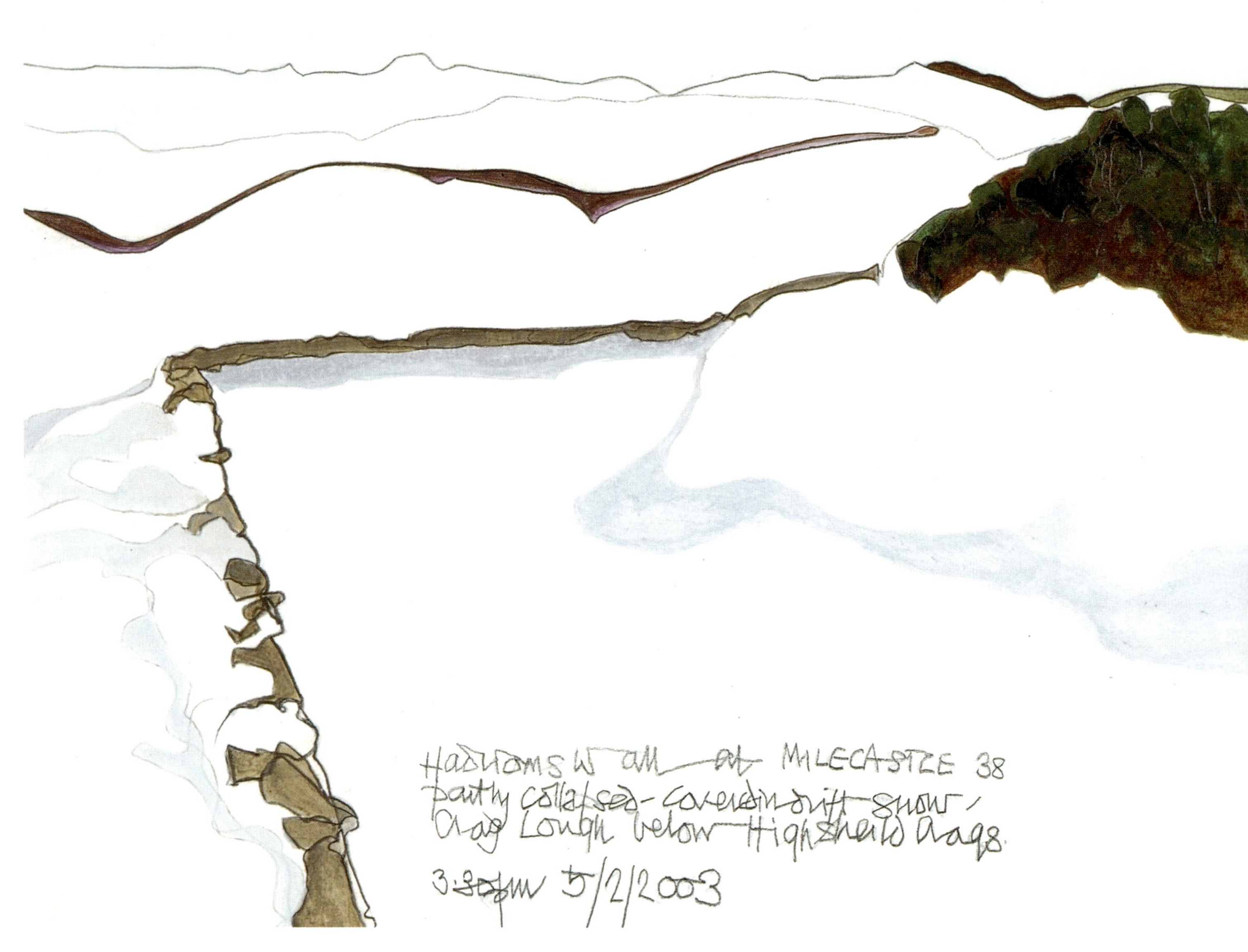

HADRIAN'S WALL: WEST FROM MILECASTLE 38 | 2003
mixed media on paper
31 × 55

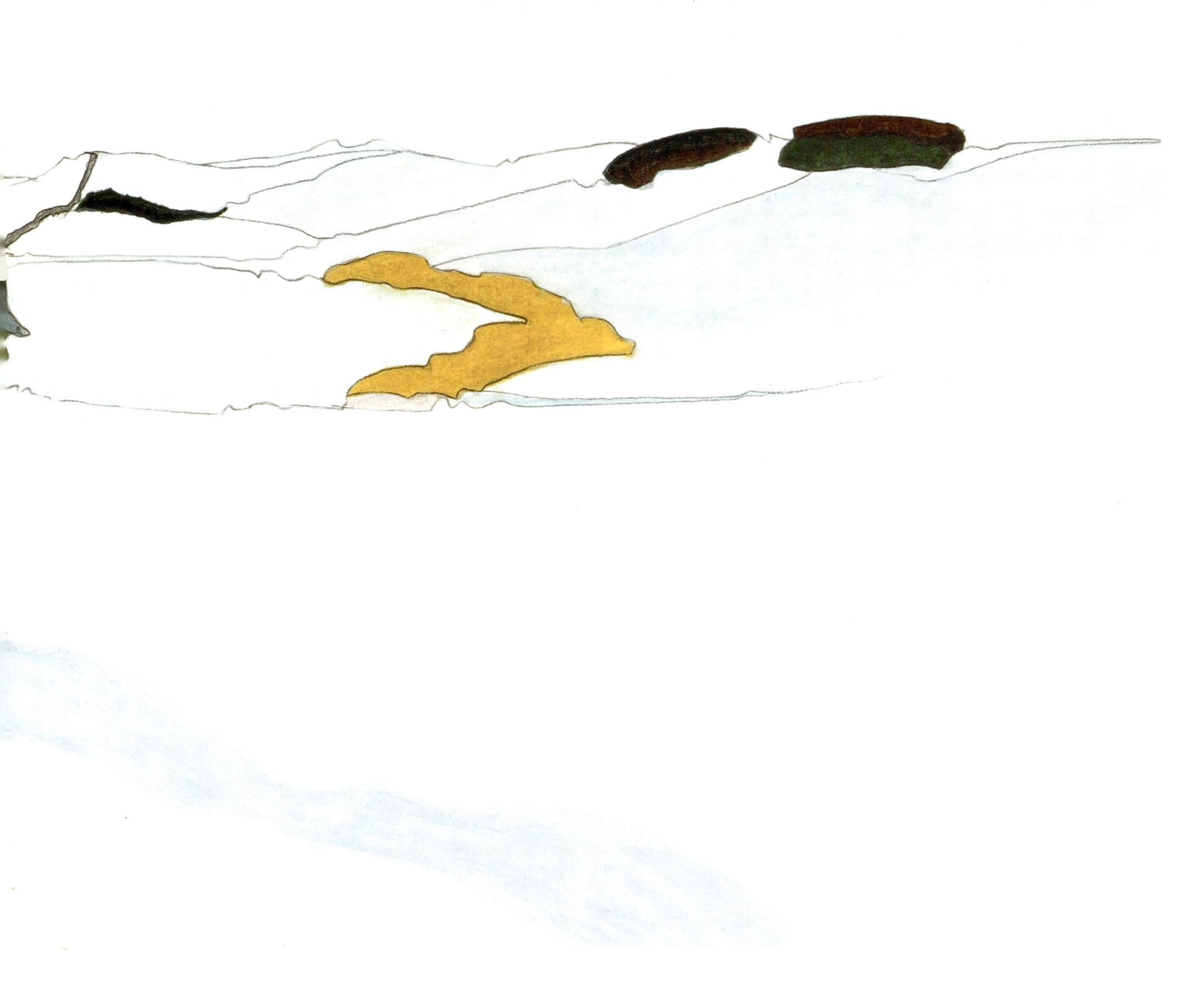

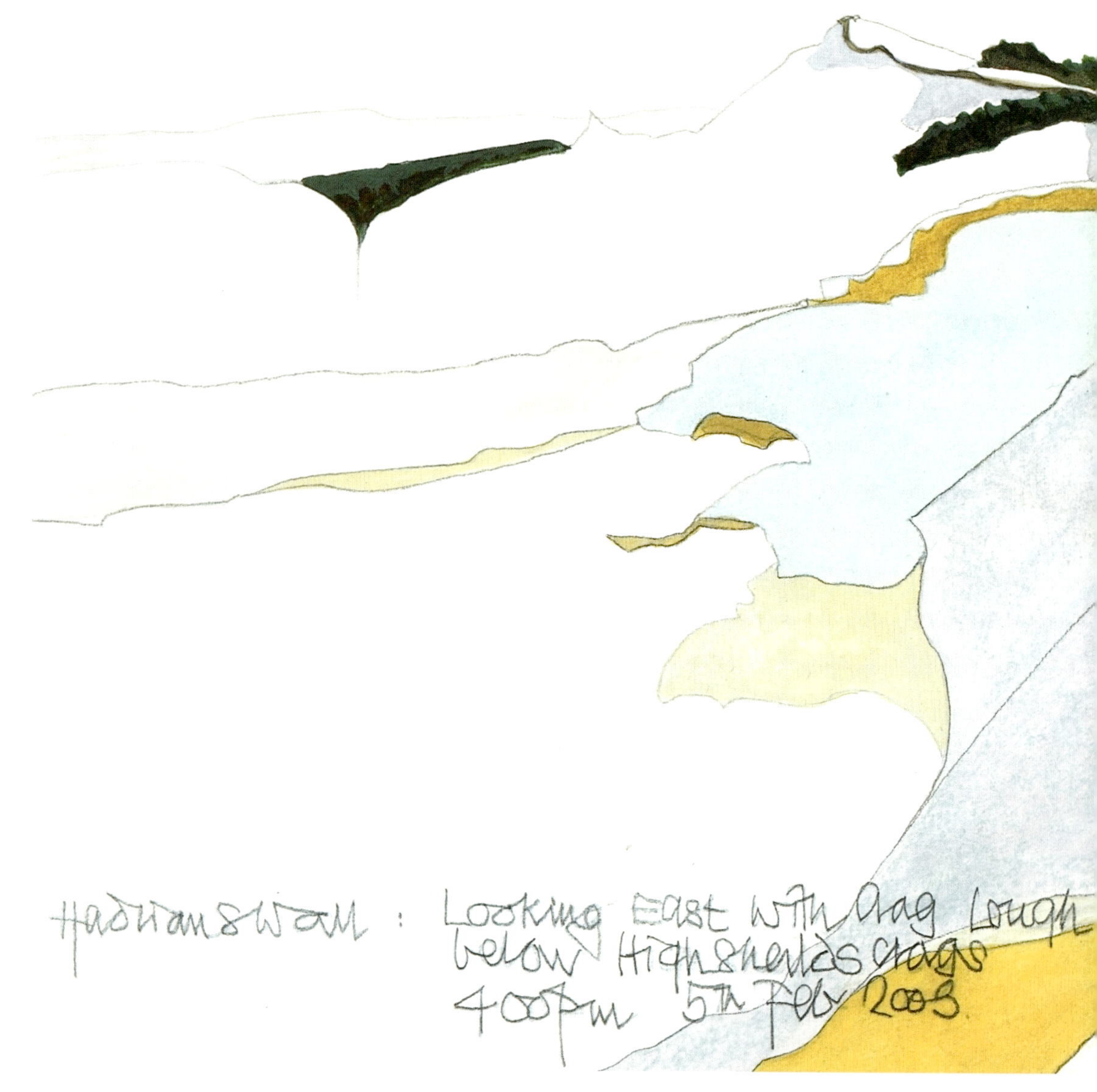

**HADRIAN'S WALL: EAST
TO CRAG LOUGH | 2003**
mixed media on paper
27×63

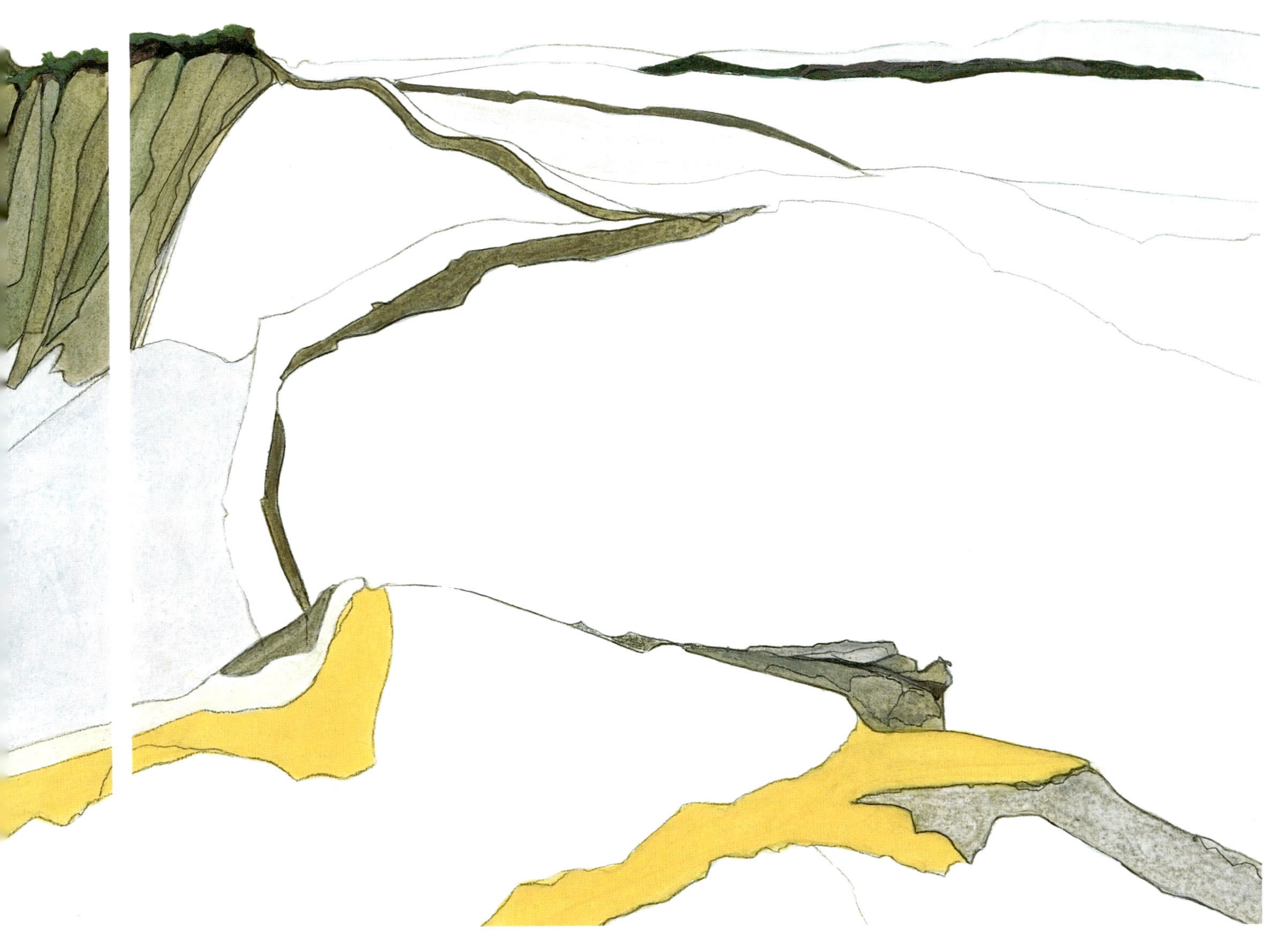

Hadrian's Wall at Milecastle 38 partly
collapsed – covered in drift snow –
Crag Lough below Highshield Crags.

3.30 PM 5 FEB 2003

THREE DAYS ON HADRIAN'S WALL: 3RD TO 5TH FEB 2003 | 2003
mixed media on paper
86 × 69

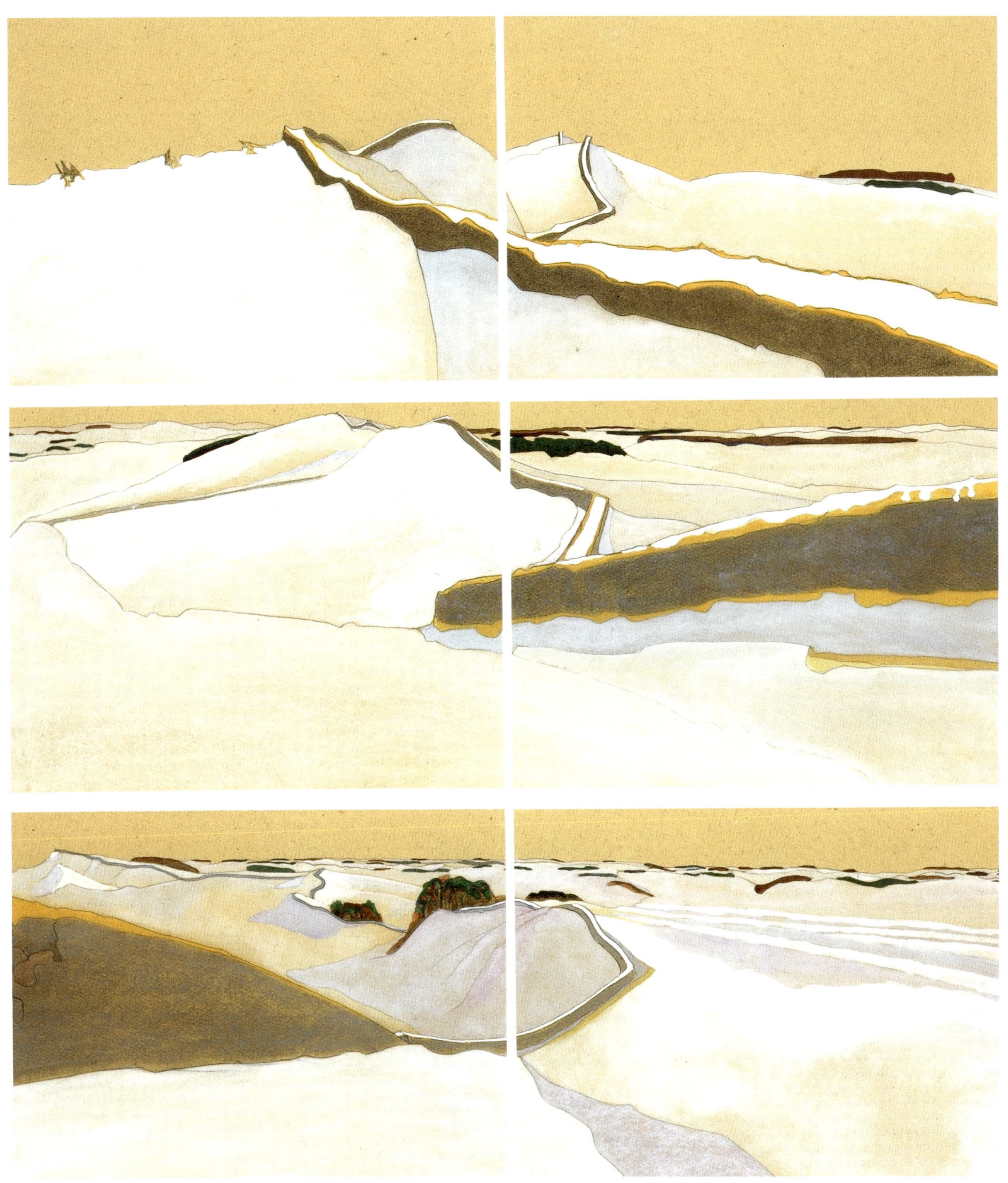

THE THREE PEAKS

The track linking the Three Peaks in Yorkshire

The Three Peaks of Pen-y-ghent, Ingleborough and Whernside lie in the west of Yorkshire, close to the Yorkshire Dales. Though not quite as dramatically distinct as the mountains of Assynt, they stand very separated in their surrounding landscape. They too have a distinctive geology – bands of limestone with sandstone and gritstone caps. Differential weathering of the stone gives Ingleborough and Pen-y-ghent their distinctive stepped form. I was so struck by the geology that I used the geological map to create a composite work that forms the endpapers of this book.

The Three Peaks are best known among walkers as an endurance challenge – climbing and descending all three peaks in twelve hours. I had no interest in attempting this feat, however long it took. My concern, rather than the peaks, was to walk and study the tracks in the valleys that connect them. These valleys are wonderful limestone plateaux, where natural rock forms have intermixed with man-made rock walls (pp. 102–03). As the rock for the walls is gathered from the surrounding exposed land, the two seem to merge together. It reminds one of the extraordinary limestone landscape of the Burren in West Ireland or the nearby Aran Islands.

In the days walking the tracks between the peaks, I mixed drawings of the longer view together with details of fragments of the stone walls and crevices in the stone land. By combining these with maps of each peak, I hope to leave an overall impression of what it is like to walk this landscape.

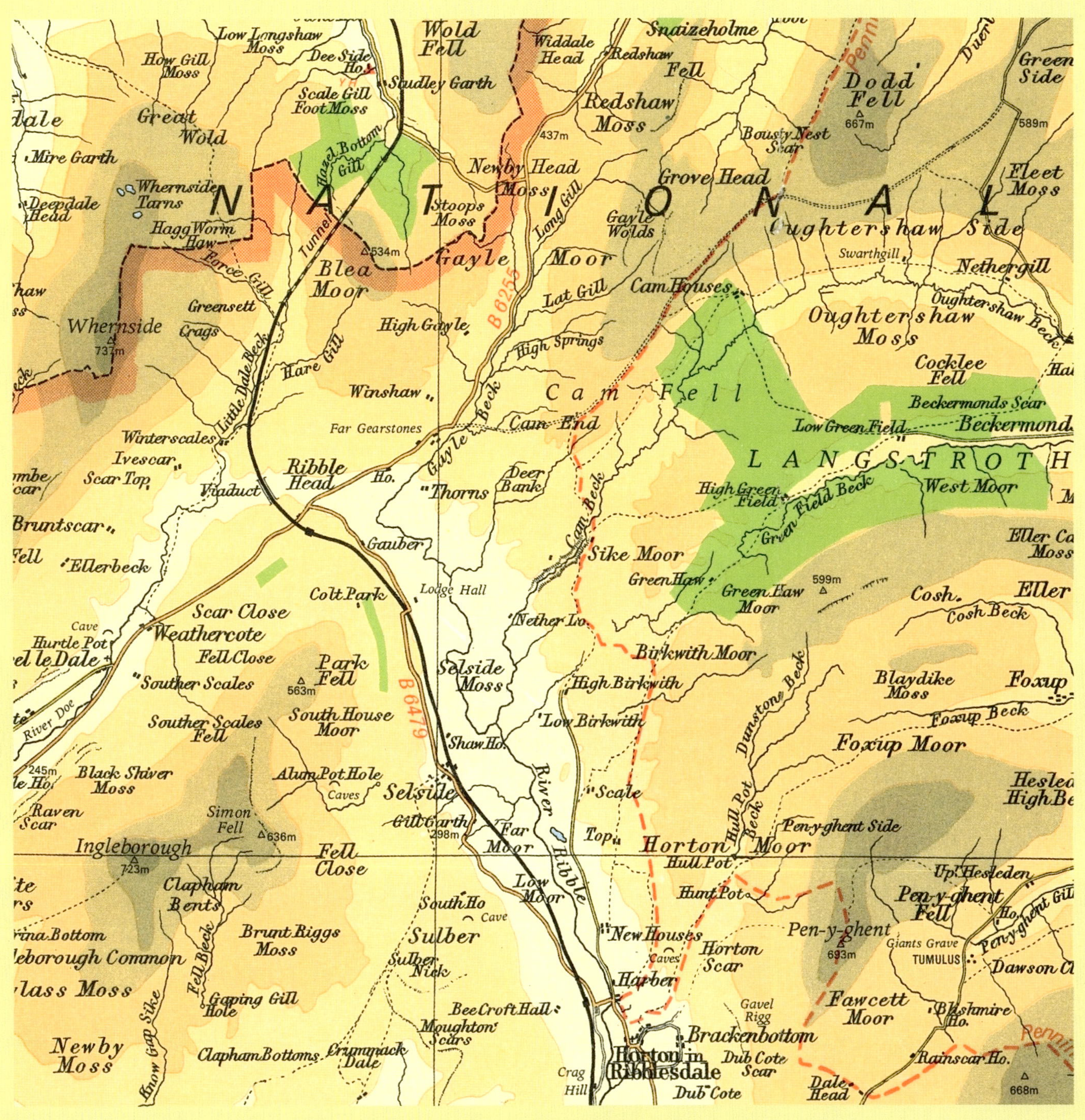

Low Longshaw Moss
How Gill Moss
Dee Side Ho.
Scale Gill Foot Moss
Studley Garth
Wold Fell
Widdale Head
Snaizeholme
Redshaw Fell
Redshaw Moss
Pennine
Dodd Fell
667m
Green Side
589m
Fleet Moss
Great Wold
Mire Garth
Deepdale Head
Whernside Tarns
Hagg Worm How
Hagg Bottom Gill
437m
Newby Head Moss
Stoops Moss
Grove Head
Gayle Wolds
Bousty Nest Scar
Oughtershaw Side
Swarthgill
Nethergill
NATIONAL
Whernside
737m
Greensett Crags
Blea Moor
534m
Gayle Moor
High Gayle
Lat Gill
Cam Houses
High Springs
Oughtershaw Beck
Oughtershaw Moss
Cocklee Fell
Winterscales
Ivescar
Scar Top
Hare Gill
Winshaw
Far Gearstones
Cam Fell
Cam End
Low Green Field
Beckermonds Scar
Beckermond
Bruntscar
Fell
Ellerbeck
Viaduct
Ribble Head
Ho.
Thorns
Deer Bank
High Green Field
Green Field Beck
LANGSTROTH
West Moor
Eller Ca Moss
Colt Park
Lodge Hall
Sike Moor
Green Haw
Green Haw Moor
599m
Cosh.
Cosh Beck
Eller
Scar Close
Weathercote
Fell Close
Park Fell
563m
Nether Lo
Birkwith Moor
High Birkwith
Blaydike Moss
Foxup
Cave
Hurtle Pot
el le Dale
Souther Scales
Souther Scales Fell
South House Moor
Low Birkwith
Dunstone Beck
Foxup Beck
Foxup Moor
River Doe
245m Ho.
Black Shiver Moss
Alum Pot Hole
Caves
Shaw Ho.
Scale
Hull Pot Beck
Pen-y-ghent Side
Hesled High Be
Raven Scar
Simon Fell
636m
Selside
Gill Garth
298m
Far Moor
River Ribble
Top
Horton Moor
Hull Pot
Up Hesleden
Ingleborough
723m
Fell Close
Low Moor
Hunt Pot
Pen-y-ghent
693m
Giants Grave
TUMULUS
Pen-y-ghent Gill
Dawson Cl
Clapham Bents
South Ho.
Cave
New Houses
Caves
Horton Scar
Pen-y-ghent Fell
Ho.
rina Bottom
leborough Common
Brunt Riggs Moss
Sulber
Sulber Nick
Harber
Gavel Rigg
Fawcett Moor
Bishmire Ho.
Rainscar Ho.
lass Moss
Gaping Hole
Bee Croft Hall
Moughton Scars
Brackenbottom
Dub Cote Scar
Pennine
Newby Moss
Fell Beck
Knaw Gap Sike
Clapham Bottoms
Crummack Dale
Crag Hill
Horton in Ribblesdale
Dub Cote
Dale Head
668m
B 6255
B 6479
Gayle Beck
Cam Beck
Little Dale Beck
Force Gill
Tunnel
River Ribble

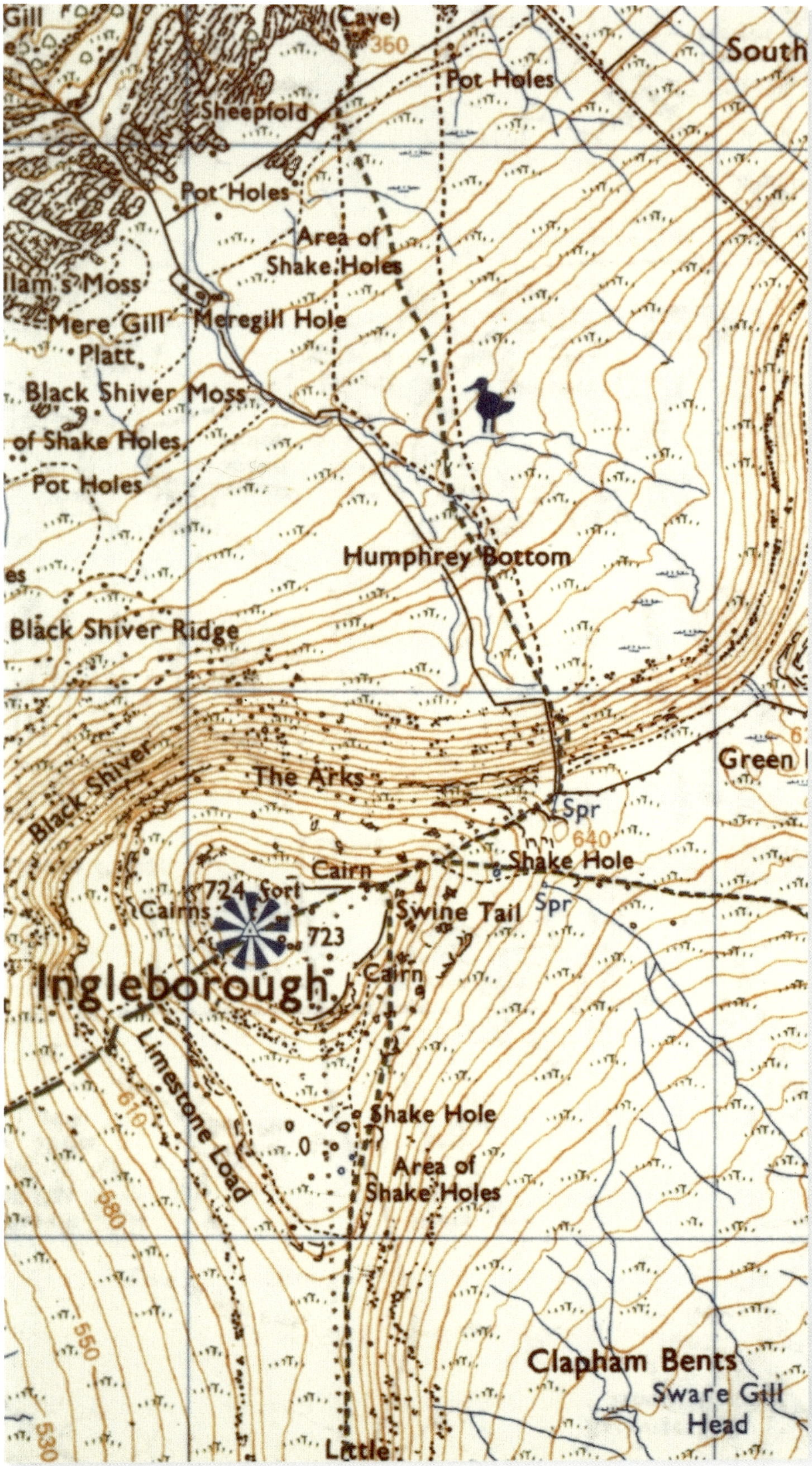

The Arks

Humphrey Bottom

Black Shiver Ridge

Black Shiver

Black Shiver Moss

of Shake Holes

Pot Holes

Mere Gill
Platt

llam's Moss

Meregill Hole

Area of
Shake Holes

Pot Holes

Sheepfold

Pot Holes

(Cave)

South

Green

Spr

Shake Hole

640

Cairn

724 Fort
Cairns

723

Swine Tail

Spr

Cairn

Ingleborough

Shake Hole

Limestone Load

610

580

550

530

Area of
Shake Holes

Clapham Bents
Sware Gill
Head

Little

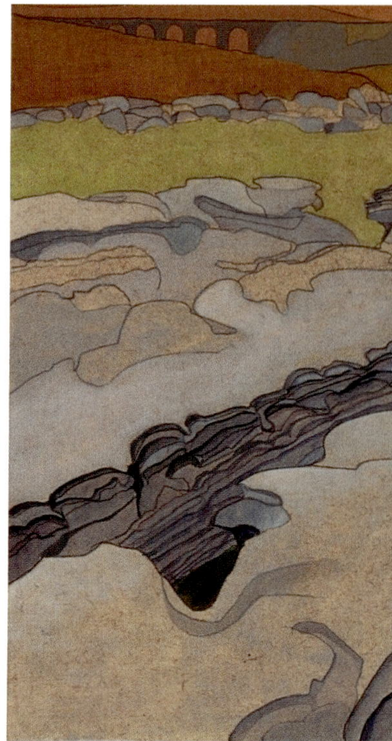

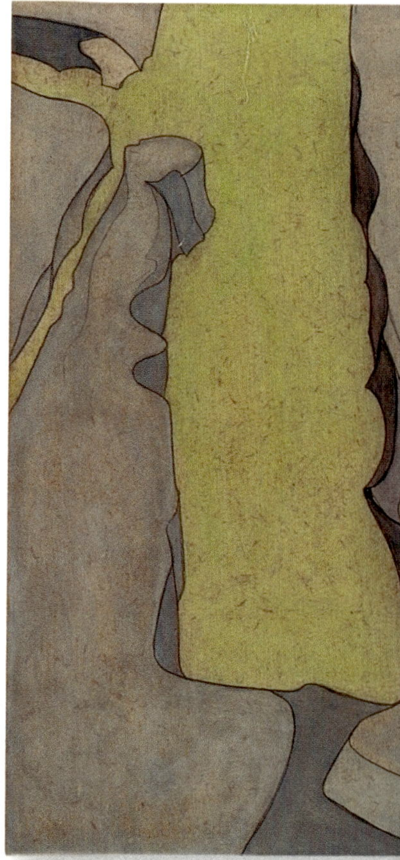

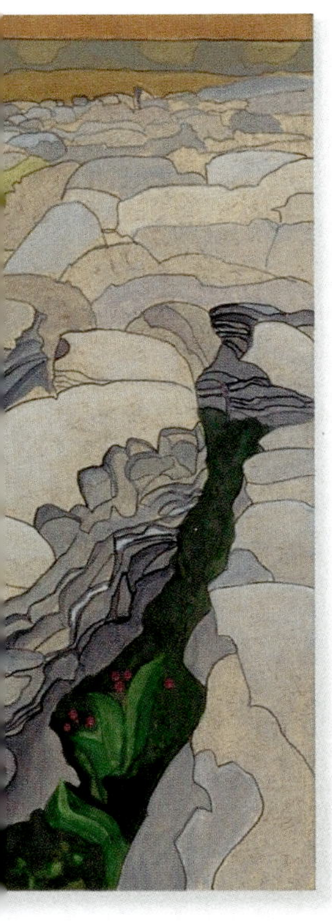
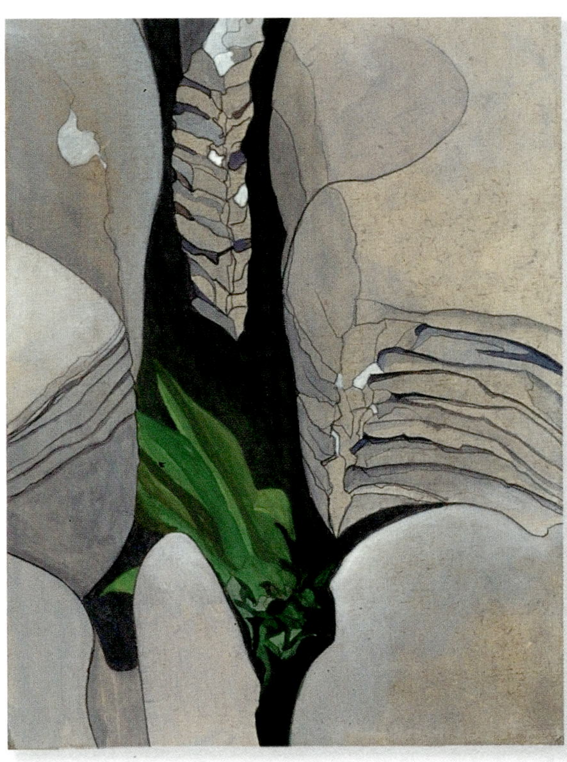
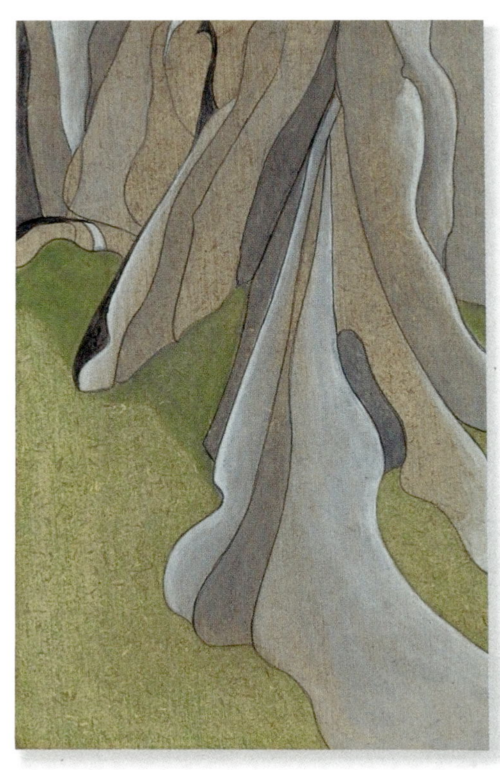
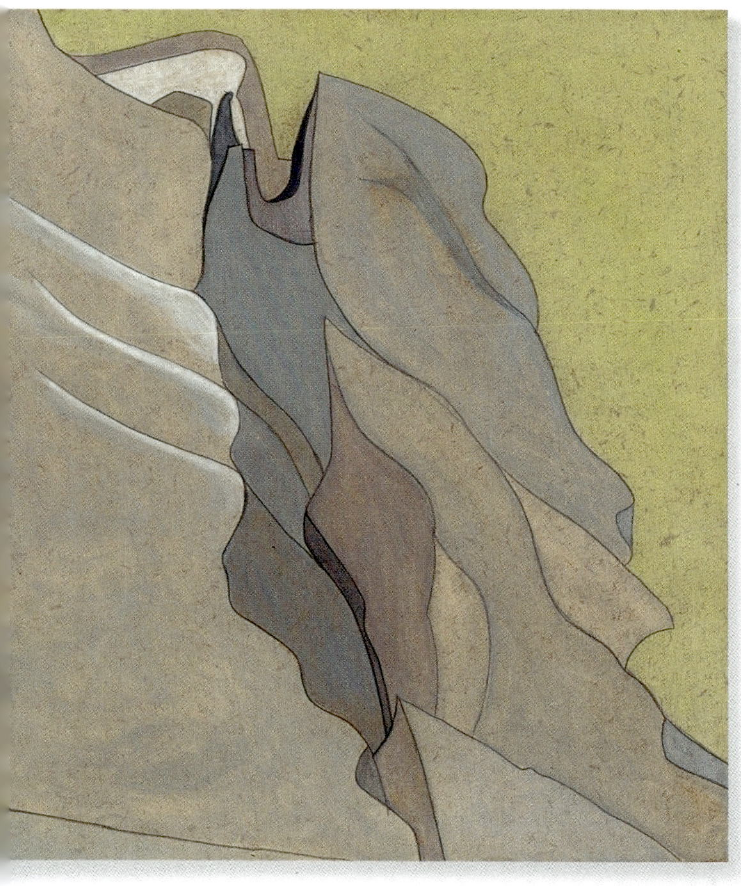
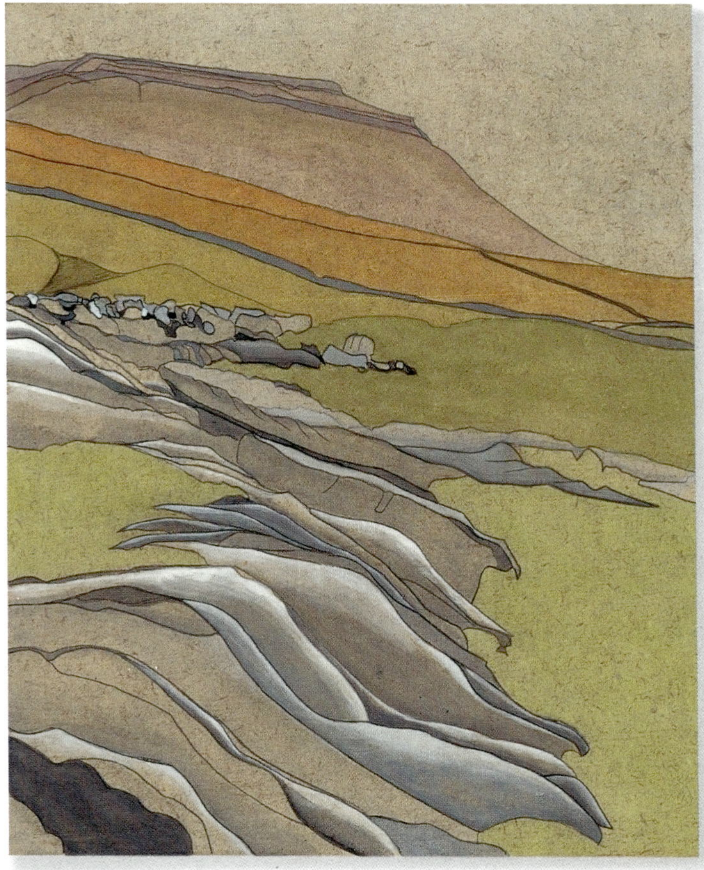

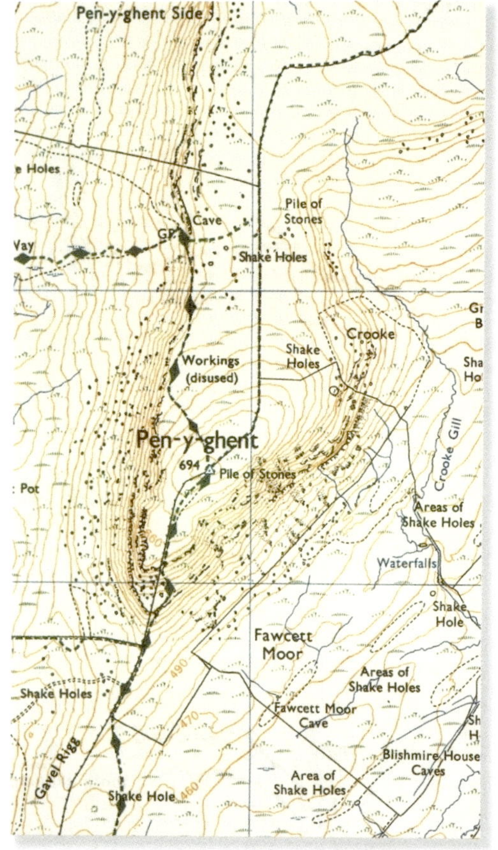

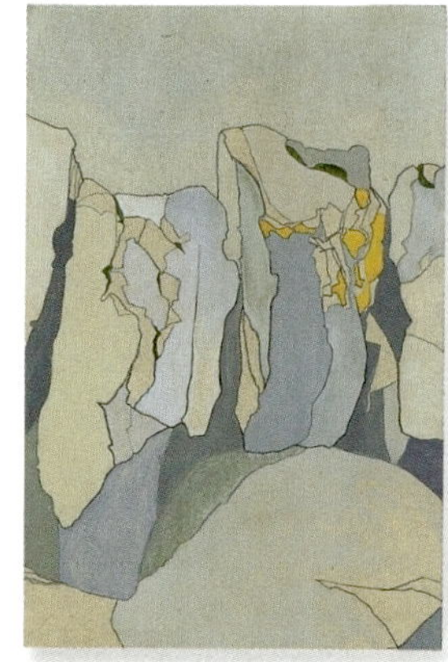

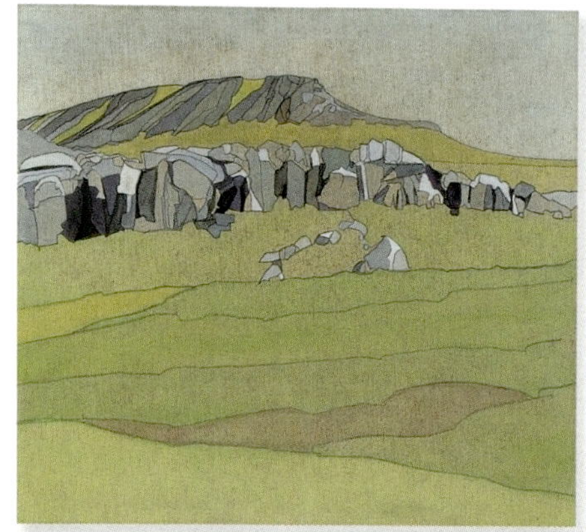

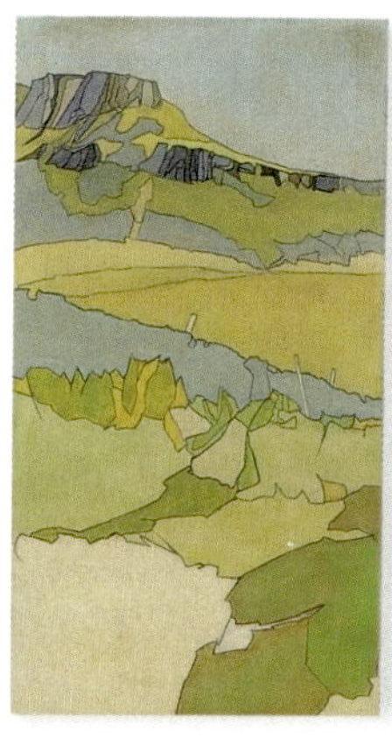

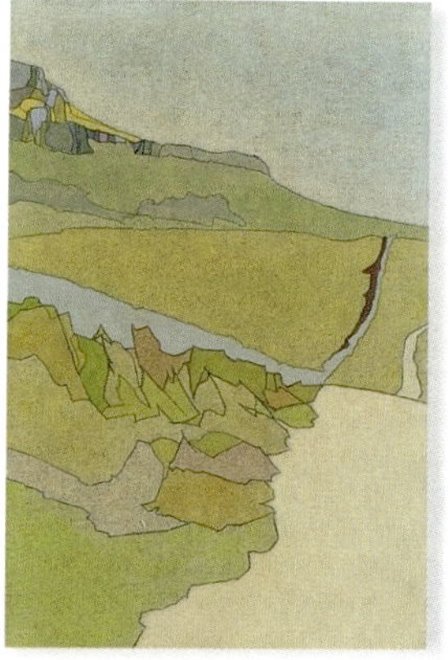

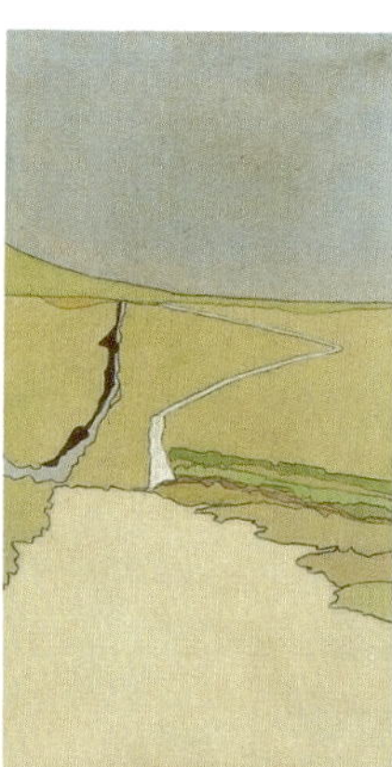

previous pages **INGLEBOROUGH | 1998**
acrylic on board with print
79 × 130

PEN-Y-GHENT | 1998
acrylic on board with print
79 × 114

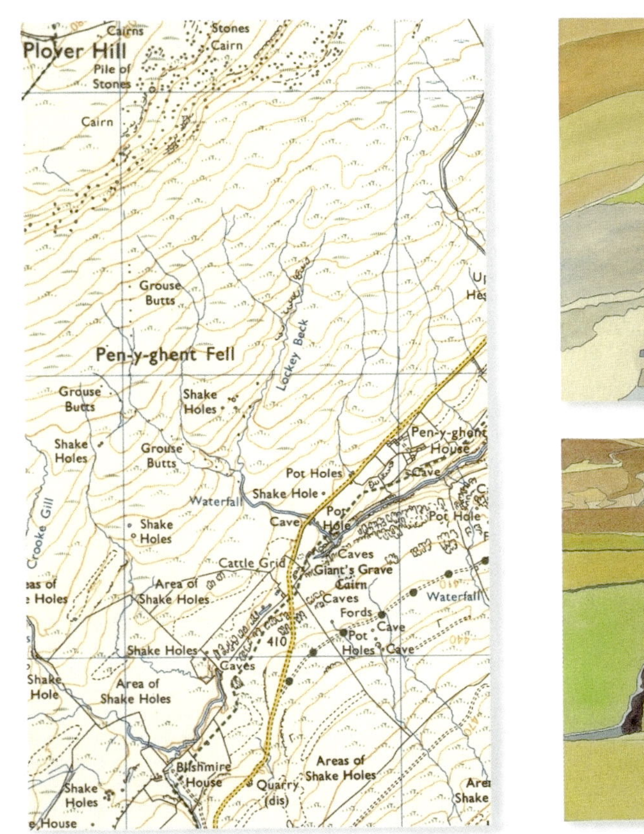

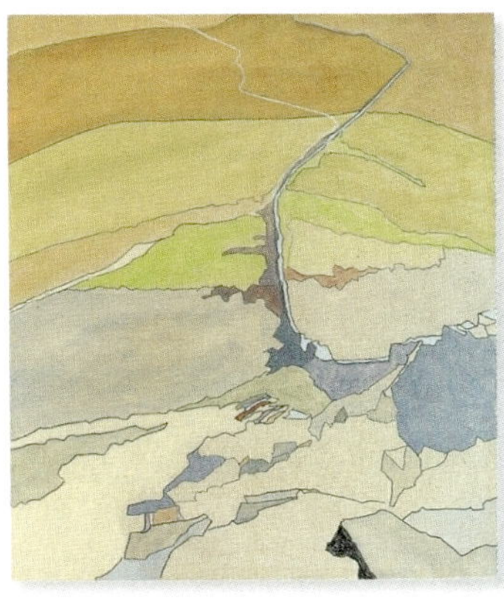

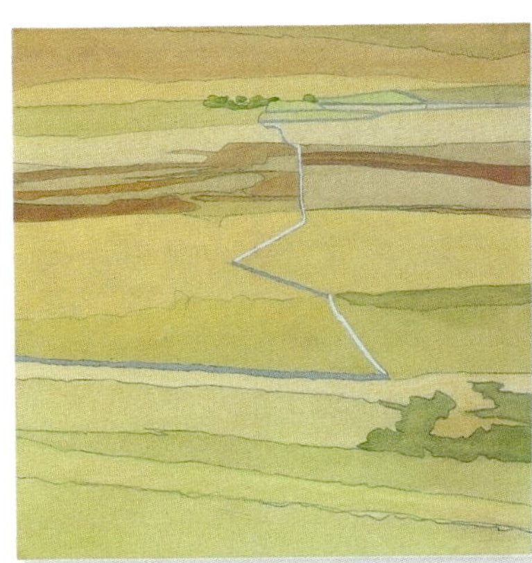

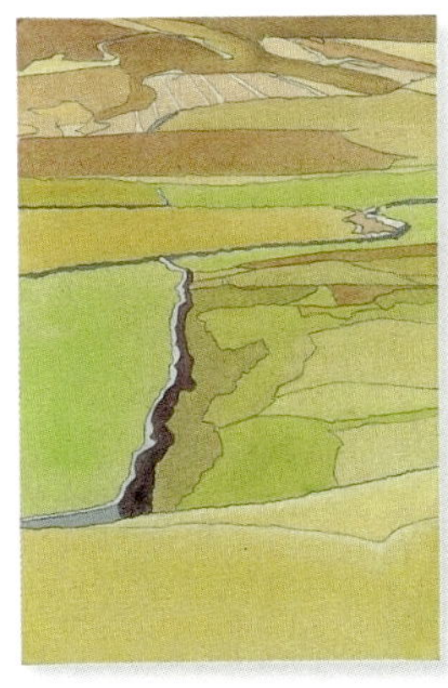

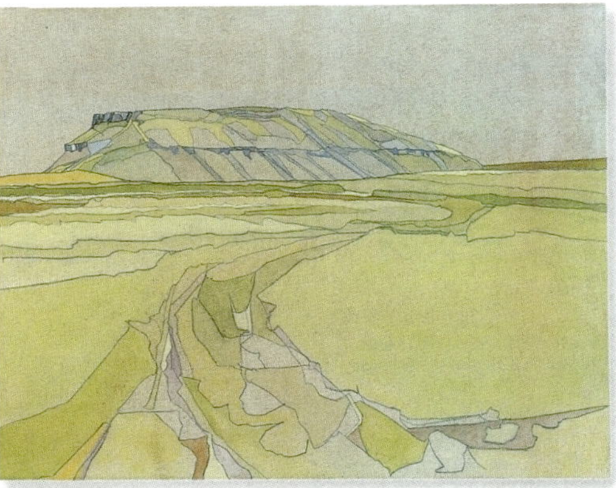

PLOVER HILL | 1998
acrylic on board with print
79 × 117

overleaf **LITTONDALE | 1998**
acrylic on board with print
79 × 130

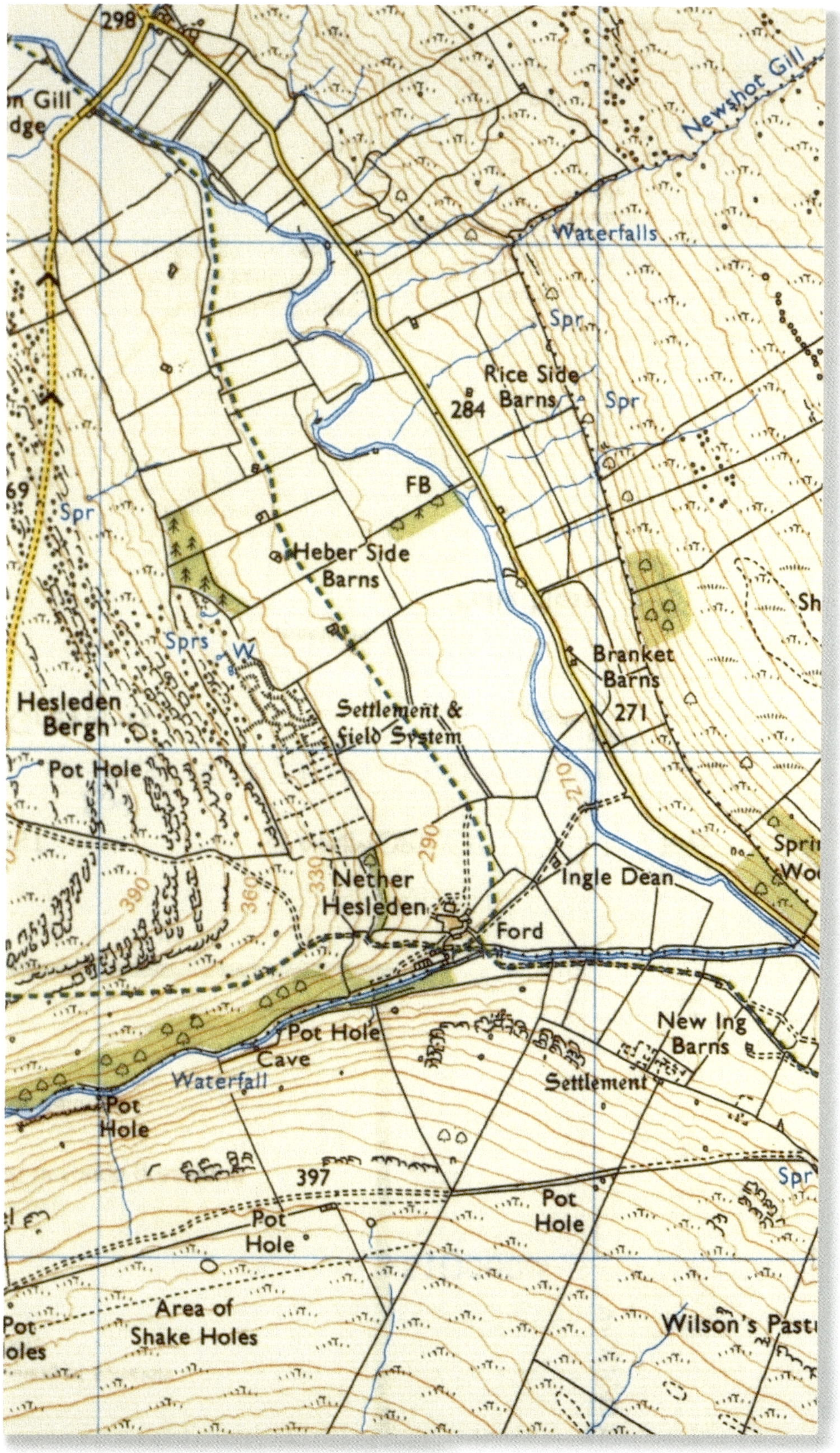

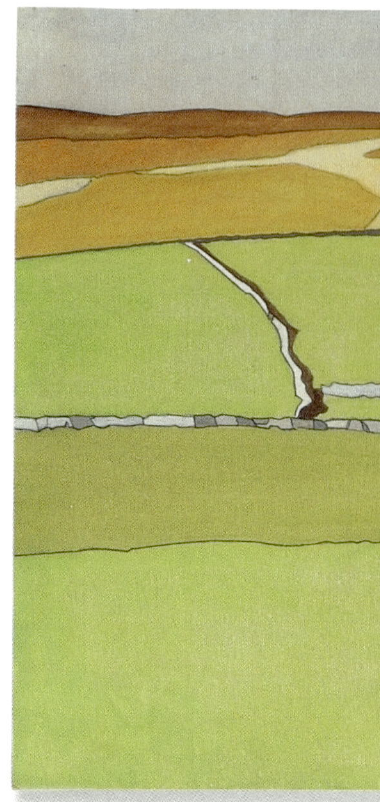

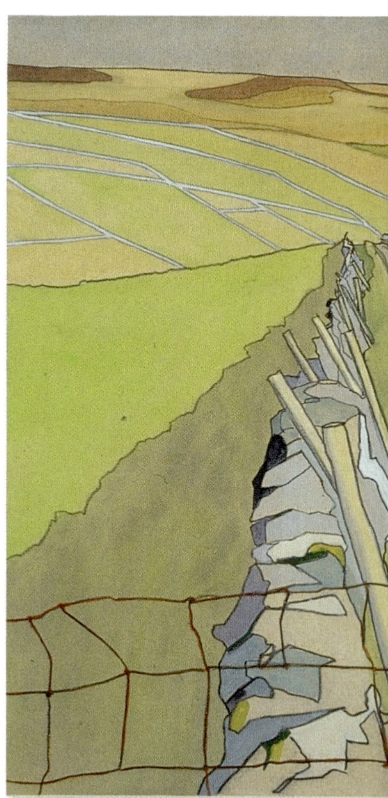

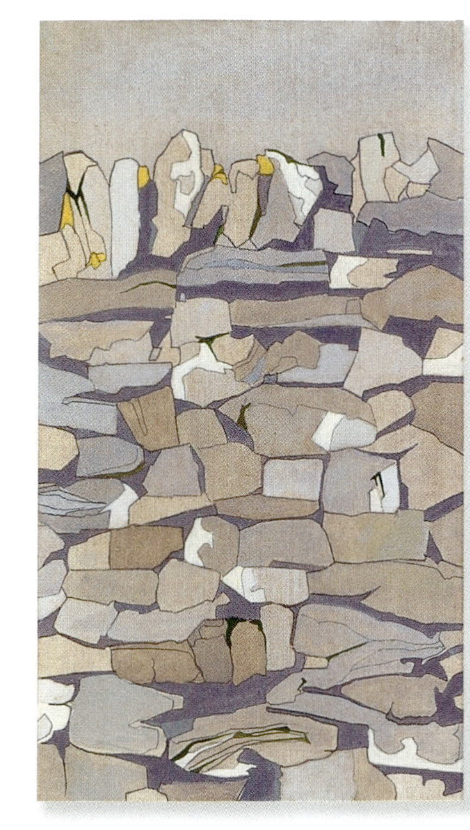
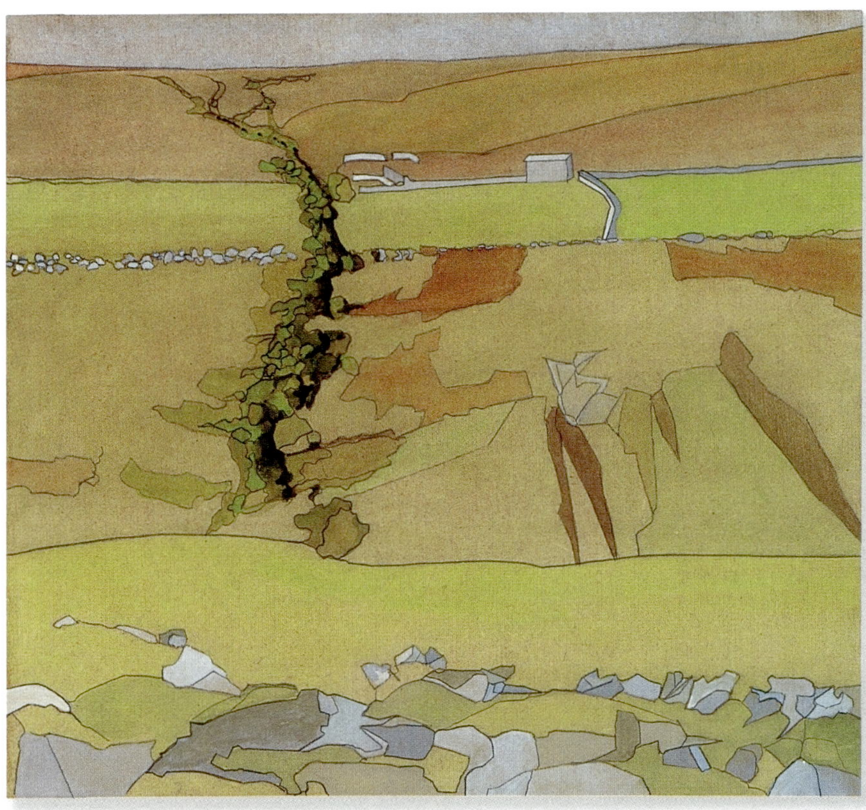
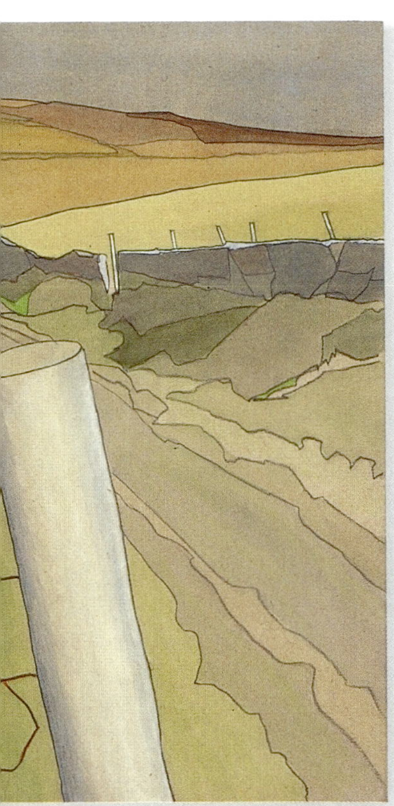
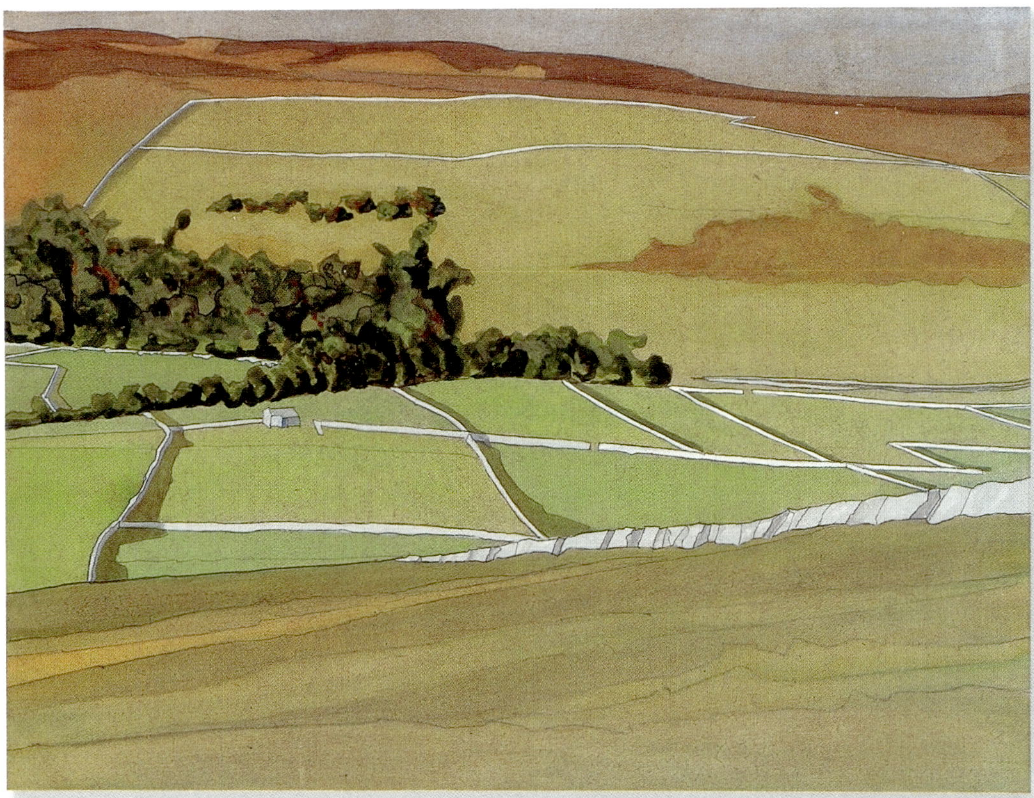

CORNWALL · SOUTH WEST COASTAL PATH

From Zennor Head to Logan Rock, following a section of the South West Coastal Path

The South West Coastal Path is over five hundred miles long, running from Minehead in Somerset, right around the southwest of England, to Poole in Dorset. This is by far the longest of all the designated long-distance walks in Britain. The part of the track that I have walked and included here is a small section in the far west of Cornwall.

The walk starts at St Ives, just beside the Tate gallery at Porthmeor Beach. For me, with my strong attraction to the St Ives school of artists, this is a 'natural' start. The landscape of this dramatic coastline influenced a number of those artists, most notably Peter Lanyon. The track nearly always keeps up high, seldom descending to the sea. Indeed, there are few points at which one can easily get down.

West Penwith, this extreme end of Cornwall, seems like a separate land, and nowhere is this more apparent than in the ancient field patterns with the myriad of banks of stone walls going back to the Bronze Age. These fascinated me, and included here are two photographic works (pp. 114 and 115) highlighting the structure of the ancient tracks and cultivation.

Penwith was the Western world's key producer of tin from the sixth century BC until the nineteenth century. I became engaged with the history of this area when I undertook a project named 'The Tin Route'. This followed the route that the tin was taken from Cornwall, across the channel, up the Seine, overland to the Saône, and then down the Rhône to the Mediterranean. This tin alloyed with copper made bronze, vital to the Greeks and the Romans.

In the project I particularly looked at this 'tin' landscape in detail, together with the upper reaches of the Seine in France. A series of paintings and drawings, many included here, come from this project.

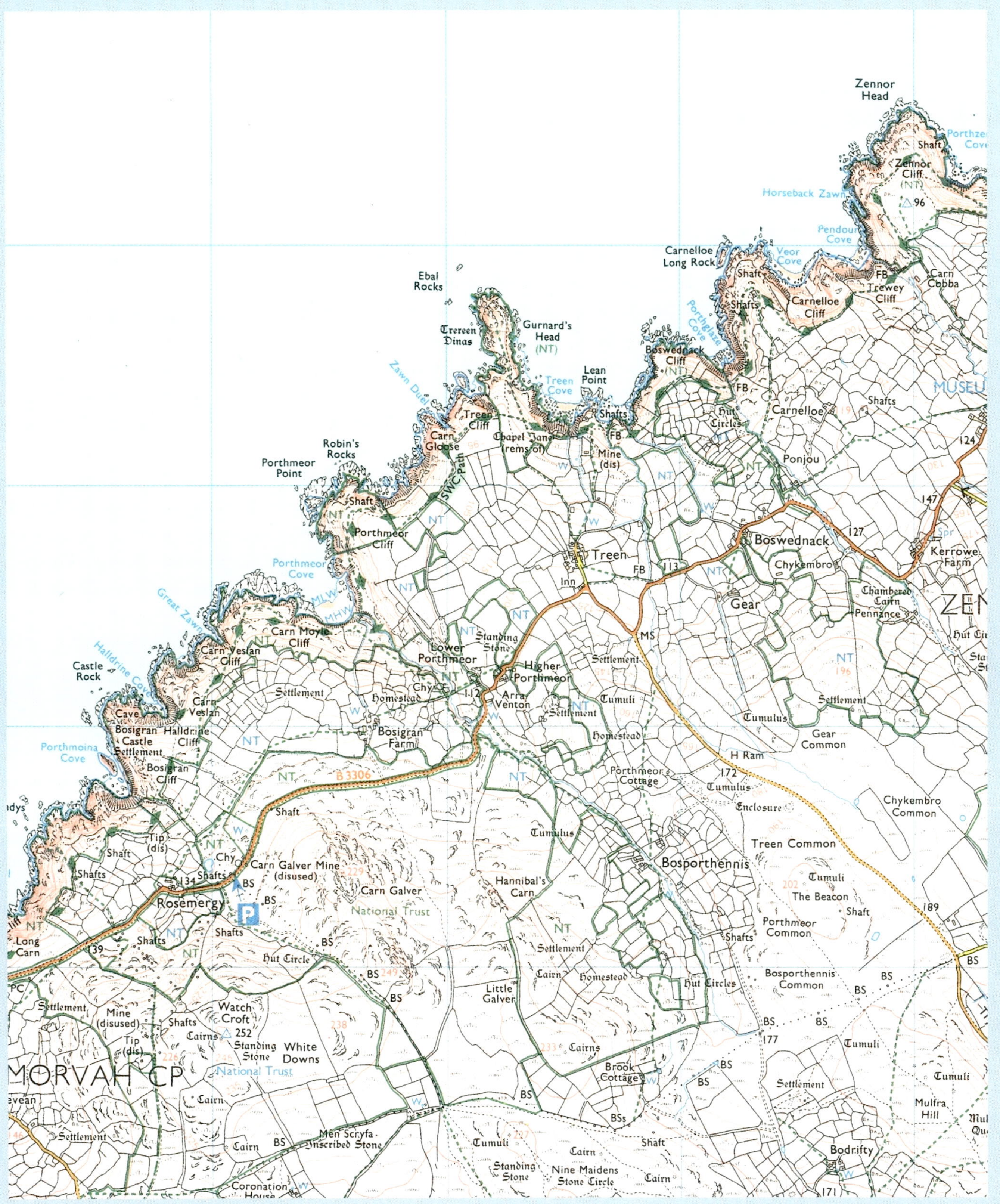

Zennor Head
Porthzeal Cove
Shaft
Zennor Cliff (NT)
Horseback Zawn
96
Pendour Cove
Carnelloe Long Rock
Veor Cove
Shaft
FB
Carn Cobba
Trewey Cliff
Shafts
Carnelloe Cliff
Ebal Rocks
Boswednack Cliff (NT)
MUSE
FB
Treryn Dinas
Gurnard's Head (NT)
Shafts
Hut Circles
Carnelloe
124
Zawn Duel
Treen Cove
Lean Point
FB
Ponjou
Treen Cliff
Chapel Jane (rems of)
Mine (dis)
NT
147
Carn Gloose
Shafts
W
Robin's Rocks
SWC Path
Spr
Porthmeor Point
W
Treen
Boswednack
127
Kerrowe Farm
Shaft
Inn
FB
113
Chykembro
Porthmeor Cliff
NT
Chambered Cairn
Pennance
ZEN
Porthmeor Cove
NT
MS
Gear
Hut Cir
Great Zawn
NT
Standing Stone
Settlement
196
Sta
MLW
Lower Porthmeor
NT
Carn Moyle Cliff
MHW
Higher Porthmeor
Tumuli
Settlement
Gear Common
Carn Veslan Cliff
Chy
112
Arra Venton
Settlement
Castle Rock
Homestead
Tumulus
Carn Veslan
Bosigran Farm
Homestead
H Ram
Halldrine Cove
Cave
NT
172
Chykembro Common
Bosigran Castle Settlement
Halldrine Cliff
NT
Porthmeor Cottage
Tumulus
Porthmoina Cove
Bosigran Cliff
B 3306
NT
Enclosure
Treen Common
dys
Shaft
Tumulus
189
Tip (dis)
W
Shaft
Bosporthennis
Tumuli
NT
Chy
Carn Galver Mine (disused)
Tumulus
The Beacon
Shaft
Shafts
134
BS
Carn Galver
Hannibal's Carn
NT
Porthmeor Common
Rosemergy
BS
National Trust
Settlement
Shafts
Long Carn
P
BS
Cairn
Homestead
Bosporthennis Common
BS
139
Shafts
NT
Shafts
Hut Circle
Little Galver
Hut Circles
BS
PC
BS
Cairn
BS
Settlement
Mine (disused)
Shafts
Watch Croft
BS
BS
Tumuli
252
Cairns
White Downs
177
Tip (dis)
Standing Stone
BS
Brook Cottage
W
Settlement
MORVAH CP
National Trust
BSs
Mulfra Hill
evean
Cairn
Shaft
Mul Qu
Settlement
BS
Tumuli
Cairn
Men Scryfa Inscribed Stone
Cairn
Bodrifty
Tumuli
Standing Stone
Nine Maidens Stone Circle
Cairn
Coronation House
171

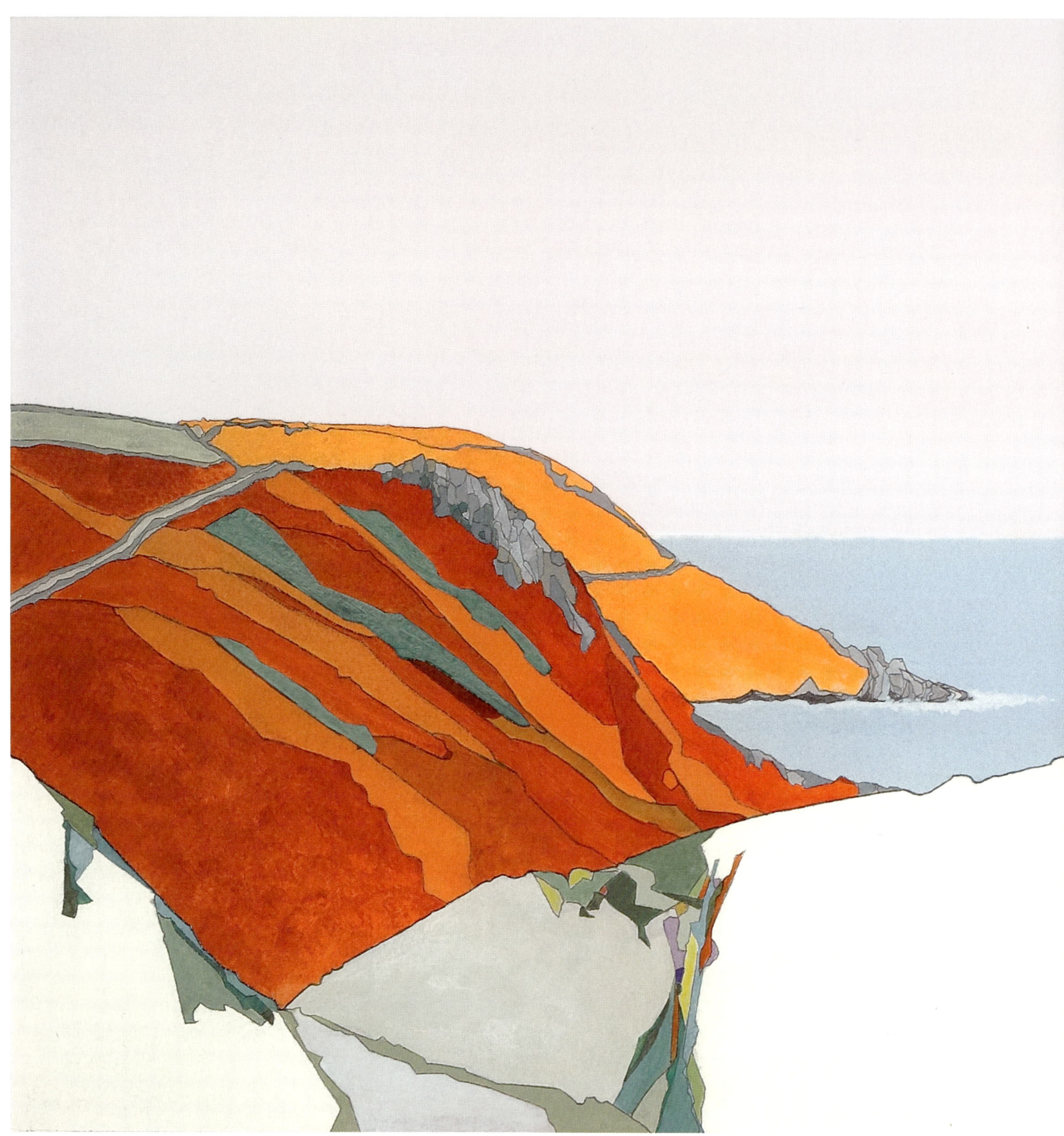

  CORNWALL

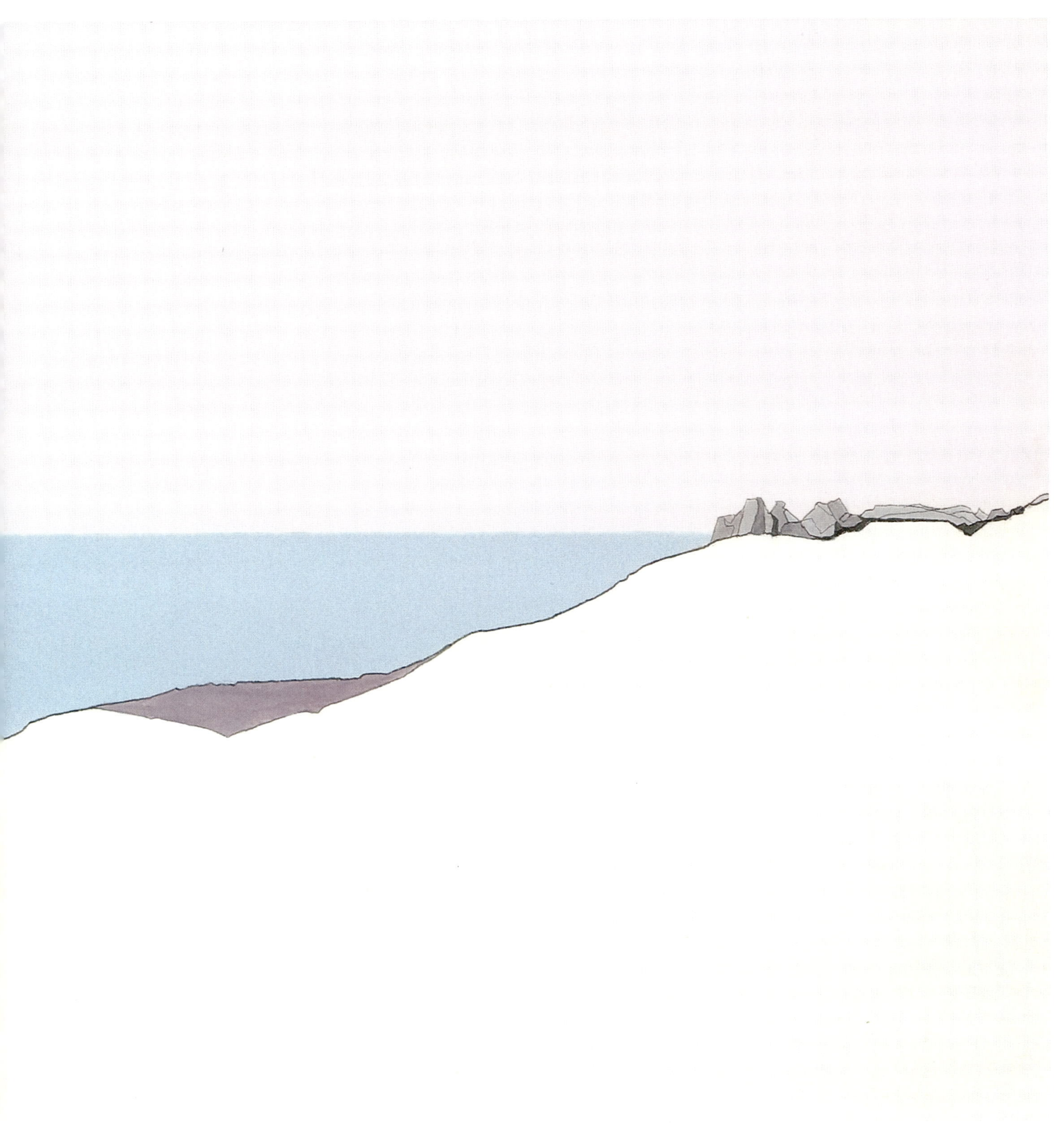

FROM ZENNOR HEAD TOWARDS GURNARD'S HEAD | 2011
acrylic on paper
44×88

The S.W. Coastal Path reaches Porthmeor
Cove: Hannibal's Carn and Carn Galver above
the ancient field patterns.

It is exactly six months to the day since I first
drew the cove, that time from upstream
looking down to the cove.

In these six months the project of the Tin
Route has advanced and I now see clearly the
importance of Porthmeor.

Surely this was one of the sources of alluvial
tin when the settlement village upstream was
occupied.

6.00 PM 23 SEPT 1999

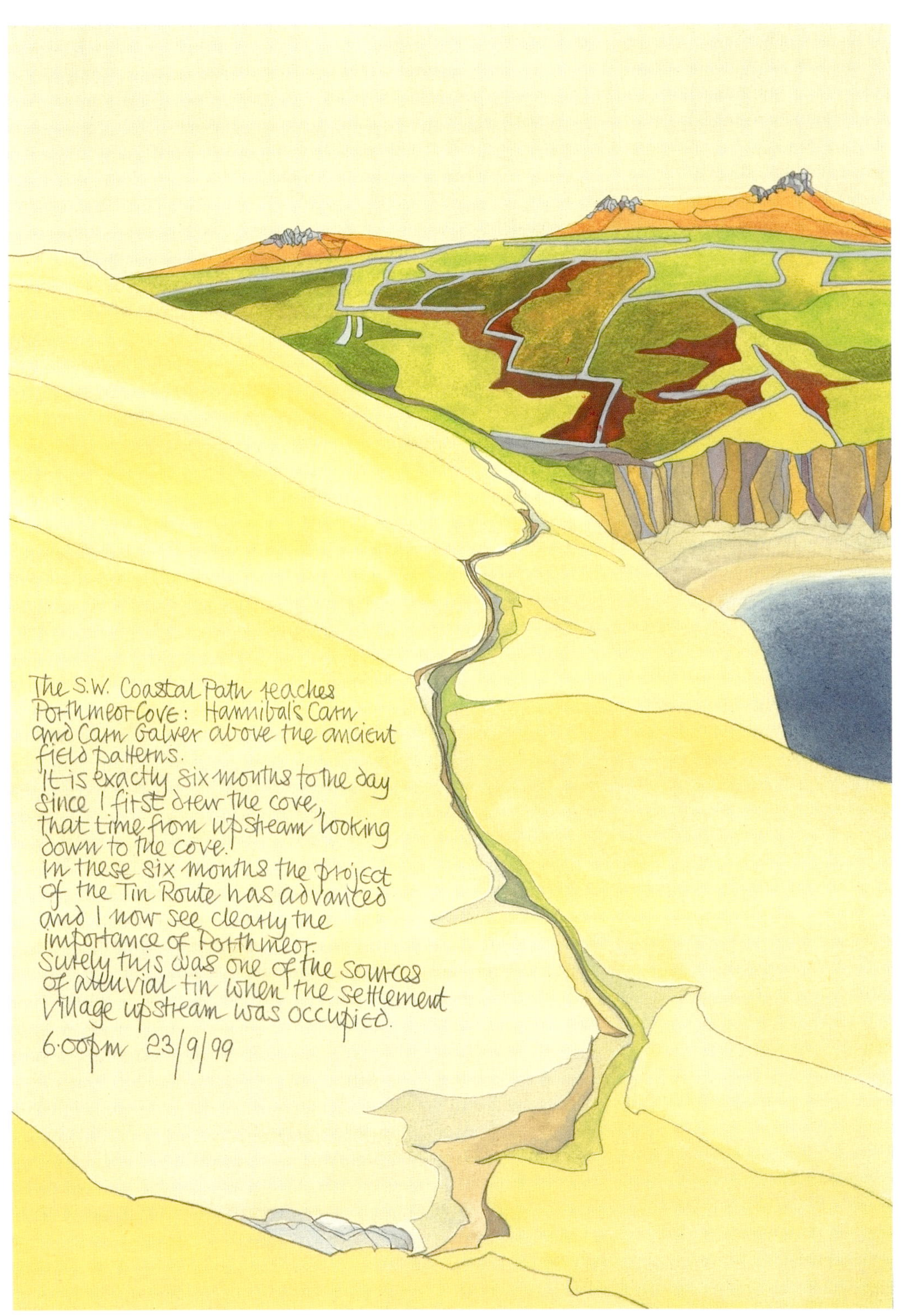

The S.W. Coastal Path reaches
Porthmeor Cove: Hannibal's Carn
and Carn Galver above the ancient
field patterns.
It is exactly six months to the day
since I first drew the cove,
that time from upstream looking
down to the cove!
In these six months the project
of the Tin Route has advanced
and I now see clearly the
importance of Porthmeor.
Surely this was one of the sources
of alluvial tin when the settlement
village upstream was occupied.
6.00pm 23/9/99

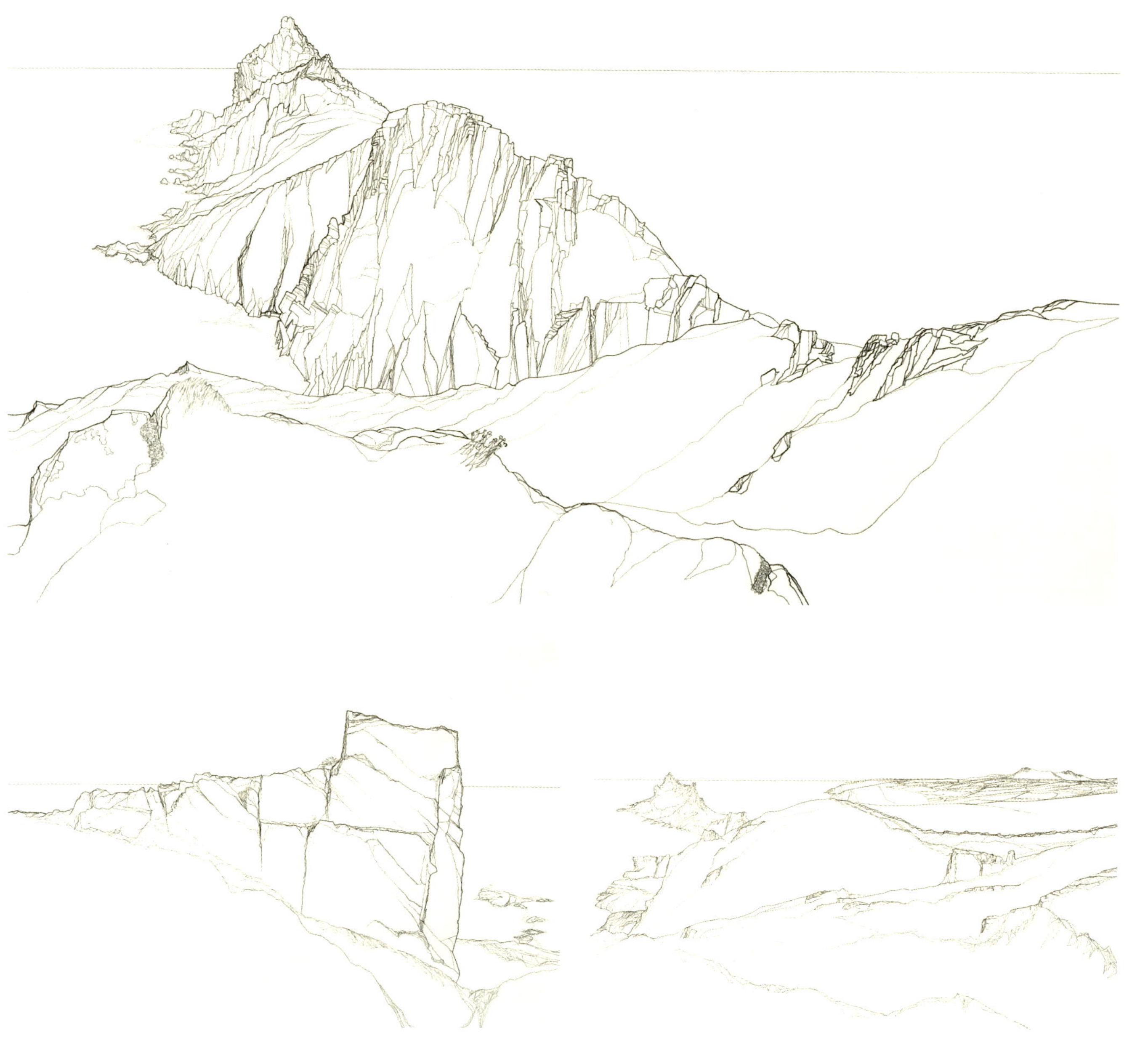

GURNARD'S HEAD | 2000
pencil on paper
88 × 123

CARN GLOOSE & GURNARD'S HEAD | 2000
pencil on paper
88 × 250

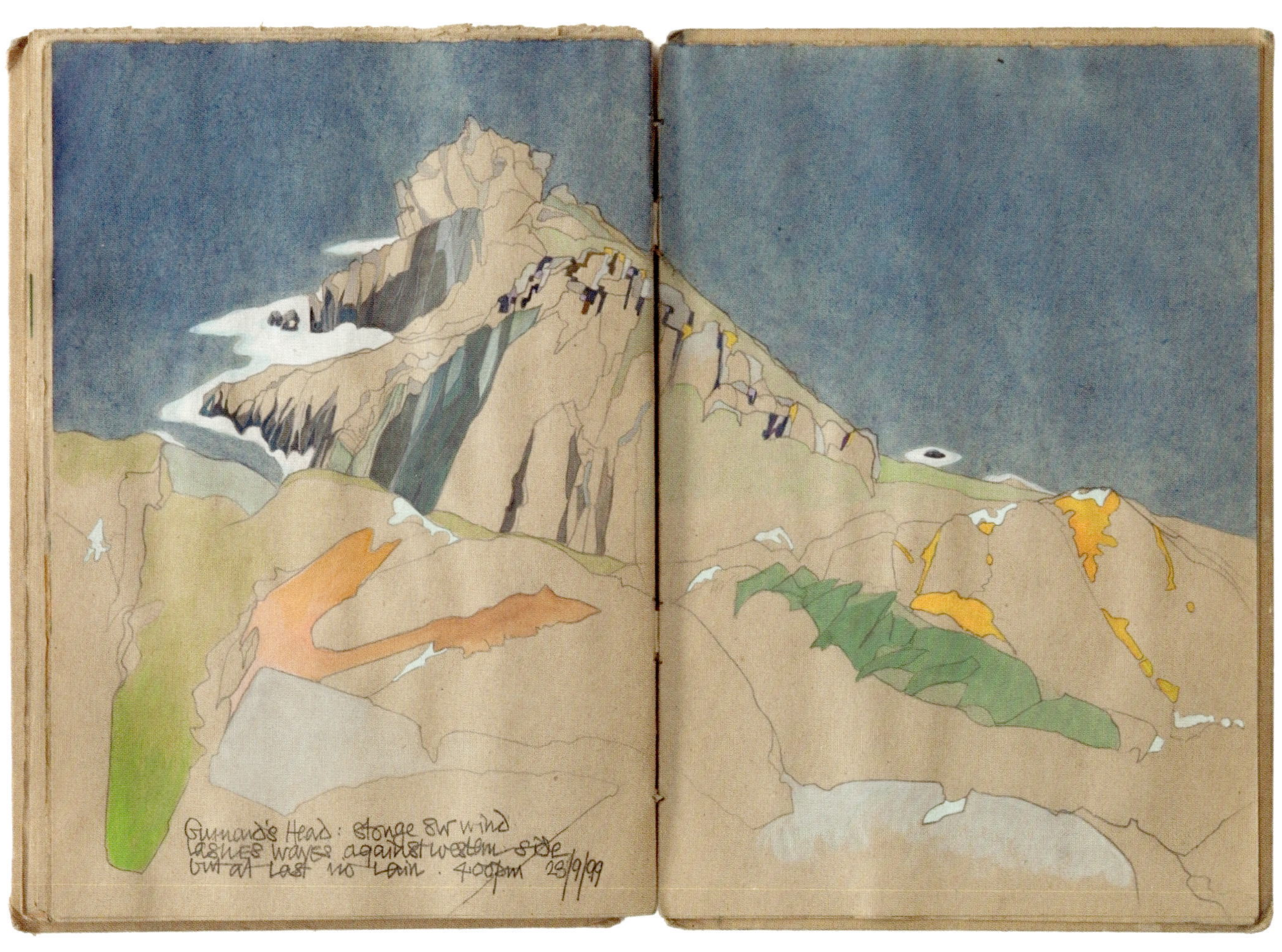

GURNARD'S HEAD, 23 SEPT 1999

NOTEBOOK | 1999

pencil & gouache on paper

32 × 45

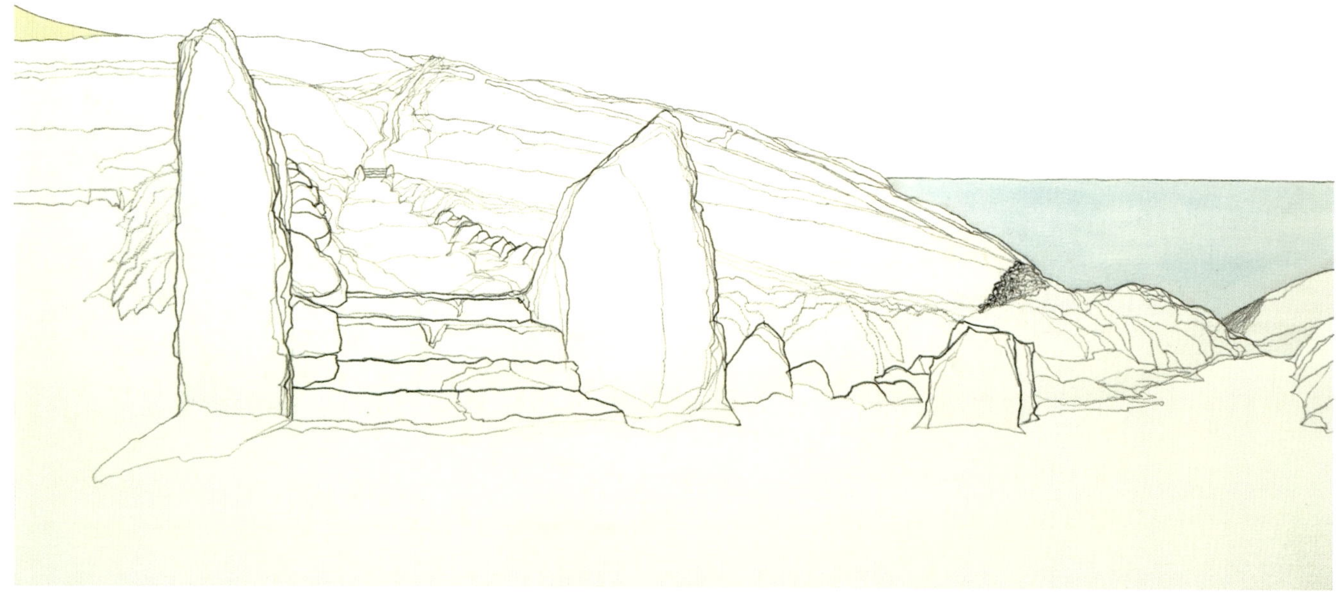

THE ANCIENT TRACK AT PORTHMEOR,
WEST PENWITH | 1999
pencil & gouache on paper
57 × 76

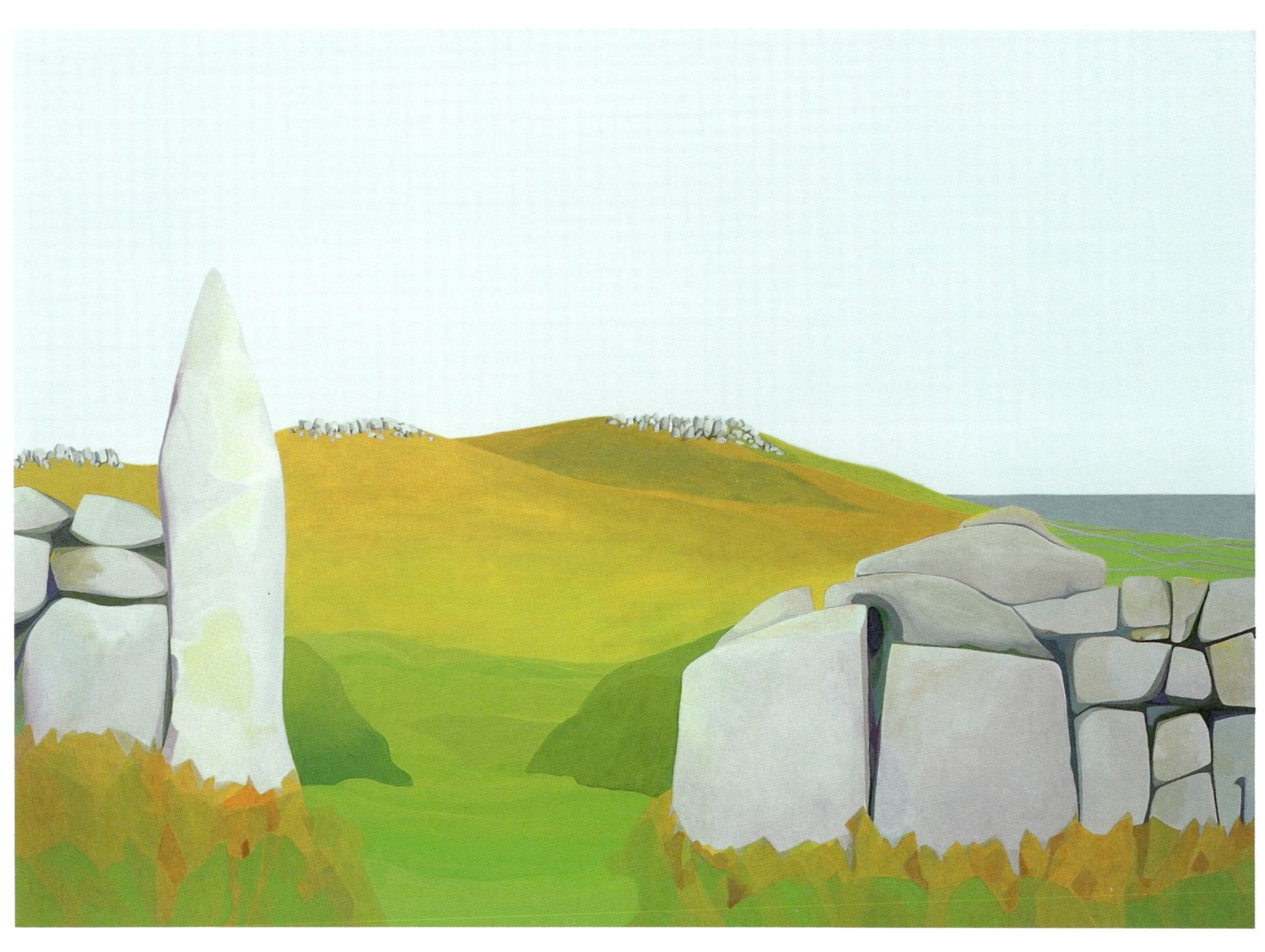

CARN GALVER | 2000
acrylic on canvas
80×112

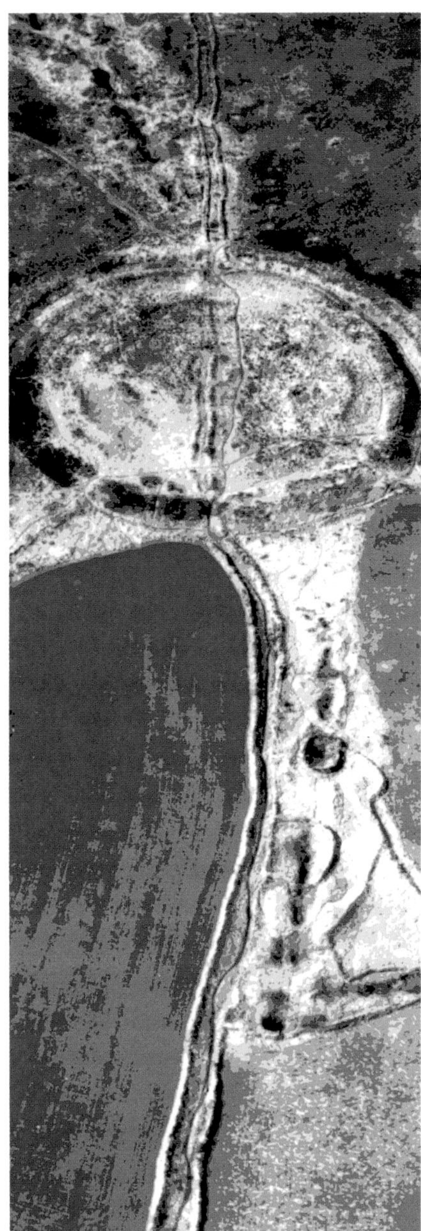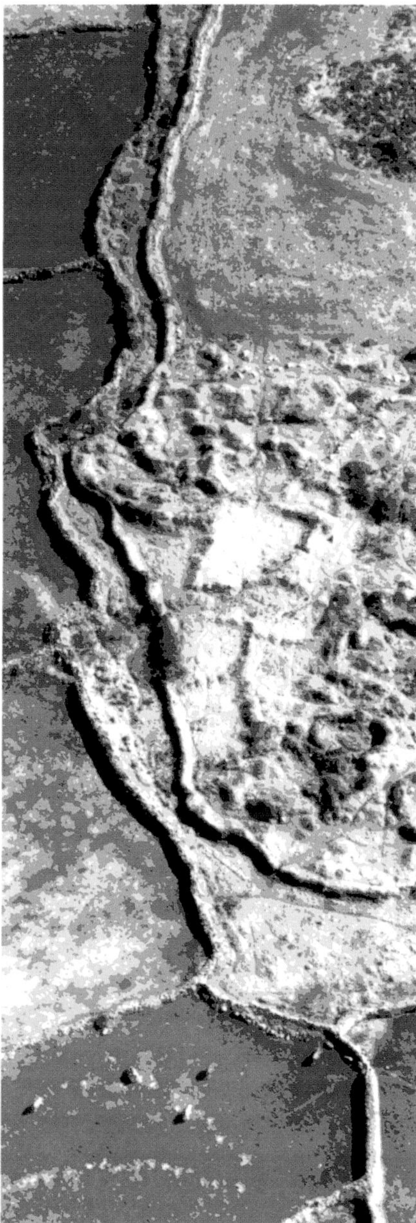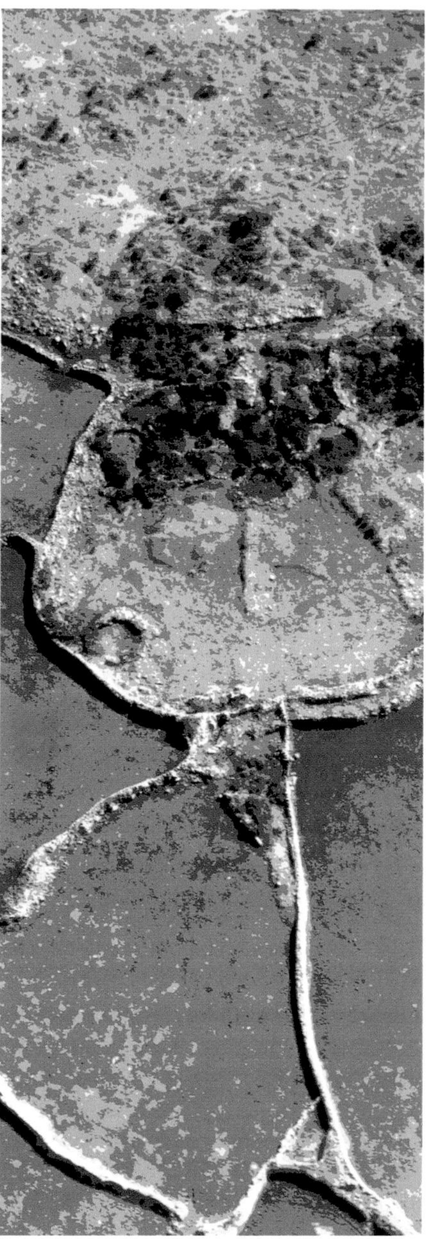

SETTLEMENTS: WEST PENWITH | 2000
print & pastel on card
95 × 103

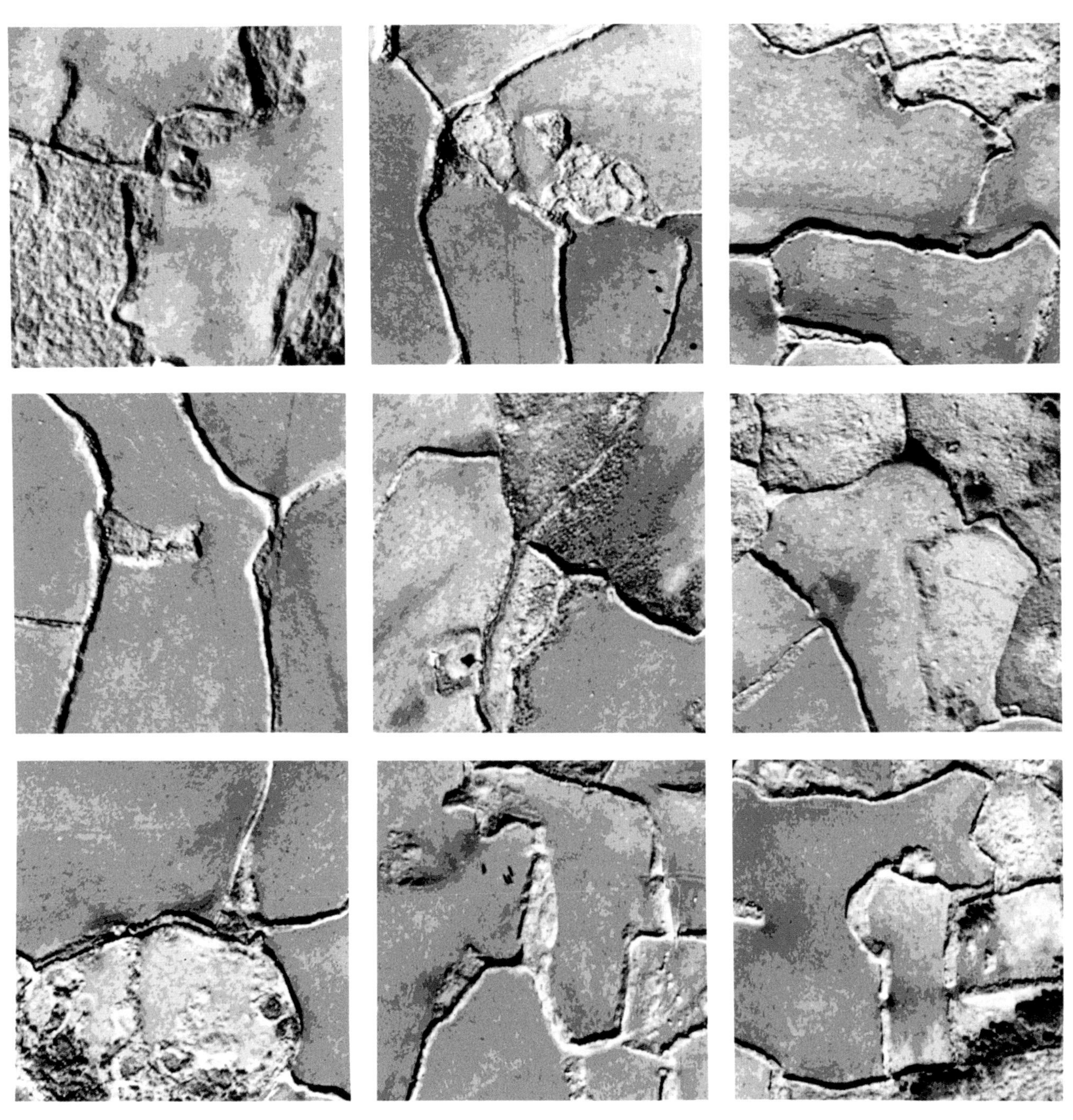

WALLS: WEST PENWITH | 2000
print on card
88×88

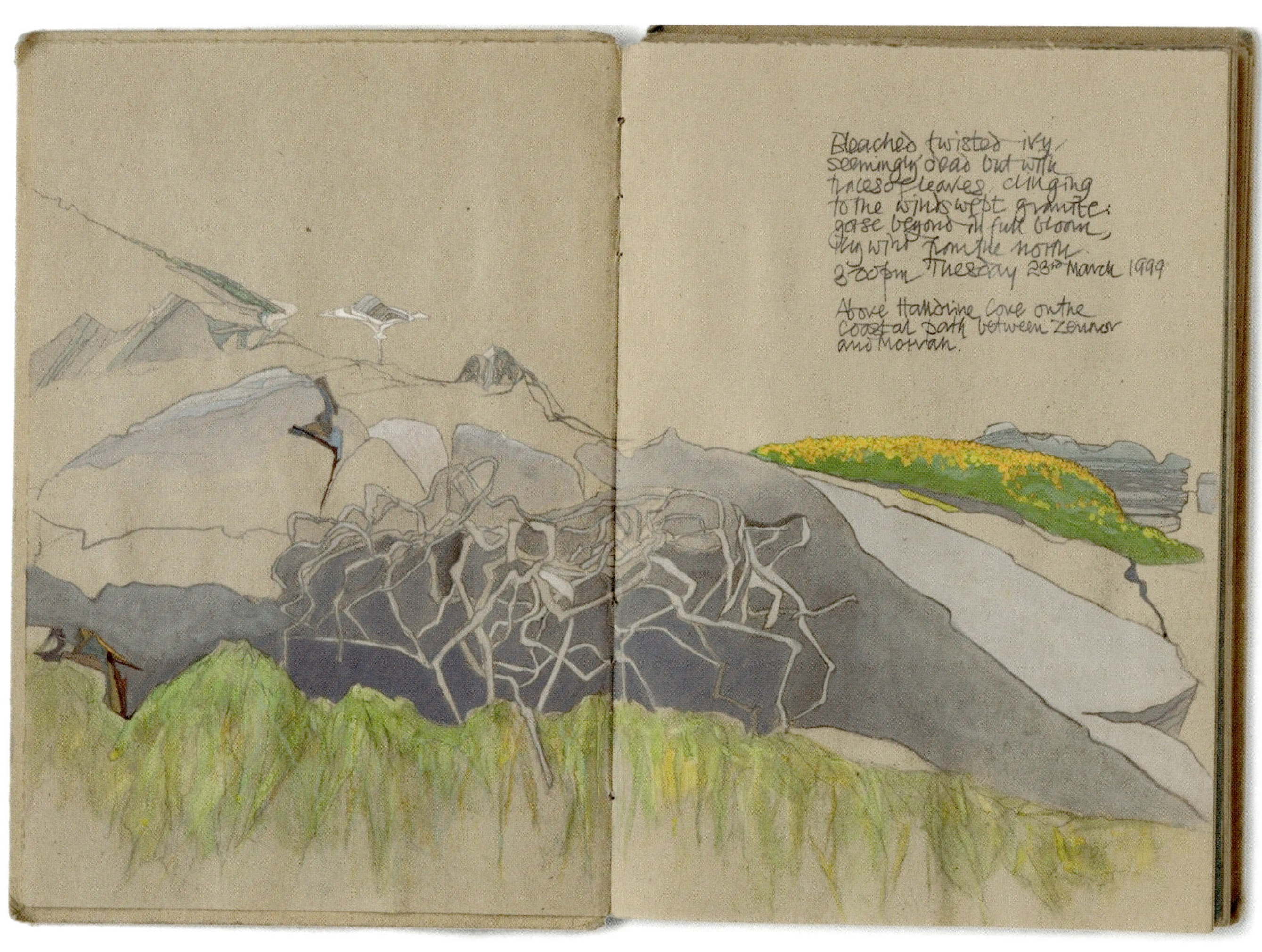

ABOVE HALLDRINE COVE, 23 MAR 1999
NOTEBOOK | 1999
pencil & gouache on paper
32 × 45

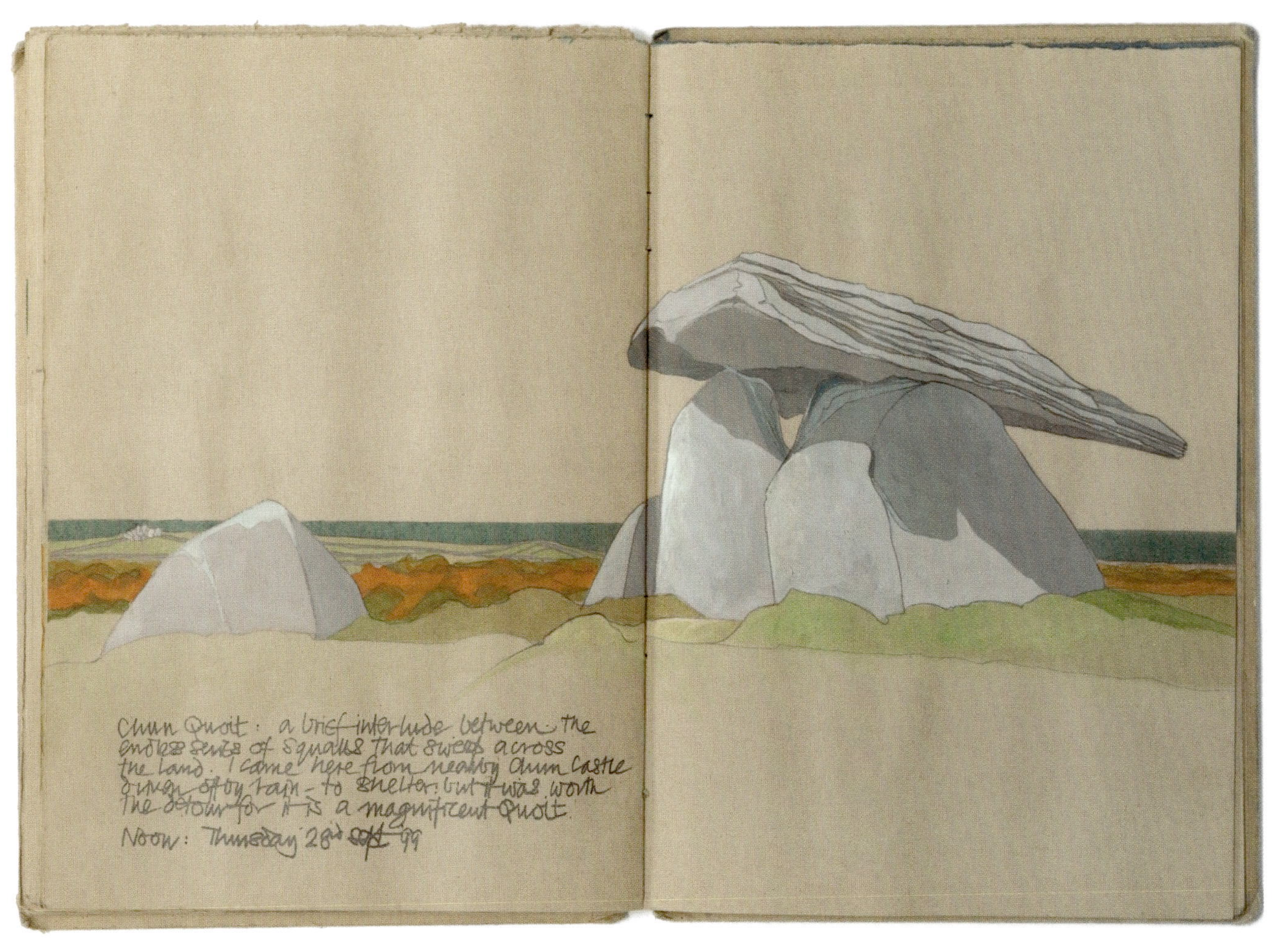

CHUN QUOIT, 23 SEPT 1999

NOTEBOOK | 1999

pencil & gouache on paper

32 × 45

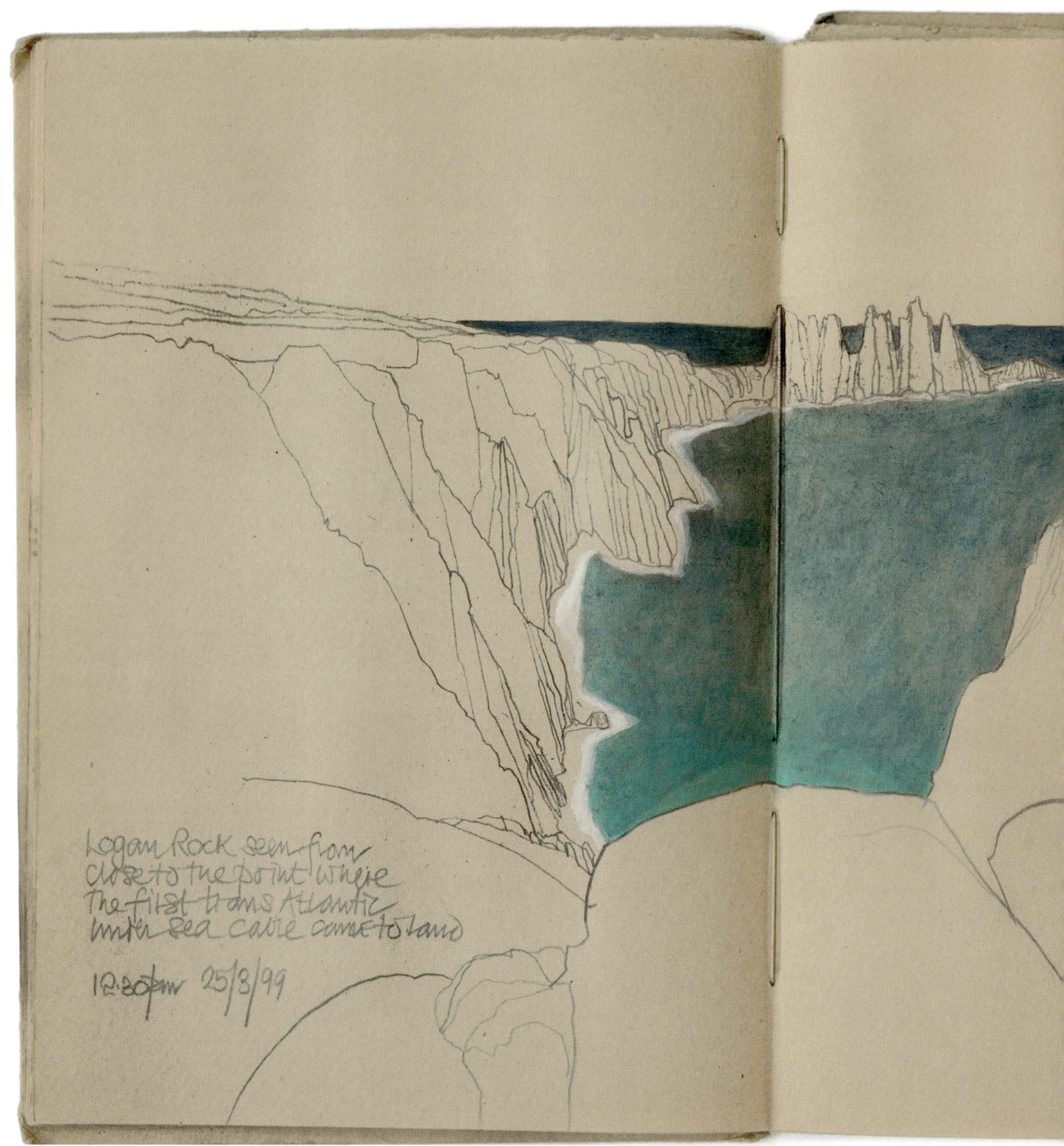

Logan Rock seen from
close to the point where
the first trans Atlantic
under sea cable came to land
12.30pm 25/3/99

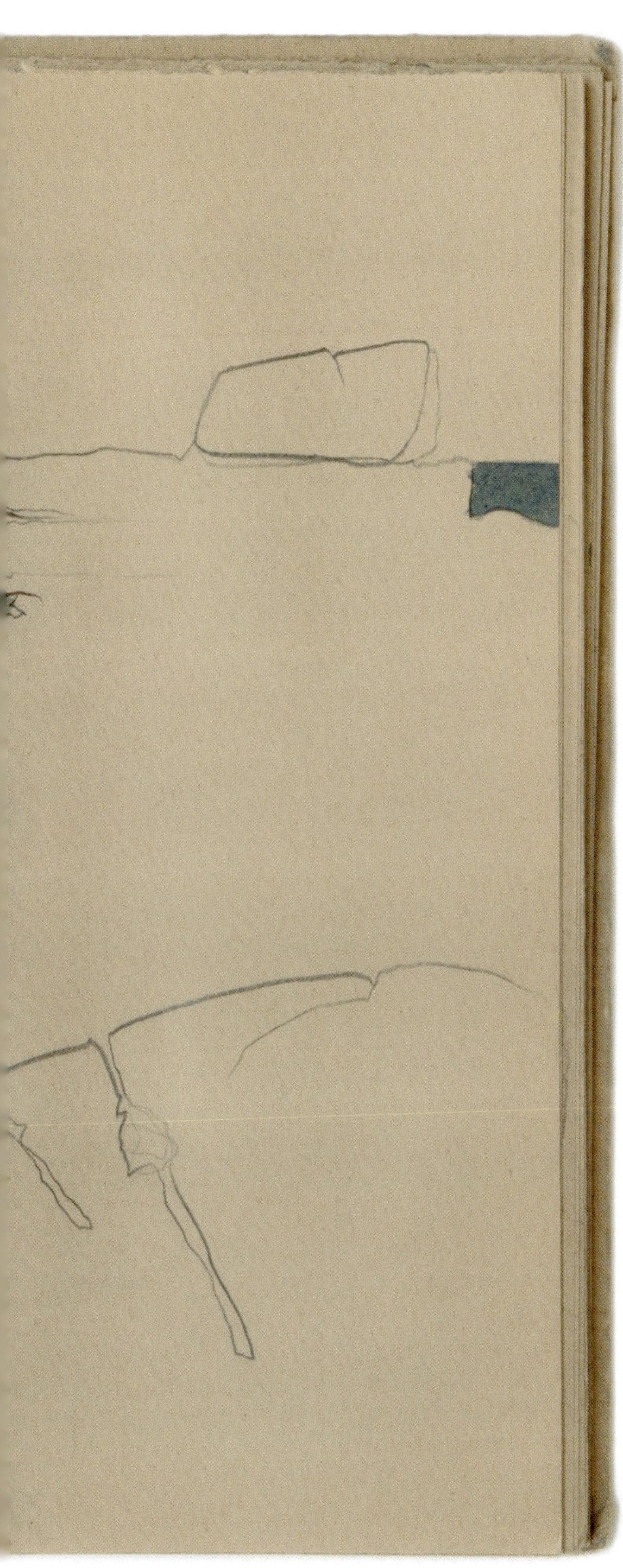

LOGAN ROCK, 25 MAR 1999
NOTEBOOK | 1999
pencil & gouache on paper
32×45

STONEHENGE

Approaching Stonehenge from the north, from The Avenue and from the south

Given my engagement with the stone circles of Britain, Stonehenge is naturally central. I can remember the time when all visitors could walk anywhere among the stones. That seems long ago. Visitors – of whom there are a huge number – are today confined to an outside track. Their experience, taking into account the proximity of roads and traffic, is now very limited.

As an artist, however, I have kindly been given permission for access to work. It used to be any time of the day, which allowed me to do a series of large drawings, two of which are shown here (pp. 128 and 129). Access is now restricted to the limited daylight outside normal public opening hours. I could not repeat the drawings.

While I have been to Stonehenge many times, it has usually been just driving to the car park and going in. Recently I have been walking various tracks to approach the circle and to try and understand its setting in the landscape. It is difficult to do this, particularly with the intense traffic on the A303 – but it is possible, and most rewarding. The features mentioned in these walks are shown in the detailed map.

To get an idea of the setting of Stonehenge you have to walk there. I have taken three approaches. The first is from the north, crossing the Cursus. The remains of this three-kilometre-long earthwork, older than Stonehenge, are clearly visible, and Stonehenge is seen over its banks and ditches.

The second is The Avenue, which was built together with Stonehenge. It starts at the River Avon, curves around and joins the monument along the line of the Heel Stone and the famous axis of the midsummer sunrise. What is striking about walking The Avenue is how Stonehenge is at one moment clear ahead, seemingly on a ridge, and then a few paces further on it disappears, as The Avenue dips into a small valley, and then close by it suddenly reappears. This theatrical effect was clearly intended. I suddenly realized the careful placement of the circle in the landscape.

The third approach is from the south along the track that also starts at the River Avon at Lake. This magnificent walk follows a valley before rising to Normanton Down with its extensive series of barrows. As you reach the crest, there is Stonehenge ahead, seeming to be on a ridge of its own (pp. 122–23).

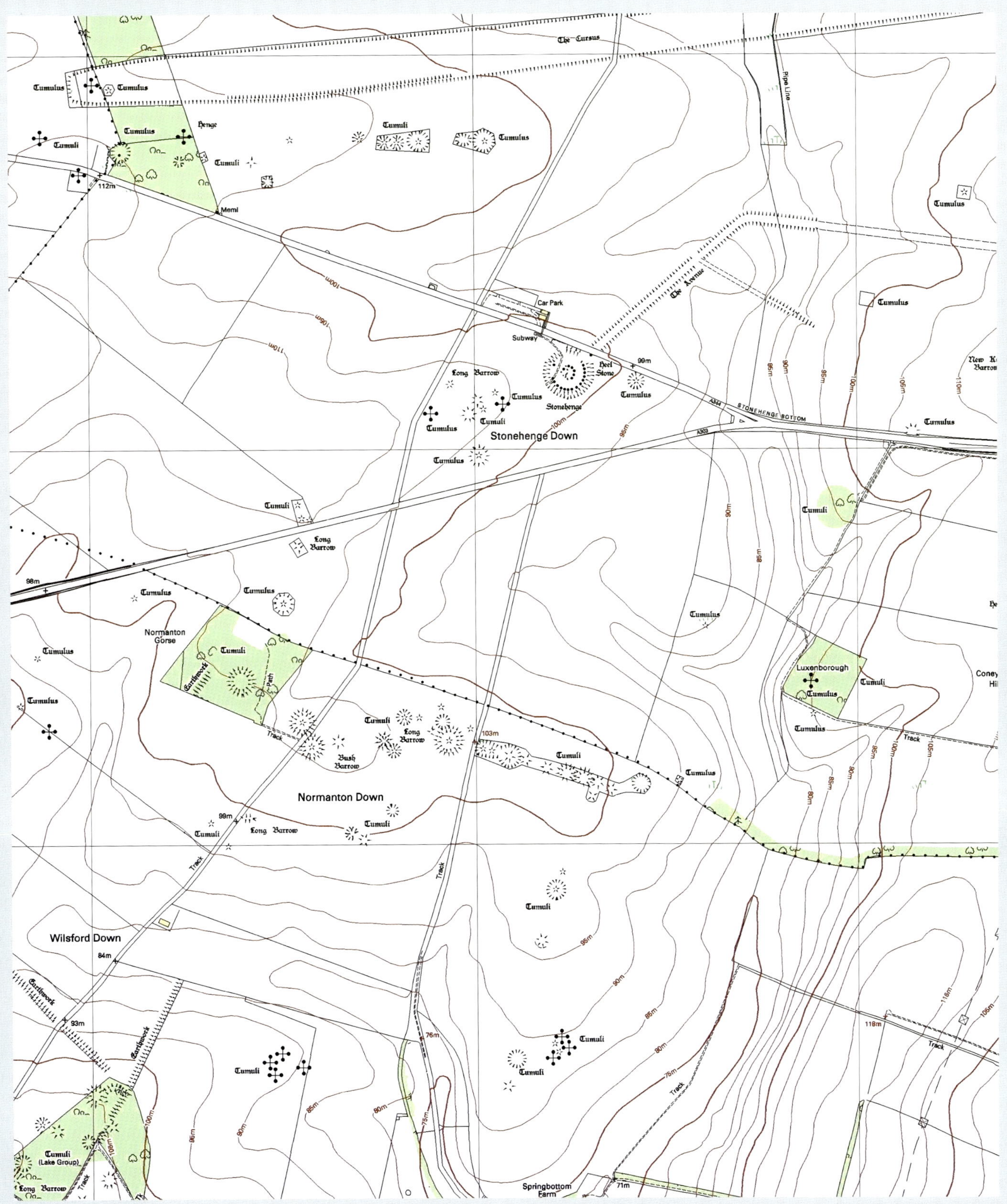

The Cursus
Pipe Line
Tumulus
Tumulus
Tumulus
Henge
Tumuli
Tumuli
Tumuli
Tumulus
Tumulus
Tumulus
Meml
Car Park
The Avenue
Subway
Heel Stone
Long Barrow
Tumulus
Stonehenge
Stonehenge Down
Tumuli
Tumulus
Tumulus
New Ki
Barrow
Tumulus
A344
STONEHENGE BOTTOM
A303
Tumulus
Tumuli
Long Barrow
Tumuli
Tumulus
Tumulus
Tumulus
Normanton Gorse
Tumuli
Earthwork
Path
Luxenborough
Tumulus
Tumuli
Coney
Hil
Tumulus
Tumulus
Tumulus
Track
Tumulus
Tumuli
Long Barrow
Bush Barrow
Track
103m
Tumuli
Tumulus
Normanton Down
Track
Tumuli
Long Barrow
Tumuli
Tumulus
Wilsford Down
84m
Earthwork
93m
Earthwork
Tumuli
Tumuli
Tumuli
Track
Track
Tumuli (Lake Group)
Long Barrow
Springbottom Farm
71m
76m
98m
112m
110m
100m
90m
80m
75m

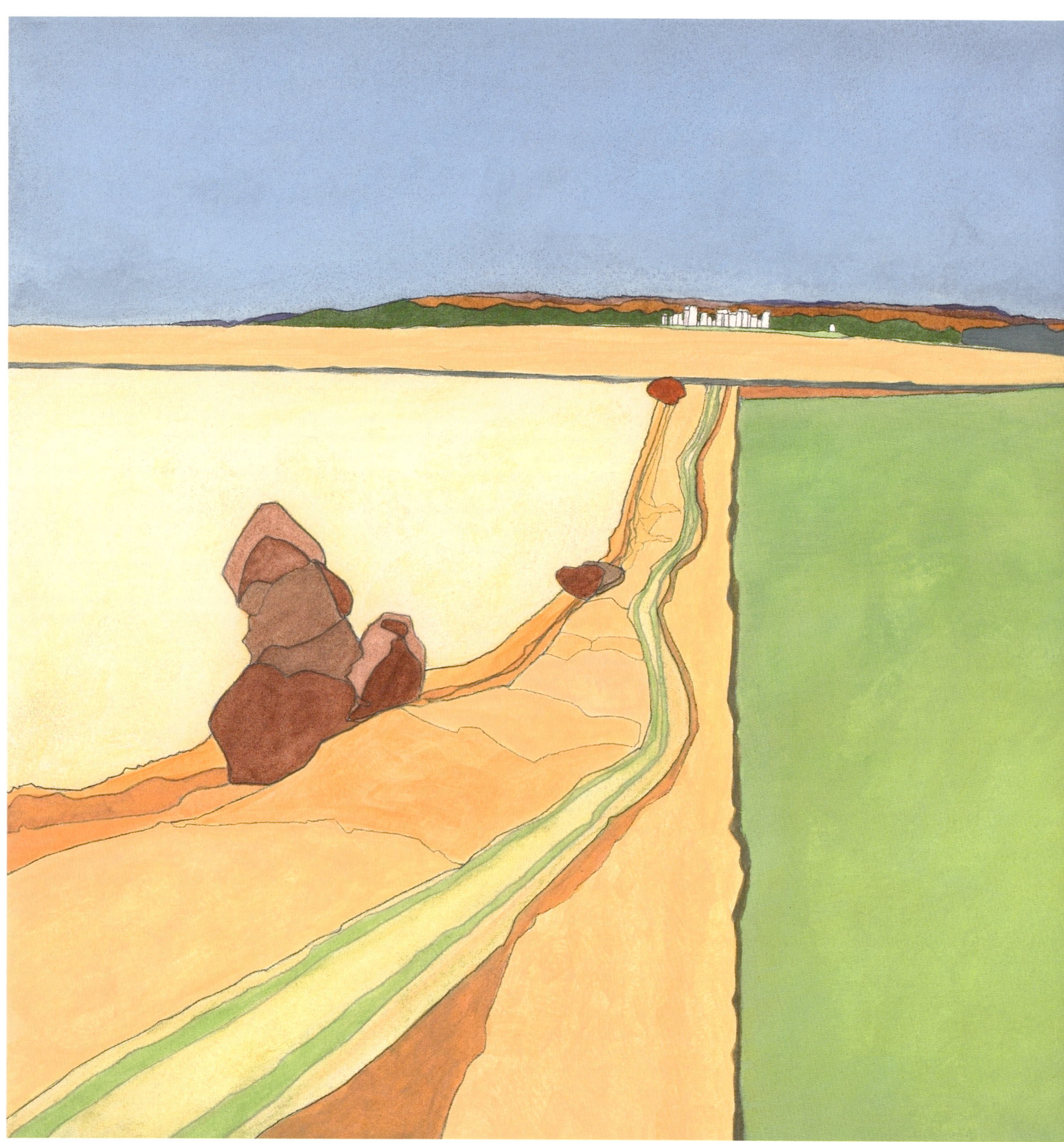

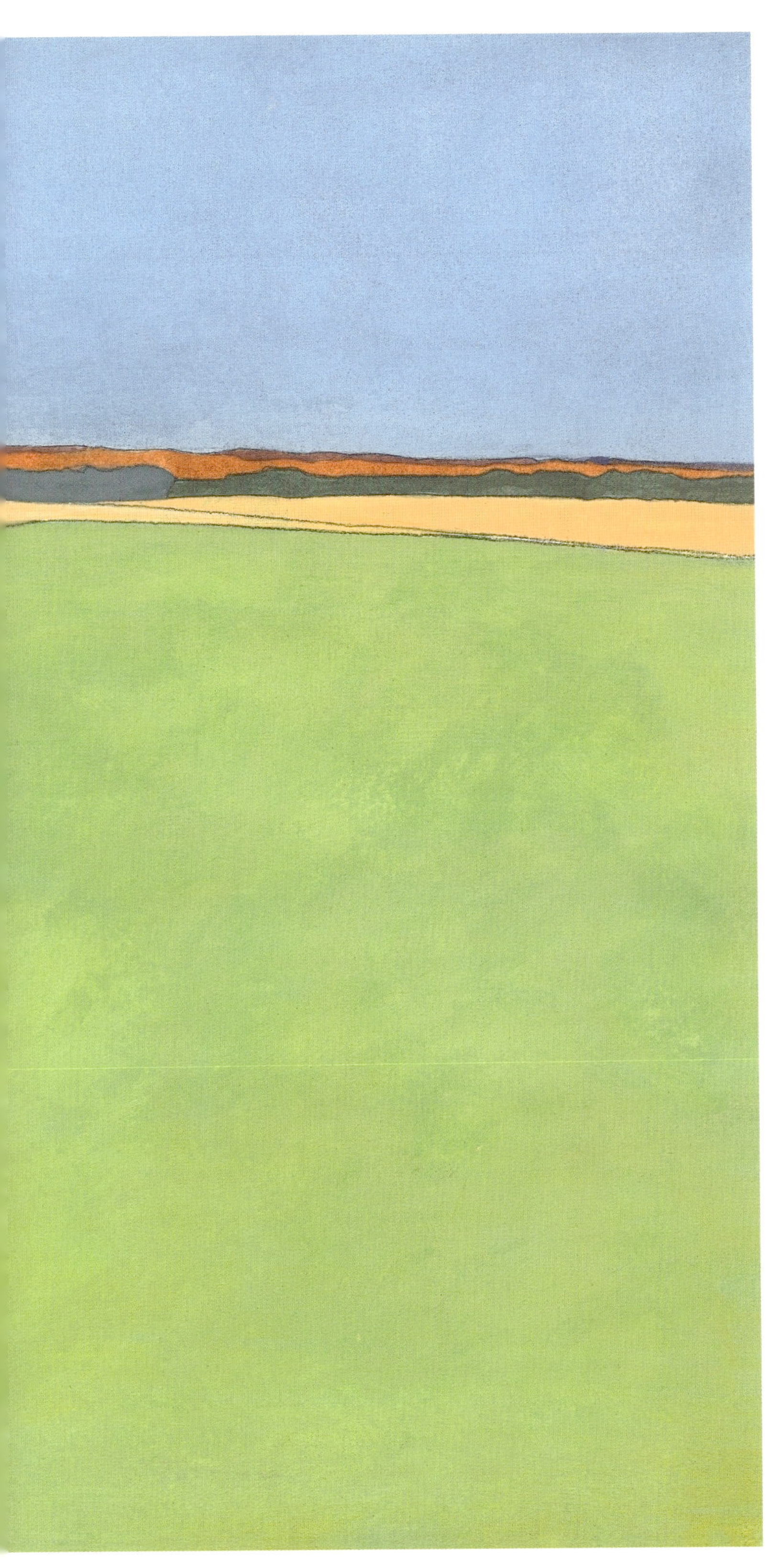

STONEHENGE: FROM THE TRACK THAT
DESCENDS FROM NORMANTON RIDGE | 2011
acrylic on paper
32×49

Stonehenge. Sunset at 4.00 pm. An icy evening, soon heavy frost. I have spent from sunrise to sunset here, now just the silhouette remains.

6 DEC 1991

Stonehenge: as I was drawing this a small hare came and tried to shelter under a fallen stone beside me.

7.20 AM 9 JULY 2008

Sitting on the most westerly of the tumuli beside the Cursus near Stonehenge. Between this and the next tumulus lies a dead hare. Last time I was at Stonehenge I shared the stones with a hare, both of us sheltering from the rain.

24 JAN 2011

STONEHENGE SEPTEMBER EVENING: STONE 12 | 1993
acrylic & pastel on paper
42 × 27

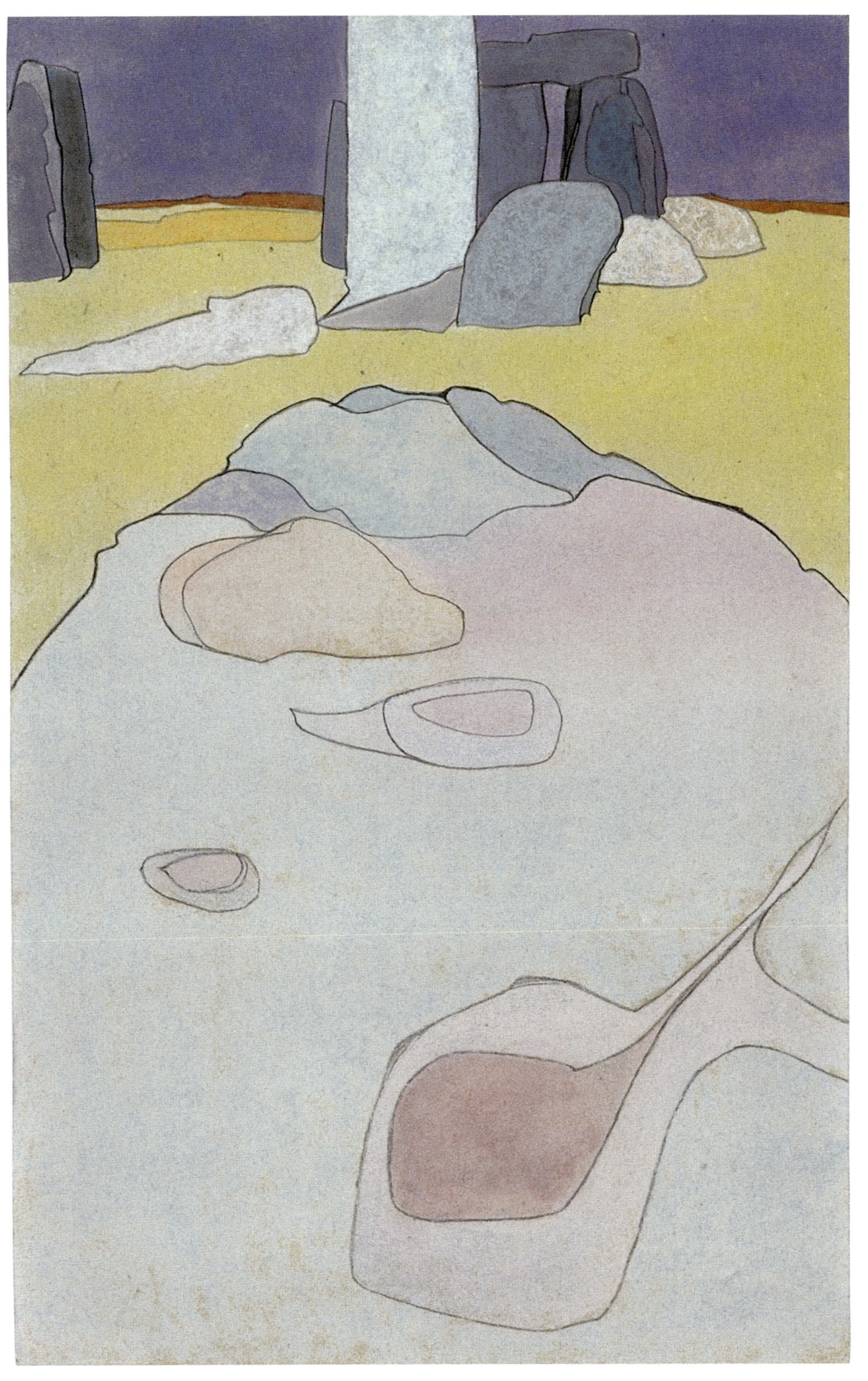

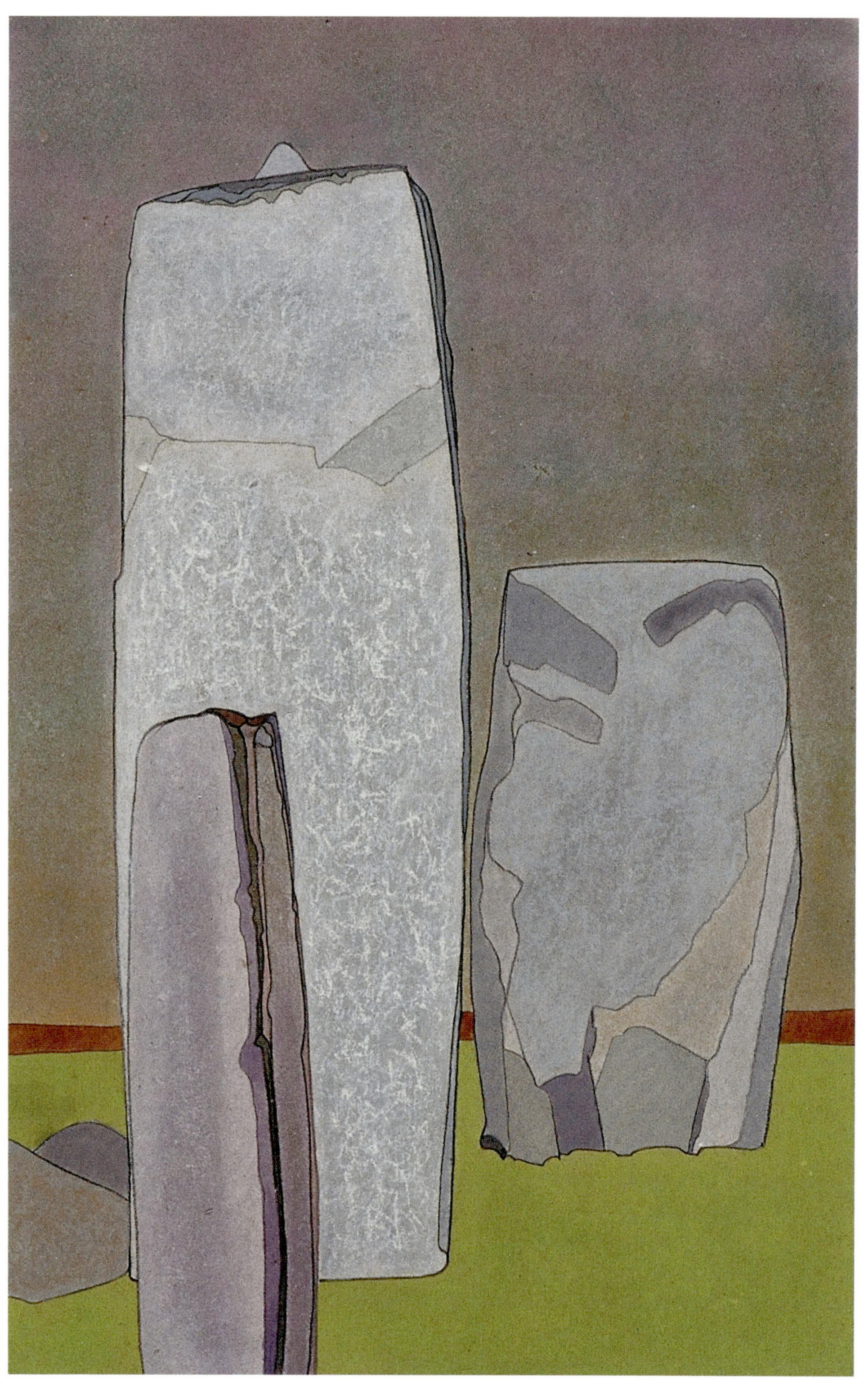

STONEHENGE SEPTEMBER EVENING: STONE 56 | 1993
acrylic & pastel on paper
42 × 27

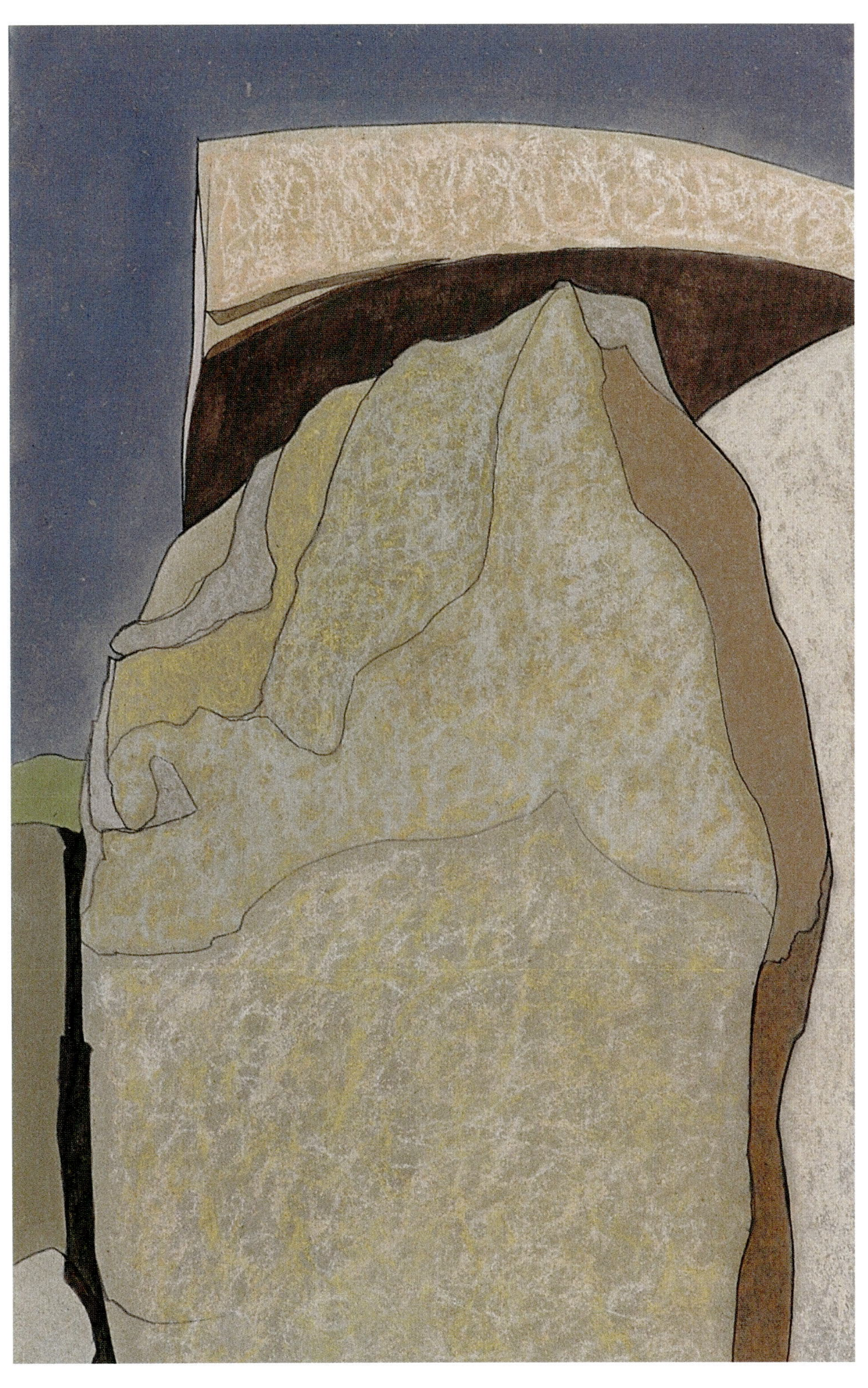

STONEHENGE SEPTEMBER EVENING: STONE 154 | 1993
acrylic & pastel on paper
42 × 27

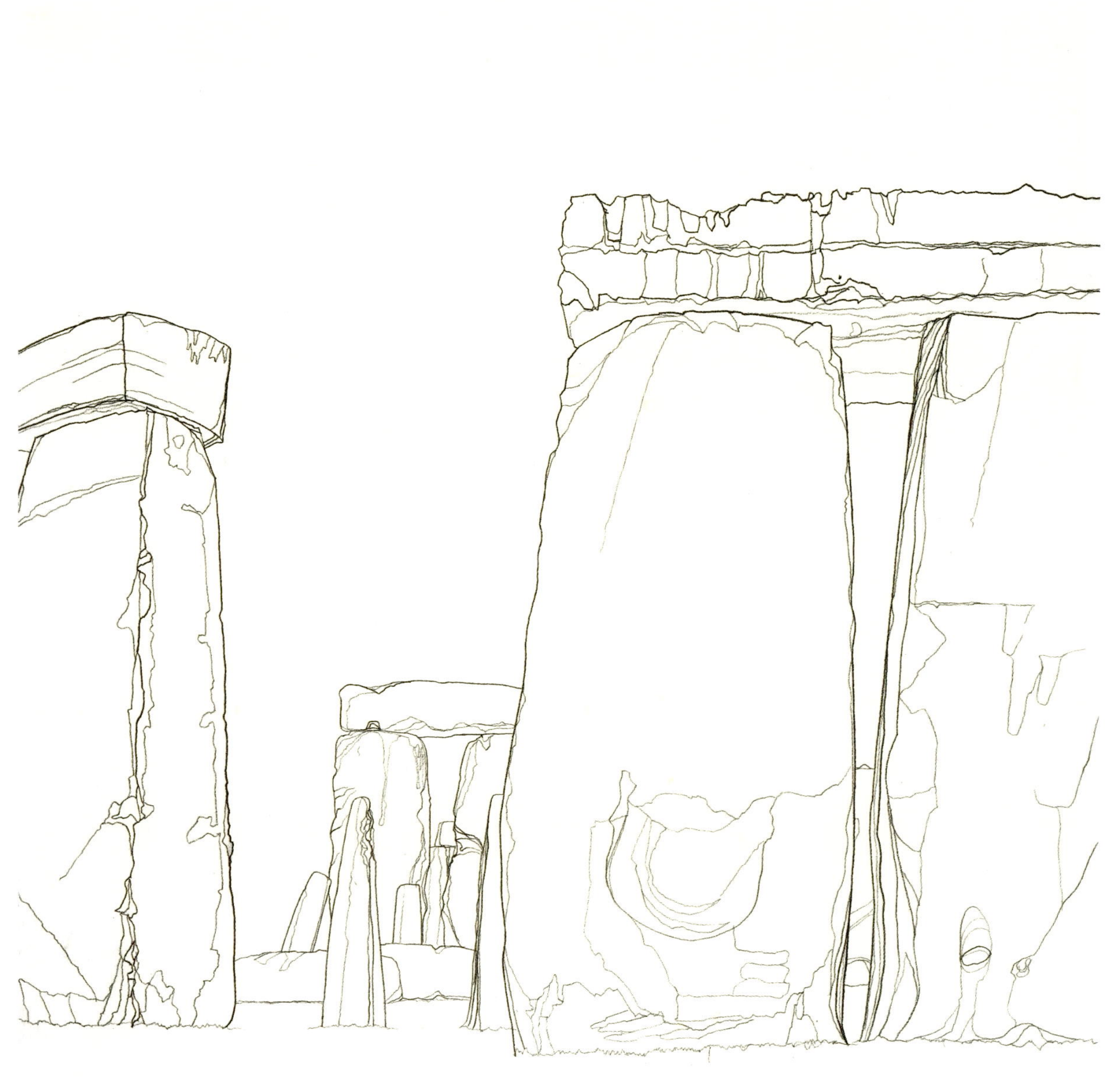

STONEHENGE: OUTER FACE OF STONES 51, 52 & 152 | 1998
pencil on paper
118 × 96

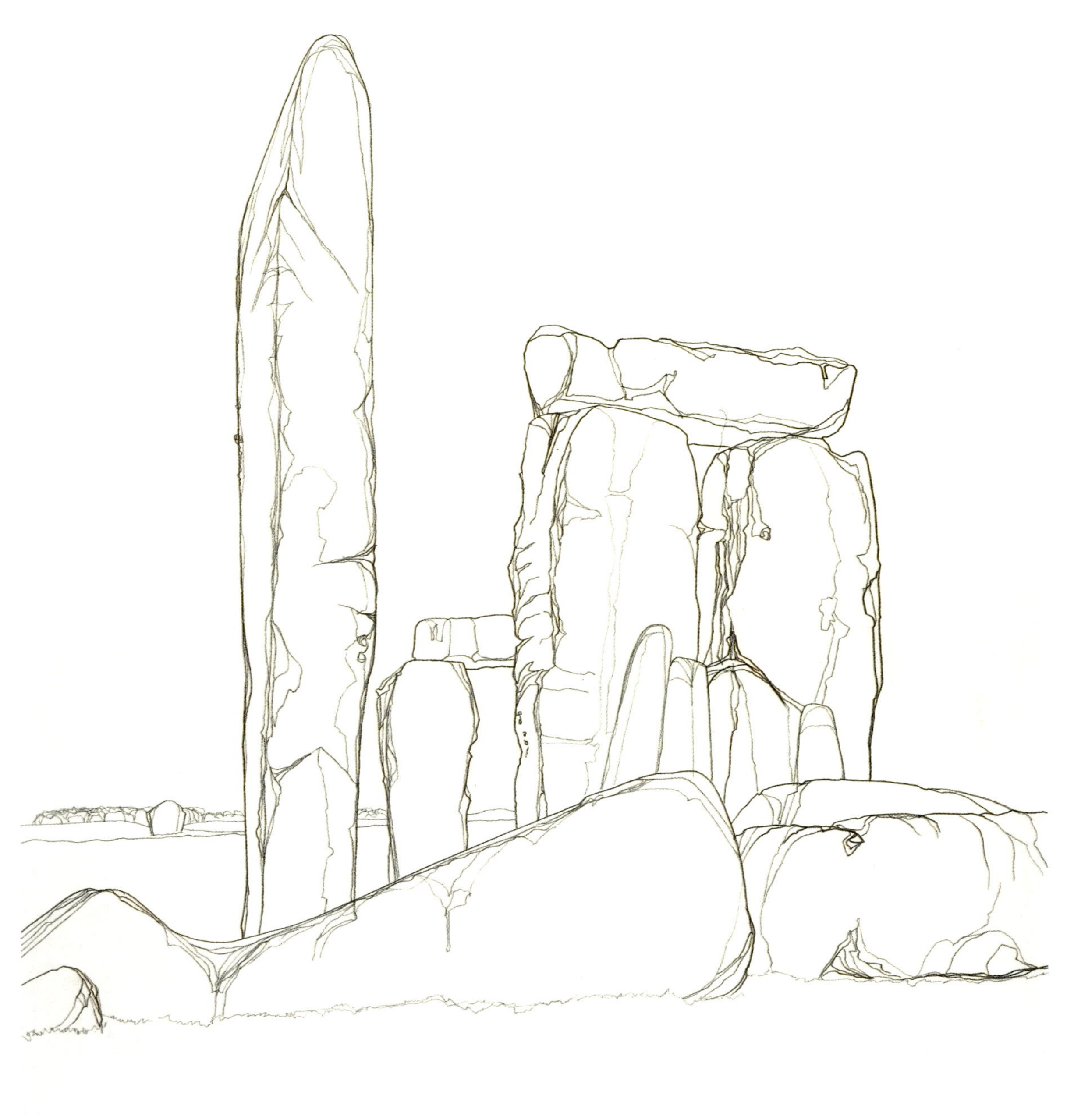

STONEHENGE: STONE 56 AND THE BROKEN 55 | 1998
pencil on paper
118×96

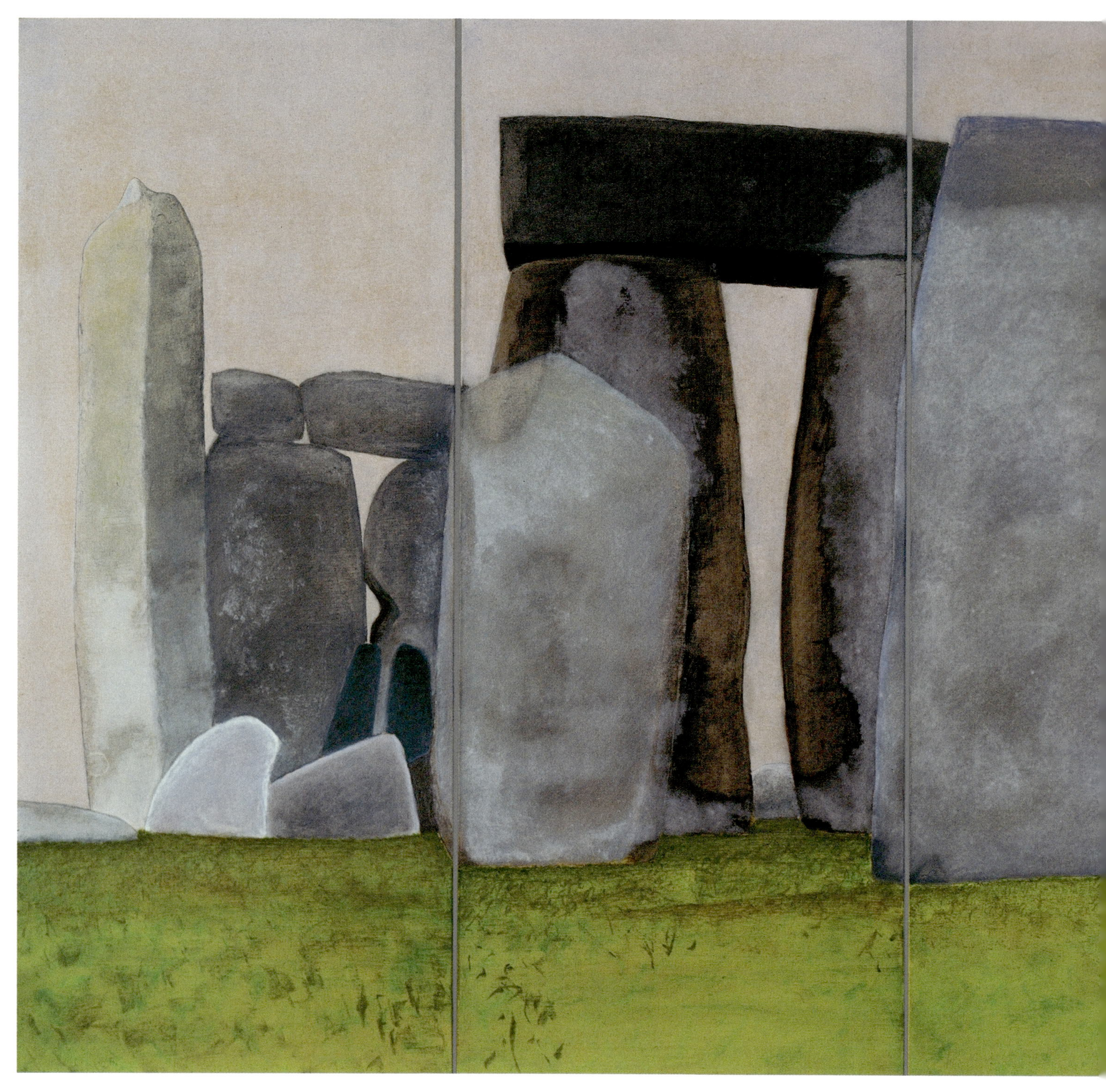

STONEHENGE: THE MAIN CIRCLE | 1994
acrylic & pastel on wood
84 × 182

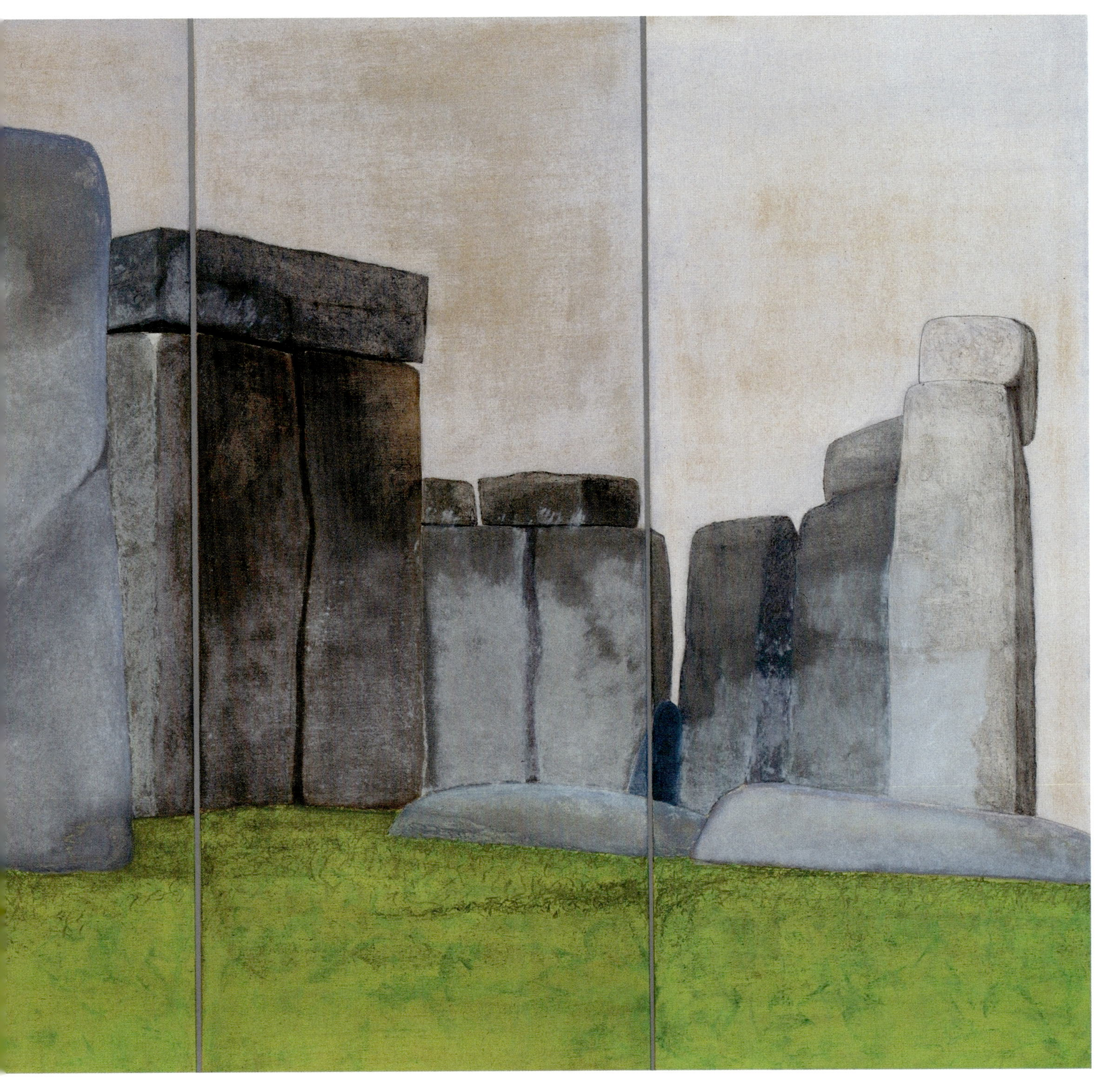

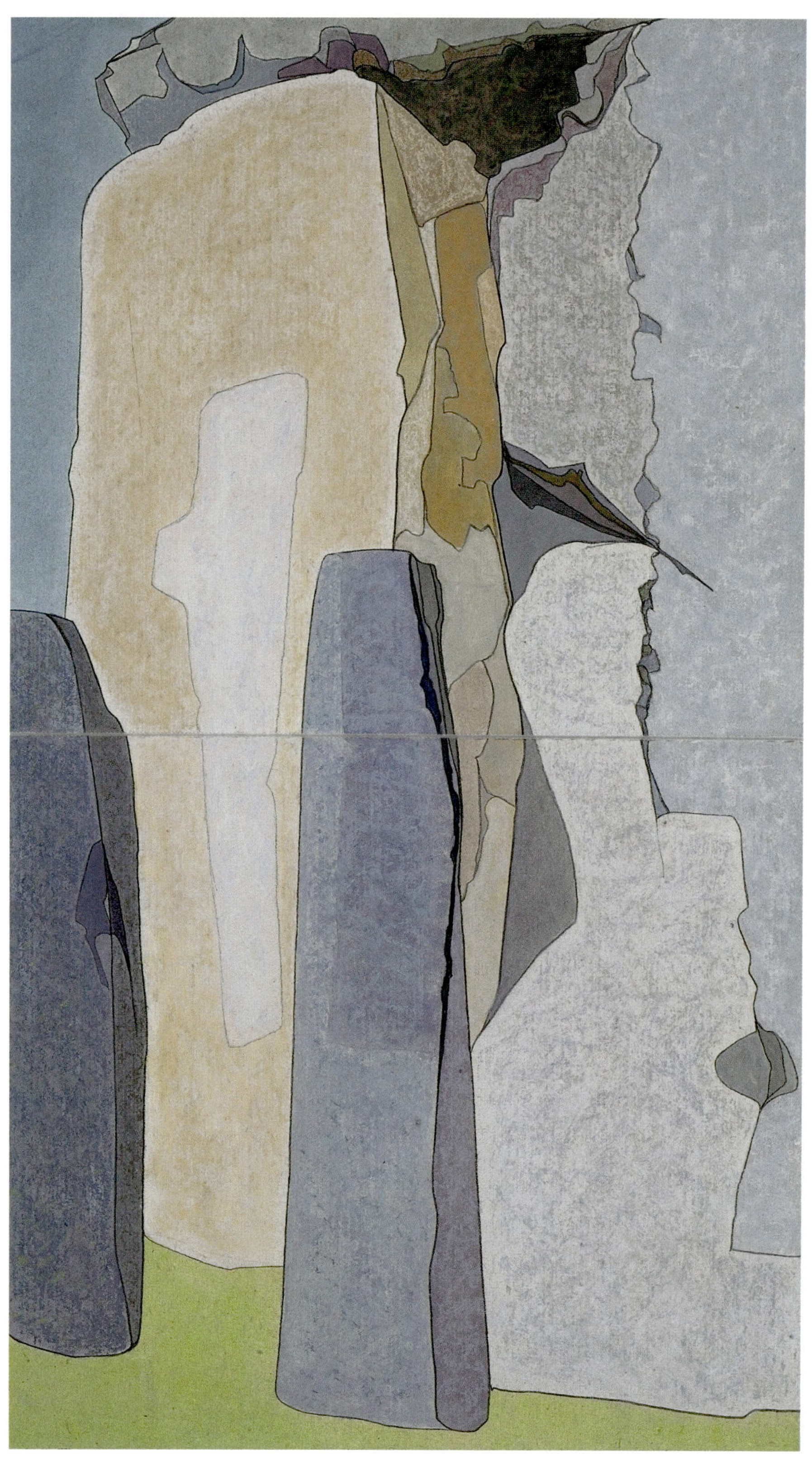

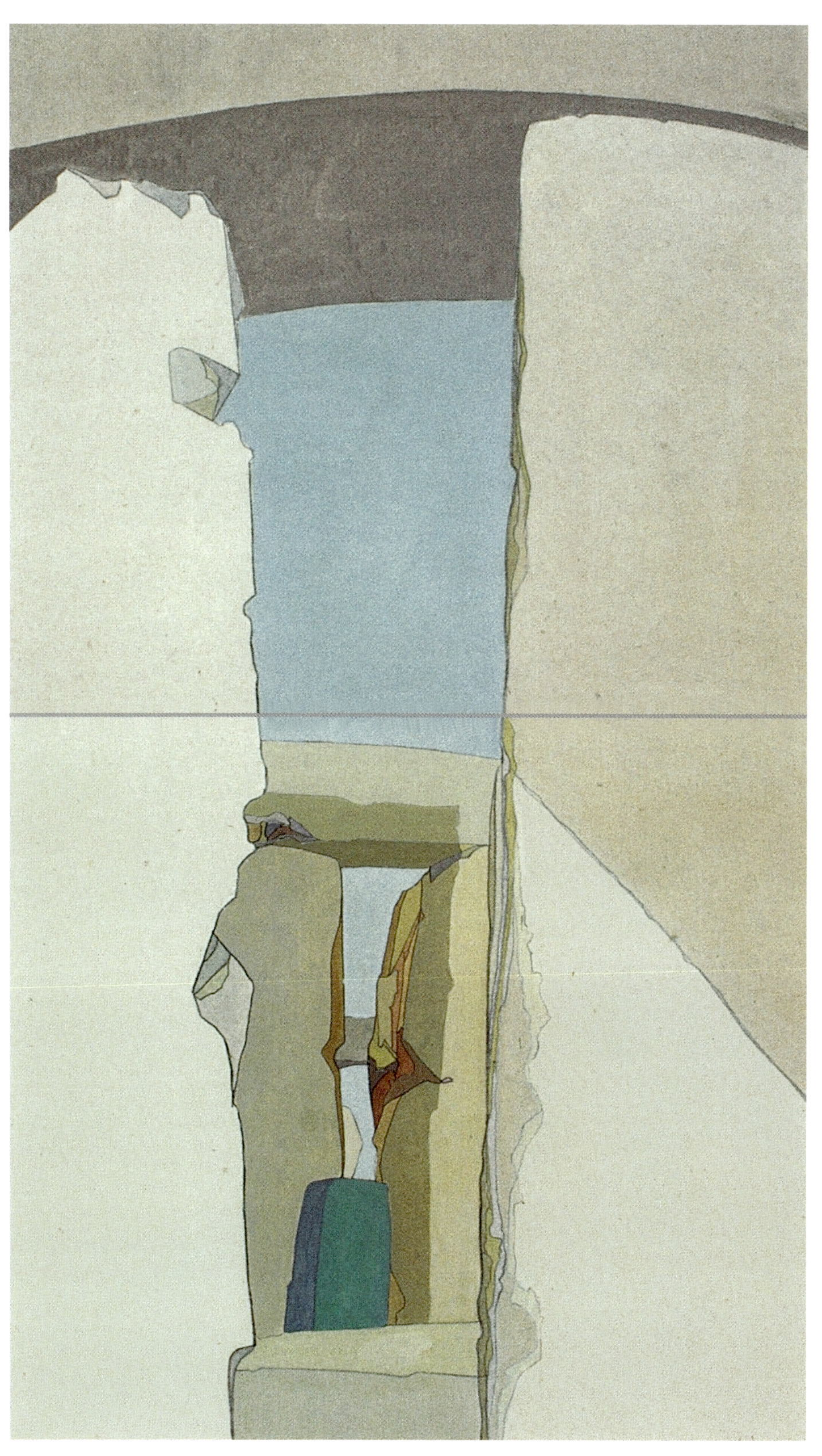

STONEHENGE DECEMBER:
THREE LINTEL STONES | 1993
acrylic & gouache on board
58 × 33

AVEBURY AND SILBURY

The linking of the ancient sites of Windmill Hill, down to Avebury, along the Kennet to Silbury, then up to West Kennet Long Barrow

Along with Mainland in Orkney, Avebury and surrounds form the most extensive group of ancient sites in Britain. The stone circle of Avebury is at the centre. From it runs The Avenue of standing stones, and beyond that is mystic Silbury. On the ridge of the Downs beyond lies the West Kennet Long Barrow. As in Orkney, you can easily walk between these sites. It is clear that their placement connects them to each other in the landscape, even though they date several hundred years apart.

Avebury is the largest stone circle in Britain, second in importance only to Stonehenge. As with Stonehenge, the experience of being there is much impaired by the road traffic. In the case of Avebury a main road runs right through the centre, and Silbury has a very busy main road almost cutting into the base of the mound. But unlike Stonehenge, the public are still allowed to wander freely among the stones and to walk the huge surrounding henge at Avebury. I have been there many, many times, always fascinated by both the individual large stones and their placement.

In walking between these sites, drawing as I go, I try to understand better the relationship between them. Gradually one can see why Silbury is so set in the landscape, but surprisingly the Avenue of Stones does not link it with Avebury. Indeed, for much of its length Silbury is hidden behind the ridge of Waden Hill (this is shown on the detailed map). But to walk the ridge is magnificent. Even though not high, nor very long, it forms the key axis. I think, however, that the true historic connection between Avebury and Silbury is along the River Kennet, which here is just a stream in its upper reaches.

The last time I was here, in midwinter with a deep freeze, Silbury was hardly visible in the fog, and the stones and grass were covered in frost. This was so different from the previous time in spring, when Silbury was covered in grazing sheep. I had never seen that before, even though the stones at Avebury are nearly always accompanied by sheep. It is nuances like this that make a visit to this area so much more involving than Stonehenge, with its press of tourists.

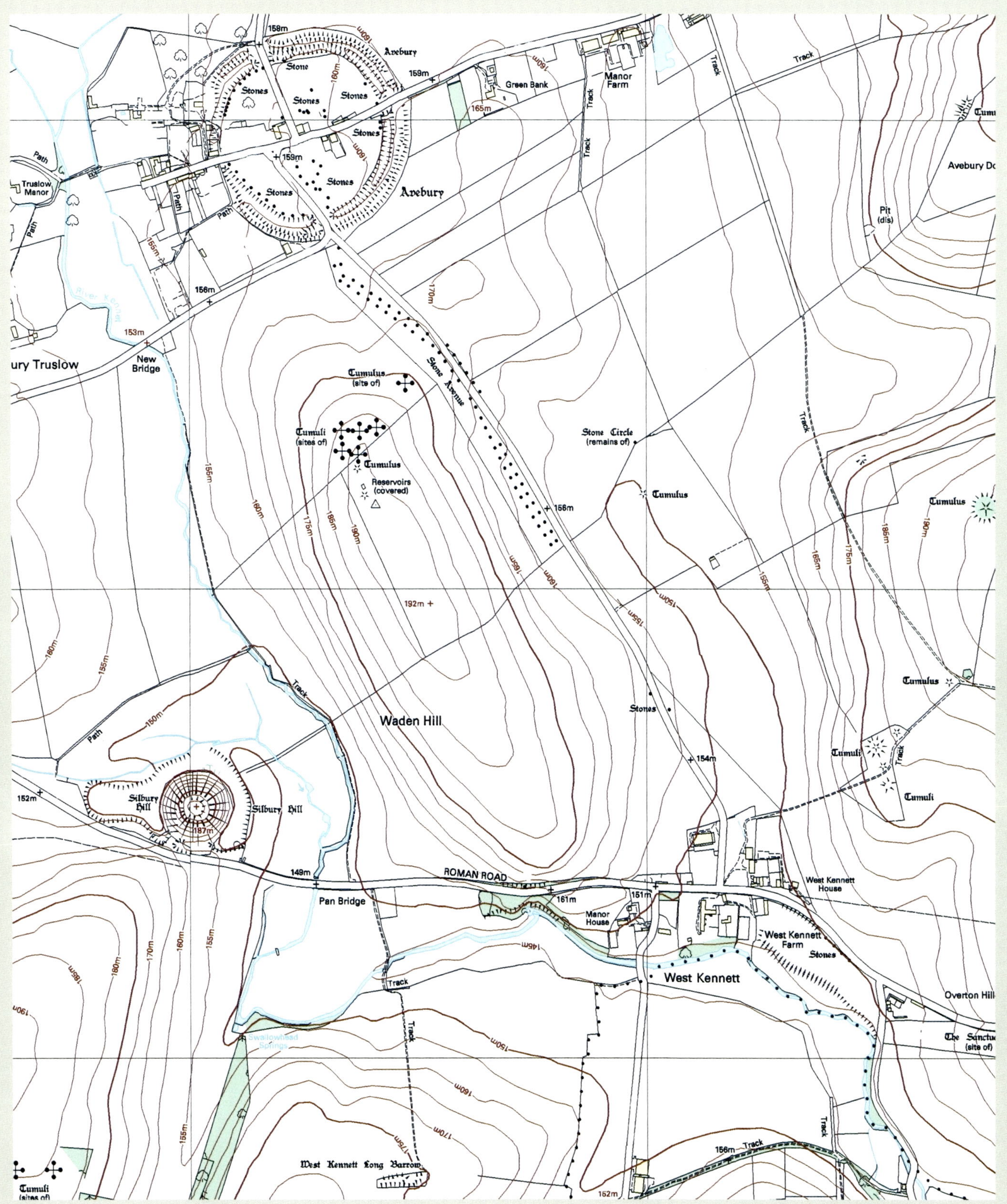

158m
Avebury
Stone
159m
Stones
Stones
Stones
Stones
Green Bank
Manor Farm
Track
Track
165m
Stones
159m
Track
Avebury Do
Avebury
Stones
Stones
Stones
Pit
(dis)
Path
Truslow
Manor
Path
Path
156m
153m
ury Truslow
New Bridge
Stone Avenue
Cumulus
(site of)
Cumuli
(sites of)
Cumulus
Stone Circle
(remains of)
Reservoirs
(covered)
158m
Cumulus
Cumulus
192m +
Track
Waden Hill
Stones
Cumulus
154m
Cumulus
Path
Cumuli
152m
Silbury Hill
Silbury Hill
187m
West Kennett House
149m
Pan Bridge
ROMAN ROAD
161m
Manor House
151m
West Kennett Farm
Stones
Overton Hill
West Kennett
The Sanctuary
(site of)
Track
Swallowhead
Springs
Track
Track
156m
Track
West Kennett Long Barrow
152m
Cumuli
(sites of)

Silbury from the top of Waden Hill.
This hill blocks the view from The Avenue.
Why? And why is the hill surrounded by
the flood plain of the River Kennet?

Wind now strong – harder to draw and
threatening grey.

2.20 PM 20 JUNE 2007

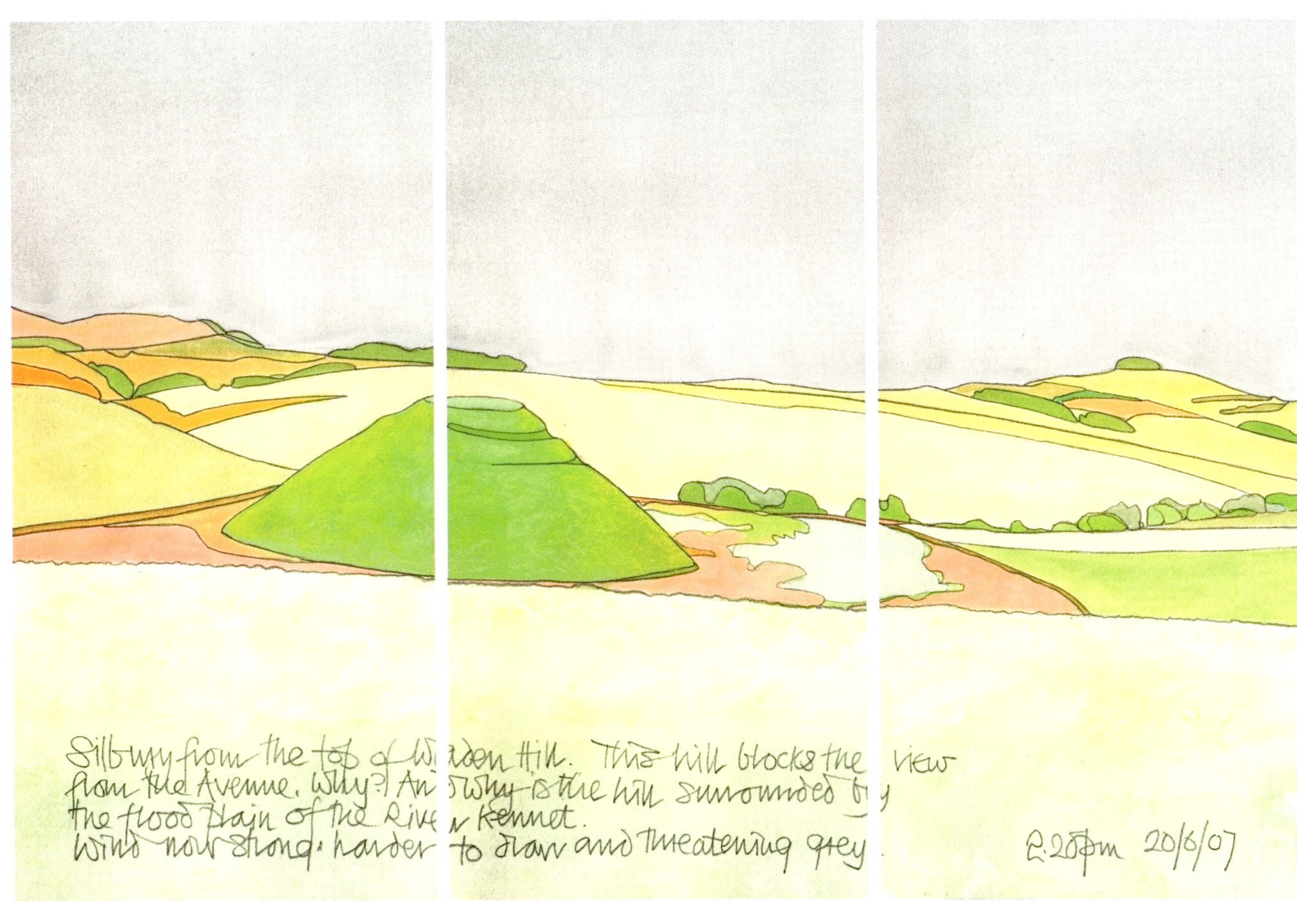

Silbury from the top of Waden Hill. This hill blocks the view
from the Avenue. Why? And why is the hill surrounded by
the flood plain of the River Kennet.
Wind now strong, harder to draw and threatening grey.   2.20pm 20/6/07

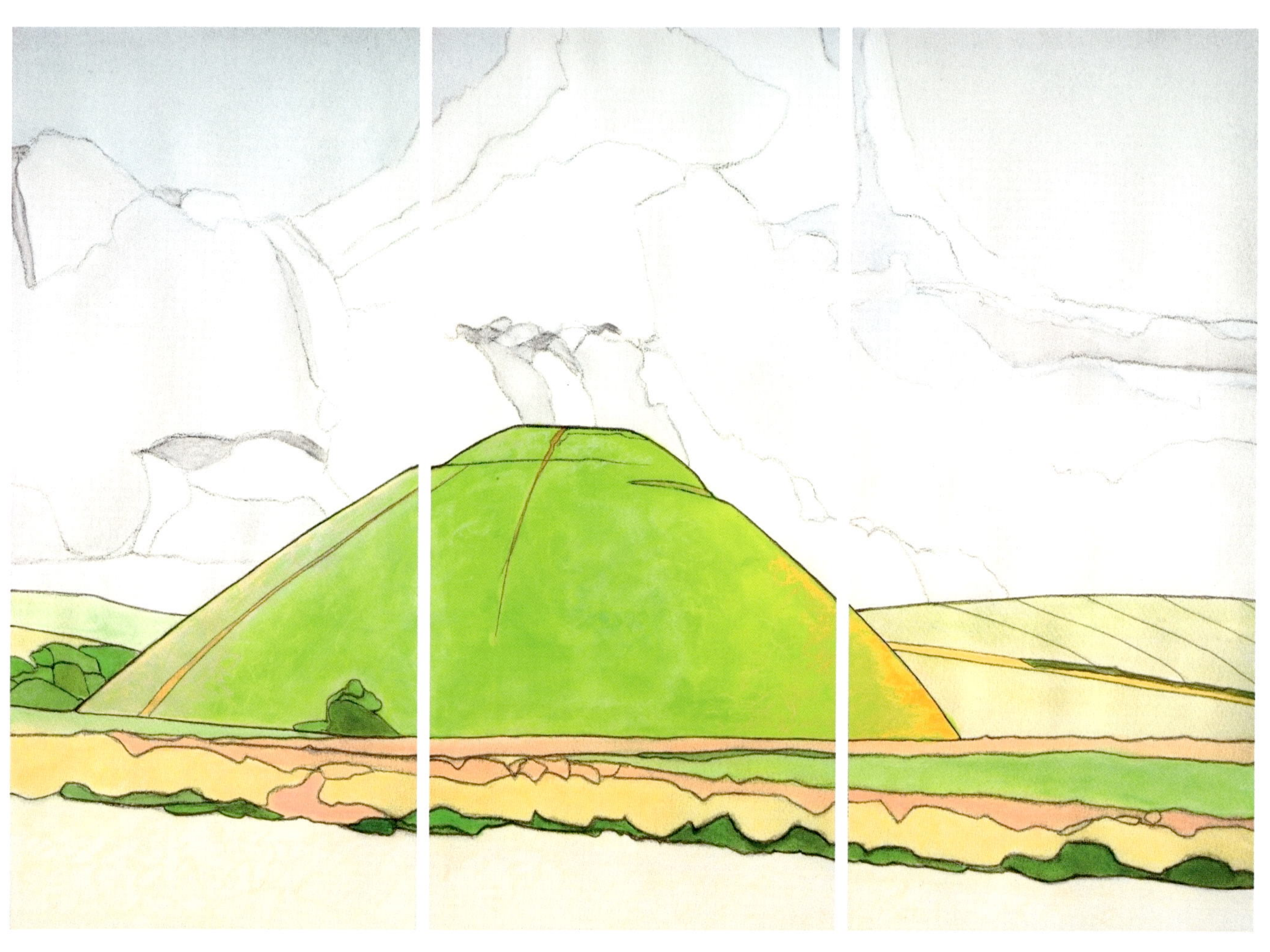

SILBURY: 10 AM 20 JUNE 2007 | 2007/08
aquacryl, pastel, gouache & print on paper
48×67

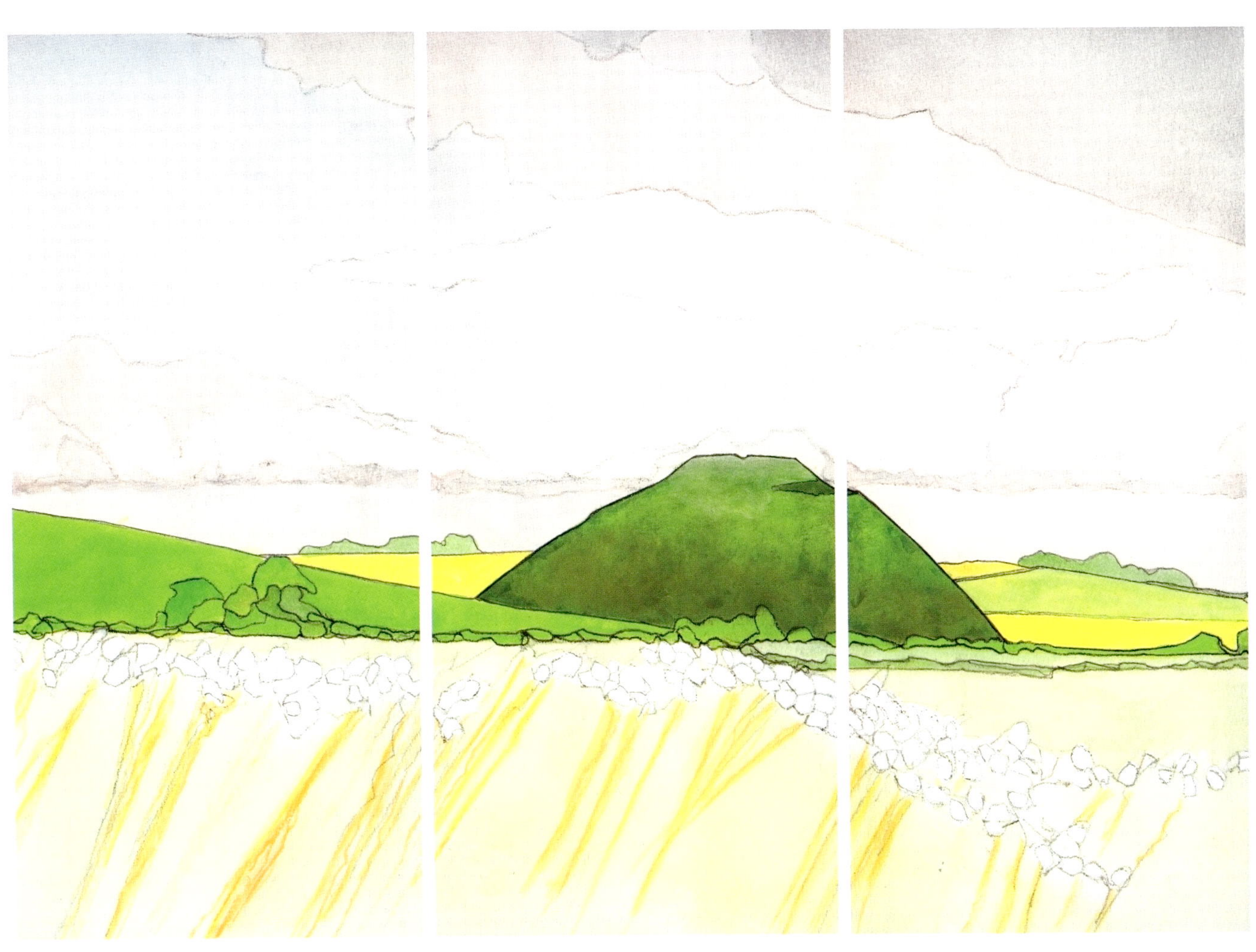

SILBURY: NOON 20 JUNE 2007 | 2007/08
aquacryl, pastel, gouache & print on paper
48×67

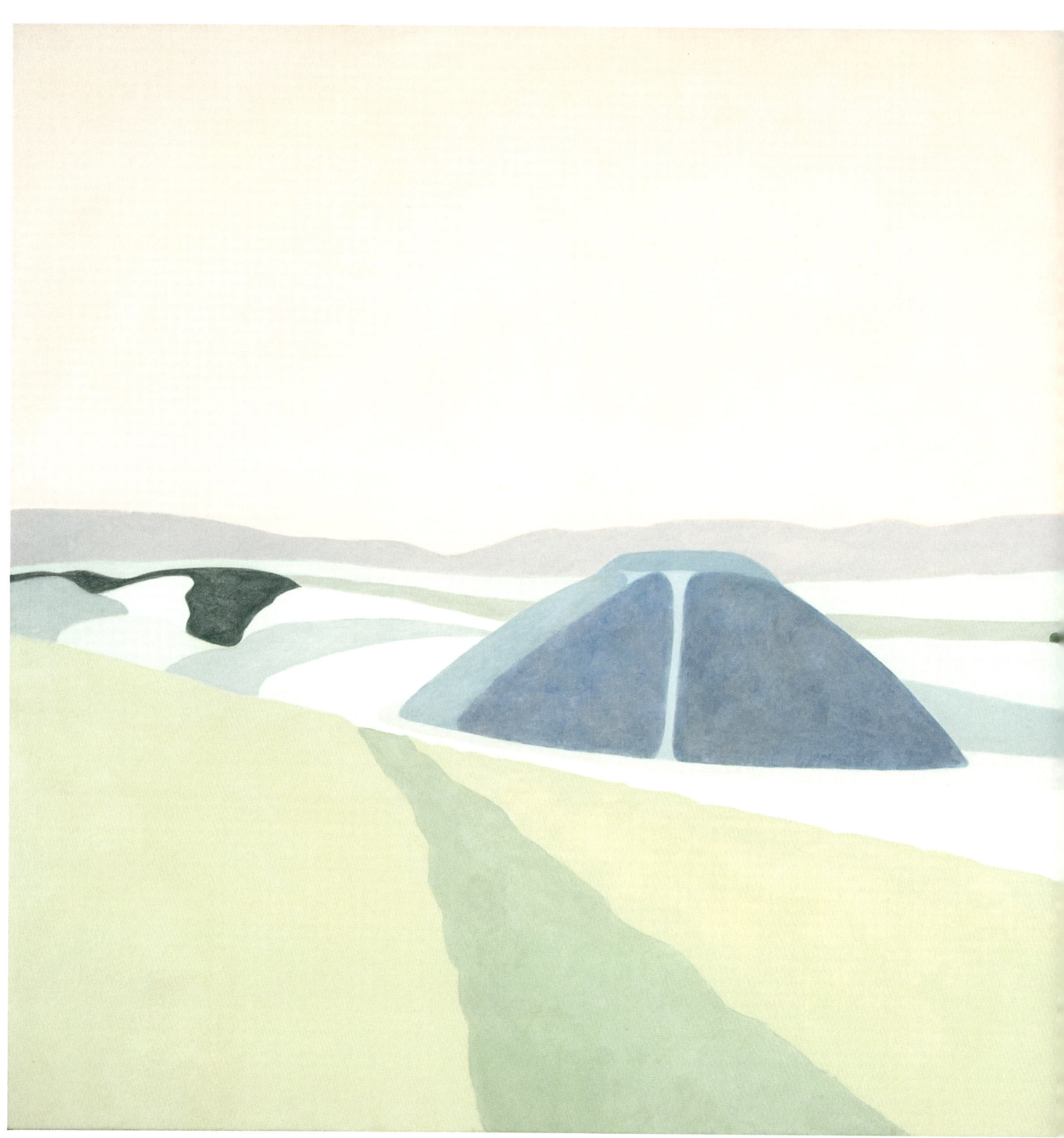

   AVEBURY AND SILBURY

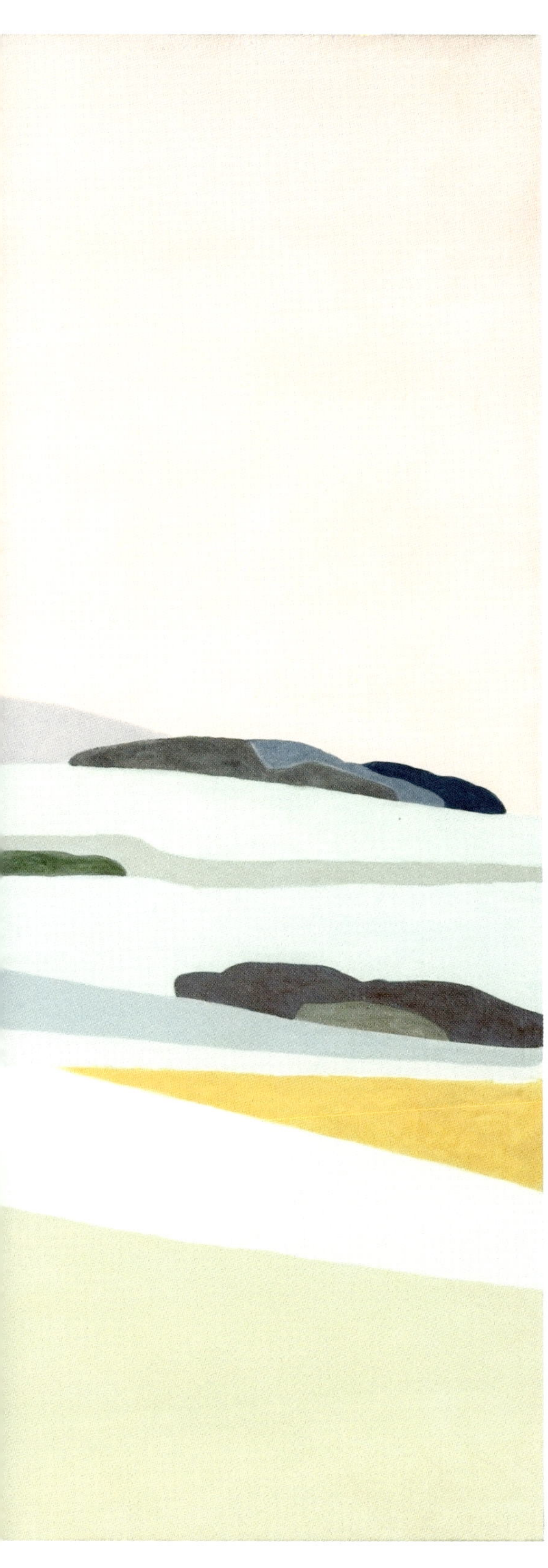

SILBURY | 2008
acrylic on canvas
70×98

I have come over the hill from Silbury.
To me the mystery of The Avenue is why
does it not run between Avebury and Silbury.
Where is it going?

A foggy, icy day. Well below freezing.
I wish the sun would break through.

2 PM 6 DEC 2010

SILBURY AND THE KENNET | 2009
acrylic on canvas
70×98

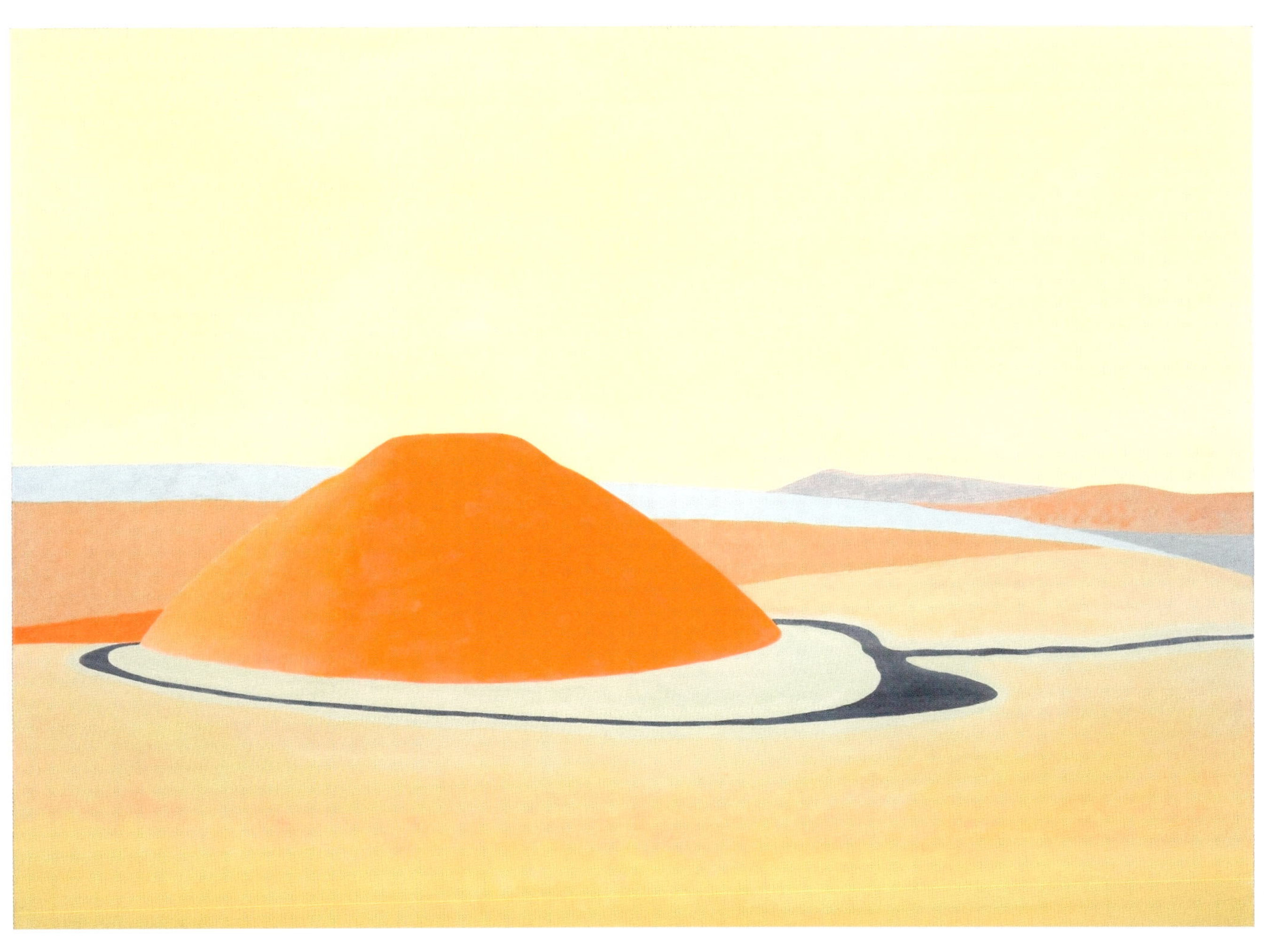

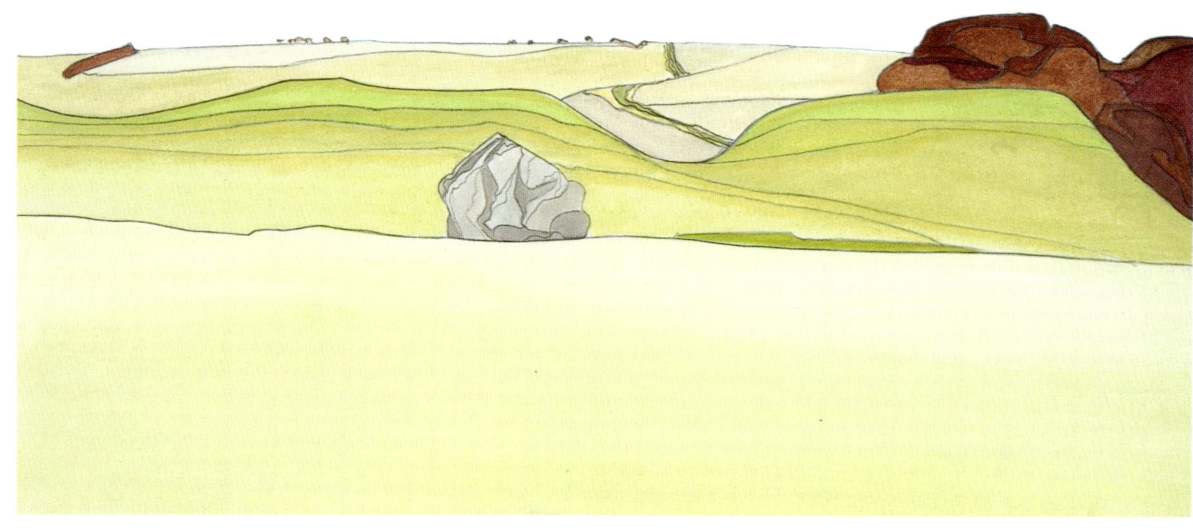

AVEBURY: LOOKING EAST, TUESDAY 9TH DEC 2003 | 2003/04
gouache on paper
31 × 35

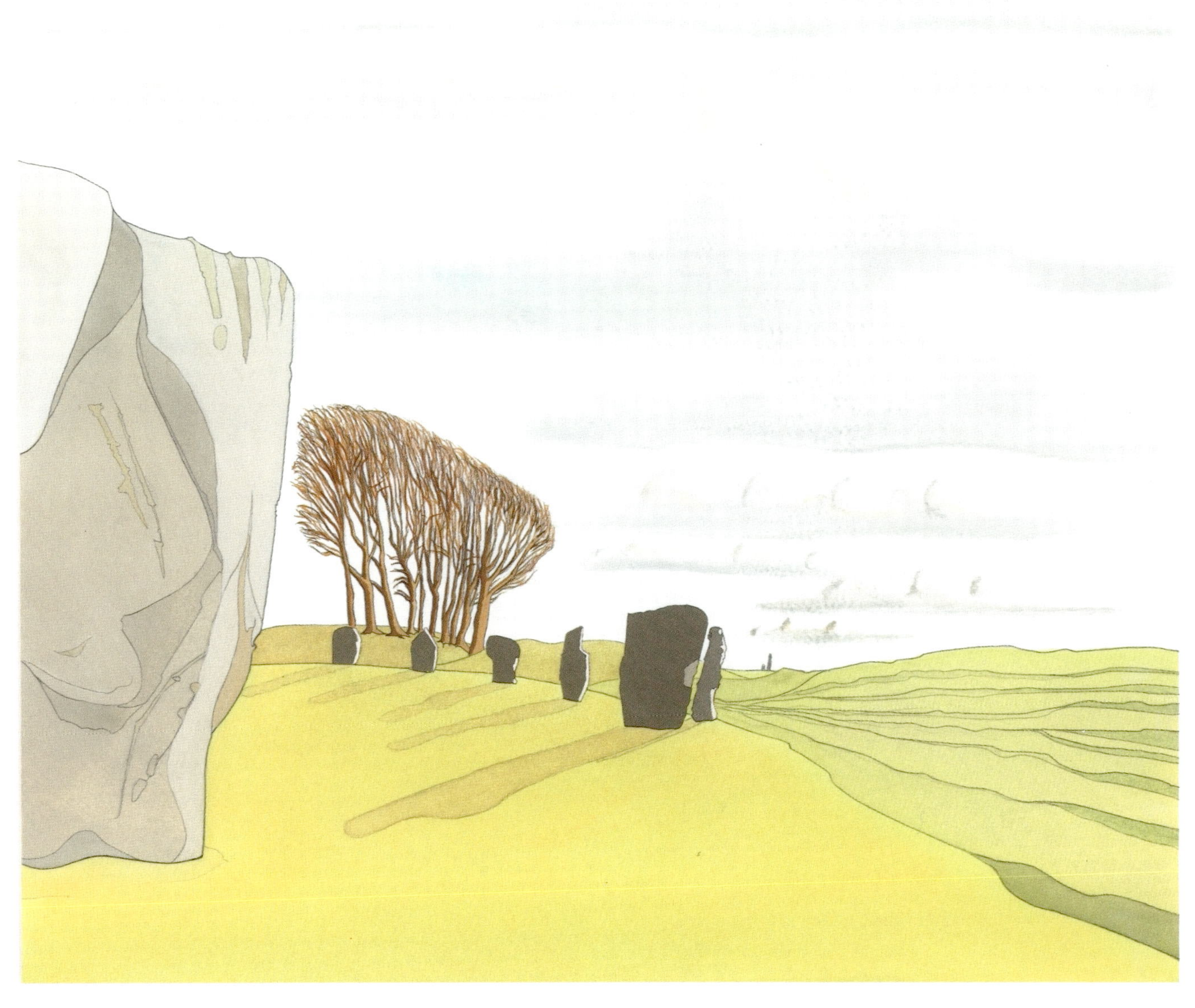

AVEBURY: LOOKING TOWARDS THE AVENUE | 1986
gouache on paper
41 × 50

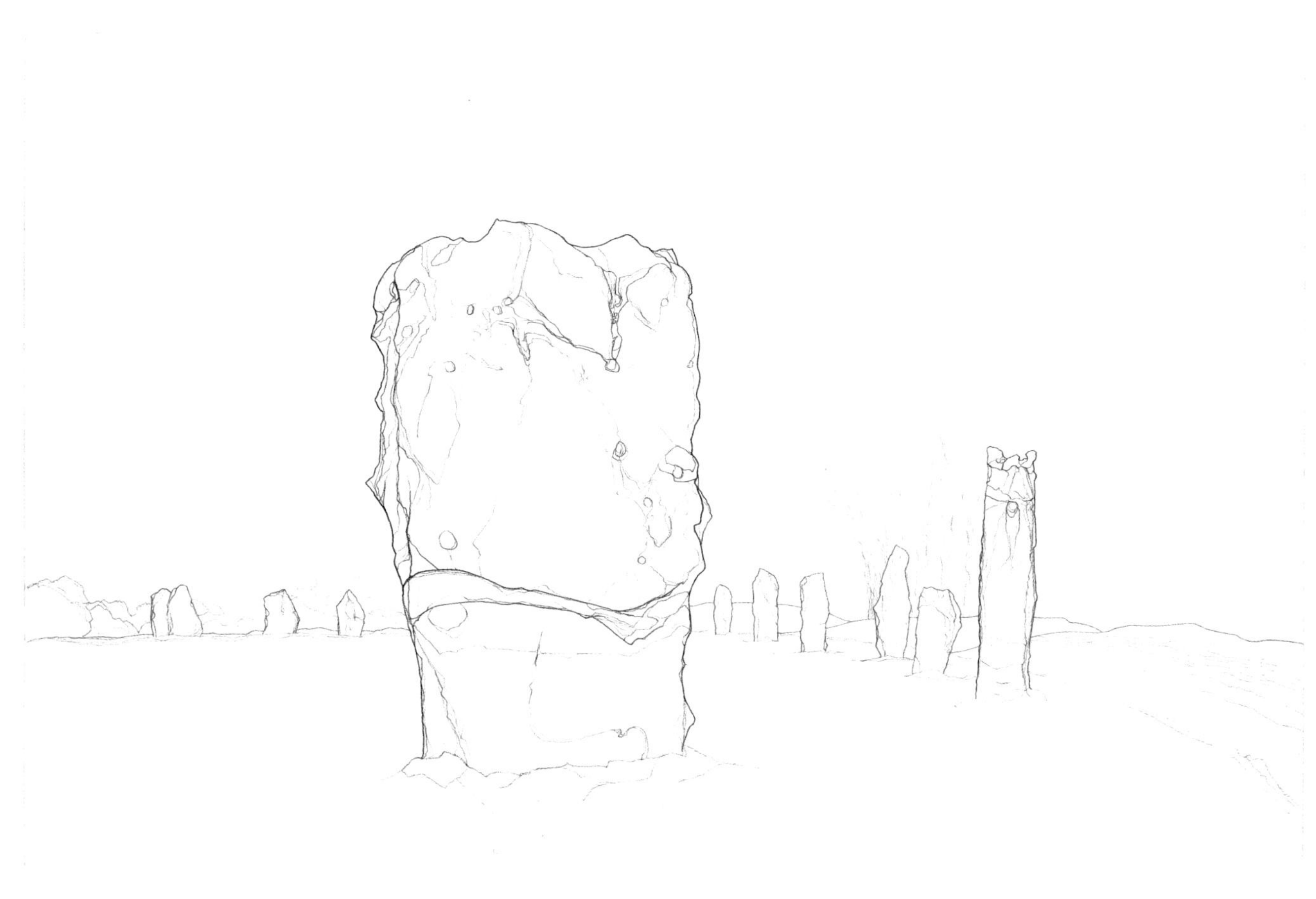

AVEBURY: SOUTH WEST ARC – LOOKING SOUTH | 2006
pencil on paper
67 × 102

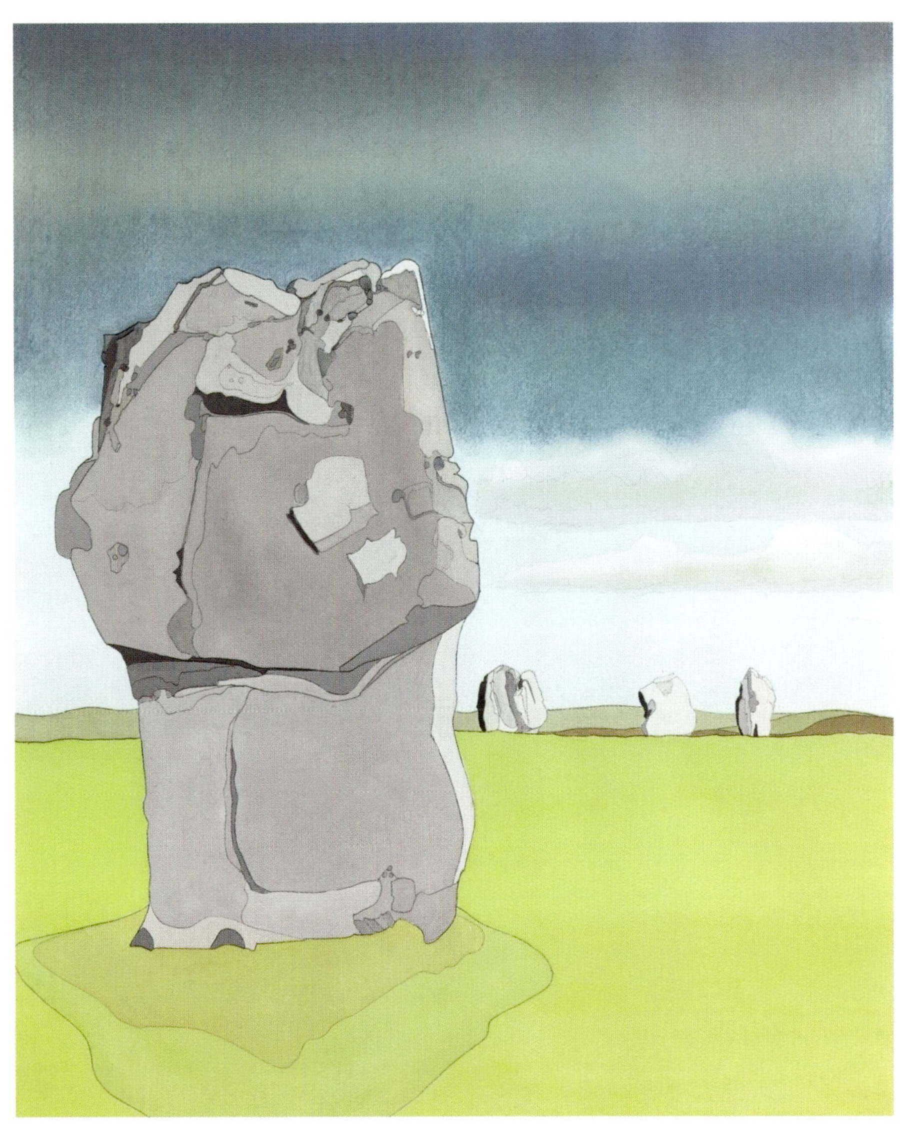

THE BARBER'S STONE, AVEBURY | 1986
gouache on paper
51×41

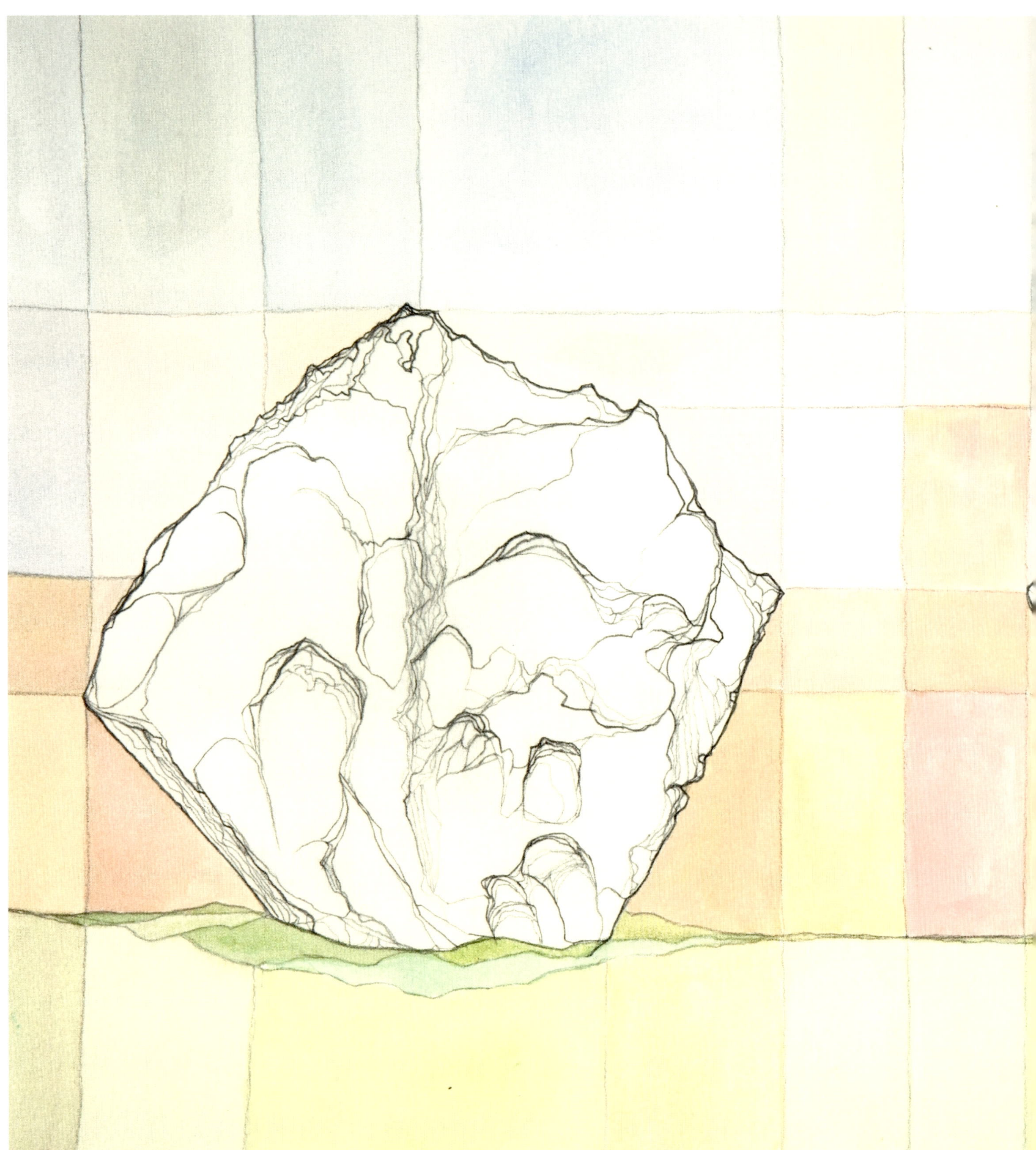

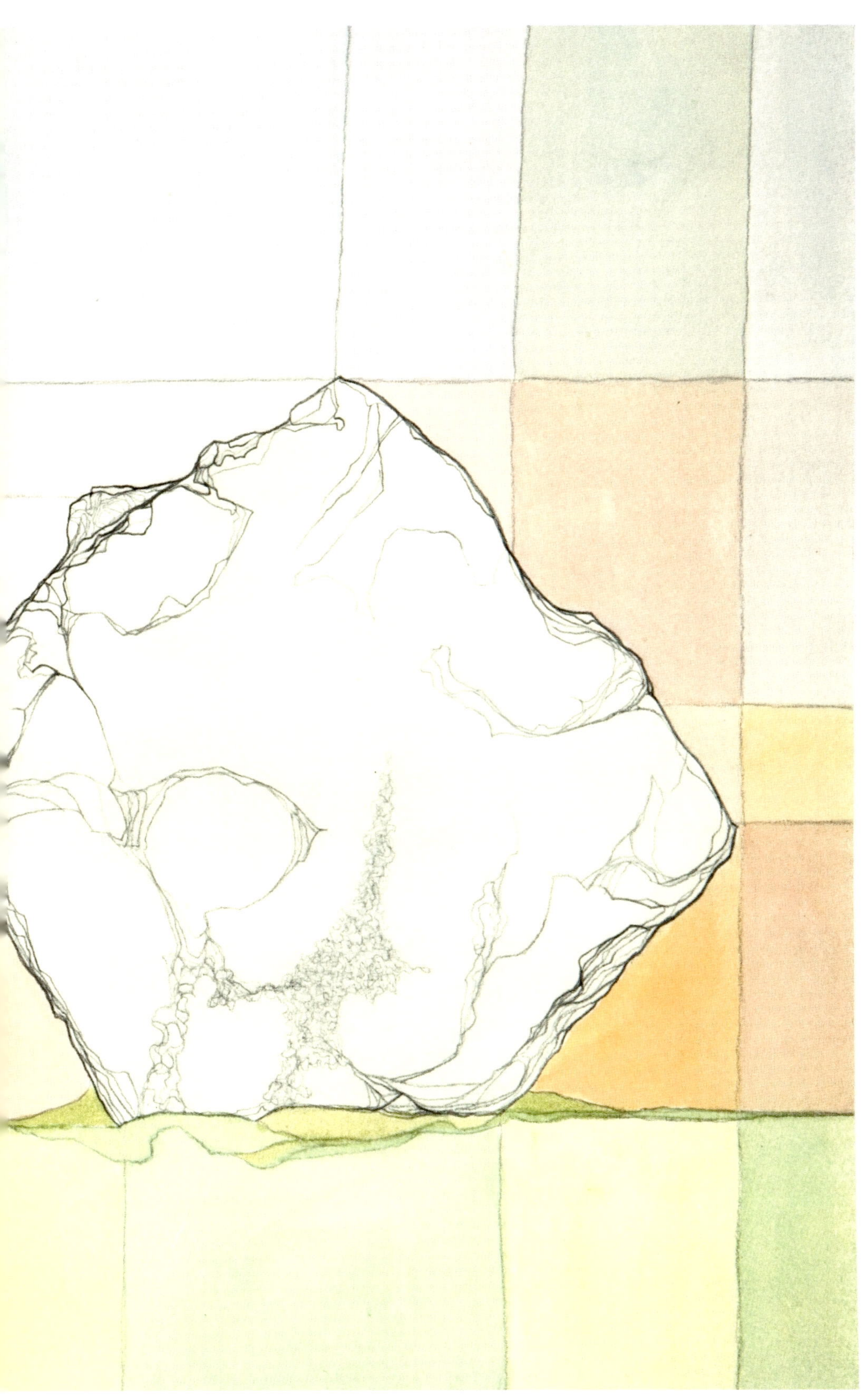

AVEBURY: ENTRANCE STONE AT THE NORTH | 2006
pencil & aquacryl on paper
31 × 51

RIDGEWAY

Overton Hill to Spasholt Firs

The Ridgeway runs from Overton Hill, just above Avebury, to the Thames at Goring. Throughout this forty-mile length it follows the ridge of the Downs, with for the most part a flat valley to its north. Sometimes the Ridgeway is defined as longer than this, reaching into the Chilterns, but I am sticking with the most generally recognized definition. The maps show two stretches, including the two most striking Iron Age hill forts of Barbury Castle and Uffington.

There are numerous guides to walking the Ridgeway. My favourite, always at hand, remains *The Oldest Road* by J. R. L. Anderson and Fay Godwin, first published in 1975. This little book includes a set of Fay's wonderful black and white photos, which remain an inspiration to me.

I keep returning to the Ridgeway to visit the various sites and to walk sections of the track. The Ridgeway also relates to the two stone circles of Avebury and Stonehenge, for it was near the track that the huge sandstone blocks were gathered to build the circles. Such blocks are called sarsen stones and, remarkably, they can still be found on the surface of the chalk downs, particularly on Overton Down (pp. 152–55).

To walk the track gives a very special feeling. You know you are in an ancient landscape. You come across numerous sites: the Megalithic tomb of Wayland's Smithy (pp. 156–57), the forts mentioned above and others, the abstracted White Horse carved into the chalk, and the strip lynchet earthbanks that are the signs of ancient agriculture.

It is not just these features that make the walk special, but the track itself. Rutted, indeed muddy in winter, it looks old. It follows the contours as if it is clinging to the ridge. It changes with the seasons. I usually go in winter, liking the low light. Once I went there to cross-country ski after a heavy snowfall (pp. 166 and 167).

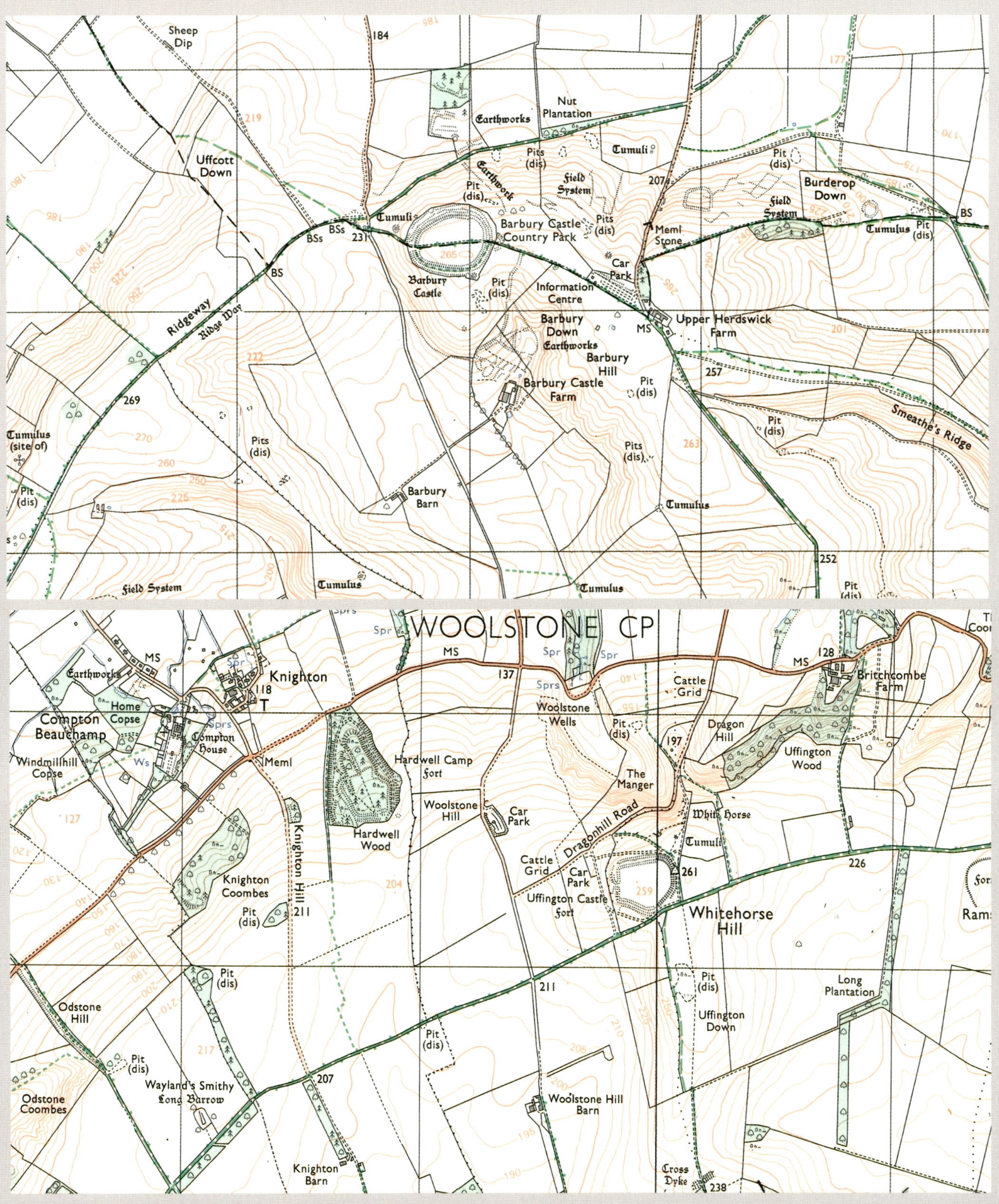

Sheep Dip
184
Nut Plantation
Earthworks
Uffcott Down
Pits (dis)
Tumuli
Pit (dis)
Burderop Down
Earthwork
Field System
207
Tumuli
Earthwork
Pit (dis)
Field System
BS
Barbury Castle Country Park
Pits (dis)
Meml Stone
Tumulus (dis)
BSs
231
BS
Car Park
Upper Herdswick Farm
Barbury Castle
Pit (dis)
Information Centre
Ridgeway
Ridge Way
Barbury Down Earthworks
MS
201
269
272
Barbury Hill
257
Barbury Castle Farm
Pit (dis)
Smeathe's Ridge
Tumulus (site of)
270
Pits (dis)
Pits (dis)
263
Pit (dis)
260
Pit (dis)
225
Barbury Barn
Tumulus
252
Field System
Tumulus
Tumulus
Pit (dis)

WOOLSTONE CP
MS
MS
128
Earthworks
Knighton
137
Sprs
MS
Britchcombe Farm
Compton Beauchamp
Home Copse
118
T
Woolstone Wells
Cattle Grid
Pit (dis)
Windmillhill Copse
Compton House
Ws
Meml
197
Dragon Hill
Uffington Wood
127
Hardwell Camp Fort
The Manger
Knighton Hill
Hardwell Wood
Woolstone Hill
Car Park
White Horse
Knighton Coombes
204
Cattle Grid
Tumuli
226
Pit (dis)
211
Car Park
261
259
Odstone Hill
Pit (dis)
Uffington Castle Fort
Whitehorse Hill
211
Pit (dis)
Long Plantation
217
Pit (dis)
Uffington Down
Pit (dis)
Odstone Coombes
Wayland's Smithy Long Barrow
207
Woolstone Hill Barn
Knighton Barn
Cross Dyke
238

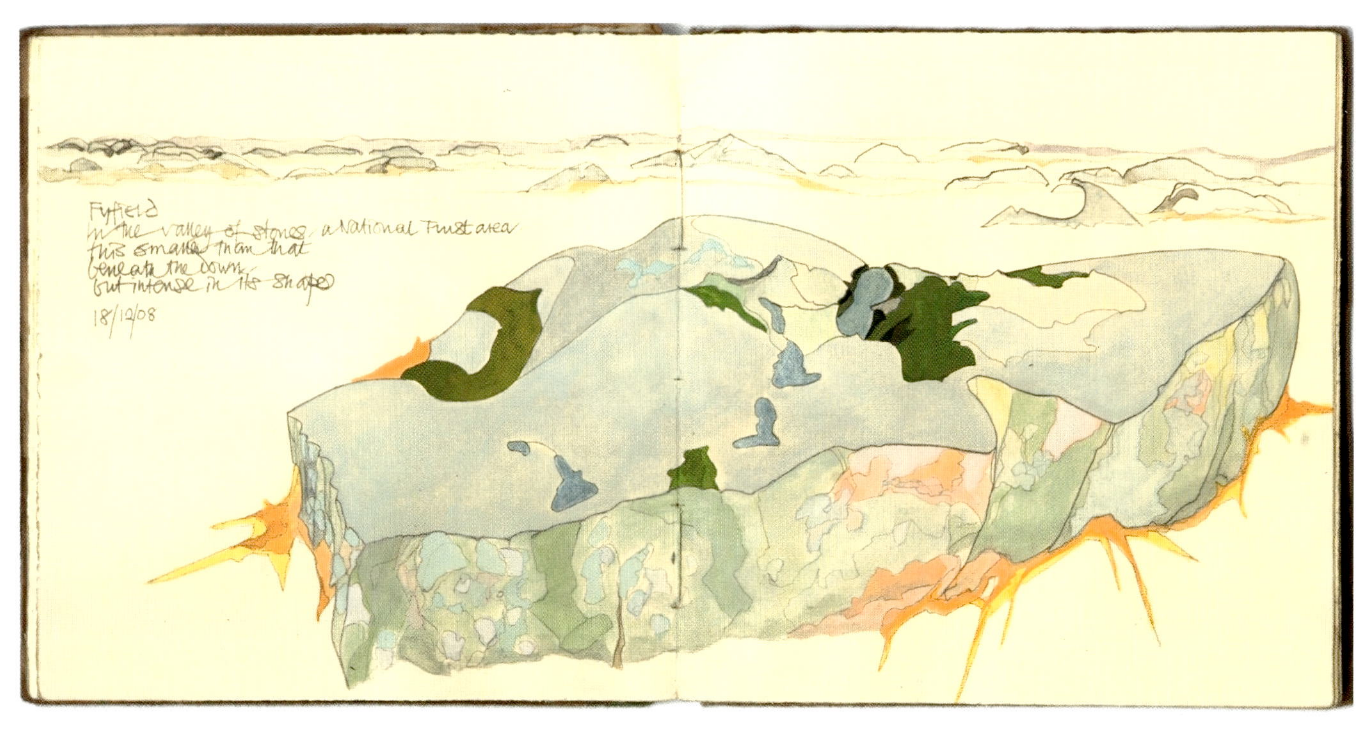

VALLEY OF THE STONES, FYFIELD, 19 DEC 2008
NOTEBOOK | 2008
pencil & gouache on paper
22 × 44

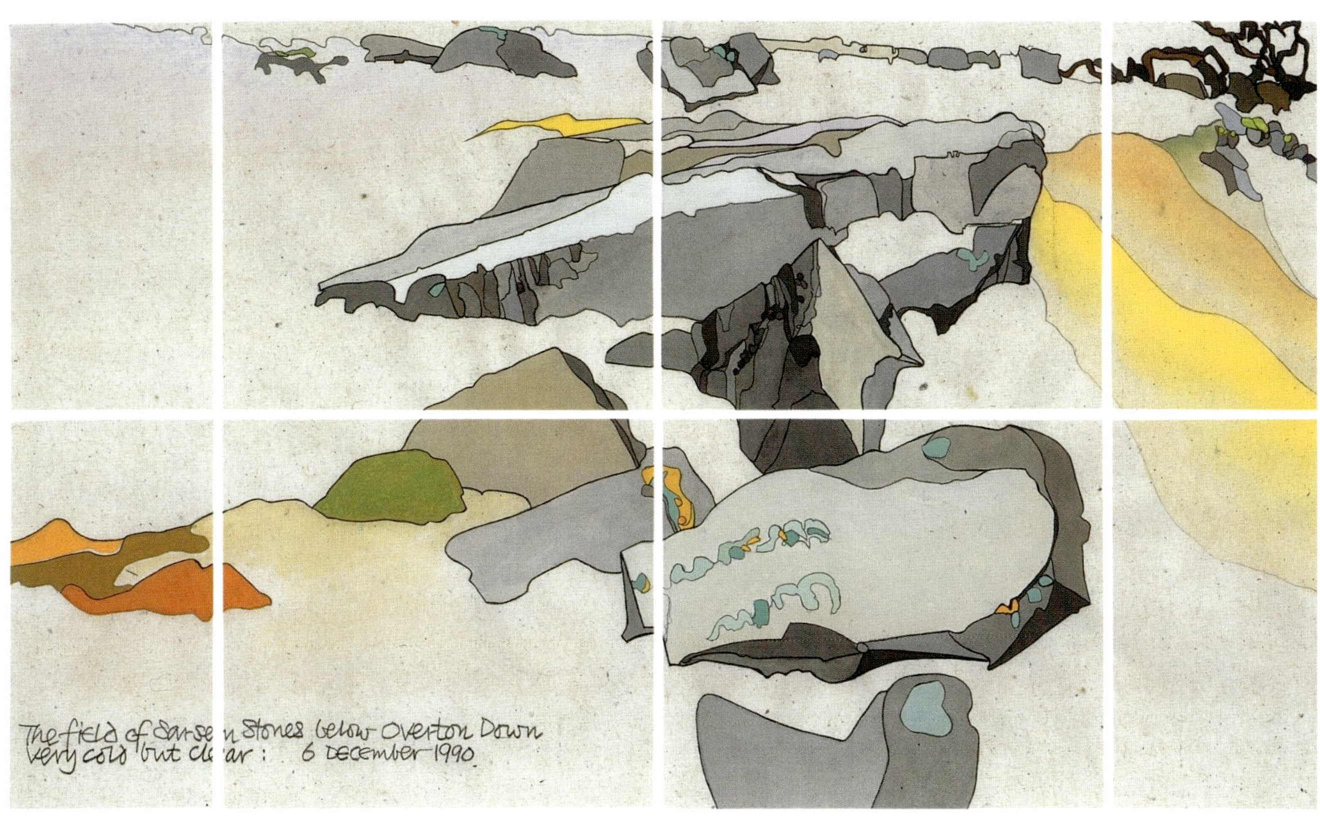

SARSEN STONES, BELOW OVERTON DOWN | 1990/91
mixed media on board
66 × 105

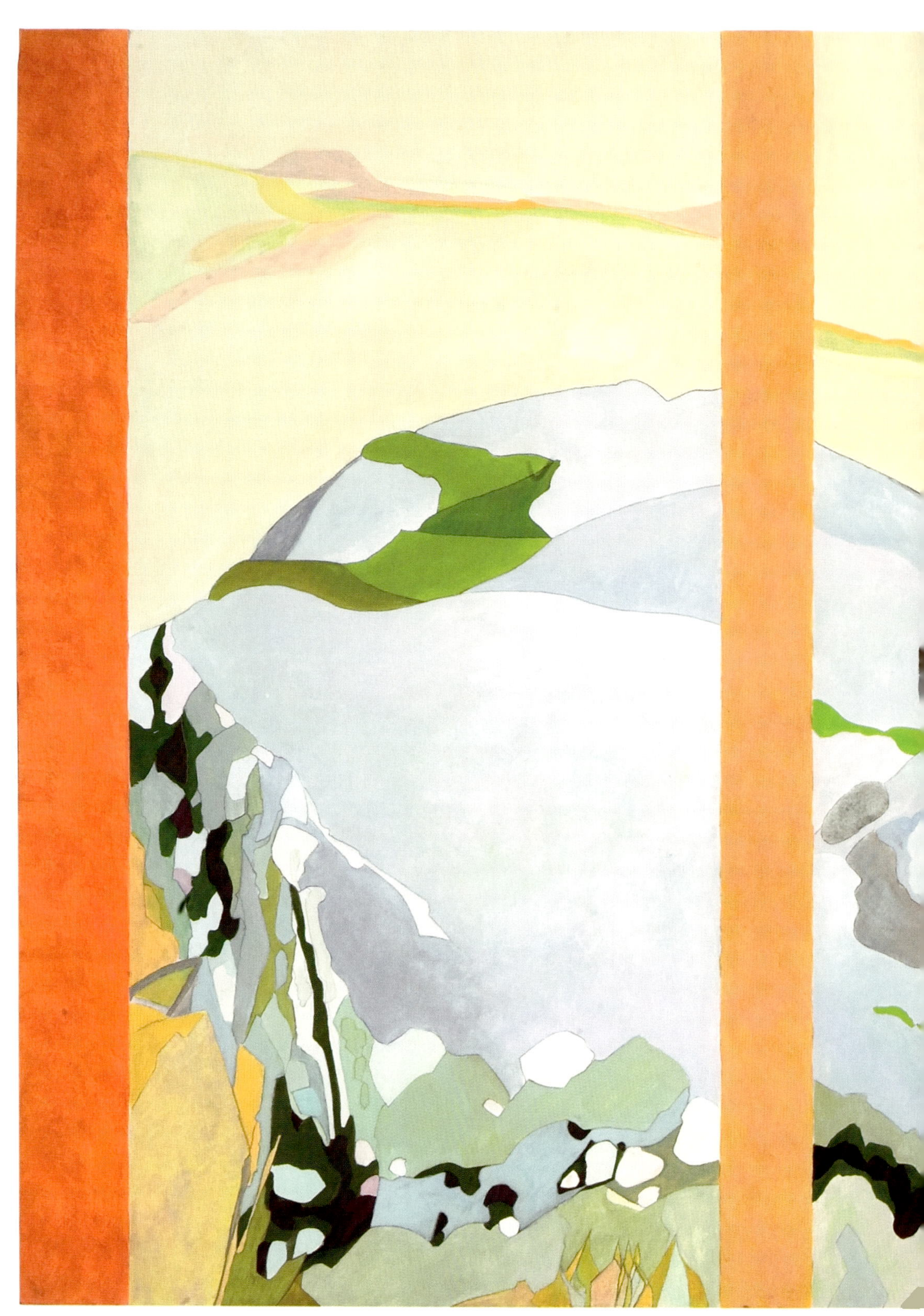

SARSEN STONES | 2009
acrylic & gouache on paper
67 × 108

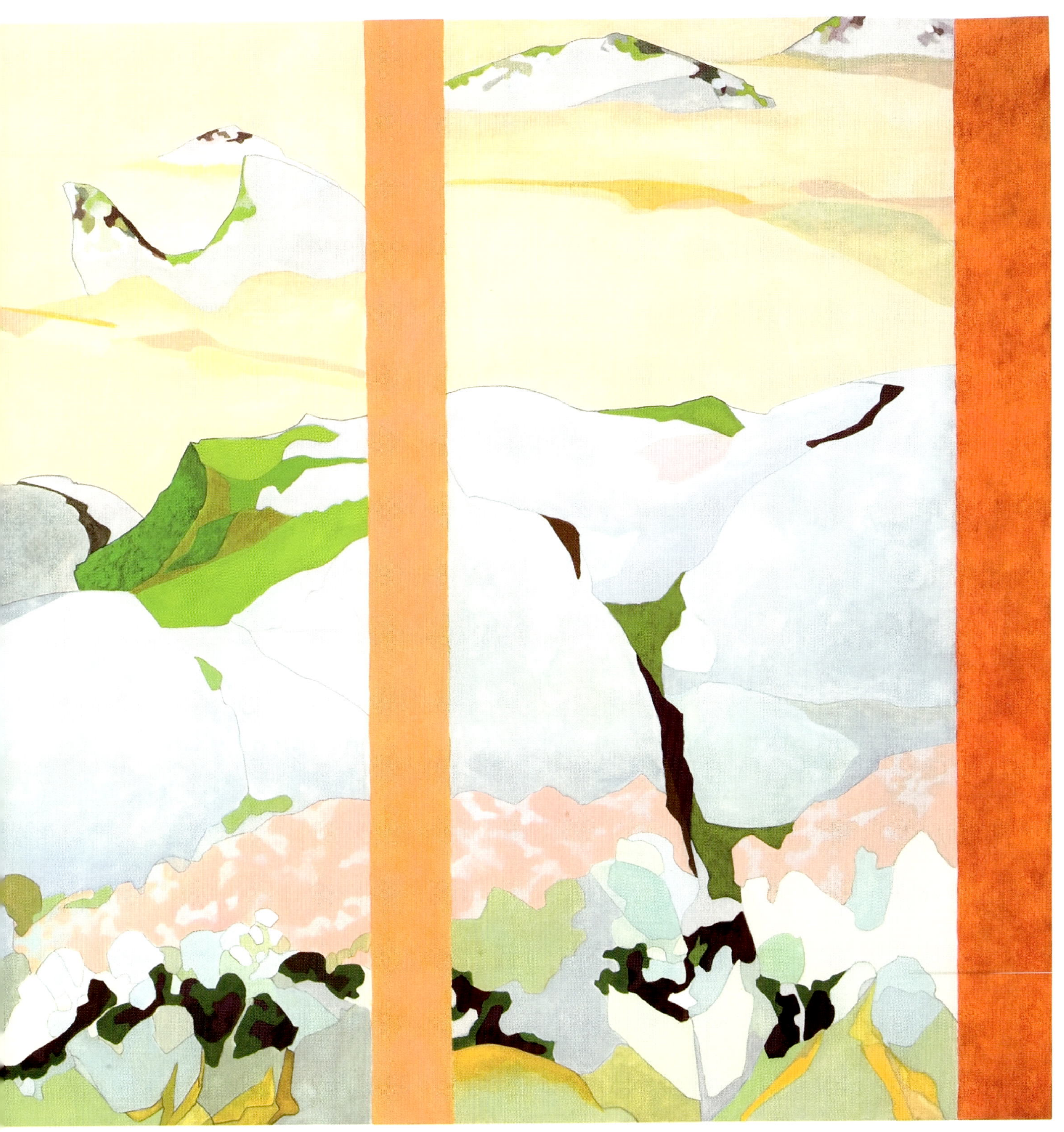

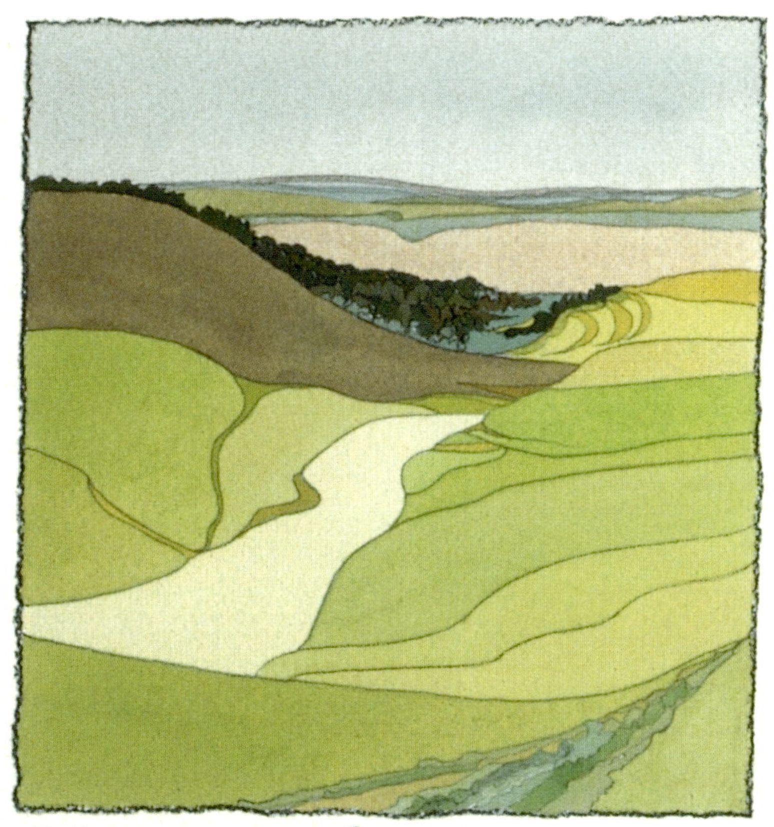

Strip lynchets near Bishopstone

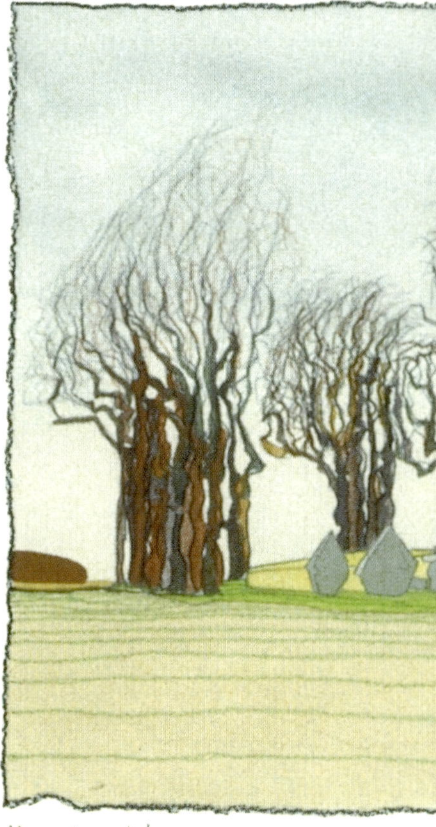

Wayland's Smithy

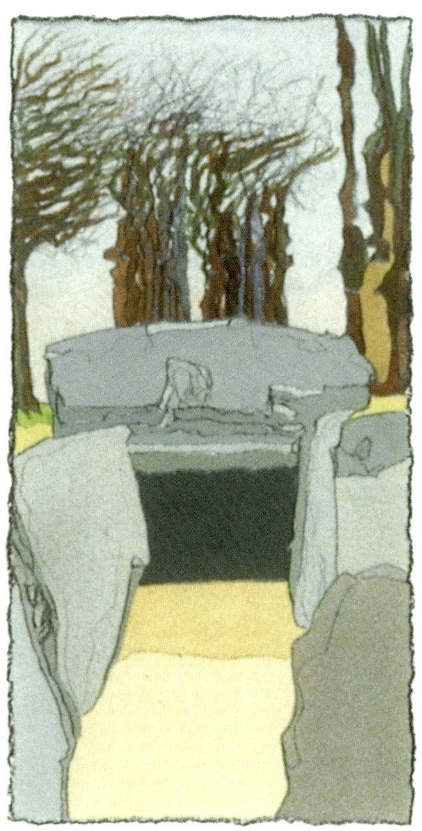

Entrance to the tomb

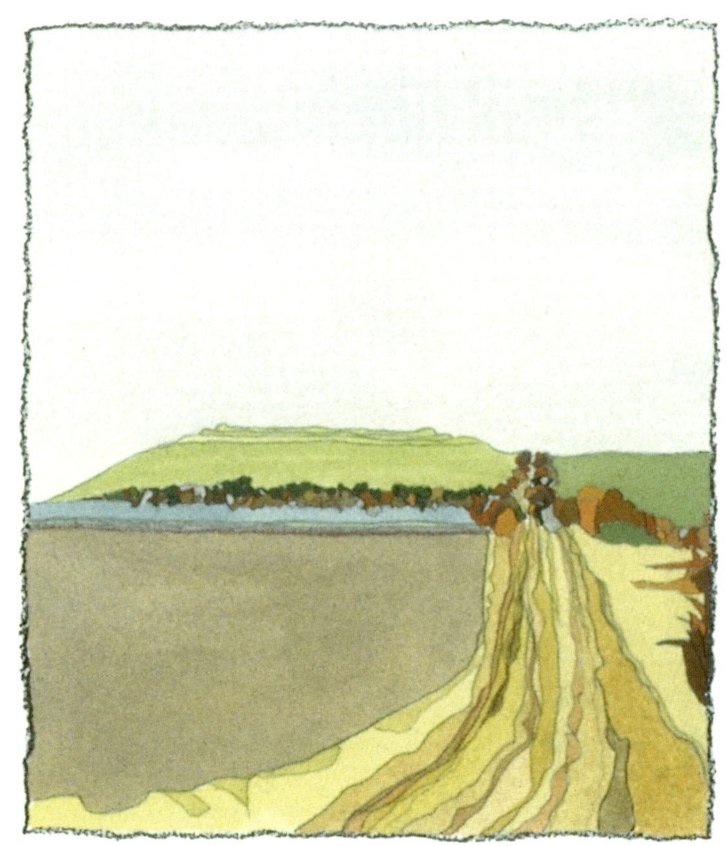

The Way rises to Uffington Castle

WALK FROM BISHOPSTONE TO WHITE HORSE HILL | 1986
gouache & pencil on paper
30×75

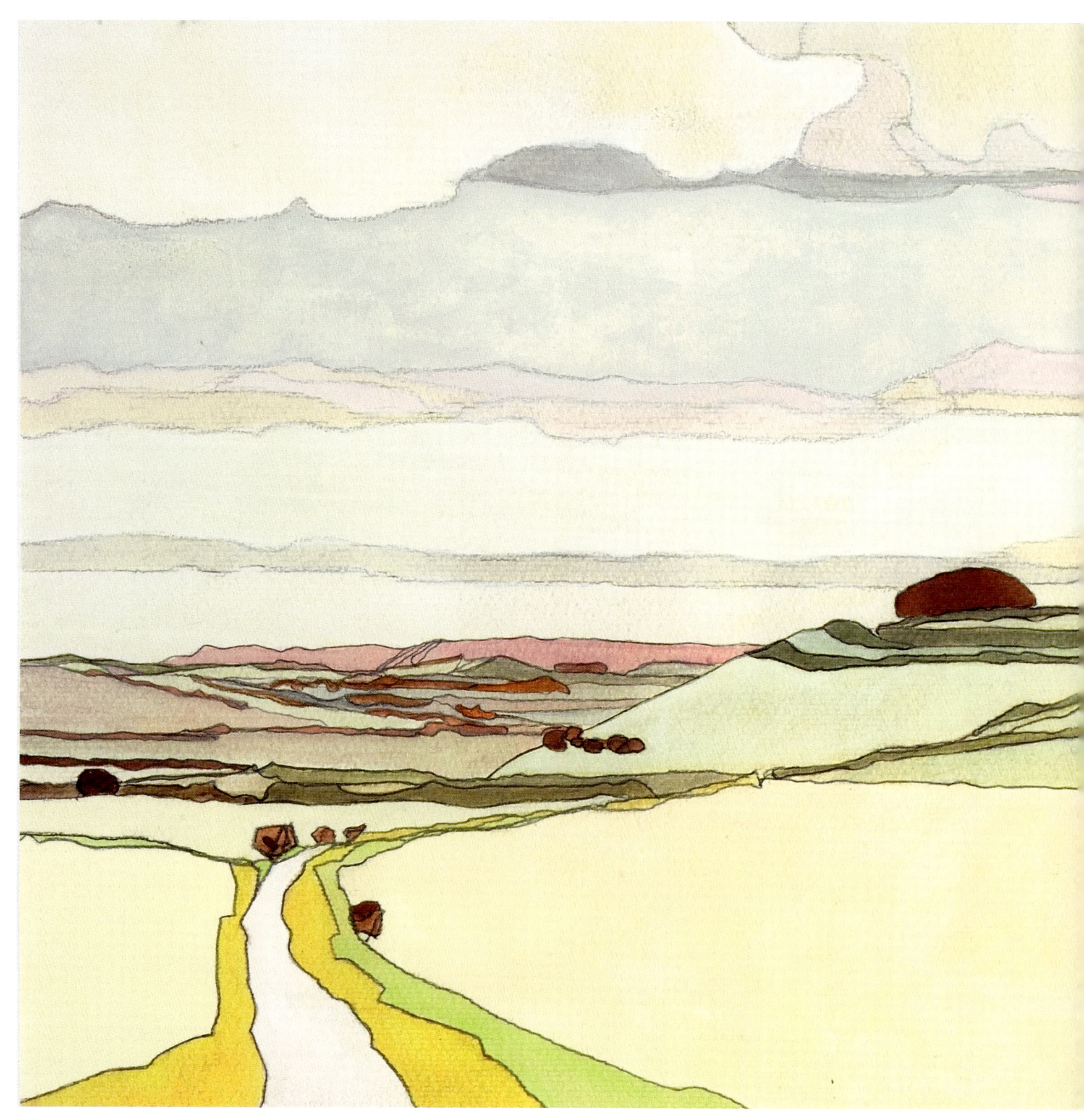

THE RIDGEWAY AND BARBURY CASTLE | 2009/10
print, acrylic & gouache on paper
32×65

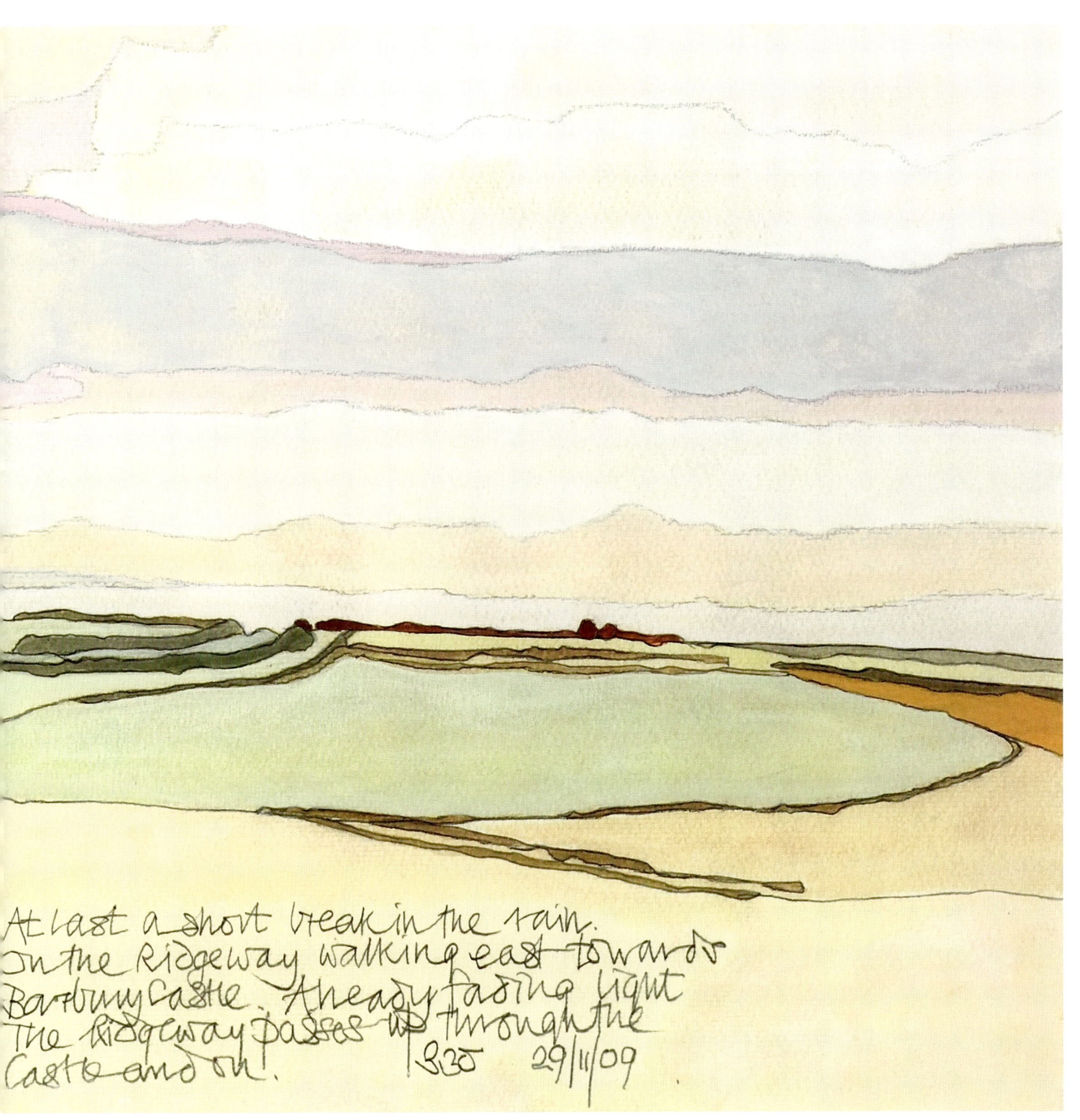

At last a short break in the rain.
On the Ridgeway walking east towards
Barbury Castle. Already fading light
The Ridgeway passes up through the
Castle and on.   3.35   29/11/09 .

BARBURY CASTLE | 1981
screenprint on paper
36×28

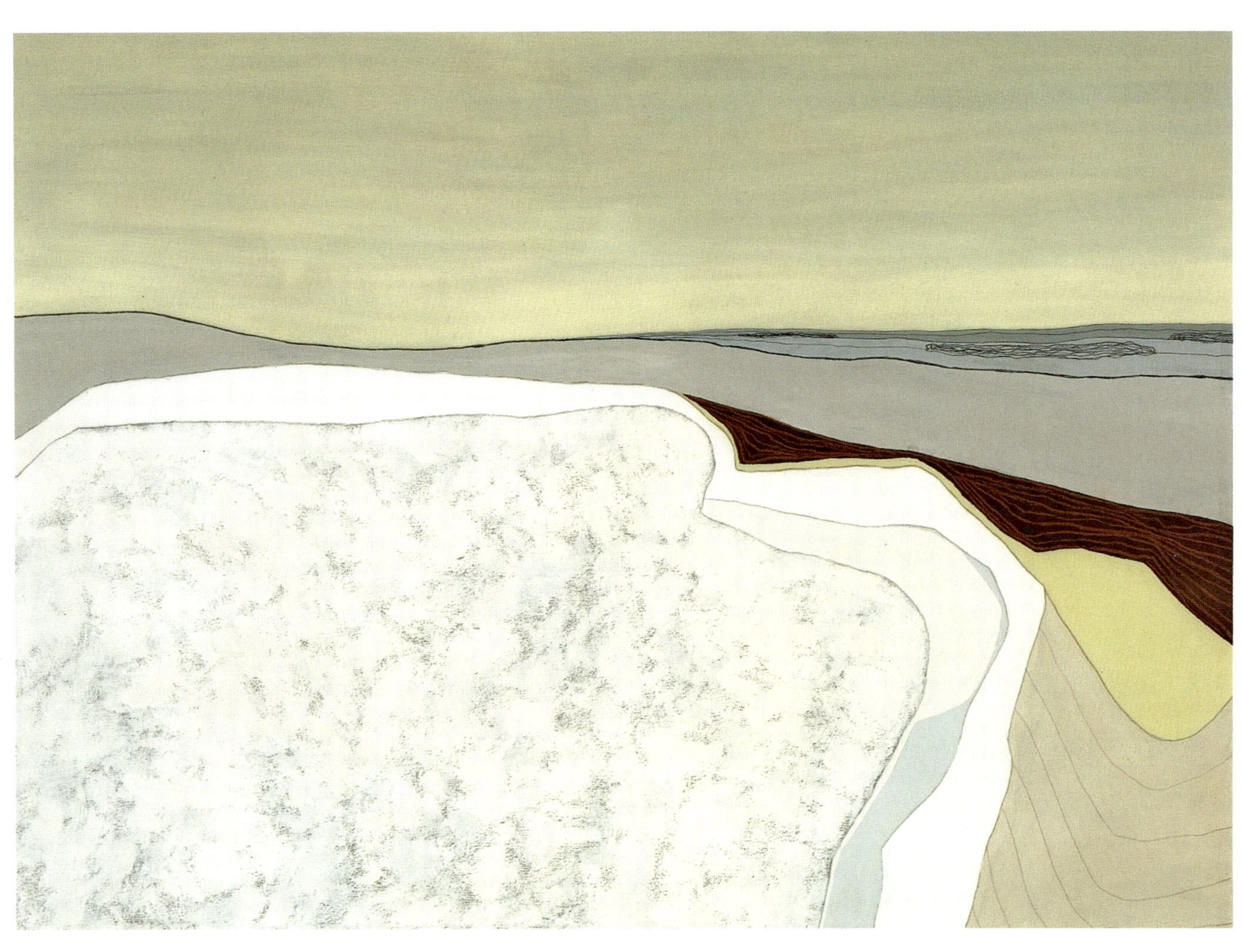

UFFINGTON CASTLE, BERKSHIRE | 1964
gouache on paper
82 × 100

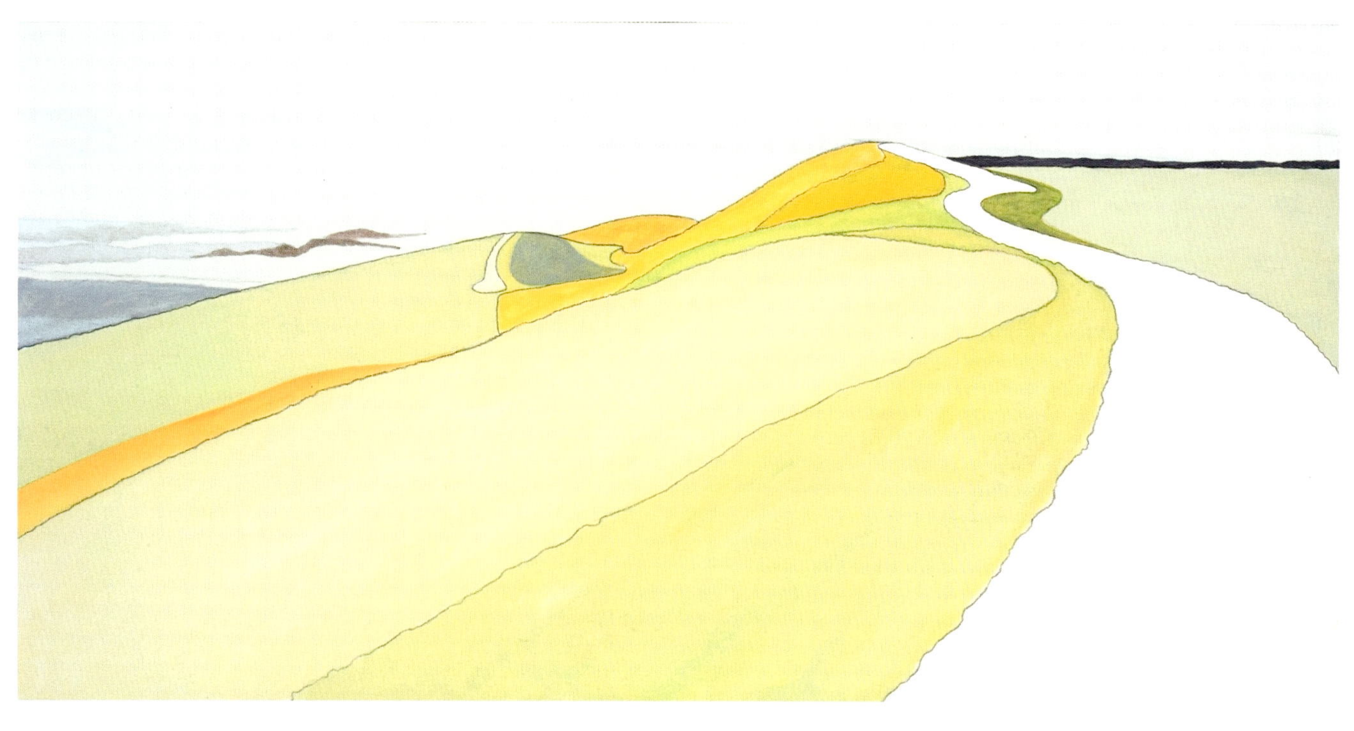

LOOKING EAST AT UFFINGTON FORT | 2003/04

gouache on paper

31 × 62

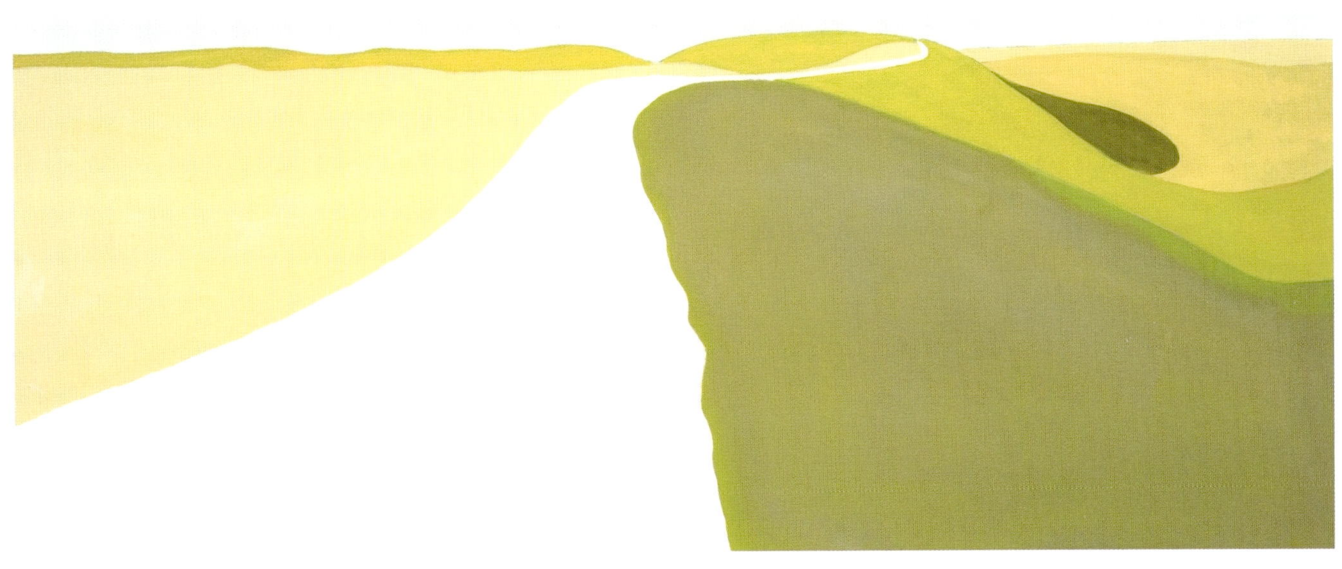

LOOKING SOUTH AT UFFINGTON FORT | 2003/04
gouache on paper
31 × 62

LOOKING WEST AT UFFINGTON FORT | 2003/04
gouache on paper
31×62

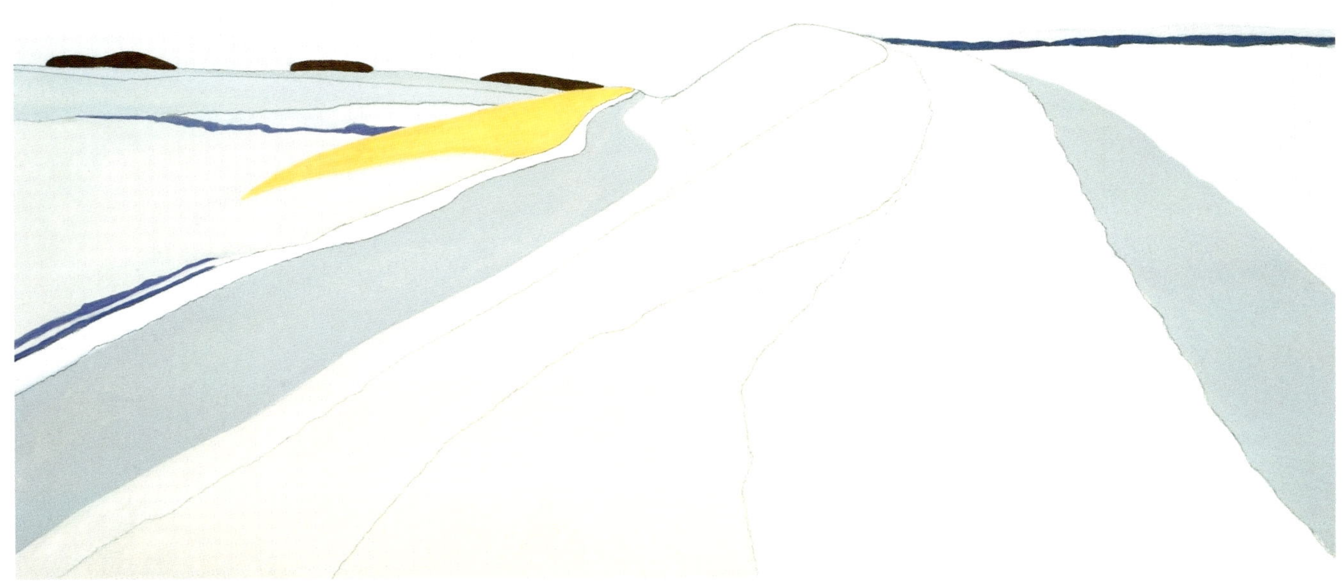

THREE CLUMPS OF BEECHES, UFFINGTON FORT | 2003/04
gouache on paper
31 × 62

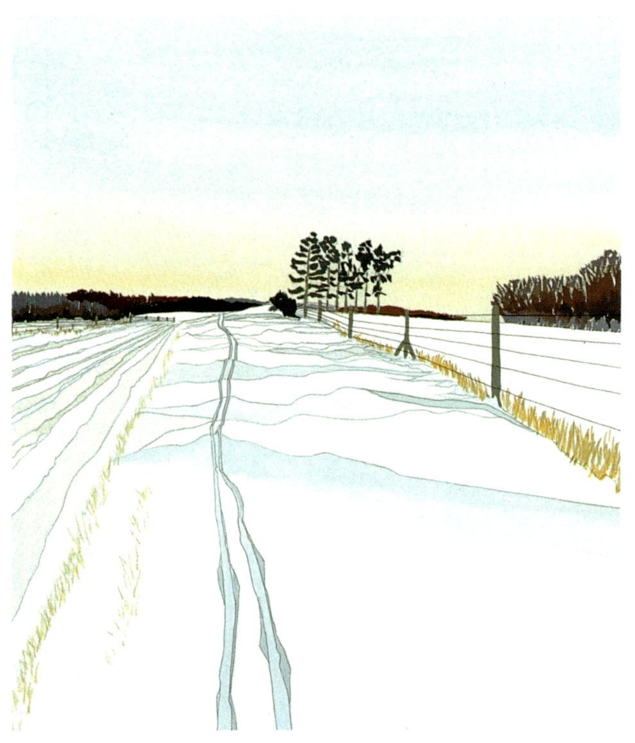 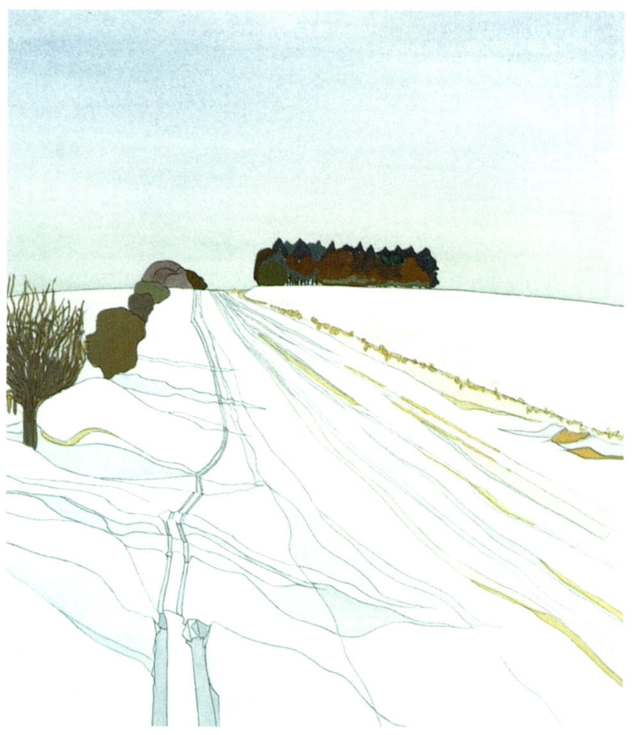

SKI TRACKS WEST | 1986
gouache on paper
32 × 22

SKI TRACKS EAST | 1986
gouache on paper
32 × 22

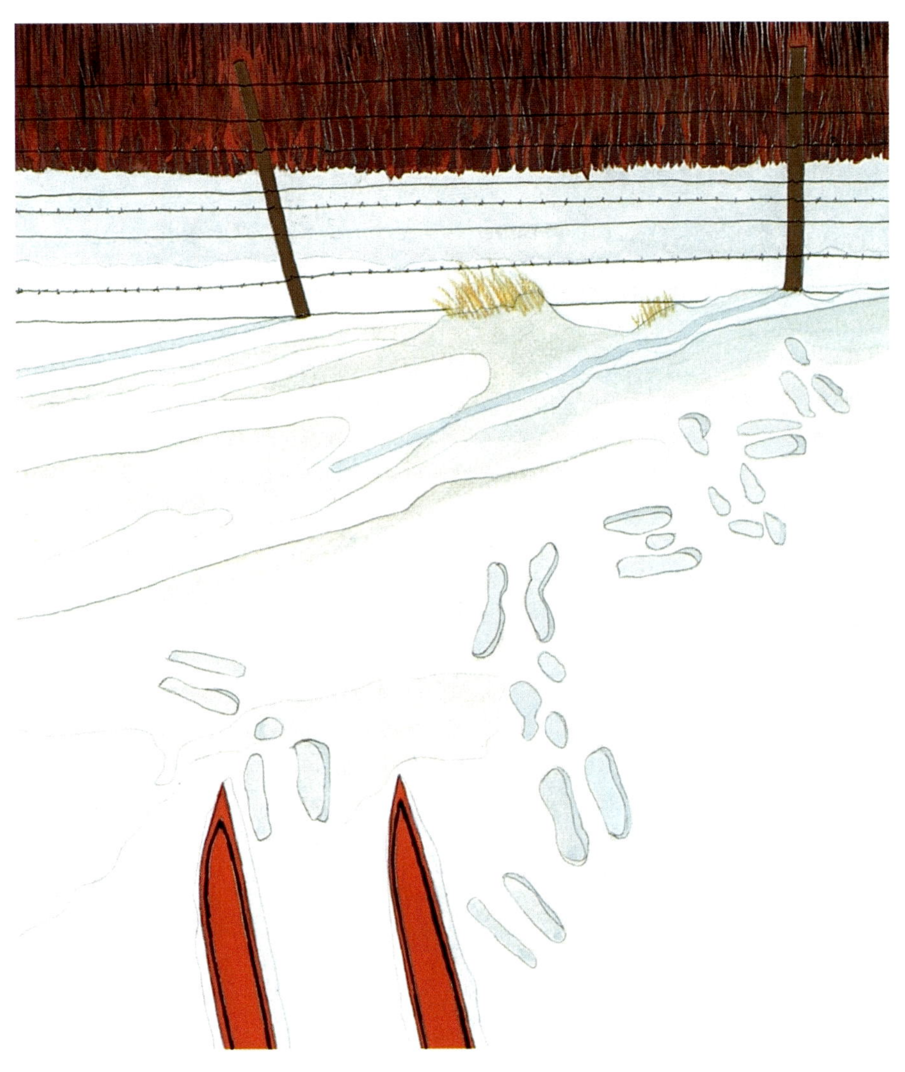

SKIS AND HARE TRACKS, RIDGEWAY | 1986
gouache on paper
32 × 28

SOUTH DOWNS WAY

Harting Downs to Beachy Head

The South Downs do not have the dramatic forms of the Yorkshire Peaks or the mountains of the Highlands, but in their own way they define the landscape of so much of the South East of England. The Downs are to me the most familiar land of all Britain. It was this landscape that I first painted. Indeed, some have commented that my paintings of the Downs are the most typical and distinctive of my work.

The South Downs Way runs for eighty miles from Hampshire to East Sussex. I know best the eastern end, where the Downs approach the sea and finally finish in the dramatic chalk cliffs of the Seven Sisters and Beachy Head. Throughout the year I walk the ridges and valleys here. As I write this, I have in my mind the images of the past two days, and in particular the way that the smooth, rounded forms suddenly come to the sheer white of the cliffs (pp. 188 and 189).

It is the landscape to which I return over and over again, to the curved forms and the changing patterns of the chalk fields. I watch the colours alter throughout the seasons. Most dramatic is when the ploughed fields become so pale, almost white, as the earth is leached away by the winter rains and the chalk becomes more and more prominent.

In walking these Downs over the years one notices the gradual change in agricultural trends. Up until the last war they were pure grasslands made over to sheep. Then during the war they were largely ploughed and cultivated. Since then the pattern of crops has varied, and now the sheep seem to be making a comeback, at least around where we live.

Right along the Downs there are numerous signs of ancient habitation, in particular the tumuli dotted along the chalk ridge. This ridge is a very ancient track. I quite recently walked the west end of the South Downs and was struck by the contrast between the way the tumuli of the Iron Age or earlier sat in the contours, but the Roman road (from Chichester to London) cut across them in a defiant straight line (pp. 174 and 175). What a contrast to the curves of the Downs!

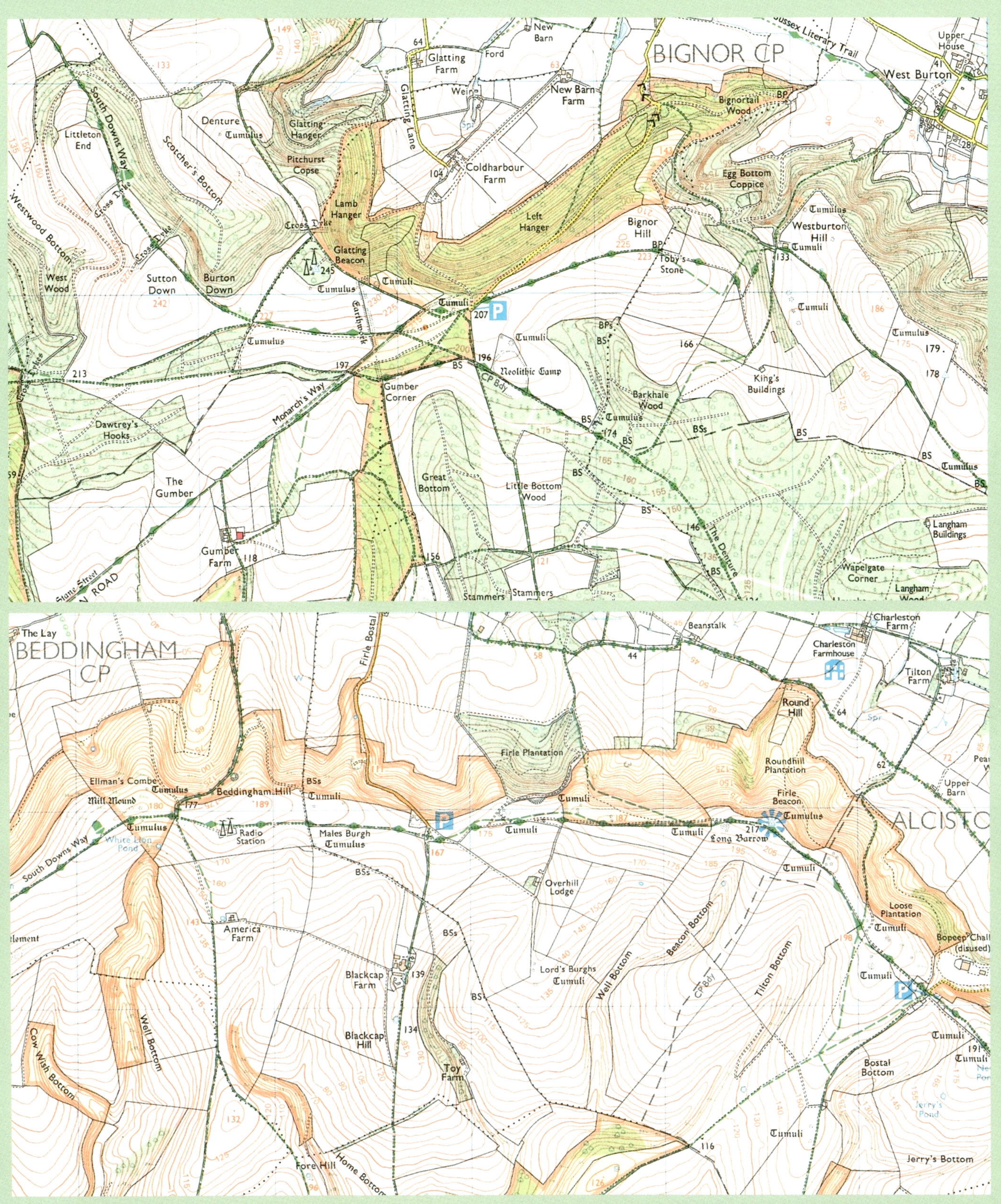

BIGNOR CP
Sussex Literary Trail
Upper House
West Burton
New Barn
Glatting Farm
Ford
New Barn Farm
Weir
Bignortail Wood
Egg Bottom Coppice
Denture
Glatting Hanger
Littleton End
Tumulus
Pitchurst Copse
Coldharbour Farm
104
Scotcher's Bottom
Lamb Hanger
Left Hanger
Bignor Hill
Tumulus
Westburton Hill
Westwood Bottom
Cross Dyke
Glatting Beacon
Tumuli
Cross Dyke
245
Toby's Stone
133
South Downs Way
West Wood
Sutton Down
Burton Down
242
Tumulus
BPs
BS
166
Tumuli
186
West Wood
207
BS
179
178
213
197
196
Neolithic Camp
King's Buildings
Dawtrey's Hooks
Gumber Corner
BS Bdy
Barkhale Wood
BSs
BS
Monarch's Way
Tumulus
174
BS
BS
The Gumber
Great Bottom
Little Bottom Wood
165
160
155
Tumulus
Gumber Farm
118
156
160
146
The Denture
Langham Buildings
Stane Street
ROAD
Stammers
Stammers
121
BS
Wapelgate Corner
Langham Wood
The Lay
BEDDINGHAM CP
Beanstalk
Charleston Farmhouse
Charleston Farm
44
Tilton Farm
Firle Bostal
58
Round Hill
64
Firle Plantation
Roundhill Plantation
62
Upper Barn
Elliman's Combe
Tumulus
Mill Mound
Beddingham Hill
Tumuli
Tumuli
Firle Beacon
Tumulus
ALCISTON
177
BSs
189
Radio Station
Males Burgh Tumulus
75
Long Barrow
217
South Downs Way
White Lion Pond
180
Tumulus
167
Tumuli
188
Tumuli
Loose Plantation
170
160
BSs
Overhill Lodge
170
Tumuli
America Farm
143
BSs
Bopeep Chalk (disused)
Blackcap Farm
139
BSs
Lord's Burghs Tumuli
Beacon Bottom
Tilton Bottom
Tumuli
Cow Wish Bottom
Well Bottom
Blackcap Hill
134
BS
Toy Farm
Well Bottom
Jerry's Pond
132
116
Tumuli
Bostal Bottom
Fore Hill
Home Bottom
Jerry's Bottom

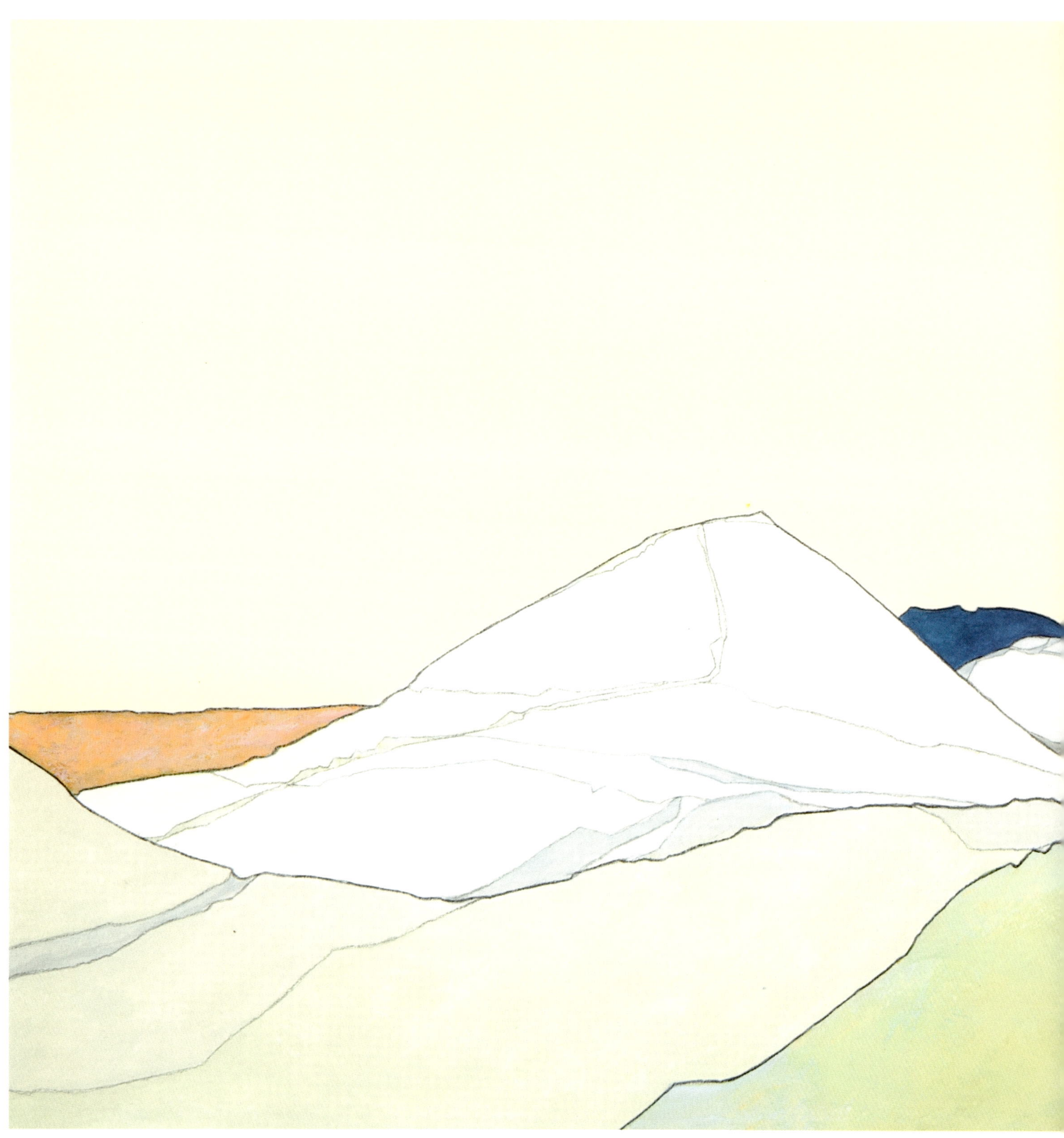

 SOUTH DOWNS WAY

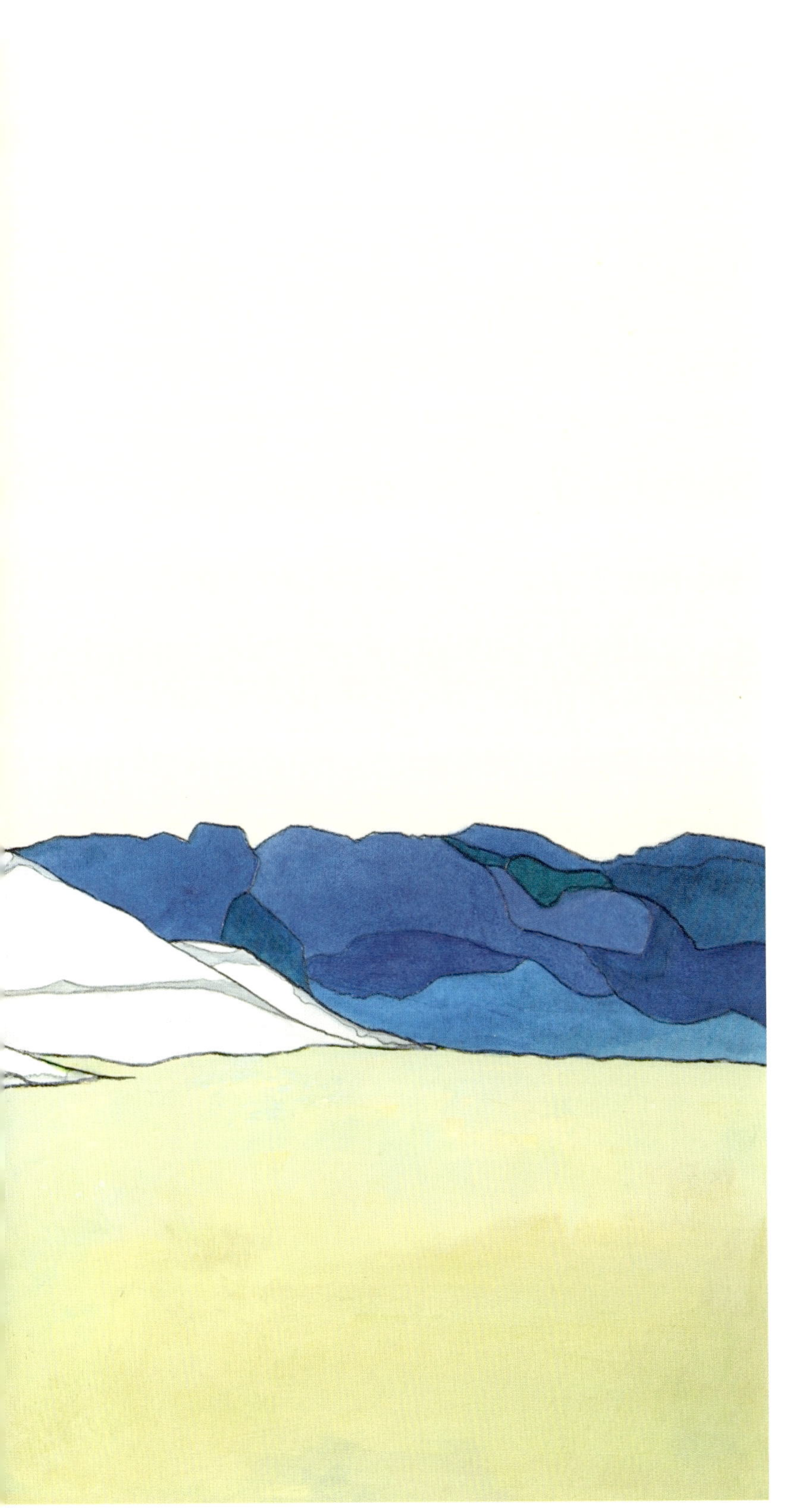

THE DEVIL'S JUMPS | 2010
aquacryl & gouache on paper
32 × 50

While here, I am exposed to two radically
different air displays. First, two huge
helicopters circling lower and lower.
I suppose they are training for Afghanistan.

Second, in contrast, three beautiful silent
white gliders going back and forth along the
escarpment of the Downs. A perfect day for
them with the wind from the north!

3 PM 11 OCT 2010

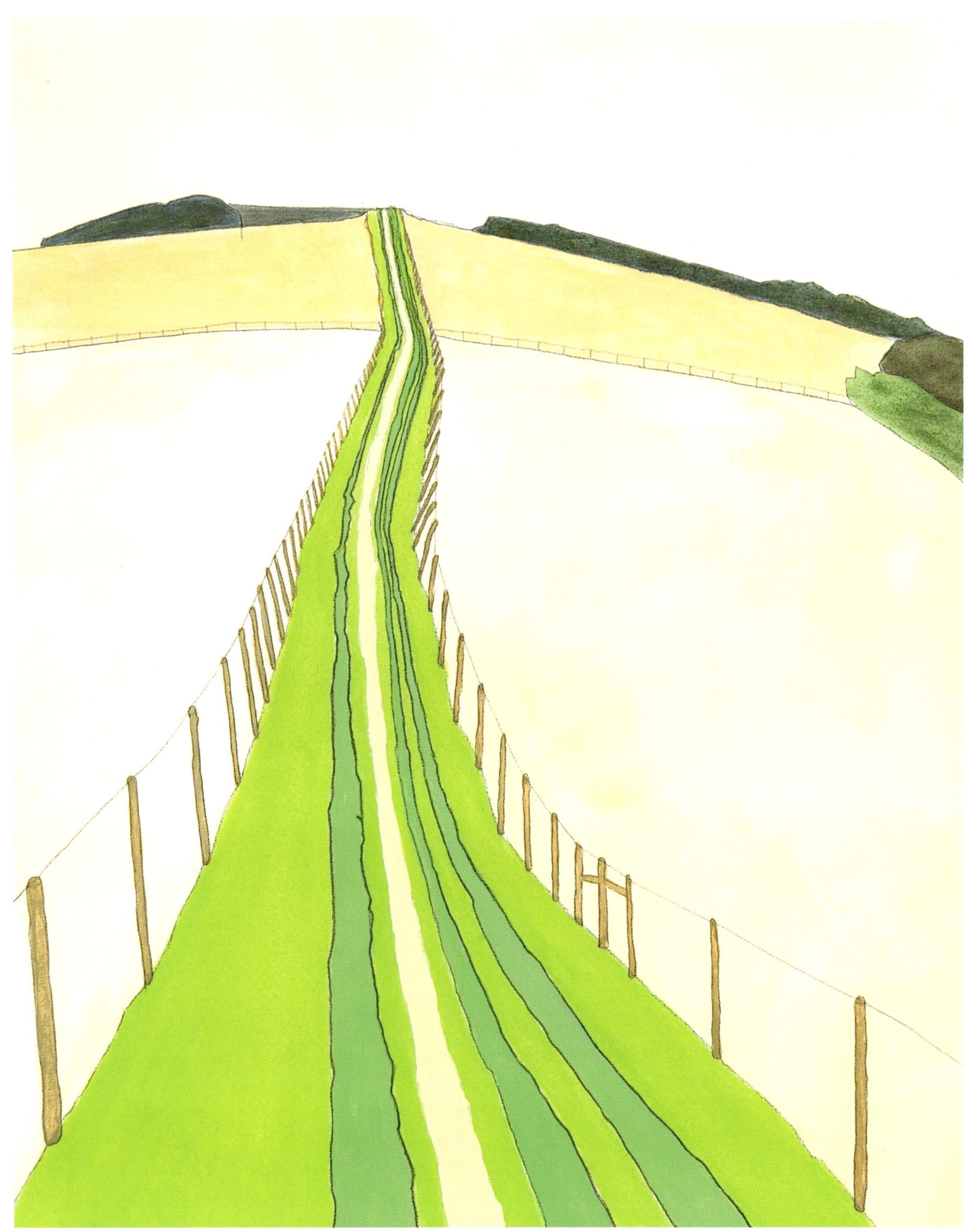

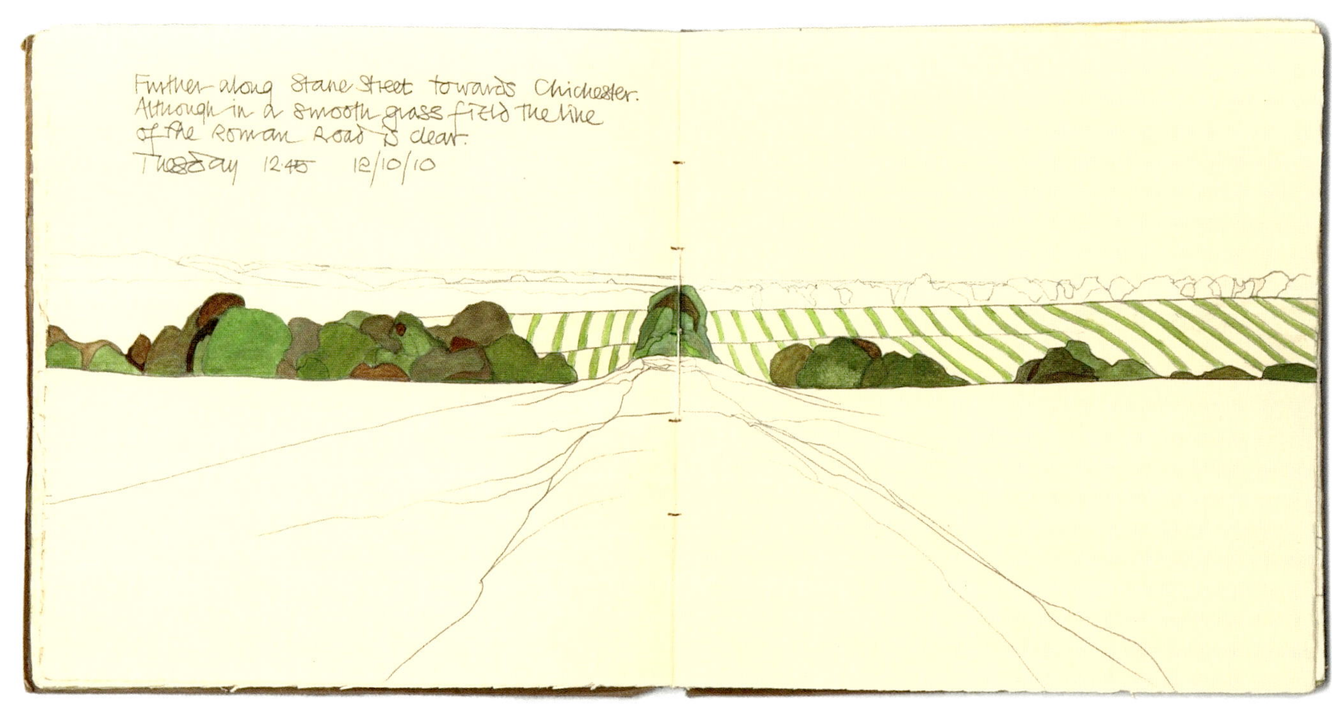

STANE STREET, 12 OCT 2010
NOTEBOOK | 2010
pencil & gouache on paper
22 × 44

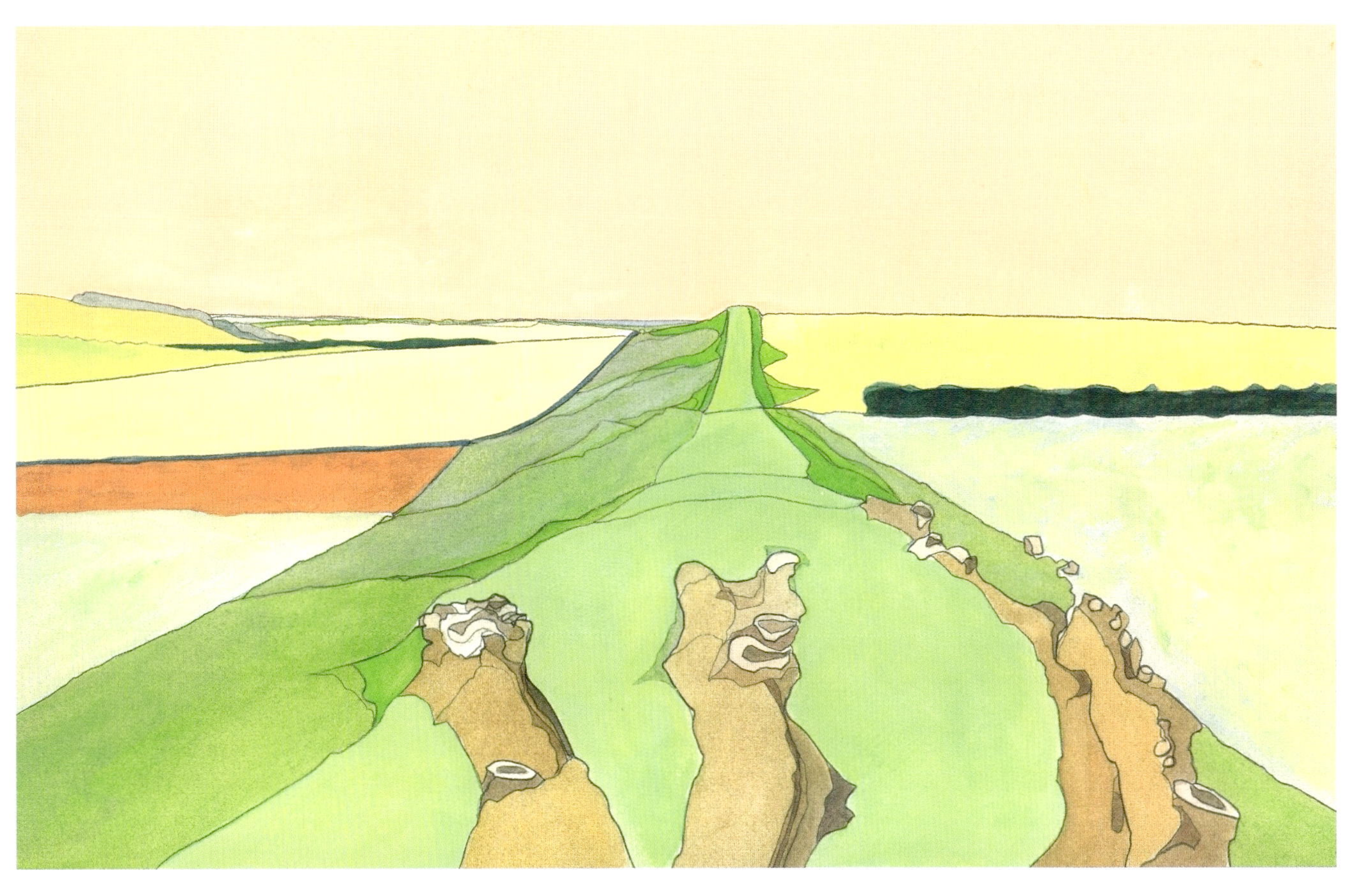

STANE STREET: THE ROMAN ROAD | 2010
aquacryl & gouache on paper
32 × 50

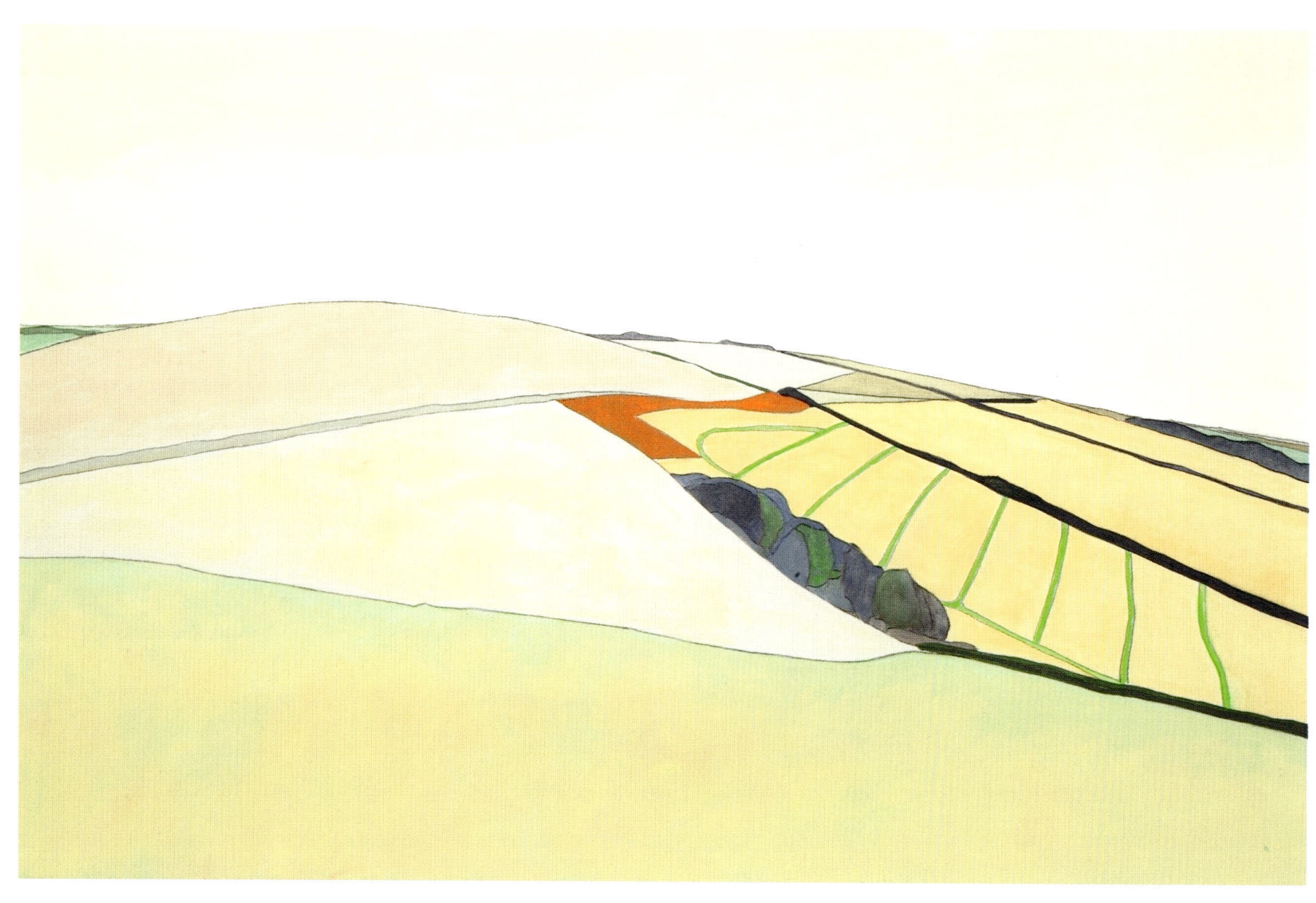

WEST BURTON HILL | 2010
aquacryl & gouache on paper
32 × 50

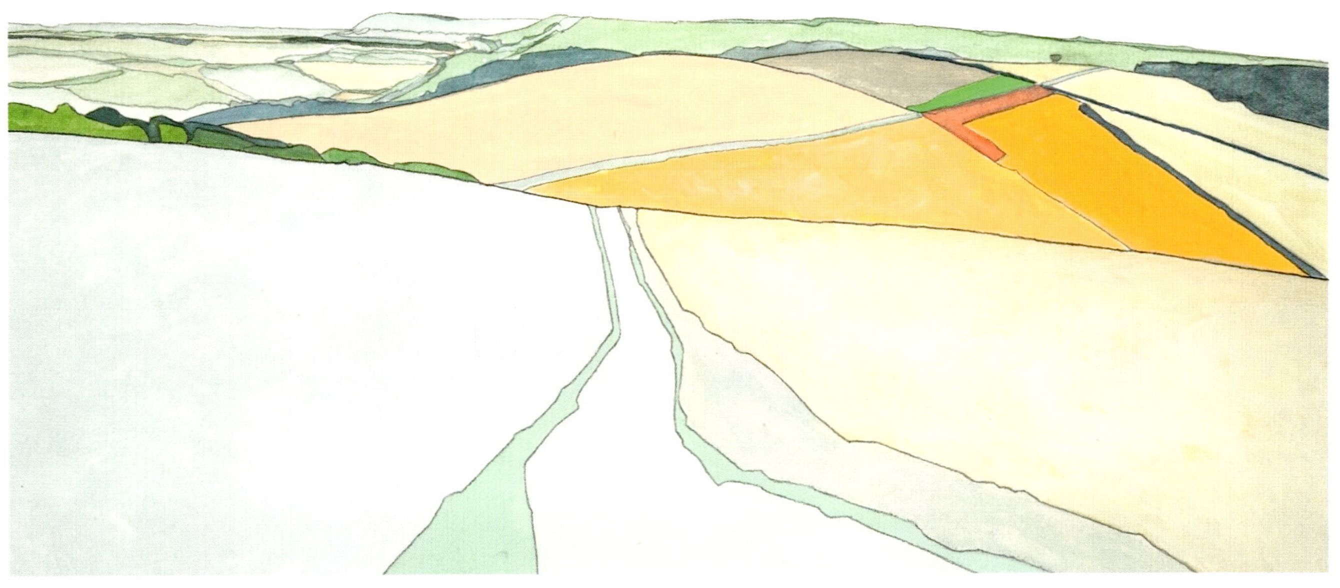

BIGNOR HILL, LOOKING EAST | 2010
aquacryl & gouache on paper
32 × 50

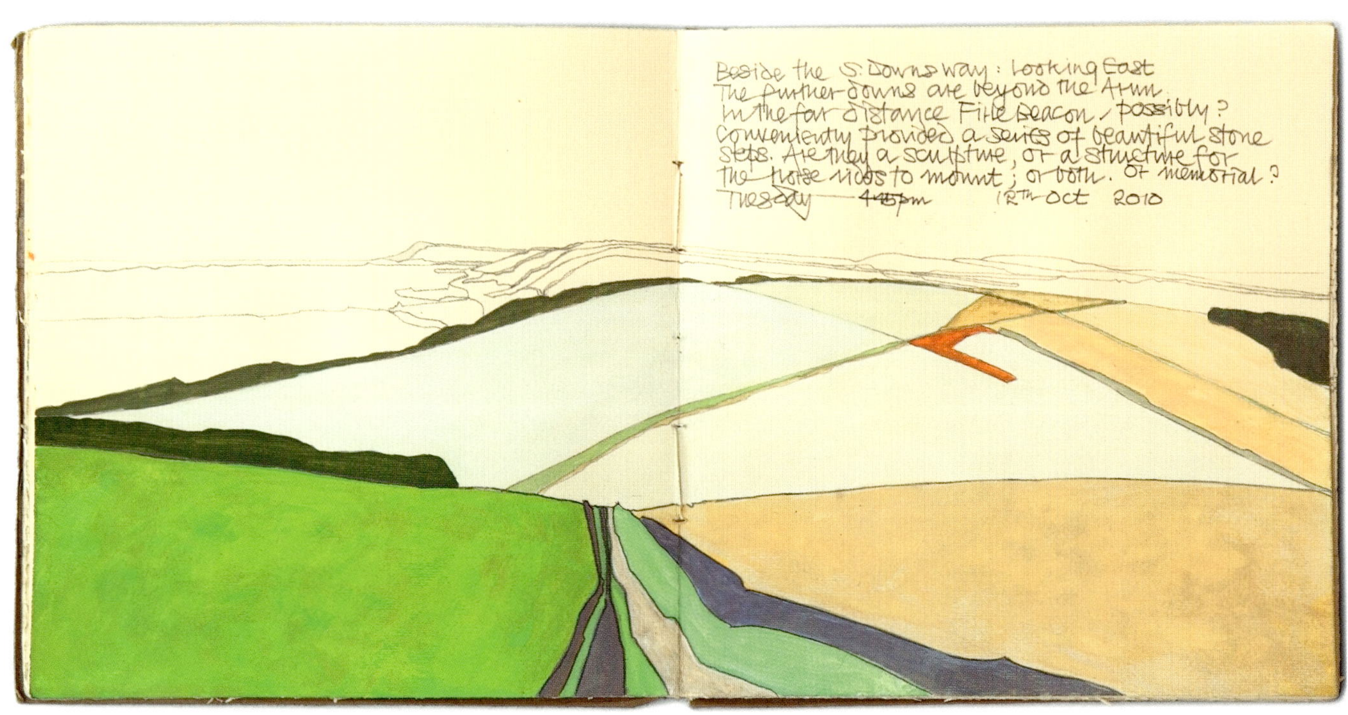

BIGNOR HILL, 12 OCT 2010

NOTEBOOK | 2010

pencil & gouache on paper

22 × 44

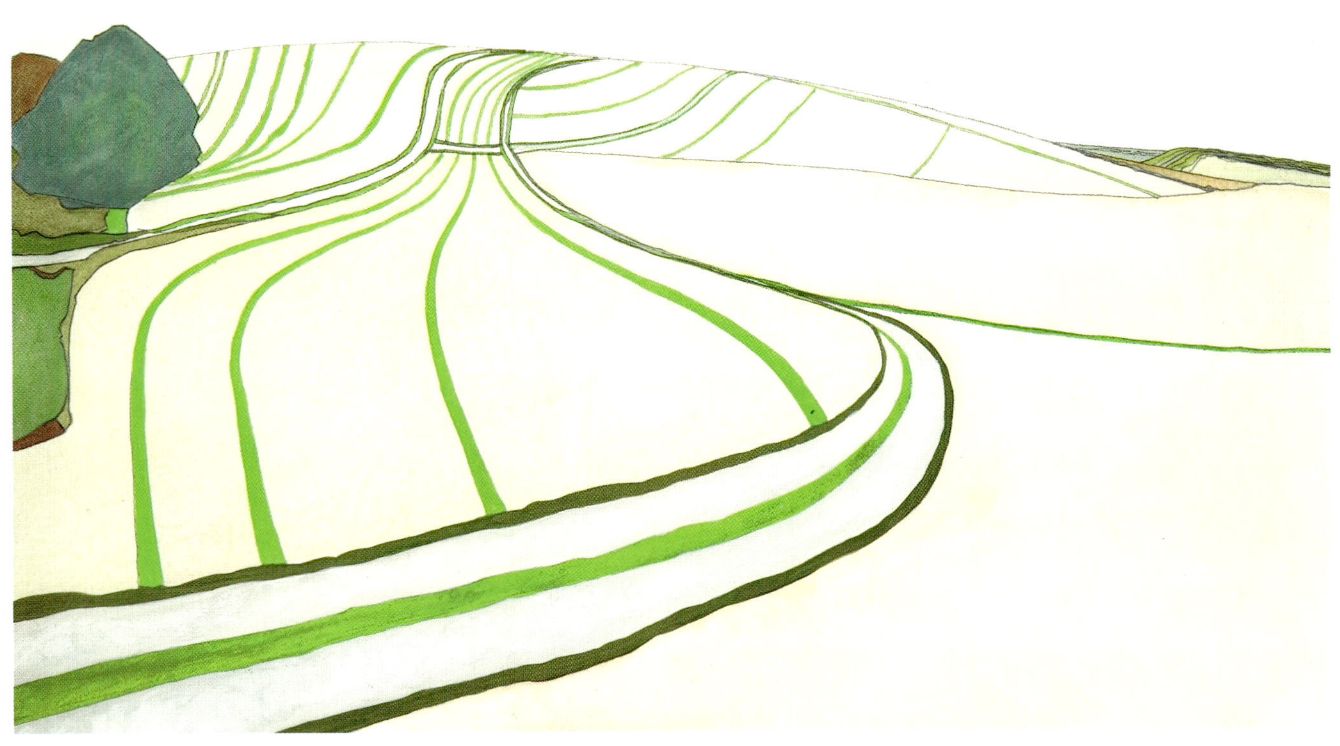

SOUTH DOWNS WAY CROSSES BIGNOR HILL | 2010
aquacryl & gouache on paper
32 × 50

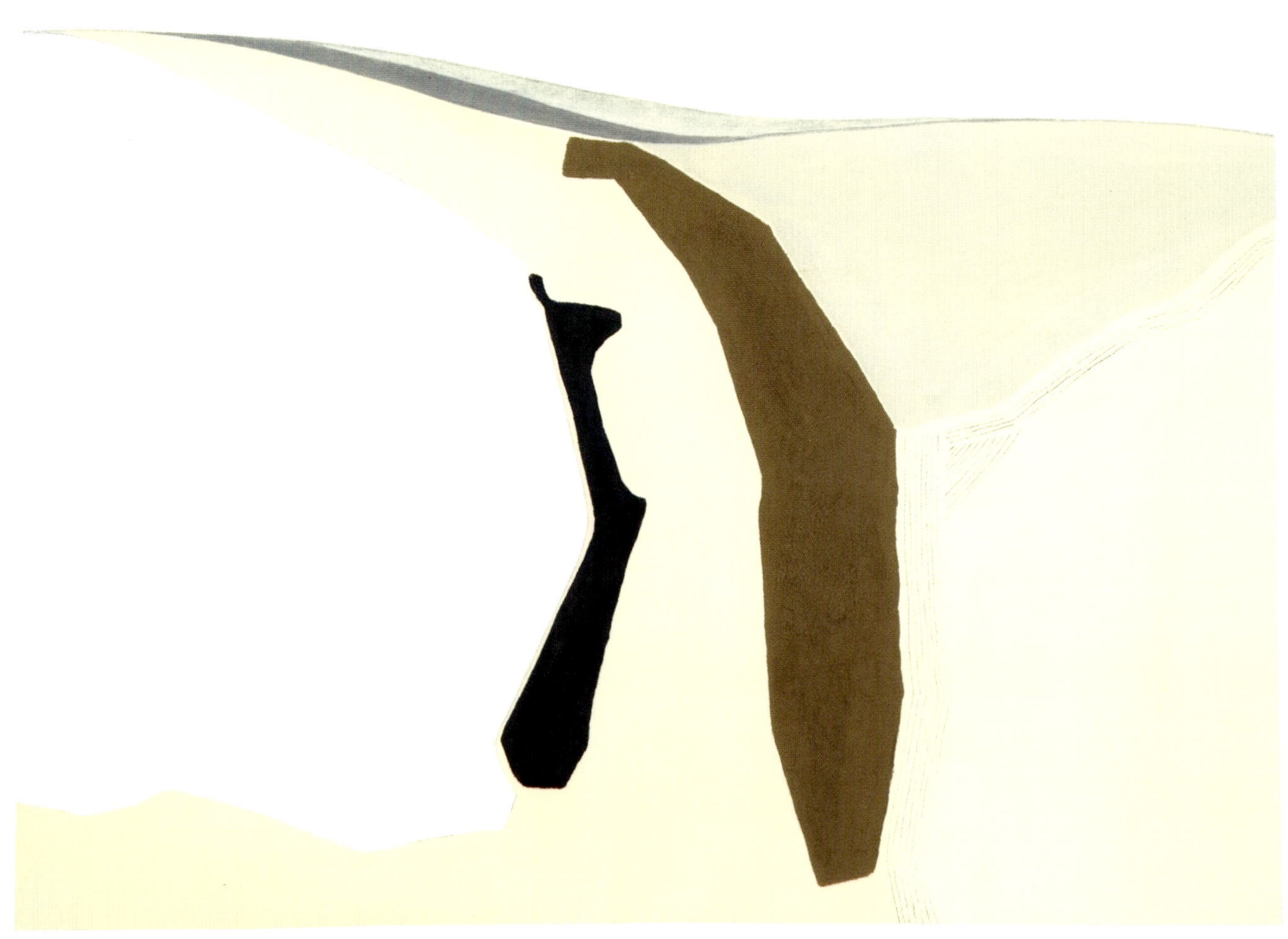

BOSTAL BOTTOM | 1974
gouache on paper
30×34

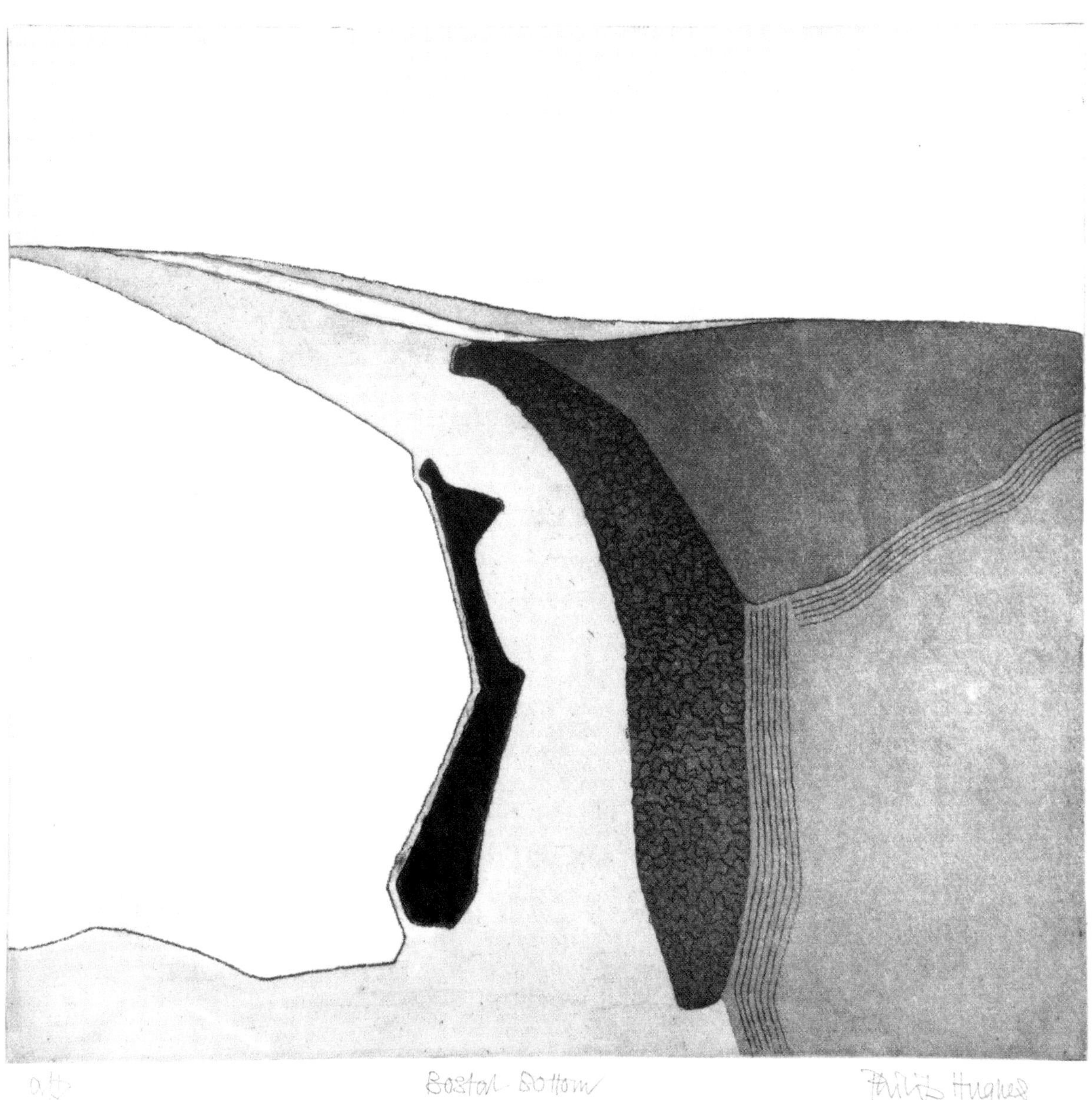

BOSTAL BOTTOM | 2010
etching on paper
48×53

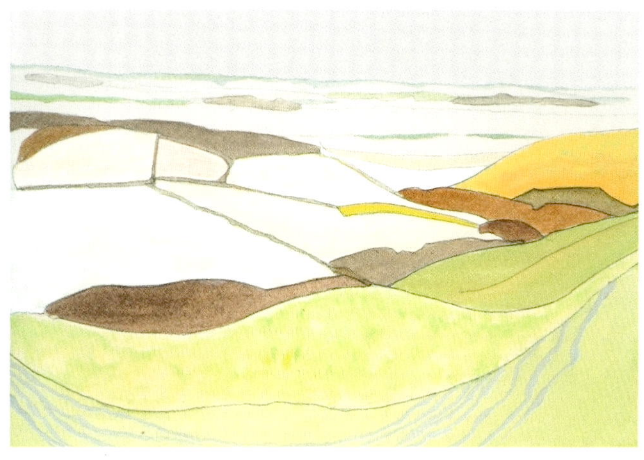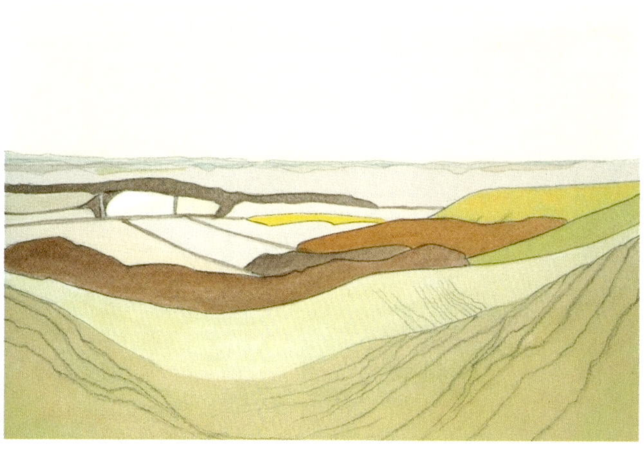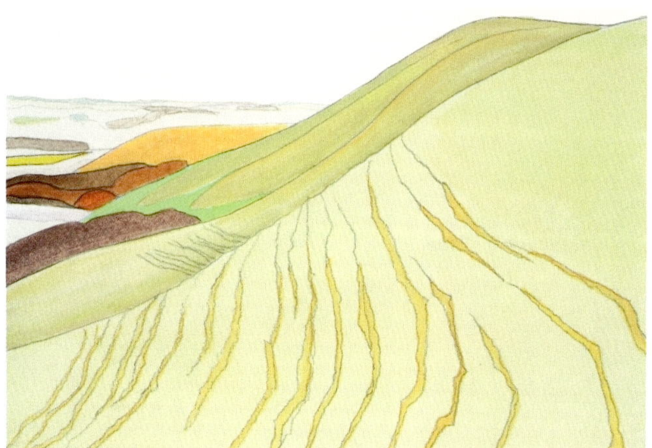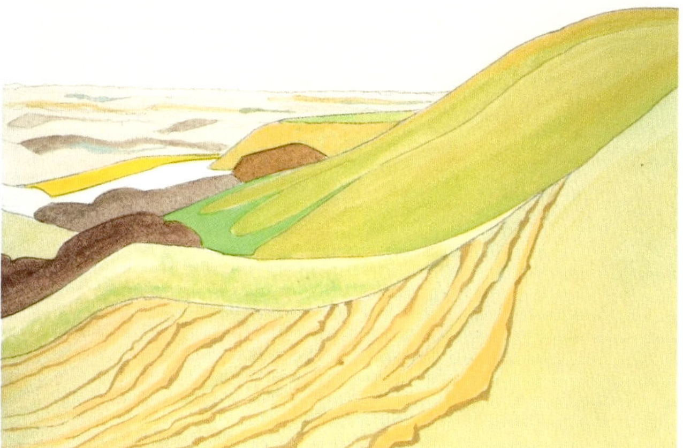

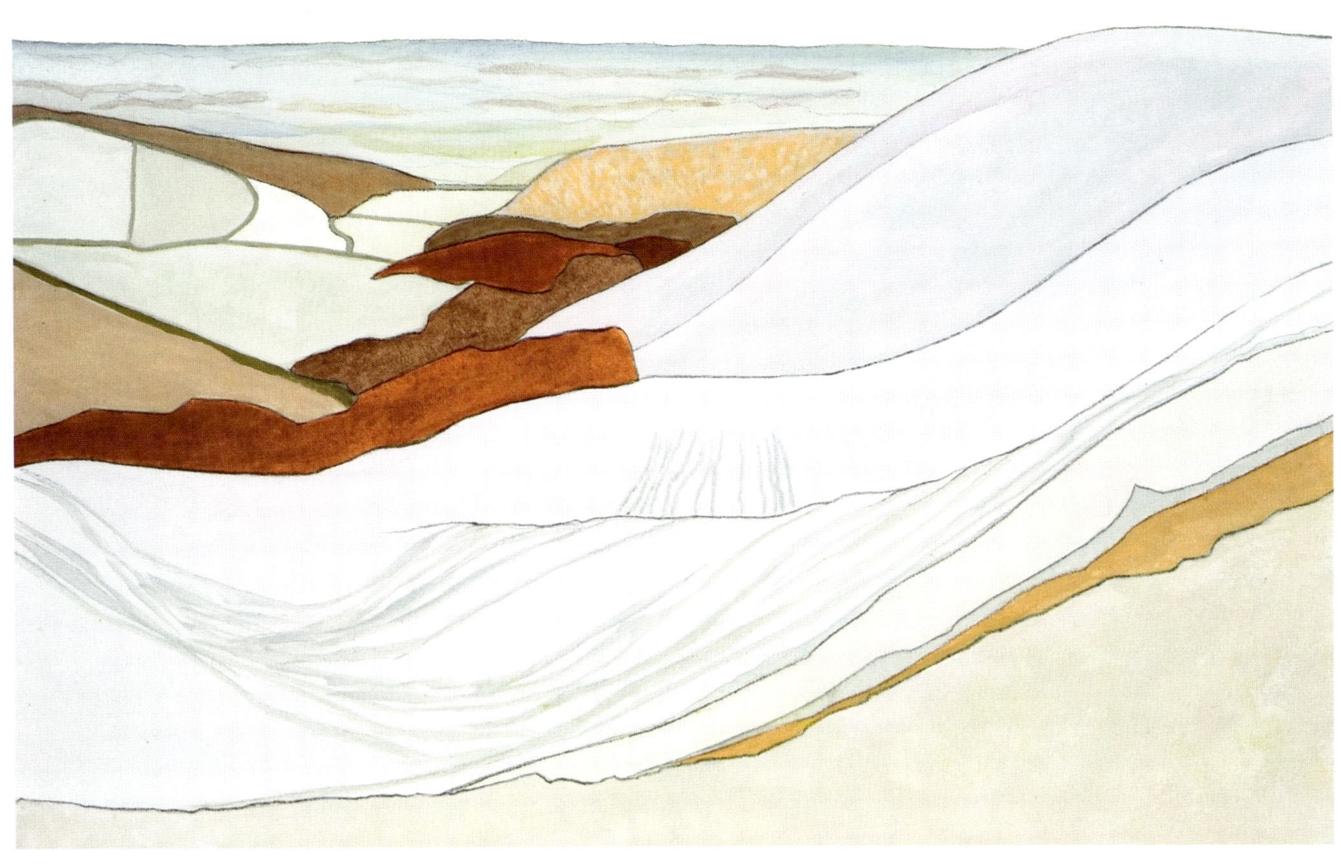

DESCENDING TO FIRLE | 2011/12
gouache & acrylic on paper
25 × 37

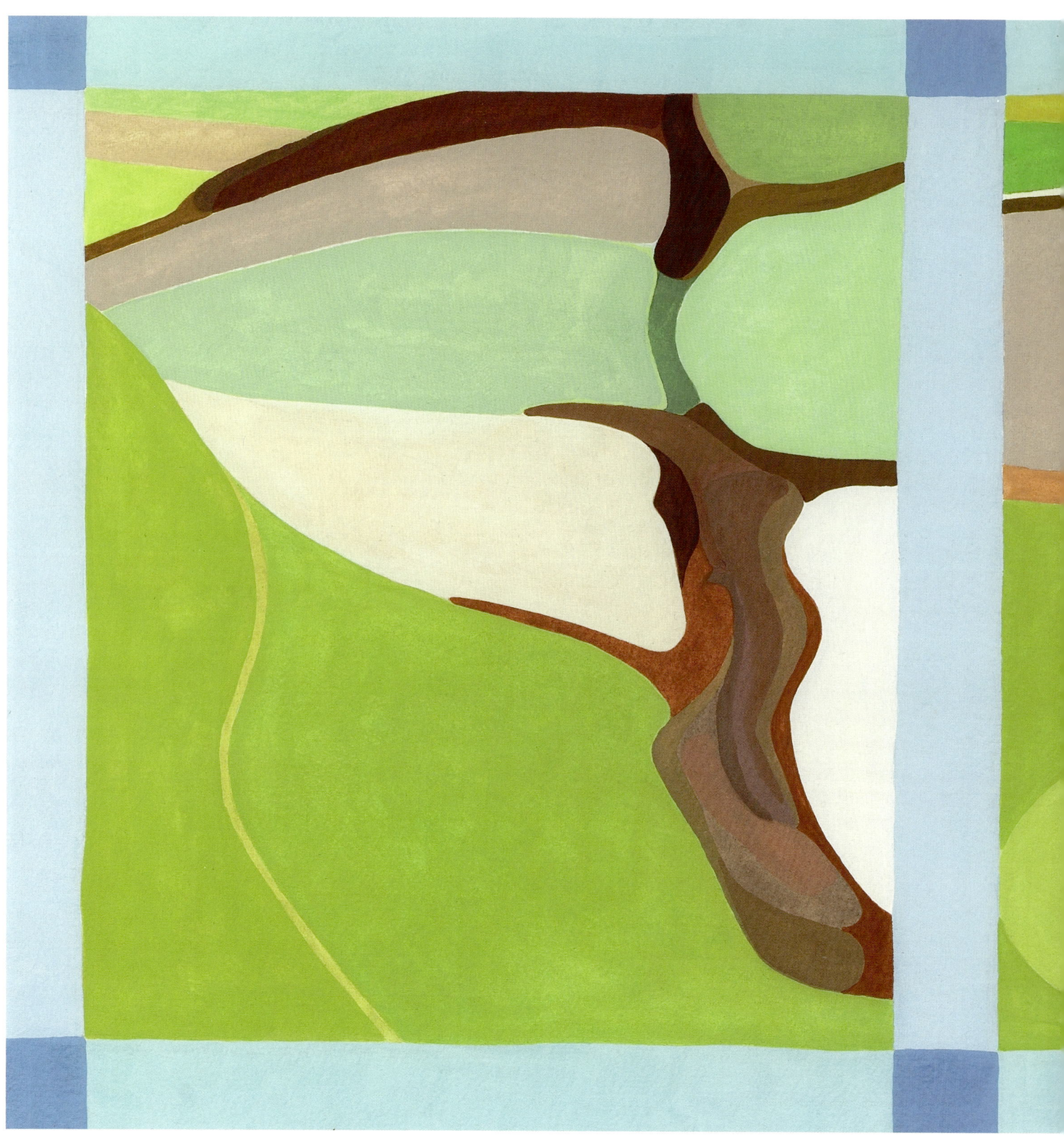

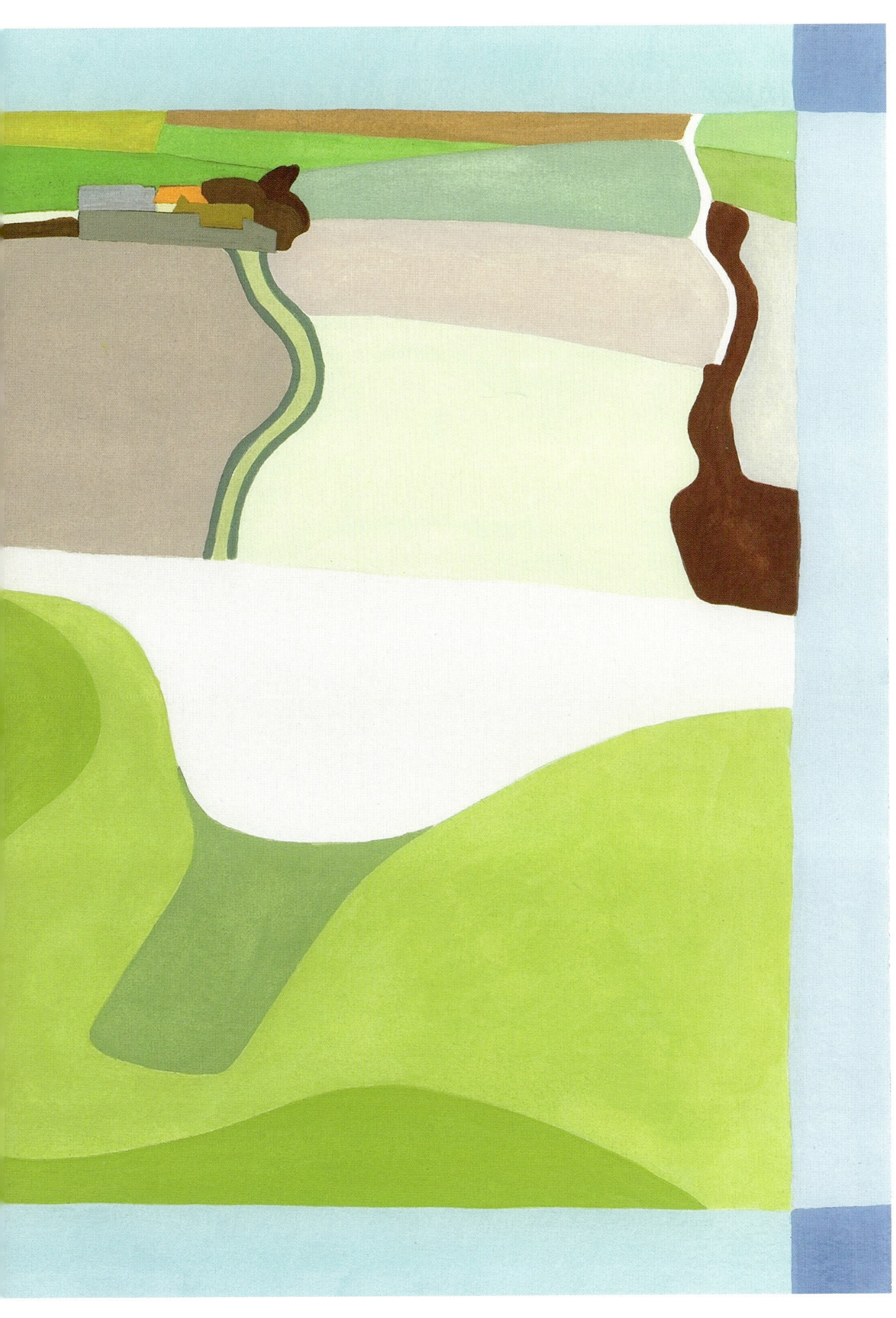

ABOVE CHARLESTON: MARCH | 1993
gouache on paper
44×76

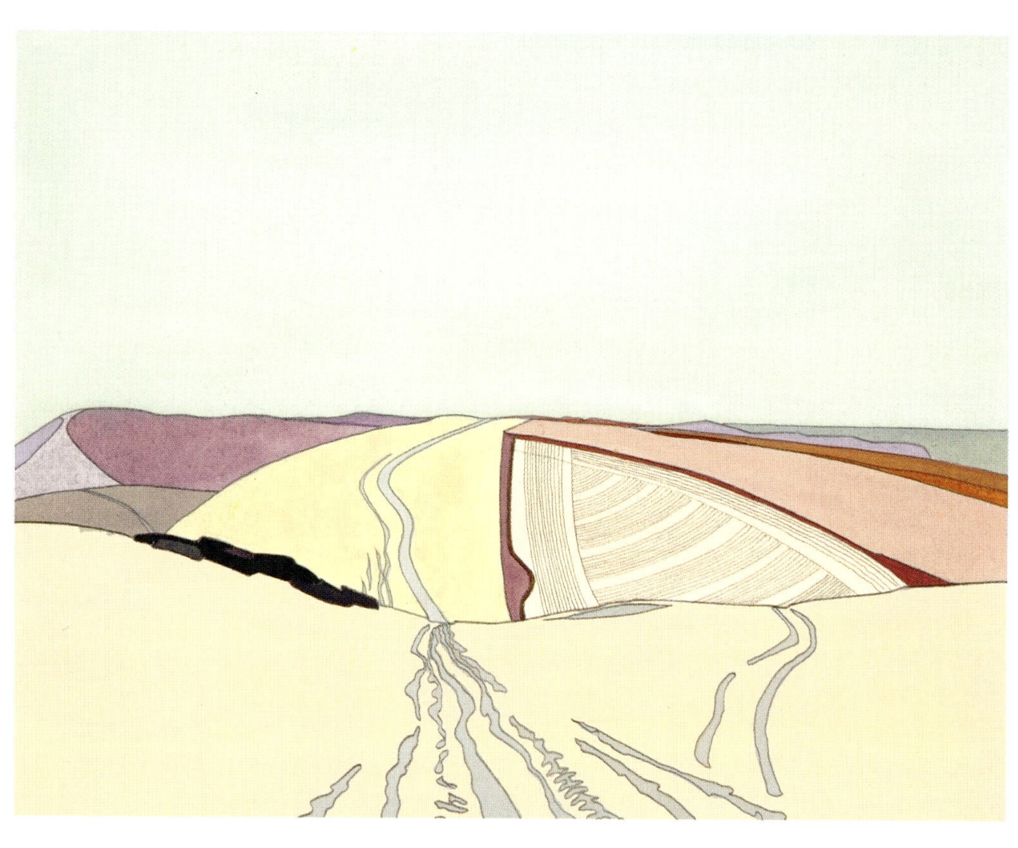

SOUTH DOWNS WAY: TOWARDS ALFRISTON | 1982
gouache on paper
23 × 29

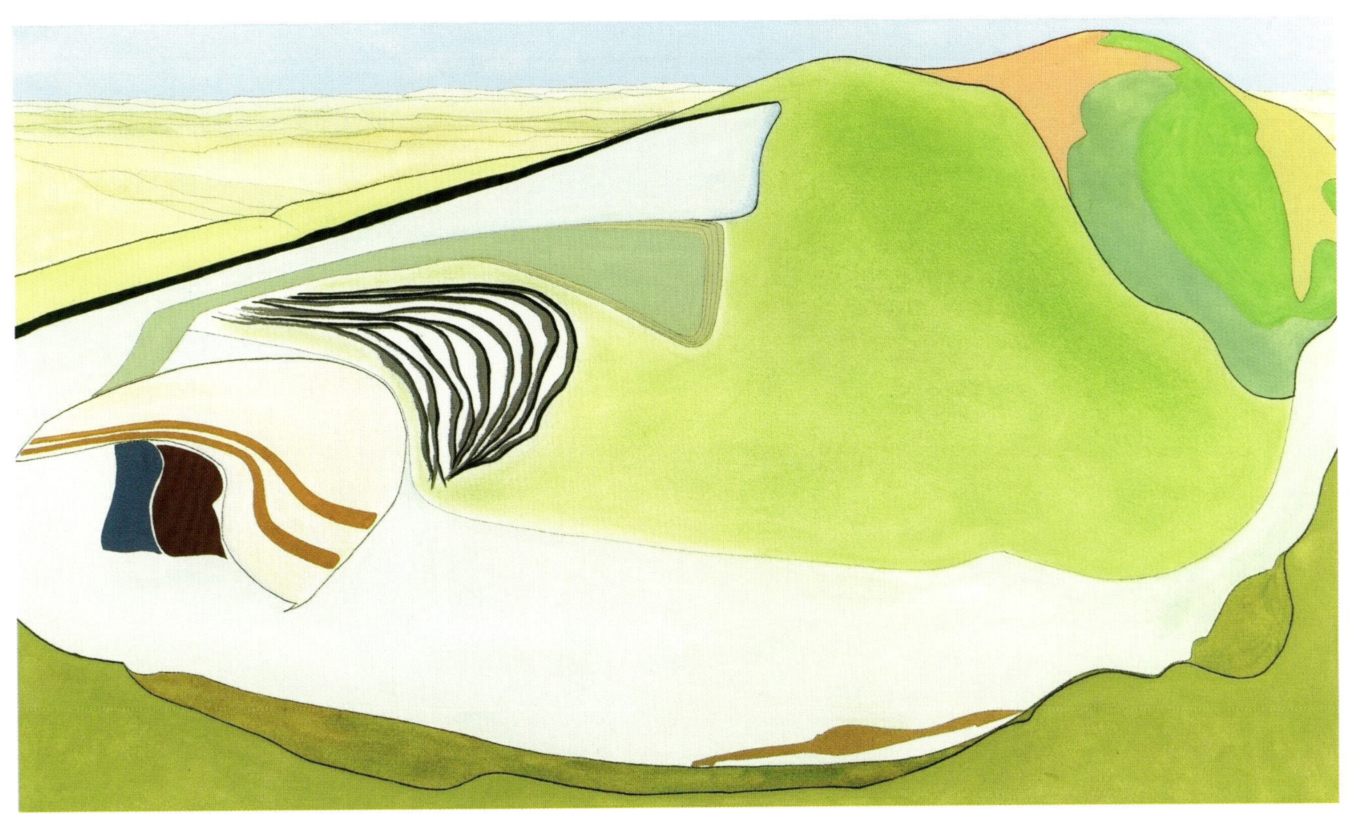

WINDOVER | 1991/93
acrylic, gouache & pastel on paper
44 × 76

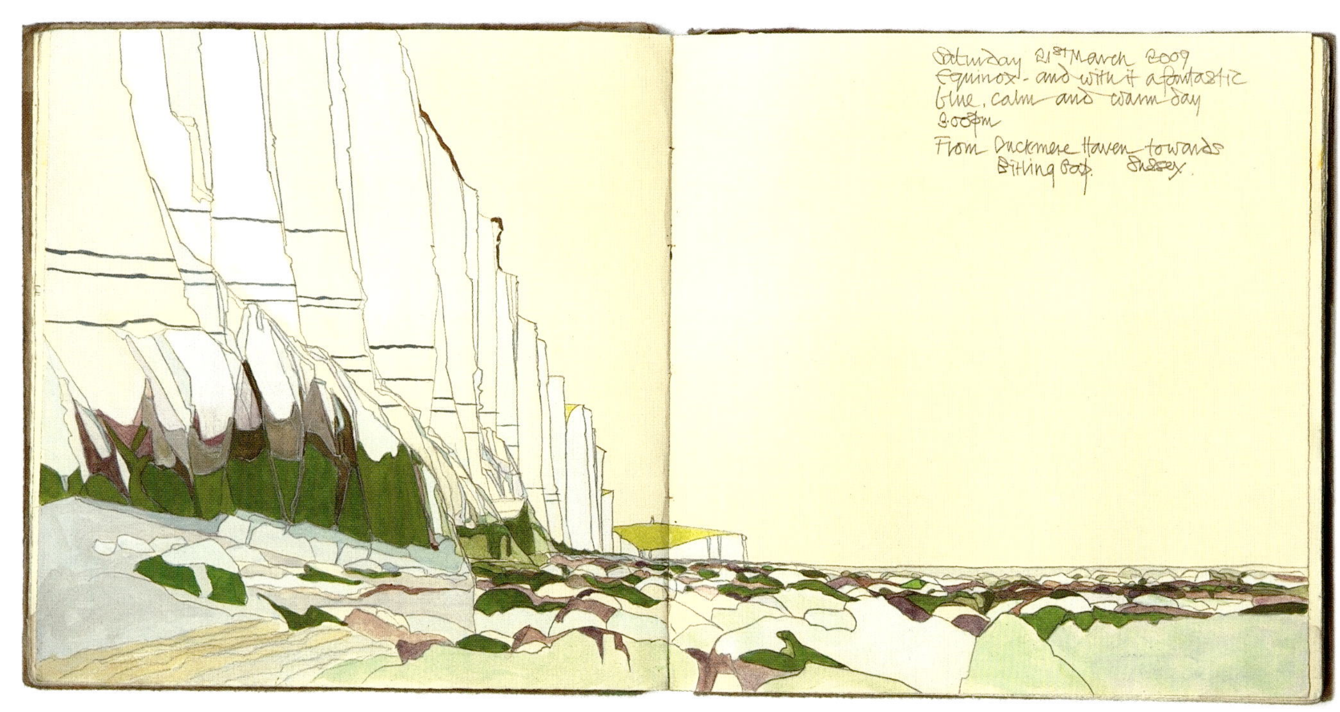

CUCKMERE HAVEN, 21 MAR 2009
NOTEBOOK | 2009
pencil on paper
22×44

SEVEN SISTERS, SUSSEX | 1998/99
acrylic & print on board
33×55

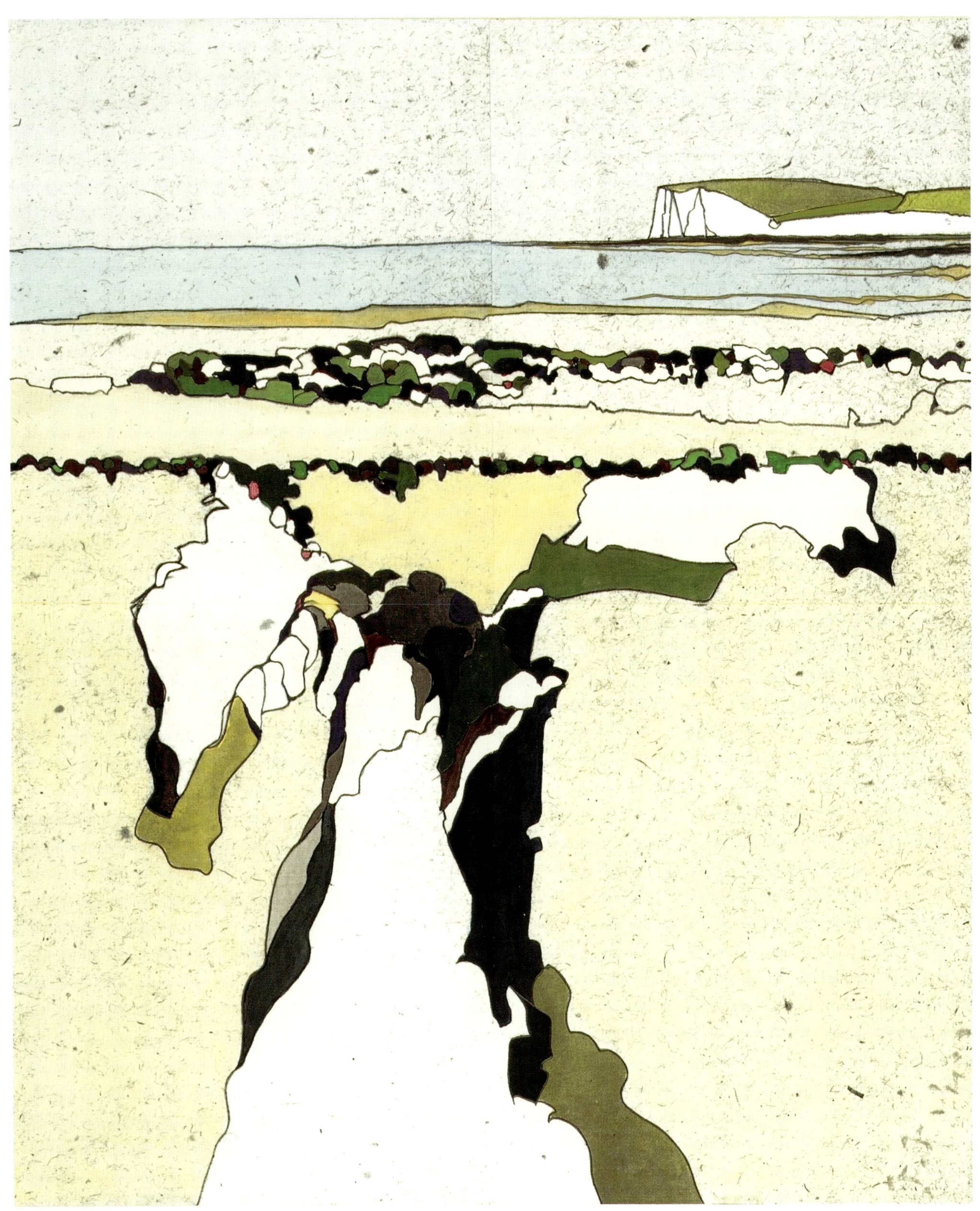

1936   Born London, UK

1957   Honours Degree, Clare College, Cambridge University, UK

1957–61   Engineer with Shell International Petroleum Company

1961–69   Computer consultant with Scicon Ltd

1969–91   Co-founder of Logica plc: Managing Director 1969–72, Chairman 1972–91

1975–76   Spent year travelling and painting in Andean countries of South America and in Provence in southern France

1981   Extensive trek in Western Himalayas to visit Kingdom of Zanskar; visit to Uluru and Olgas in Australia

1982   Visit to pre-Columbian sites in Mexico, particularly Palenque and Monte Albán

1984   Took part in protest in Tasmania against proposed damming of Franklin River and flooding of virgin temperate rainforest; paintings exhibited in London to increase publicity

1987–92   Member of the Council of the Royal College of Art

1987   Walked the Inca Trail to Machu Picchu in Peru; paintings exhibited later that year

1990–96   Member of Board of Design Museum, London

1993   Mural commission for new Quaglino's Restaurant, London

1995   Extensive visit to the north of Western Australia, Kimberley and the Bungle Bungles

1996–2000   Chairman, Board of Trustees of the National Gallery, London

1997   Lithograph illustrations for Carmen Boullosa's epic poem *The Elysian Garden* (limited edition produced onsite at Taller Magenta, Monterrey, Mexico); subsequently exhibited at museums in Mexico

1998   *Patterns in the Landscape: The Notebooks of Philip Hughes* published by Thames & Hudson, with foreword by Glenn Murcutt

2000–02   Trustee of The National Gallery, London

2001–02   Visiting Artist to Antarctica with the British Antarctic Survey for two months

2002   Illustrated the artist's book *Jump of the Manta Ray*, a long poem by Carmen Boullosa, translated by Psiche Hughes, and published by the Old School Press, UK

2004–06   Extensive work in Northern Highlands of Scotland

2007–08   Project to do large drawings on site of the major stone circles of Scotland and England

2009–10   Working in collaboration with archaeologists researching in Orkney

2011   Visited the remote northern edge of Lake Eyre in Central Australia to work on aerial images in that region

2012   *Tracks: Walking the Ancient Landscapes of Britain* (first edn) published by Thames & Hudson, with foreword by Kay Syrad

2014   Extensive work in Dungeness for exhibitions in Jerwood Gallery, Hastings and Studio 3 Gallery, University of Kent, Canterbury, England

2018   Illustrated the artist's book *Alchimia de los Planetas* (*Alchemy of the Planets*) with Amy Petra Woodward; a series of poems by Carmen Boullosa, translated by Psiche Hughes, and published by the Old School Press, UK

Awards include the CBE and honorary Doctorates/Fellowships a the Universities of Stirling, Kent, Queen Mary's College and Royal Holloway

ONE-PERSON EXHIBITIONS

Parkway Focus, London 1976

Angela Flowers Gallery, London 1977

Galerie Cance Manguin, Luberon, France 1979, 1985

Francis Kyle Gallery, London 1979, 1982, 1984, 1987, 1989, 1992, 1994, 1997, 2000, 2003, 2007, 2010

Museum and Art Gallery, Inverness, Scotland 1990

La Tour des Cardinaux, L'Isle-sur-la-Sorgue, France 1993

L'Ambassade d'Australie, Paris, France 1995

Museo de Arte Contemporaneo, MARCO, Monterrey, Mexico 1997

Lesley Craze Gallery, London 1998

Museo Rufino Tamayo, Mexico City, Mexico 1998

Drill Hall Gallery, Canberra, Australia 1998, 2002, 2008

Volvo Gallery, Sydney, Australia 1999

The George Adams Gallery, Victorian Arts Centre, Melbourne, Australia 1999

Artothèque, Luberon, Vaucluse, France 2000

The Tate Gallery, St Ives, Cornwall 2000

The Victoria and Albert Museum, London 2001

University of Lecce, Memmo Gallery, Lecce, Italy 2001

Musée du Châtillonais, Châtillon-sur-Seine, France 2002

Star Gallery, Lewes, Sussex 2004

Watermill Gallery, Aberfeldy, Scotland 2005

Rex Irwin Art Dealer, Sydney, Australia 2005, 2008

Galerie Pascal Lainé, Ménerbes, France 2007, 2010

La Maison de la Truffe et du Vin, Ménerbes, France 2007

Charleston, near Lewes, East Sussex 2008

The Pier Arts Centre, Stromness, Orkney, Scotland 2008

Galerie Gimpel & Müller, Paris, France, together with Chris Drury and Nicolas de Staël 2011

Francis Kyle Gallery, London 2012

Salisbury Museum, Wiltshire, England 2012

Stirling University, Scotland 2012

Pier Arts Centre, Stromness, Scotland 2012

Cromarty Arts Trust, Scotland 2012

Brighton Museum & Art Gallery, England 2012

Jerwood Gallery, Hastings, England 2014

University of Kent, Canterbury, England 2015

The Watermill Gallery, Aberfeldy, Scotland 2016
Studio 3 Gallery, Jarman Building, Canterbury, England 2016
Galerie Pascal Lainé, Ménerbes France 2018
Maison de la Truffe et du Vin, Ménerbes, France 2018
Charleston, East Sussex, England 2019

TWO-PERSON EXHIBITIONS

The Monks Gallery, Sussex (with Beryl Bainbridge) 1972
Francis Kyle Gallery, London (with Fay Godwin) 1976
Lesley Craze Gallery, London (with Francis Bendixson) 1992
Sherman Galleries, Sydney, Australia (with Philip Wolfhagen) 2002
Churchill College, Cambridge (with Keith Grant) 2003
Château la Nerthe, Châteauneuf-du-Pape, Vaucluse, France
  (with Antoine Poncet) 2004
The Perse, Cambridge, England (with Amy Petra Woodward) 2018
European Space Agency, Darmstadt, Germany (with Amy Petra
  Woodward) 2018–19

SELECTED GROUP EXHIBITIONS

Aldeburgh Festival, Suffolk 1969
'Artists for Vietnam', London 1970–76
Angela Flowers Galley, London 1974, 1983
Thumb Gallery, London 1976
La Roche Gallery, London 1981
Acme Gallery, London 1981
 Seven Dials Gallery, London 1982
L'Hôtel de Ville, Bonnieux, France 1982
Pintura Britanica Contemporanea, Museo Municipal, Madrid 1983
Royal Festival Hall, London 1985
Museum and Art Gallery, Swindon 1986
Francis Kyle Gallery, London 1988, 1991, 1993, 1994, 1995, 2003,
  'Lair of the Leopard' 2005, 'Everyone Sang' 2006, 'That Gong-
  Tormented Sea' 2009, 'This Twittering World' 2011
Mount House Gallery, Marlborough, Wiltshire 1988
Camden Arts Centre, London 1988
The London Group, Royal College of Art, London 1988
Sotheby's, London 1991, 1997
Eddie Glastra Gallery, Sydney, Australia 1991
Galerie Jaquester, Paris 1992
Art-Asia Convention, Hong Kong 1992
Art '93, Contemporary Art Fair, London 1993
Lesley Craze Gallery, London 1993, 1994, 2004
Royal Society of Arts, London 1994
John Jones Gallery, London 1995
Royal Academy Summer Exhibition, London 1997
Rex Irwin Gallery, Sydney, Australia 1999, 2000
The Prince of Wales's Institute of Architecture, London 1999

The Museum of Fine Arts, Houston, USA 2000
'Trentside', Djanogly Art Gallery, Nottingham 2001
'White Horizons: British Art from Antarctica, 1775–2006',
  Edinburgh, Scotland 2006
'Nature in Art', Wallsworth Hall, Twigworth, Gloucester 2007
'Landscapes of Exploration', Peninsula Art Gallery, Plymouth 2012
Francis Kyle Gallery, London 2013
Lesley Craze Gallery, London 2014
The Gallery, Arts University Bournemouth, England, *Landscapes of
  Exploration* 2015
Belgrave Gallery, St Ives, England 2017
Stromness Museum, Orkney, Scotland 2018

COLLECTIONS

The British Library, London
The British Museum, London
The Victoria and Albert Museum, London
The UK Government Collection
Clare College, Cambridge
Musée du Châtillonais, Châtillon-sur-Seine, France
The National Gallery, Canberra, Australia
The City Library, New York, USA
Columbia University, New York, USA
The Library of Congress, Washington, DC, USA
The Museum of Fine Arts, Houston, Texas, USA
The University of Georgia, USA
The University of Iowa, USA
Washington University, St Louis, Missouri, USA

Numerous corporate and private collections in the UK, France,
the Netherlands, USA and Australia.

INDEX